The Motherless State

THE MOTHERLESS STATE

Women's Political Leadership and American Democracy

EILEEN MCDONAGH

The University of Chicago Press
Chicago and London

Eileen McDonagh is professor in the Department of Political Science at North-eastern University and visiting scholar at the Institute for Quantitative Social Science at Harvard University. She is the author of *Breaking the Abortion Deadlock: From Choice to Consent* and, with Laura Pappano, *Playing with the Boys: Why Separate Is Not Equal in Sports.*

The University of Chicago Press, Chicago 60637
The University of Chicago Press, Ltd., London
© 2009 by The University of Chicago
All rights reserved. Published 2009
Printed in the United States of America

18 17 16 15 14 13 12 11 10 09   1 2 3 4 5

ISBN-13: 978-0-226-51454-3   (cloth)
ISBN-13: 978-0-226-51455-0   (paper)
ISBN-10: 0-226-51454-4   (cloth)
ISBN-10: 0-226-51455-2   (paper)

Library of Congress Cataloging-in-Publication Data

McDonagh, Eileen L.
   The motherless state : women's political leadership and American democracy / Eileen McDonagh.
       p.cm.
   Includes bibliographical references and index.
   ISBN-13: 978-0-226-51454-3 (cloth : alk. paper)
   ISBN-13: 978-0-226-51455-0 (pbk : alk. paper)
   ISBN-10: 0-226-51454-4 (cloth : alk. paper)
   ISBN-10: 0-226-51455-2 (pbk : alk. paper)   1. Women in politics—United States.
2. Leadership in women—United States.   3. Political leadership—United States.
4. Democracy—United States.   I. Title.
   HQ1236.5 .U6M3925 2009
   320.973082—dc22
                                                                          2008038372

♾ The paper used in this publication meets the minimum requirements of the American National Standard for Information Sciences—Permanence of Paper for Printed Library Materials, ANSI Z39.48-1992.

To Edward and Robert
and to
Robert Edward

CONTENTS

ACKNOWLEDGMENTS

Earlier versions of portions of this book's materials appeared in "Forging a New Grammar of Equality and Difference: Progressive Era Suffrage and Reform," in *Formative Acts: Reckoning with Agency in American Politics*, ed. Stephen Skowronek and Matt Glassman (Philadelphia: University of Pennsylvania Press, 2007); "Political Citizenship and Democratization: The Gender Paradox," *American Political Science Review* 96, no. 3 (September 2002): 535–52; "Race, Class, and Gender in the Progressive Era: Restructuring State and Society," in *Progressivism and the New Democracy*, ed. Sidney M. Milkis and Jerome M. Mileur (Amherst: University of Massachusetts Press, 1999); "Gender Politics and Political Change," in *New Perspectives on American Politics*, ed. Lawrence C. Dodd and Calvin Jillson (Washington, DC: Congressional Quarterly Press, 1994); and "The 'Welfare Rights State' and the 'Civil Rights State': Policy Paradox and State Building in the Progressive Era," *Studies in American Political Development* 7, no. 2 (1993): 225–74.

This book is about the power of a maternal political context for enhancing women's access to political leadership, and that precept applies to the book itself. Long in the writing and rewriting, it would never have seen the light of day without the incalculable nurturing of a wide range of men and women plus one canine who together make up a diverse group of friends, colleagues, and family. There are four who wrote extensive critiques of an earlier version of this manuscript that paved the way for cutting and clarifying, without which this project could not have moved forward. For their time, care, and crucial insights, it is with the deepest appreciation that I thank Mary Katzenstein, Stephen Skowronek, Rogers Smith, and Sidney Verba. In addition, I thank Ira Katznelson for a series of extended conversations at this stage in the process that pointed the way out of the maze. Others, having been given leaner versions, also took the time to read and comment in writing, thereby providing additional stepping stones for moving forward for which I am also deeply grateful. My thanks for their advice and help go to Edwin Amenta, Lisa Anderson, Karen Beckwith, Elisabeth Clemens, Cyndi Daniels, Nancy Hirschmann, Peter Katzenstein, Sherry Martins, Suzanne Mettler, Edward Price, Robert Price, Kimberly Weaver, Susan Welch, and Wade Woodson for the time and effort it takes to do such things.

The American Association of University Women (AAUW) extended invaluable resources in the form of a two-year visiting professorship and research fellowship to be hosted by City College of New York (CCNY). I thank Joyce Gelb at CCNY for inviting me to apply for the AAUW grant, Joyce Gelb and Ellen Smiley at CCNY for their assistance in writing the grant application, and CCNY for extending their facilities to me for two years. I thank the AAUW for their generous support, which included funding a conference to discuss the issues raised by this book. For their perspicacious critiques, I thank the conference participants, who included Edwin Amenta, Elisabeth Clemens, Victoria Hattam, Nancy Hirschmann, Mary Katzenstein, Robert Lieberman, Suzanne Mettler, Carol Nackenoff, Stephen Skowronek, Dan Tichenor, as well as Jen Gaboury for her assistance with the conference. I also thank Drew Faust when she was Dean of the Radcliffe Institute for Advanced Study, and Gary King, Director of the Institute for Quantitative Social Science at Harvard University, for my appointments as a visiting scholar, which greatly facilitated the research for this book and which provided the community of researchers so necessary for all such enterprises. In addition, a number of special conferences and academic invitations presented forums for testing a number of suppositions. I thank Karen O'Connor at the American University for splendid conferences on women's political leadership, Martha Fineman for her feminist and legal theory workshops, Mary Katzenstein for her invitation to present this material at Cornell, Stephen Skowronek for his invitation to present this material at a conference at Yale, Sunshine Hillygus and Claudia Gay for including me in American Politics Workshops at Harvard, Debby Kaufman at Northeastern University for inviting me to be a speaker for her "Gender Matters" series, and Kay Lehman Schlozman for including me in a conference she organized for the Ash Center at the Kennedy School at Harvard University. I also thank Christina Wohlbrect for organizing and hosting an excellent conference on gender and American democracy at Notre Dame University and Karen Beckwith and Lisa Baldez for their pioneering vision evident at this conference and in their launching of the new journal, *Politics and Gender*.

Two people, Jason Wittenberg and Robert Price, met with me on a regular basis for over a year to discuss each of our ongoing projects—each finished theirs much earlier than I did mine, but now that mine is in hand, it is with great appreciation that I recall how important were our conversations. Others lent me their ear for extended conversations over extended months and years, and for their time and advice, I thank Martha Acklesberg, Lee Ann Banaszak, Amrita Basu, Alice Bierhorst, Elin Bjarnegård, Eileen Boris, Chris Bosso, Ellen Browning, Andrea Campbell, Mary Churchill, Nancy Cott, Daniel Carpenter, Cynthia Enloe, Bob Davoli, Gary King, Laura Frader, Danny Goldhagen, Sarah Williams Goldhagen, Kristin Goss, Christine Harrington, Mala Htun, Mary Katzenstein, Mona Krook, Barbara Lee, Robert Lieberman, Jane Mansbridge, Richard Matland, Linda McClain, Sid Milkis, Carol Nackenoff, Steve Nathanson, Pippa Norris, Ruth O'Brien, Karen Orren, Paul Pierson, Paul Quirk, Steve Quatrano, Gretchen Ritter, Wendy Sarvasy, Shauna Shames, Molly Shanley, Theda Skocpol, Victoria Steinberg, Jennifer Yvette Terrell, Sue Tolleson-Rinehart, Mary Wolf, Veronica Zebadua Yanez, and Katherine Zippel. I also thank President of Ireland, Mary Robinson, for her advice about the legacy of women's political leadership, and Laura Liswood, cofounder of the Council of Women World Leaders, for promoting women's political leadership.

I have been more than fortunate to work with brilliant research assistants whose enthusiasm for this project over the years along with their skills and expertise made this a less lonely enterprise than are many academic ventures. For their belief in this book and their invaluable work, I thank Laura Cobb, Nicholas Cornell, David Daniels, Jen Darrah, Kristen Eichensehr, Jen Gaboury, Susan Lee, Eric Liu, Deolinda Martins, Daniela Nogueira, Eunice Park, Toni Pole, Rain Robertson, Shauna Shames, and Amy Wasserman. To De Kallgren special thanks for her patience and expertise in coding biographical information on over four thousand women leaders. For assistance with coding the constitutions of the world's countries, thanks to Angela Millard, Anna Niestadt, and Autumn Elliott. For editorial assistance and preparation of the manuscript for publication, my thanks go to Nadia Berenstein, Dawn Hall, Natalie Greenberg, Virginia LaPlante, Robert Price, Rodney Powell, Pat Rimmer, and Amy Wasserman.

Then there is the question of the book's title, which it has, of course, but not after consultation with a myriad of folks whose patience in resolving this issue rivals that of Job. I thank all of you for enduring the endless grilling you got from me, but especially Martha Acklesberg, Marcia Angell, Amrita Basu, Karen Beckwith, Bob Davoli, Cynthia Enloe, Danny Goldhagen, Kristin Goss, Heide Hatry, Nancy Hirschmann, Kimberly Jones, Mary Katzenstein, Pat McDonagh, Sidney Milkis, Laura Pappano, Edward Price, Robert Price, Katie Sigelman, Shauna Shames, Molly Shanley, Stephen Skowronek, Rogers Smith, Jason Wittenberg, and John Wronoski who were marathon participants in this sport, and, most especially, Scott Brown, who actually came up with the title. Accolades, also, to the captain of the editorial ship, John Tryneski at the University of Chicago Press, who consistently combined over what ended up being years a seamless joining of intellectual insight with sensitive consideration for author and manuscript.

I am very fortunate to have a supportive family, and my thanks and love go to Edward Price, Robert Price, Ellen Browning, Alice Bierhorst, Zachary Price, Dexter Price, and Louisa Price. To my second best buddy, Lesko, thanks for starting my every day with such tail wagging zest, and to my best buddy, Bob Davoli, all my love and thanks for so much for so long.

Eileen McDonagh
Lincoln, MA   July 2008

Confronting the Puzzle 1

In the United States, we pride ourselves on our democratic and egalitarian values. As the world's oldest contemporary democracy and among the most stable, equality is crucial to our national self-image. Yet there are many groups in the United States to whom the country has consistently failed to keep its promise of equality. For African Americans the heritage of racialized slavery that marks the very founding of the American state is a blight upon our past. The virtual genocide of Native Americans in the wake of the expansion of the American state constitutes wrongdoing of gargantuan proportions. And today Americans and their government still struggle to find ways to guarantee the rights of massive numbers of immigrants whose lives belie the promise that America is a land of plenty for newcomers as well as for those already privileged to have access to its bounty.[1]

Yet another group stands out for its long history of inequality in the American state, persisting tenaciously to this day: women.[2] To be sure, women are not relegated to a subordinate role in every aspect of contemporary society. Despite the earning gap between men and women that stubbornly refuses to close, women in the United States currently have high rates of education and comparable, if not higher, rates of entry into the professions and business than do women in other industrial democracies. In the United States, for example, 52% of college students are women, compared to 50% in Britain, 48% in the European Union, and only 26% in Japan.[3] As political scientists Nancy Burns, Kay Schlozman, and Sidney Verba note, "in comparative terms, when it comes to the proportion of women in managerial and administrative positions outside government, the United States tops the list—ahead of all fifteen countries in the European Union and in just about every nation in the world."[4]

Yet there remains a crucial arena in the United States where women's inequality is appalling, namely holding national political office. As of 2006 women made up only 15.2% of the U.S. House of Representatives, ranking the United States a lowly eighty-third among the world's nations in terms of the percentage of women elected to national legislative office, as Table 1.1 indicates.[5] America's percentage of women in office is in no way comparable to our wealthy Western, industrial counterparts, such as Sweden (45.3%), Norway (37.9%), Finland (37.5%), Denmark (36.9%), the Netherlands (36.7%), Spain (36%), Belgium (34.7%), Austria (33.9%), Iceland (33.3%), Germany (31.8%), New Zealand (28.3%), Bulgaria (26.2%), Switzerland (25.0%), Australia (24.7%), or even our next door neighbor Canada (20.8%). The United States has an even lower percentage of women in its House of Representatives than do some less wealthy and less industrialized countries, such as Uganda (27.6%), Vietnam (27.3%), Namibia (26.9%), and Suriname (25.5%), as shown in table 1.1.

In addition, consider that since the beginning of the twentieth century eighty-five other countries, comprising nearly half the world's political systems (44.3%)—have elected women to serve in the executive office as president, prime minister, vice president, or deputy prime minister.[6] Until Hillary Clinton's 2007–8 campaign for the presidency, however, no woman in the United States even came close to being nominated as a presidential candidate of a major political party, much less being elected to that office.

Women's Political Representation

Women's political equality in terms of their representation as elected leaders in the United States is not only a serious problem but also a puzzle. The country's long-standing liberal democratic tradition of individual equality, the parity in women's education as compared to men's, and the significant presence of women in the salaried workforce, including the professions and business, are generally thought to bolster the election of women to political office. The United States should therefore be a pacesetter when it comes to women's political inclusion.[7] Yet it is not. In terms of women's political representation, the United States is a laggard.[8]

Table 1.1 Percent women elected to national legislature[a], 2006

Political System		Political System		Political System	
RANK (50%–26%)	PERCENT	RANK (25%–16%)	PERCENT	RANK (15%–11%)	PERCENT
1st Rwanda	48.80	30th Iraq	25.50	80th Philippines	15.70
2nd Sweden	45.30	31st Suriname	25.50	81st Czech Republic	15.50
3rd Costa Rica	38.60	32nd Timor Leste	25.30	82nd Cape Verde	15.30
4th Norway	37.90	33rd Laos	25.20	83rd United States	15.20
5th Finland	37.50	34th Switzerland	25.00	84th Angola	15.00
6th Denmark	36.90	35th Australia	24.70	84th Chile	15.00
7th The Netherlands	36.70	36th Liechtenstein	24.00	86th Bangladesh	14.80
8th Cuba	36.00	37th Honduras	23.40	87th Sudan	14.70
9th Spain	36.00	38th Luxembourg	23.30	88th Sierra Leone	14.50
10th Argentina	35.00	39th Tunisia	22.80	89th Cyprus	14.30
11th Mozambique	34.80	40th Mexico	22.60	90th Israel	14.20
12th Belgium	34.70	41st Taiwan	22.20	91st Guinea Bissau	14.00
13th Austria	33.90	42th Bulgaria	22.10	92nd Malawi	13.60
14th Iceland	33.30	43rd Eritrea	22.00	93rd Korea, South	13.40
15th South Africa	32.80	44th Lithuania	22.00	94th St. Kitts & Nevis	13.33
16th New Zealand	32.20	45th Ethiopia	21.90	95th Barbados	13.30
17th Germany	31.80	46th Moldova	21.80	96th Ireland	13.30
18th Guyana	30.80	47th Croatia	21.70	96th Gambia	13.20
19th Burundi	30.50	48th Pakistan	21.30	98th Greece	13.00
20th Tanzania	30.40	48th Portugal	21.30	99th Dominica	12.90

Table 1.1 continued

Political System	50%–26%	Political System	25%–16%	Political System	15%–11%
22nd Seychelles	29.40	50th Singapore	21.20	100th Zambia	12.70
22nd Peru	29.20	51st Latvia	21.00	101st Liberia	12.50
23rd Belarus	29.10	52nd Canada	20.80	102nd Niger	12.40
24th Andorra	28.60	53rd Monaco	20.80	103rd France	12.20
25th Uganda	27.60	54th Nicaragua	20.70	103rd Slovenia	12.20
26th Afghanistan	27.30	55th Poland	20.40	105th Colombia	12.05
26th Vietnam	27.30	56th China	20.30	106th Congo, Dm Rep	12.00
28th Namibia	26.90	57th Korea, North	20.10	107th Maldives	12.00
29th Grenada	26.70	58th The Bahamas	20.00	108th Serbia & Monténégro	12.00
		59th Dominican Rep	19.70	109th Syria	12.00
		59th United Kingdom	19.70	110th Burkina Faso	11.70
		61st Trinidad & Tobago	19.40	110th Jamaica	11.70
		62nd Guinea	19.30	110th Lesotho	11.70
		63rd Senegal	19.20	110th San Marino	11.70
		64th Estonia	18.80	114th Azerbaijan	11.30

Rank	Country	Value		Rank	Country	Value
65th	Macedonia	18.33		114th	Fiji	11.30
66th	St. Vincent	18.20		114th	Indonesia	11.30
66th	Equatorial Afr	18.00		117th	Romania	11.20
68th	Venezuela	18.00		118th	Botswana	11.10
69th	Tajikistan	17.50		118th	Uruguay	11.10
69th	Uzbekistan	17.50				
71st	Italy	17.30				
72nd	Mauritius	17.10				
73rd	Bolivia	16.90				
74th	Bosnia-Herzeg	16.70				
75th	El Salvador	16.70				
76th	Panama	16.70				
76th	Ecuador	16.00				
78th	Slovakia	16.00				
79th	Turkmenistan	16.00				
79th	Zimbabwe	16.00				

a) Lower House, IUP Data.

The puzzle is, therefore, why the United States fails to elect women to political leadership positions? Or to put it another way, what do other comparable democracies have that the American state lacks that would explain why most of them elect higher percentages of women to their national legislatures, if not also to their chief executive offices?

Many have long pointed to how political structures, such as proportional representation, parliamentary systems, multiple parties, and gender quotas improve women's electoral prospects.[9] In addition, women's political representation tends to increase in relation to demographic characteristics, such as having a higher percentage of women in the paid labor force in general or in the public sector in particular.[10] Some cultural norms and traditions are thought to enhance women's election to political office, such as egalitarianism, Protestantism, and postmaterialist values.[11] On the other hand, when it comes to what blocks women's political representation, researchers note the disjuncture between women's sociological roles within the domestic sphere of the home and their political leadership roles within the public sphere of the state.[12] Psychological variables also pose problems by predisposing men more than women to run for political office.[13]

There is yet another explanation that has not been so fully explored, the *state* itself. The state's public policies teach voters which traits are associated with political governance and, by extension, who are suitable as political leaders. The key to women's political leadership, therefore, is a political context generated by state policies that teach voters that the traits associated with men as well as with women signify inclusion in the public sphere of political governance.

The basic duty of all states—if they are to be defined as such—is to maintain law and order within their own borders and to defend against intruders from outside their borders by means of police and military forces.[14] The public associates the police and the military with men. Hence, the state's basic public policies are gendered as male, promoting the view that men are particularly suited for political leadership. In addition, one of the basic duties of a liberal democratic state, such as the United States, is to guarantee individual equality by treating everyone the same "in spite of" their ascriptive group differences, that is, the traits they acquire by birth, such as race, class, or sex.[15] In the United States, the Equal Protection Clause of the Fourteenth Amendment of the Constitution is a good example of liberal individualism, as is Title VII of the Civil Rights Act of 1964. The Amendment requires the government to treat individuals the same "in spite of" race or sex differences, and, barring extraordinary circumstances, Title VII makes it a federal crime for an employer to treat employees differently in hiring, promotion, or retention "because of" their race or sex, unless a person's sex is a bona fide occupational qualification (BFOQ).

Public policies based on liberal individualism, which typify democracies, promote the view that what makes women suitable for public office is their individual equality in comparison to men, that is, their *sameness* with men. For this reason, when women run as candidates for political office, one of their first tasks is to establish that they, too, can be "male." Women candidates must show that they are the same as men, which includes the same ability to wield the state's coercive force in order to ensure law and order at home and national security abroad. Yet voters also need reassurance that women candidates remain "female," or different from men. In the eyes of voters, women typically differ from men by having maternal traits, such as a predisposition to nurture and care for others. As a result, women running for political office typically end up becoming *hybrid candidates,* who go to great efforts to represent both male and female traits by establishing that they are both the same as and different from men.

Hybrid Candidates

In 2007 the presidential primaries marked the entry of the first viable female candidate for nomination by a major political party, Hillary Rodham Clinton. As remarkable as is her participation as the lone woman running, the precedent for women's acceptance as candidates in presidential contests harks back to 1984, when Geraldine Ferraro made history as the Democratic Party's vice presidential candidate, the first woman in the United States to run on a major party's presidential ticket.[16] One of the central challenges she faced in this precedent-setting role was to convince the American public that she could be just as "tough" as any man, especially when it came to the military defense of the nation. During her vice presidential campaign Geraldine Ferraro was challenged repeatedly on her capability of handling international military crises.

Recognizing that she had to establish her credibility on masculine political issues, Ferraro was explicit about how she would deal with military situations. For example, when questioned during the vice presidential debate by John Mashek, a correspondent for *U.S. News & World Report,* as to how her three terms in the House of Representatives stacked up against the experience of George Bush, the incumbent Republican nominee for vice president, who had been "ambassador to the United Nations, ambassador to China, Director of the Central Intelligence Agency," *and* vice president for the last four years, she emphasized her analytical ability and capacity to make "hard" decisions:

> There's not only what is on your paper resume that makes you qualified to run for or to hold office. It's how you approach problems and what your values are. I think if one is taking a look at my career they'll see that I level with the people; that I approach problems analytically; that I am able to assess the various facts with reference to a problem, and I can make the *hard* decisions.[17]

Later in the debate, Robert Boyd, Washington bureau chief for Knight Ridder newspapers, questioned whether Ferraro would have what it takes to protect the United States against nuclear threats by asking her,

> Congresswoman Ferraro, you have had little or no experience with military matters and yet you might someday find yourself commander-in-chief of the armed forces. How can you convince the American people . . . that you would know what to do to protect this nation's security, and do you think in any way that the Soviets might be tempted to try to take advantage of you simply because you are a woman?[18]

Ferraro replied emphatically:

> Quite frankly I'm prepared to do whatever is necessary in order to secure this country and to make sure that security is maintained. . . . If the Soviet Union were to ever believe that they could challenge the United States with any sort of nuclear forces or otherwise, if I were in a position of leadership in this country, they would be assured that they would be met with swift, concise and certain retaliation.[19]

Given the continuing struggle for women's equal rights in this country, it is no small matter for women to be treated by the government and to be viewed by the public as individuals who are the same as men in spite of their sex difference. The recognition of women as individuals who can be considered on the same terms as men, however, has not had the effect of replacing their traditional identity as maternalists who differ from men. Women's identities as individuals have rather been added on to their maternal identities, producing hybrid, dual identities as both individuals who are the same as men and maternalists who are different from men. Thus, as explained by Barbara Lee, Director of the Barbara Lee Family Foundation, a nonpartisan, not-for-profit organization that promotes women's election to state and national public office in the United States, women not only must prove their toughness, meaning their ability to compete as equal individuals with men in terms of strength, courage, and intelligence, but also must prove their warmth and relational ability expressing the ethic of care associated with mothers.[20]

The public's association of maternal traits with women is here to stay. The consequence for women political candidates is that in addition to demonstrating that they are as good or the same as any man when it comes to national security, they are also no slouch when it comes to fulfilling women's traditional, maternal roles. Ferraro established her "feminine," maternal credentials by baking blueberry muffins. As she recalls in her autobiography, "In no way was I going to deny my femininity during the [1984] campaign. I not only stood up for loving flowers, but when asked by the Mississippi agriculture commissioner during the campaign if I can 'bake a blueberry muffin,' I replied: 'I sure can—Can you?'"[21]

It is only fair to ask: What could be the political significance of baking blueberry muffins? And if there were any political significance to baking them, why would a man not be required to testify about his prowess with a muffin tin? After all, blueberry muffins are hardly on any doctor's list of what to eat to maximize health. Why not point proudly instead to one's ability to boil broccoli, steam spinach, or turn out low-carb, high-protein tofu concoctions? The answer is that blueberry muffins, like chocolate chip cookies, are comfort foods associated with *social maternalism*, or mothering. It is presumed that a mother will supply her children with the utilitarian baseline nutrients needed for growth and material well-being. Yet mothering also implies the provision of warmth and love—something more difficult to find on a plate of brussels sprouts, perhaps, but abundant in a basket of warm muffins or cookies. To mother is not only to care for people in the utilitarian sense of the word but also to care for people in the emotional, feel-good sense of the word—to indulge, to coddle, and to serve. The demand that Ferraro demonstrate both her toughness as a leader and her catering character as a mother may explain why media questioners had trouble accepting that she could perform either of these roles capably.

This double standard may also explain why in 1992 Hillary Rodham Clinton, who was then merely the spouse of presidential candidate Bill Clinton, got herself and her husband into trouble with the public when she announced that, when Bill had been governor of Arkansas, she had decidedly *not* wanted to "stay home and bake cookies." Instead, she had used her Yale law degree to practice as an unusually successful attorney. The public outcry over her statement was so ferocious that Hillary had to reassure voters of her acceptance of the traditional role by proclaiming her love for baking chocolate chip cookies for her daughter, Chelsea. While such a plain assertion may have been enough in Ferraro's time, by 1992 maternalism had taken on a new and more competitive edge. Consequently Hillary had to prove her baking skills to the public by means of a notorious competition with first lady Barbara Bush over who had the "best" chocolate chip cookie recipe. *Family Circle* published both recipes, and the public was invited to vote for the one they thought superior.[22] Barbara's cookie recipe beat Hillary's, although Bill beat George Bush in the presidential election.[23]

For women to be considered viable political candidates, therefore, they must add individualistic if not masculine roles to their traditional maternal ones, thereby establishing a dual or hybrid candidate identity. This balancing act involves the risk of adding "too much" masculinity to women's identities when running for political office, as illustrated by Hillary Clinton's bid for the White House in the primaries in 2008. While presenting herself to mothers and daughters as a role model who is "making history" as a viable female candidate for the Democratic presidential nomination, she also "for the most part predicated her candidacy on the masculine virtues of toughness, resolve, and her extensive experience in the (male-dominated) realm of politics and government." The latter position generated questions about her likeability, prompting her rival, Senator Barack Obama, to utter assurance that she was "likable enough," albeit in what some took to be a patronizing and dismissive tone.[24]

Hybrid State

Women's mixed identities as hybrid candidates who as individuals are the same as men *and* as maternalists who are different from men are currently thought to bolster the public's acceptance of women's participation in politics. What has yet to be recognized, however, is the role of the state in fostering public attitudes about women as political leaders. When the state represents the hybrid combination of individual sameness and maternal group difference, voters learn that the maternal traits they associate with women signify a location not only in the private sphere of the home or in the service sector of the market, but also in the public sphere of political governance.[25]

The joining of two opposite traits in the construction of the state is not uncommon. As political scientists Karen Orren and Stephen Skowronek show, the simultaneous operation of opposite trends, developments, and institutional components is more often the norm than the exception in political processes. This characteristic, which they term, intercurrence, refers to the "operation of asymmetric standards of control and incongruous rules of action," which is the foundation "around which historical-institutional theories of politics may be more securely built."[26] When their principle of intercurrence is applied to a study of women's political leadership, it shows that women's political representation improves in a political context defined by a hybrid state that combines in its public policies the apparently incongruous principles of women's sameness with men and women's maternal difference from men. Not only is this combination the norm for most of the world's democracies, but it is crucial for improving women's access to elected political leadership because of the lesson it imparts to voters, namely, that to be a man or an individual as well as to be maternal signifies a location in the public sphere. In order to elect women to political office, therefore, it is not enough for women themselves to be hybrid candidates. The state has to be a hybrid entity. In short, when it comes to democracies, liberal policies that treat everyone the same in spite of their group differences by sex are necessary, but not sufficient, for generating a political context supportive of women's access to political leadership. What is also required is a government that adopts public policies representing the maternal traits that voters attribute to women.[27]

Why Women Matter

The election of women to political office in percentages that are at least roughly comparable to their percentage in the population at large matters for both normative and instrumental reasons. From the normative perspective, it matters because the core definition of democracy is rule by the people.[28] Except in very small communities, rule by the people means representative democracies in which people elect officials to make decisions on their behalf.[29] These elected representatives take the place of the people who vote for them. *Descriptive representation* refers to the norm that elected representatives should look like the population they represent. In other words, if 51% of the population is composed of women, something close to that percentage of the Congress should be composed of women. Serious underrepresentation of major groups in society undermines the normative claim that a country is a representative democracy. Or as political scientist Virginia Sapiro puts it, a democracy minus women is not a democracy.[30] Hence, descriptive representation has an intrinsic value related to the very definition of democracy as a representative form of government.

Descriptive representation also leads instrumentally to *substantive representation*. As Janet Clark observes, members of relevant groups may not always entirely share the policy perspectives of their constituents. Some men may represent women's interests better than some women.[31] Yet the reverse is more often the case, where members of a demographically defined descriptive group, as identified by race, class, or gender, do support the interests of their demographically consonant constituents. For example, both Republican and Democratic women elected to political office are more supportive than are men of legislation that benefits women in particular according to feminist principles of individual equality, such as abortion rights and publicly funded day care. Political scientists Susan Carroll and Michelle Swers demonstrate that women officeholders are more likely than their male counterparts to promote agendas that are women-friendly, advancing policies that reflect women's different interests from men's as a group.[32] In an analysis of the 103rd and 104th Congresses, from January 1995 to January 1999, Swers finds that both Republican and Democratic women were more likely to support a feminist agenda than their male partisan counterparts. As Clark notes, "female officials do appear to be committed to supporting women's issues," such that their presence in office has both descriptive and substantive value.[33]

What is more, political scientists Alana Jeydel and Andrew Taylor find that once in office, female members of the House of Representatives are just as effective as their male counterparts when it comes to turning their policy priorities into law.[34] Similarly, in a study of twenty-two industrial democracies Valerie O'Regan finds that electing women to policy-making positions improves the passage of legislation addressing women's needs and interests.[35] Political scientist Kira Sanbonmatsu also depicts descriptive representation as providing the "potential" for women's substantive concerns to be addressed.[36] Legislatures without women end up disproportionately representing issues more associated with the concerns of men than of women.[37]

In addition, women more than men, regardless of their political party, lend more support to legislation that benefits all people, such as peace, education, and welfare policies. This is true in the United States and elsewhere. Carroll finds that women in the general population compared to men are "less militaristic on issues of war and peace, more opposed to the death penalty, more likely to favor gun control, more likely to favor measures to protect the environment, and more supportive of programs to help the economically disadvantaged."[38] Political scientist Lise Togeby finds the same pattern in Denmark, where by the 1980s there was a clear gender gap in public attitudes about war and foreign policy, with women being more peace-loving and dovish."[39] Torben Iversen similarly finds that gender has the "greatest impact" on support for social spending policies.[40]

Since it matters whether women are adequately represented in political office, the question becomes, what bolsters that representation?[41] The answer is a hybrid state that combines public policies representing individual equality with public policies representing the maternal traits voters attribute to women. Such a state produces a political context that teaches voters that the maternal traits attributed to women signify women's suitability not only in the kitchen baking muffins but also in the Congress passing legislation, if not in the Oval Office executing policies.[42] All democracies by definition adopt public policies representing the first principle, women's sameness with men. The question then becomes: How can governments adopt public policies representing the second principle, maternal traits?

Maternal Traits

The term *maternal* encompasses both gender and sex. Gender conventionally refers to the social roles ascribed to people on the basis of their socialized identities as female or male, while sex refers to their biological classification as female or male. The general assumption is that all people can engage in all roles associated with being human, including gender roles characteristically attributed to women. As a biological construction, however, sex denotes a physical, material component, such as sex-specific genetic characteristics, female versus male reproductive organs, and varying levels of the reproductive hormones estrogen and testosterone.

To date, there appears to be no way to alter the defining genetic differences that are used to classify people as female or male, although there are ways to alter reproductive organs and hormone levels. Thus, although sex difference as a physical trait is more malleable than it used to be, when it comes to the capacity to reproduce the species by becoming pregnant and bearing a child, physical sex difference remains virtually static and rigid. People who are initially classified as "male" can become "female" by means of surgical procedures that transform male reproductive organs into female ones and convert male hormonal levels into female ones, but to date such physical transformations do not convey the female capacity to be pregnant and bear a child. For this reason sex difference is still not synonymous with gender difference.[43] In this book, rather than using either gender or sex, I employ the term maternal, by which I mean social and biological reproductive labor, that is, the care and generation of human beings respectively.

Caring for people once they are born is social maternalism (what is usually termed *gender*), and bearing them in the first place is biological maternalism (what is usually termed *sex*). Study after study emphasizes that voters attribute both social and biological maternal traits to women, whether women seek those attributions or not.[44]

Social Maternalism

Social maternalism includes the care-work people need after they are born and throughout their lives, but most desperately when they are infants, children, ill, disabled, or elderly. Such work at the very least includes the provision of health care, education, food, clothing, and shelter. In terms of its *recipients*, care-work is gender neutral. However, the *caregivers* are *not* gender neutral. To the contrary, as sociologist Ann Orloff establishes, the public associates *care-workers* with women.[45] As Paul Herrnson and his colleagues note, "voters view women as better able to handle [social maternalist] issues, such as child care and education, but less able to handle 'masculine' issues, including the economy and war."[46] Sapiro finds that the public assumes women will be better than men at handling "such issues as education, assisting the poor, and encouraging the arts," and that men will be better than women at directing the military and "handling business and labor, and strengthening the economy."[47] On this basis, as Herrnson and his colleagues state, "voters use gender to assess a candidate's policy positions and potential performance in office in much the same way they use party identification and other traditional voting cues."[48]

Care not only is needed by all people but can be done by all people, men as well as women, and in an ideal society it would be. As political theorist Joan Tronto argues, in a pluralistic democracy all citizens would engage in the "practice of care." To care for others would refer not merely to a sentiment or an affective emotion but also to an ongoing practice of meeting the needs of others.[49] The fact of the matter, however, is that we are not there yet. To date, despite the closing of the mothering gap, women still do more care-work than do men. A 2005 "American Time Use Survey" conducted by the Bureau of Labor Statistics[50] found that women employed in the labor force do just under two hours of housework a day, compared with an hour and ten minutes for comparable men. Workingwomen devote about forty-five minutes a day to caring for family members compared to only twenty-four minutes a day for workingmen.[51] Similarly, an Australian study found that "when women and men work the same number of paid hours, women tend to do more total hours of work per week than men," because of the additional household and care-work that employed women contribute to the family.[52]

Because of the greater involvement of women both in the home and in the service sector of the market, in a pattern that most likely will continue for the foreseeable future, the public will most likely continue to attribute social maternal traits to women in general and to women candidates in particular, whether women want that identification or not. As researcher Monika McDermott notes, "candidate gender, unlike other demographic cues, can usually be determined by the candidate's first name. For this reason, even when a voter knows nothing about the candidate except what the ballot says on election day, candidate gender can be a source of information about a candidate's views. As such, candidate gender has significant potential to influence voting behavior."[53] As political scientists Kim Kahn and Ann Gordon find, women running as candidates for the U.S. Senate in the 1980s were more likely to use commercials focusing on issues of health care and education than were male candidates, who were more likely to focus their commercials on the economy, military defense, and foreign policy, thereby strengthening the public's view of gender stereotypes.[54]

Biological Maternalism

In addition to social maternal traits, the public associates women more than men with the biological maternal traits involved in generating a new human being. This process depends upon two things that the public specifically associates with women: the sexual capacity to bear offspring and the actual bearing of offspring by means of pregnancy and birth.

Although the public also views men as necessarily involved in biological reproduction because they are the donors of sperm, without which there could be no generation of a new human being, the public assumes that unless at least some individual women also allow a fertilized ovum in the form of an embryo to implant itself in their uteruses and consent to be pregnant and to give birth, no new human being will ever come into existence. Since the public views pregnancy and birth as distinct to females as a group, the public disproportionately associates women as a group with biological reproductive labor, regardless of whether individual women affirm that association by actually being pregnant and giving birth.

The public's association of women with biological maternalism, defined by a female sex classification and the bearing of children, is reinforced every time such fundamental issues as abortion rights or teenage pregnancies get onto the political agenda, which is often. The potential, if not the actuality, at least for some women—and no men—to be pregnant can also take center stage in the political process when a woman candidate actually is pregnant while running for office. Such was the case with Jane Swift who was the Republican candidate for lieutenant governor of Massachusetts in 1998 while being pregnant and expecting to give birth just two weeks before the general election. Her pregnant condition generated enormous attention and enormous criticism, proof positive that the public not only attributes to women biological maternalist identities but also, when faced with an actual woman about to become a biological mother, finds that identity relevant to her suitability as a political leader.

As Evelyn Reilly, executive director of the Christian Coalition of Massachusetts, said about Swift, "My first reaction was, 'Thank God she's not having an abortion,' and my second reaction is, 'I hope she'll have enough time to spend with the child.'"[55] Similarly, as Elizabeth Sherman, director of the Center for Women in Politics and Public Policy at the McCormack Institute of the University of Massachusetts at Boston, noted, "On the one hand, a lot of people have been saying, 'This is great, it's as it should be; of course, we have more and more women candidates, naturally we'll inevitably have a woman who's pregnant.' On the other hand, there's been a backlash by . . . [those] who've said, 'This is wrong, she shouldn't be doing this.'"[56]

Public Policies Representing Maternal Traits

Women can modify their maternal identities by adopting masculine traits, such as becoming a warrior, if not a military hero. Jingū-Kōgō of Japan, who became empress when her husband died, ruled from 343 to 380 CE. Among her duties was to lead her troops in battle. When Japan decided to invade Korea in 366, she was at the head of her military troops, despite the fact that she was pregnant. Her solution was to have adjustable armor made to fit her pregnant body, thereby dramatically illustrating that even when engaged directly in biological maternalism by being pregnant, it is still possible to excel at military tasks associated with masculinity.[57]

The key point about women's identities, however, is that masculine traits can be added, but not substituted, for maternal ones. In the case of an empress, if she does not become pregnant and give birth, her direct contribution to the pool constituting the dynastic family to which she belongs will vanish. Certainly she can lead in battle, as many women political leaders have done. However, in ancient times and still today women's mastery of masculine skills and accomplishments serves more as an addition to maternal identities than as a substitution. Whether individual women wish to affirm their social and biological maternal identities or not, the public's association of maternalism with women is all but constant across historical time and political place.

While women's maternal identities in the eyes of the public do not change over time, what does change is the way the government itself, the state, becomes associated with maternal traits vis-à-vis its public policies.[58]

Welfare Policies as a Representation of Social Maternalism

Most would concede that when the state itself engages in care-work by means of *welfare provision*, it is engaging in social maternalism, whether or not the beneficiaries of public welfare provision are women. This is because everyone needs care-work, not just women. The beneficiaries of care-work, therefore, can be gender neutral. What are not perceived by the public to be gender neutral are the *care-givers*. Hence, what makes state-provided care-work a form of social maternalism is that it is a government activity based on a social maternal trait the public associates with women.

When the state takes on the job of providing care-work to others, the government becomes associated with the social maternal activities the public attributes to women as the usual providers of care-work in the home and in the service sector of the market, regardless of whether the recipients of government provided care are male or female. For this reason, I characterize government provided care-work—that is, welfare provision—to be a social maternal public policy, even when that care-work is directed to people in a gender-neutral way, such as by the government provision of health care.

Gender Quotas as a Representation of Biological Maternalism

The state can represent a female sex classification as a component of biological maternalism by adopting *gender quotas*. These are really female sex quotas, which designate a minimum percentage of women to serve in national legislatures or to be included as candidates in electoral processes simply "because of" their sex classification as female. Currently, gender quotas are usually analyzed as a type of political structure similar to proportional representation in terms of giving women an advantage at the polls. To place them in the category of political structures, however, loses sight of their gendered character. Political structures such as proportional representation, multiple parties, and parliamentary or presidential systems are gender-neutral public policies because they reference no traits particularly associated with men or women. Not so when it comes to gender quotas, which specifically single out women as worthy of legislative representation simply because of their sex classification as female.

For this reason, it is more appropriate to think about gender quotas as a public policy that represents biological maternalism. In this sense, gender quotas are more similar to welfare policies than to such political structures as proportional representation. Gender quotas and welfare provision represent biological and social maternalism respectively, and by so doing, teach the public that to have maternal identities is to signify one's suitability inside the state, a lesson that gender-neutral political structures fail to convey. Many study the utilitarian impact of gender quotas on women's election to national legislatures. However, much less recognized is the way they represent biological maternalism and much less studied is their *symbolic impact on public attitudes*. Yet by definition gender quotas highlight a biological maternal trait, the sex classification as female, and a state that adopts them conveys to voters that being female has the political meaning of making one suitable to be a member of the legislature.

Hereditary Monarchies as Another Representation of Biological Maternalism

When a woman becomes a biological mother by bearing a child, she is necessarily generating family-kinship networks. The mother-child relationship constitutes one family connection, the fact that a woman needs a male genetic partner to bear a child constitutes another family connection, in turn both she and he necessarily had biological parents, and so on and so on. Bringing a child into the world biologically is thus the same thing as generating multiple family-kinship networks.

Government can adopt public policies that represent this biological maternal trait of generating family-kinship networks through *hereditary monarchies*. As Vernon Bagdanor notes, in its essence a monarchy is a hereditary institution, the archetypal fusion of the family with the state, albeit only one family, the dynastic family.[59] The political viability of any particular dynastic family and of hereditary monarchical rule in general is utterly dependent on and ultimately determined by women, who must be pregnant and give birth to replenish the pool of those eligible to be sovereigns. A monarchy is therefore a public policy based on women's biological maternalism, defined by the actual bearing of children. When women in the dynastic family give birth, they are doing *political work*, so to speak.[60] Incorporating a hereditary monarchy into the government, however symbolically, associates the government with the public's attribution of actual biological motherhood to women.

As John Stuart Mill declared, "the legal subordination of one sex to the other . . . is wrong itself, and now one of the chief hindrances to human improvement . . . it ought to be replaced by a principle of perfect equality, admitting no power or privilege on the one side, nor disability on the other."[61] When seeking to establish the principle of women's equality with men, this classic liberal theorist turned to none other than monarchical political rule. It is difficult, he argued, to establish that women are as capable as men in literary, philosophical, artistic, or musical endeavors, because we have no examples of women as great as Homer, Aristotle, Michelangelo, or Beethoven. Women might hypothetically be as capable as men in these areas, but in Mill's view, that the question remains uncertain and open to debate and discussion.

In the case of political leadership, however, as Mill pointed out, there is no doubt that women are as capable as men because we have examples of women, such as Queen Elizabeth I and Queen Victoria, who exercised political authority with excellence comparable to men. As Mill emphasized, the reason we know about these women is precisely because they were given a chance to excel in a political context, a hereditary monarchy, where their familial identities signified their inclusion, not their exclusion, in the pool of those eligible to be political rulers. As he noted, "When, to queens and empresses, we add regents and viceroys of provinces, the list of women who have been eminent rulers of mankind swells to a great length."[62] More important, "had they not inherited the throne," these women would have had no chance to prove that they could be "entrusted with [even] the smallest of . . . political duties," much less the leadership of the entire country. Yet once women are given the chance by monarchical forms of government to be political leaders, they prove that they have "vigour," "intelligence," and "talents for rule."[63]

To classify hereditary monarchies as a form of maternalism might seem questionable in view of the fact that historically and still today, most monarchies prefer men when selecting a sovereign. Yet preference for men in choosing a sovereign hardly excludes women. Throughout history thousands of women have ruled because they were in a political context, monarchical government, that defined their familial identities as signifying inclusion in political authority. That pattern continues in constitutional monarchies today, which despite their preference for male sovereigns include women as sovereigns. Among the world's twenty-four democracies in the twentieth century that have hereditary monarchies open to women, eighteen, or 75%, have *selected* at least one woman to be their sovereign. In comparison, among the world's ninety democracies that have *elected* a woman to be head of state in the twentieth century, only forty-eight, or 53%, have done so. It therefore appears that constitutional hereditary monarchies, a type of government representing biological maternalism, are *more* open to choosing women as heads of government than are democratic countries.

Making Politics a Woman's Game

The Power of Political Context

As Burns, Schlozman, and Verba established, when women candidates run for public office, women in general become more engaged in the political process. Making politics look like a woman's game as well as a man's has a clear impact on women's interest in politics.[64] Political scientist Kathleen Dolan concurs. She examined the power of a gendered political environment to enhance women's election to national office by counting the number of newspaper stories devoted to women candidates appearing in local and national newspapers from September 1 to the day before the election for each year from 1990 to 2000.[65] It turned out that a gendered political environment increases the probability of voting for a woman candidate for the House of Representatives by 0.19.[66] In addition, media coverage of issues that have a "manifest gender content," such as abortion and the women's movement, have a greater impact on voter choice than do issues with a "latent gender content," such as education and the environment.[67] As Dolan found, the key aspect of the electoral environment is "the amount of gendered information that is available to voters."[68]

As Kim Kahn notes, there is no way around the stereotypical views of men and women in general and of male and female candidates in particular. What changes is the "electoral climate," an environmental factor that renders being male or female as a candidate an advantage or a disadvantage.[69] When the traits stereotypically associated with being female correspond to an electoral climate that is also defined as female, women have a political advantage. By measuring the proportion of issues and traits that represent male versus female themes in the coverage of political campaigns, Kahn validates that "people have favorable (or warm) attitudes toward women who run in campaigns highlighting 'female' issues while their attitudes toward women competing in 'male'-oriented environments are significantly cooler."[70] This relationship is even stronger for nonincumbents than for candidates who are already in office. The more positive view of women in a female-centered electoral climate also translates into more people voting for women.[71]

Undoubtedly the media plays a crucial role in determining the amount of gender information available to voters. However, so, too, does a democratic state's maternal public policies affect voter attitudes. While the media coverage of campaigns, including women candidates and women's issues, waxes and wanes in response to election cycles, the state's public policies are ongoing, quasi-permanent sources of gender information. By defining what the state "does," they in effect define what it means to be political. Therefore, an even more powerful mechanism for electing women to office than either the women candidates themselves or the media coverage is the *state* itself. When it embodies the characteristics associated both with women's individual sameness with men and their maternal group difference from men by adopting public policies representing maternal traits, it boosts public attitudes about the suitability of women as political leaders and women's election to national political office.

Public Policies Cause Political Attitudes

It is common, of course, to view public attitudes as leading to the adoption of public policies rather than the other way around.[72] For example, a public with more egalitarian attitudes about gender would be expected to endorse policies that promote women's political equality, such as abortion rights, family leave, and child care, if not gender quotas. A growing body of evidence, however, reverses the causal path, showing that once public policies are in place, whatever has caused them, those policies can then have an impact on public attitudes, as shown in figure 1.1.

Once public policies are in place, they can exert an influence on the very attitudes that undoubtedly were involved in their establishment in the first place. Public policies that promote women's equality, for example, such as gender quotas, could not come into being without preliminary public support for such quotas. After gender quotas are in place, their very existence has a feedback effect that reinforces attitudes about women's equality that were crucial to their initial adoption.[73] Policy feedback does *not* replace the initial importance of attitudes for generating support for policies. Rather, both factors are needed. Public attitudes affect policies, but so do public policies, once in place, affect attitudes.

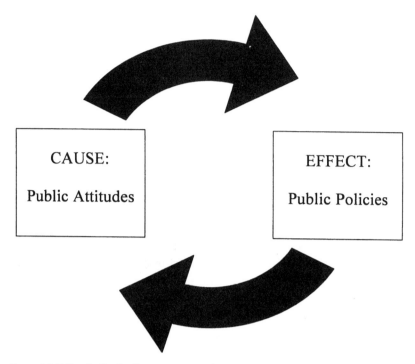

Figure 1.1: Policy feedback effects—reversing the causal arrow.

Solving the American Puzzle

A hybrid state that represents both women's individual sameness with men and their maternal difference is the norm for most democracies comparable to the United States. The United States affirms public policies representing individual equality, but falls short when it comes to representing maternal traits. In terms of social maternalism, although the United States has some care-giving policies, such as Medicaid and Medicare, it does not come close to funding health care, for example, at the levels of comparable democracies. Nor does the American Constitution define the state as having an affirmative duty to meet the basic economic needs of the people, in contrast to the constitutions of most other comparable democracies that do.

In addition to failing to adopt policies that represent social maternalism, the United States also lacks public policies representing biological maternalism. It has not yet adopted gender quotas, and at its founding it destroyed its monarchical heritage. Hence, the American state is a "motherless democracy" in two senses. First, it has a dearth of women represented in political office, thereby lacking the support women supply for the passage of policies oriented toward nurturing and care. Second, it is motherless in the sense that it lacks public policies representing maternal traits, whether socially or biologically defined. Failure to assign maternal traits to the government produces a political context that by default leaves maternalism located solely in spheres outside the state, such as the home, the market's service sector, or private charitable institutions. Consequently, people who are viewed as having maternal traits, such as women, also are relegated to realms outside the state.[74]

For advancing women's representation as elected political leaders, the motherless status of the American state is a disaster that starts with its origins. When the United States destroyed the first type of state maternalism, hereditary monarchies, at its founding, this did not mean that women no longer had maternal identities in relation to familial roles. Rather, it meant that those roles no longer connected women to the government as members of a ruling, dynastic family, much less as sovereigns of the political realm. To the contrary, once the family was cut-off from the state, the maternalism attributed to women signified only women's location in the home. It was from this private sphere location that women were then supposed to make informal political contributions, not as voters or officeholders in the state, but rather as Republican Mothers outside the state who would raise children to be good citizens.[75]

Since the public attributes maternal traits to all women, whether women actually are or want to be social or biological mothers, once maternalism is absolutely cut off from the state by means of a violent revolution that ideologically and institutionally demolishes the first form of state maternalism, monarchies, all women are assigned solely to the private sphere, whatever their actual motherhood status. Thus, for example, by 1808, every state in the United States barred all women from voting rights, that is, from a location inside the state, not just mothers who were taking care of children. Lest we think this was only a phenomenon of the bygone past, let us recall that in much more recent times, the Supreme Court did exactly the same thing in regard to jury duty.

The Sixth Amendment of the Constitution mandates that individuals who have been accused of a criminal offense be tried by an impartial jury.[76] Courts have interpreted an impartial jury to mean that jurors are drawn from a representative cross section of the community. As the court explained in 1942 in *Glasser v. United States*, "the proper functioning of the jury system, and, indeed, our democracy itself, requires that the jury be a 'body truly representative of the community' and not the organ of any special group or class."[77] As law scholar Joanna Grossman notes, a *representative* jury requires that *defendants* in criminal prosecutions have juries composed of members of their community.[78]

Another requirement of jury duty, however, is citizenship. The jury is a crucial instrument of self-governance, whereby citizens can make decisions about the criminal status of an individual prior to the state imposing punishment on that individual.[79] As such, "the jury has been the symbol of a democratic people zealous of freedom and afraid of centralized government power."[80] Jury duty, therefore, denotes not just the right of the criminal defendant to be tried by his or her peers, but also the right of a citizen to be a *juror*. In *Powers v. Ohio*[81] the Supreme Court reaffirmed the importance of citizenship to jury duty when it noted, "With the exception of voting, for most citizens, the honor and privilege of jury duty is their most significant opportunity to participate in the democratic process."[82]

Statutes that exclude individuals solely on the basis of their group characteristics, such as race, class, or sex, violate both the "fact-finding ability of the jury" and the political citizenship rights of the individuals excluded. Yet throughout American history states did just that, using characteristics of subordinate groups to exclude individuals from jury duty, thereby violating both representative and citizenship standards of political inclusion. Many states, for example, once routinely excluded people from jury duty on the basis of their race. The Supreme Court put an end to that in 1879. In *Strauder v. West Virginia*, the Supreme Court ruled that the exclusion of individuals from jury duty on the basis of race violated the Equal Protection Clause of the Fourteenth Amendment.[83]

A different story, however, emerged with regard to sex discrimination as a principle for composing jury pools.[84] As late as 1961, in three states all women were absolutely prohibited from participating on juries, and in eighteen states and the District of Columbia all women were absolutely exempted from jury duty, which meant that they had to make an explicit request to be included in the jury pool. Florida was one of the eighteen states that gave women an automatic exemption from jury duty, whereby no female could serve on a jury unless she personally requested to be put on the jury list. No wonder that in such states the overwhelming proportion of people in the jury pools were men.

Mrs. Gwendolyn Hoyt, who lived in Florida, got into an unusually violent argument with her husband after he had admitted to being unfaithful and proclaimed that he was leaving her forever. In what she described as a moment of "temporary insanity," she grabbed a baseball bat, assaulted her husband, and killed him. Because of the Florida statute that used sex as a criterion for jury duty, out of the 10,000 people eligible for jury duty in her district, only ten were women. The result was an all-male jury, which tried and convicted Mrs. Hoyt of second-degree murder. Mrs. Hoyt appealed on the grounds that she was denied equal protection of the law by virtue of the fact that the jury pool discriminated against women, thereby producing a jury without women. She claimed that the Florida legislation was unconstitutional because, by denying her the right to be tried by women as well as men, she was denied access to women jurors who might "have been more understanding or compassionate than men in assessing the quality of [her] act and her defense of 'temporary insanity.'"[85]

What had worked for race in 1879, however, did not yet work for sex in 1961. In *Hoyt*, rather than striking down state statutes that discriminated on the basis of sex, the Court declared instead that the use of sex as a criterion for jury duty "in no way resembles . . . [the use of] race or color."[86] The reason given by the Court was that states have a rational foundation for using sex as a criterion for jury duty, namely preserving the "general welfare" by relieving women "from the civic duty of jury duty," so that "woman [*sic*] [who] is still regarded as the center of home and family life," can fulfill the domestic responsibilities so crucial for the well-being of society.[87] The Court acknowledged that the Florida statute made no distinction between married and unmarried women, between women responsible for child care and those who were not, or between women with young children and those with adult children. As the Court explained, "Florida could have limited the [jury] exemption . . . only to women who have family responsibilities . . . [nevertheless] we cannot regard it as irrational for a state legislature to consider preferable a broad exemption" that excludes all women solely on the basis of sex.[88]

This is a classic example of how a state can profess the value of maternalism without giving it a political meaning that locates women inside the public sphere, rather than outside. In the *Hoyt* decision, women's group difference is defined in terms of their maternal capacities and roles, and the Court acknowledges the importance of maternalism for the well-being of society. However, rather than serving as a reason for women's political inclusion as jurors, the maternal traits attributed to women serve instead as a pretext for their political exclusion. The *Hoyt* decision is especially significant in that it was made by the Warren Court, the very same justices who in 1954 ruled in the landmark case *Brown v. Board of Education*[89] that "separate is not equal" in the context of racially segregated public schools. Yet when it came to sex discrimination, this progressive, forward-thinking, stereotype-breaking, "liberal" Court, as it is remembered today, had no vision. It seemed perfectly reasonable to the Court, as it had to the American Founders, to exclude women from a political institution, the jury, so central to American democracy, "because of" women's maternal group difference from men. The Supreme Court came to its senses only in 1975, when it ruled in *Taylor v. Louisiana*[90] that it is just as unconstitutional to use sex as a criterion for jury duty as it is to use race.

In the United States, therefore, women's maternal identities have regularly been used against them to justify their exclusion from the state by denying to women such basic political rights as the right to vote, the right to hold political office, and the right to serve on juries. Small wonder that many feminists balk at the very mention of the word, maternalism. For them, it is a risky enterprise to invoke maternal identities in the context of advancing women's political inclusion, one that does little but stimulate divisive controversies about such issues as reductionism, essentialism, intersectionality, and the normative and instrumental value of a liberal state for promoting women's political representation. See Appendix 1 for a discussion of such concerns. However, women's maternal identities are part and parcel of electoral arenas, like it or not, and, presumably the public's attribution of maternal identities to women is here to stay for the foreseeable future. A constructive question, therefore, is what makes maternal identities signify women's political inclusion rather exclusion. The answer provided here is that it is the state itself that defines the political meaning of maternalism vis-à-vis its public policies. When the public policies of a democratic state that by definition represent individualism also represent maternalism, the public learns a lesson, namely, that it is both women's sameness with men and women's maternal difference from men that signifies their location inside the state as elected officeholders in the public sphere of governance.

The laggard status of America with respect to women's political inclusion stems from its failure to combine public policies based on individualism with those representing social or biological maternalism, in contrast to most comparable democracies. The one exception to America's motherless trajectory occurred in the early decades of the twentieth century, when many states and the federal government briefly adopted welfare provision as a form of state maternalism. Significantly, in this period women finally achieved the right to vote when the 19th Amendment was added to the Constitution in 1920, thereby locating women inside the state on the basis of a federal guarantee. However, the United States subsequently failed to sustain its early maternalist public policies, and it is the current absence of such policies that explain why today the United States lags behind comparable democracies in the election of women to national political office.

Defining Maternal Public Policies **2**

"The Personal Is Political"

The early 1960s and 70s witnessed a remarkable women's rights movement in the United States, the impact of which is felt to this day. Following in the wake of a civil rights revolution that challenged racism, women began to see that the problems of American society included another -ism: sexism. As African Americans demanded the right to attend schools and to enter occupations of their choice "in spite of" the color of their skin, so, too, at this time did women inaugurate new demands for educational and occupational rights as individuals who should be treated the same as men "in spite of" their sex.

Activists launching Second Wave Feminism, as this movement is called, are notable for coining the saying, "the personal is political." By this they meant that the acquisition of individual rights alone was not enough to secure women's equality with men in the American state. Rather, to achieve that equality, women also needed government policies, such as day care funding and family leave guarantees, which expanded maternal roles identified with the home or the service sector of the market to the state itself. Consequently, the mantra of the women's rights movement that the "personal is political," demanded that the state recognize that many of the problems faced traditionally and individually by women as caregivers to their families should be faced collectively with government assistance in the public sphere. Child care, for example, should be defined as the public responsibility of the government, not solely as the private personal responsibility of individual mothers alone. "The personal is political," therefore, called upon the state to guarantee more than public policies representing individualism. The state should also guarantee public policies representing maternalism.

State Individualism: Negative Individual Rights

By definition, democracies are countries that base public policies on individualism and guarantee *negative individual rights*. These rights refer to what the state will *not* do—specifically, it will not interfere with people's lives any more than is necessary to ensure a modicum of law and order, and it will not treat people differently because of their ascriptive group differences, such as their race or sex. Negative individual rights thus guarantee that the state will treat all individuals the same. In the 1960s and 70s, in the United States, congressional legislation and the Supreme Court expanded negative individual rights to guarantee sex equality. This expansion included women's rights to employment and educational opportunities, to obtain financial credit ratings, to participate in military training, and to use contraceptives—all on the same basis as men. Women also acquired the right to choose an abortion as individuals constitutionally entitled to make decisions about their reproductive options without undue government interference.

State Maternalism: Positive Group Rights

While negative individual rights are vital for women's full inclusion in society, they are not enough. Also needed are government guarantees of *positive group rights*, that is, policies guaranteeing that the government will offer benefits, protections, and privileges to people precisely because of their group differences by virtue, for example, of being ill, disabled, elderly, a parent, or poor. "The personal is political" mantra, therefore, demands that the state adopt public policies representing not only women's sameness with men, but also women's maternal group difference from men. It is a demand for policies affirming positive group rights, namely, that the state should act maternally by providing child-care funding for women or for parents in general because they are groups in need of government assistance. "The personal is political" therefore demands that the *state itself* adopt public policies constituting the maternal traits voters attribute to women.

Representation, Not Regulation

All countries regulate maternalism by means of marriage, abortion, and parenting laws. In some, such as China, there are regulations on the number of children it is permissible to generate. In others, such as the United States, the distribution of welfare benefits can be tied to a recipient's marital status. A case in point is the Personal Responsibility and Work Opportunity Act (PRWOPA), passed in the United States in 1996, which imposes middle-class and racially biased norms on recipients. One of its components, called Temporary Assistance to Needy Families (TANF), for example, ostentatiously strives to establish two-parent families by requiring mothers to identify the biological father of their children, regardless of the many reasons women might be reluctant to do so, such as the threat of domestic violence. It also requires single mothers to engage in market work without concern for how such regulations interfere with women's parenting decisions and child-rearing options. The family formation stipulations also automatically confer on biological fathers social and financial connections to their children regardless of the consent of the biological mothers. Such policies prevent poor, single women from exercising their right to control their intimate associations and to form a family on their own terms.[1] These are but a few of the many ways in which welfare policies can have a punitive impact on disadvantaged groups.[2]

What benefits women, of course, is not coercive policies that undermine their independence, but rather the way the government itself becomes associated vis-à-vis its public policies with the maternal traits voters attribute to women. To the degree that government policies do connect the maternal to the state as a characteristic of government activity, the public will learn to associate maternalism with government and along with that lesson, to associate maternalists—women—with the government. In other words, what the state does matters to individual recipients of policies, but also to the public at large. I draw upon the perspective that "what the state does matters" by analyzing how state individualism and state maternalism generate more favorable public attitudes about women's suitability as political leaders and higher percentages of women elected to political office.

What the State Does Matters

The state creates political contexts that affect public attitudes in a variety of ways. Political scientist Lee Ann Banaszak shows, for example, that political regimes have a long-term impact on the public's policy preferences.

The German Democratic Republic (GDP, East Germany) was a strong supporter of women's employment outside the home while both the GDP and the Federal Republic of Germany (FRG, West Germany) preferred to support women's roles within the family. The GDP adopted public policies to promote women's employment, such as state-subsidized child care, extensive maternity leaves, and reduced work hours for women with two or more children.[3] By contrast, the public policies of the FRG discouraged mothers from working. There was a dearth of child-care facilities available for employed women, and West German policies used tax incentives to encourage women with children to remain in the home.[4]

Banaszak finds that the heritage of gendered public policies in East and West Germany continued to influence public attitudes about appropriate gender roles long after German unification, regardless of demographic differences between the regions of East and West Germany. Even after public policies supporting women's employment were reduced in the aftermath of German unification, East Germans were more supportive of women's nontraditional roles as workers than were West Germans. The effects of the GDP public policies on public attitudes lasted fifteen years beyond the date of unification with West Germany, which indicates that the impact of gendered public policies on citizen attitudes about the suitability of women for traditional versus nontraditional roles in society can endure even after the initial policies have all but vanished.[5] Similarly, political scientist Jason Wittenberg, establishes how public attitudes on policy issues, as initially established in the context of one political regime, can persist even "amid prolonged social upheaval, disruptive economic development, and demographic transformations."[6]

When it comes to the formation of public attitudes, therefore, what the state does matters. In the case of women, state policies generate more favorable public attitudes about the suitability of women as political leaders, which subsequently lead to the election of more women to political office. Thus, women's political leadership is promoted in democracies by a political context in which the government's public policies represent both individual equality and the maternal traits voters associate with women. That is, the best political context for advancing women's political leadership is generated by a hybrid state that represents both individualism and maternalism.

Contemporary democracies necessarily endorse individualism—negative individual rights—by means of government policies guaranteeing that all individuals will have equal civil and political rights "in spite of" their ascriptive group differences, such as race, class, sex, religion, linguistic heritage, or other such identities. One measure of whether a country has such public policies is the survey of freedom in the world conducted by Freedom House. For over sixty years Freedom House, founded by Eleanor Roosevelt, Wendell Willkie, and others interested in the international prospects for democratic governance,[7] has evaluated the degree of democratic practice characterizing countries around the world. This organization has measured how adequately the practices of a country protect the political rights and civil liberties of individuals "in spite of" their ascriptive group differences.

In the words of Freedom House, its survey "provides an annual evaluation of the state of global freedom as experienced by *individuals*. Freedom is the opportunity to act spontaneously in a variety of fields *outside the control of the government* and other centers of potential domination. Freedom House measures freedom according to two broad categories: political rights and civil liberties. Political rights enable people to participate freely in the political process, including through the right to vote, compete for public office, and elect representatives who have a decisive impact on public policies and are accountable to the electorate. Civil liberties allow for the freedoms of expression and belief, associational and organizational rights, rule of law, and personal autonomy *without interference from the state*."[8]

Freedom House, therefore, measures democratic practice as the degree to which a government guarantees negative individual rights. Because the goal of Freedom House is to assess "the real-world rights and freedoms enjoyed by individuals," scores are not based on the constitutional arrangement of governmental bodies or on legislation per se. Freedom House scores instead reflect democratic practice, or the way people experience political rights and civil liberties. The specific rights that Freedom House regards as indicators of a state's practice of democracy derive from the United Nation's Universal Declaration of Human Rights,[9] which in turn reflects what Americans are most familiar with in the form of the Bill of Rights that was added to the American Constitution in 1791. Freedom House considers a "free" state one that performs "individualism" as a public policy, in terms of guaranteeing to individuals their civil and political rights.[10]

Other public policies guarantee *positive group rights,* that is, government guarantees to individuals of benefits, protections, or privileges specifically "because of" their ascriptive group statuses, such as their race, sex, religion, and so forth. Public policies that guarantee positive rights to groups representing social or biological traits associated with women constitute what I mean by the term *state maternalism*. The three public policies by which the government can associate itself with social and biological maternal traits are welfare provision, gender quotas, and hereditary monarchies.[11]

Welfare Provision

Care-Work as Social Maternalism

One of the ways the public associates women with social maternalism is as providers of care to people after they are born. Women are more likely than men to nurture and to care for others. Not surprisingly, the dictionary definition of maternalism, defines it by the verb "to mother," that is, to engage in nurturing and care. As the *OED* notes, the verb "to mother," is a sex-neutral term; anyone, male or female, or "anything" can take on mothering roles by caring for or protecting someone or something. In nautical terms, one can ask for a torpedo boat to be "mothered," to be protected, as in the "torpedo craft could also be 'mothered.'"[12] However, when men, women, and even things do "mother," their activity is characterized as a form of maternalism, not paternalism. The reason, undoubtedly, is that over historical time and political place, and still today, though men and things can mother, women mother the most. The disproportionately greater involvement of women in mothering, compared to male mothering, renders the social construction of women's sex group difference from men to be social maternalism, defined by care-work.[13]

The most obvious example of state maternalism is the provision of state welfare. The basic question for all people everywhere is where and how to obtain food, shelter, clothing, health care, and education.[14] People satisfy their dependency needs for the care provided by others through four major delivery systems: the family, the market, charities, and the state.[15] The first three systems are private, and the last is publicly funded.[16]

The family is the basic private delivery system. The *OED* defines a family as "people who are descended or claiming descent from a common ancestor . . . the group of persons consisting of the parents and their children, whether actually living together or not; the unity formed by those who are nearly connected by blood or affinity." Traditionally, the family is the institution that cares for people. It is the primary institution that satisfies people's dependency needs. Historically, unities formed by blood or affinity, namely families, gathered or grew their own food, built their own shelters, made their own clothes, and provided for their own health care and education. The family, and disproportionately women within the family, is also historically the institution that cares for its members when they become ill, elderly, or disabled.[17]

The market and charities are additional private delivery systems of care. The market, defined as the commercial resources of a nation and financial resources of people, is a resource for care in the sense that people who are employed and who receive sufficient financial remuneration from the market or have other financial resources can purchase the materials and services necessary to satisfy their dependency needs. Thus, a person who earns sufficient funds can purchase food, shelter, clothing, health care, and education. For people without access to family or market resources to satisfy their dependency needs, namely the poor, those needs can be met by charitable institutions, such as churches and nonprofit assistance organizations. Charitable institutions provide food, clothing, shelter, health care, and education to those who lack family or market resources.

In many countries, the work of care as originally performed by the family is transferred to the *state*. As Alva Myrdal notes, prior to the advent of state social security policies, people were protected from disabilities resulting from illness, old age, and other infirmities by the care provided in the context of the family as an institution.[18] Women within the family were typically identified as the primary performers of such work in their roles as wives and mothers. Thus, the social construction of women's maternal group difference from men was defined in terms of "care-work."[19]

As Mrydal observes, however, in the development of a welfare state, the "protective tasks which earlier had been provided for within the family are . . . transferred to more expert public bodies . . . a whole series of institutions . . . [forming] an interlocking system of social assistance."[20] Not surprisingly, women perform more work in the public provision of social assistance as paid professionals. They disproportionately choose service occupations, such as social work, primary school education, nursing, or unpaid volunteer social service. Hence, women's disproportionate engagement in care, whether performed within or outside the home, culturally defines such work, or welfare provision, as "women's work."[21] As Jane Jenson notes, it is important not to equate unpaid work with care, since care also can be paid for as a market commodity. She suggests distinguishing between where the care is provided (the family, charities, the market, the state), who cares (women or men), and who pays (women, men, charities, or the state).[22]

The idea of a welfare state is based on dual assumptions: that all human beings have a right to life that includes basic care, such as the provision of food, clothing, shelter, health, and education; and that the state guarantees the provision of care to meet the needs of people. The textbook definition of a welfare state, according to Gosta Esping-Andersen, therefore, "involves state responsibility for securing some basic modicum of welfare for its citizens."[23] When the state fuses itself with welfare by guaranteeing that it will provide care for people, the result is what is termed "social citizenship." As defined by T. H. Marshall, social citizenship refers to the right of people to receive the state-provided care necessary for their survival.[24] For others, social citizenship refers to the right of people, men and women, to be providers of care or to be free from providing care as a result of the assumption of that work by the state.[25] For still others social citizenship requires transforming a welfare state into a feminist social democracy expanding our understanding of citizenship, socializing our definition of rights, finding new loci for participation, and privileging gender in defining equality.[26]

Types of Welfare States

According to Esping-Andersen, there are different types of welfare states with varying degrees of development. First, for a state to be a genuine welfare state, "a majority of its daily activities must be devoted to the welfare needs of households."[27] Second, if the state provides care-work only when the family or market delivery systems fail, it is a residual welfare[28] state, in contrast to an institutionalized welfare state that "extends its commitments to all areas of distribution that are necessary for welfare . . . [and] is universal . . . [embodying] an institutionalized commitment to welfare."[29] Finally, there are theoretical models of welfare states that can be used to assess particular welfare state construction.[30]

Esping-Andersen classifies the relation between welfare state policies and the market into three major types: liberal, conservative or corporatist, and social democratic.[31] The liberal welfare regime provides care-work to people only when they cannot provide it for themselves, by means of either family, charitable, or market resources. In a liberal welfare regime there is no development of a person's right to care, only a person's need for care. Thus, acceptance of care from the state is stigmatized as the failure of people to secure care for themselves, particularly the failure to provide for that care by means of market employment. According to him examples of liberal welfare regimes are the United States, Canada, and Australia.[32] The conservative or corporatist welfare regime in Esping-Andersen's typology does incorporate the principle that all individuals have a right to care and that the state should replace the market as its main provider. However, these regimes make no attempt to restructure the stratification and inequality of the market. Instead they are committed to preserving traditional market structures based on class inequalities. His examples of corporatist welfare states are Austria, France, Germany, and Italy.[33]

According to Esping-Andersen, social democratic welfare regimes, like corporatist welfare regimes, establish that individuals have a right to care and that the state should be its main provider. However, they also seek to dismantle inequalities that structure the family and the market by equalizing class relations within the market. Scandinavian countries, although they retain some liberal characteristics, are primarily social democratic states.[34] From the perspective of women's political citizenship, among the more serious failings of these types of welfare state, is their gender bias. Scholars Ann Shola Orloff, Julia S. O'Connor, and Sheila Shaver have written convincingly that attention to the relationship between welfare state policies and the market fail to appreciate how welfare policies affect stratification within the family for women or women's relationship to market employment. They invoke Helga Maria Herne's idea of a woman-friendly welfare state as one that promotes women's independence, both within the family and in relation to the market.[35] They also challenge the classification of Esping-Andersen's liberal regimes, arguing that the only true liberal welfare state is the United States.[36]

Others direct attention to how welfare policies can decrease women's equality and economic independence. As Eileen Boris and Peter Bardaglio show, in American society, the implementation of welfare policies did little more than shift women's subordination within a patriarchal family to women's subordination within a patriarchal state.[37] Consequently, the nineteenth- and twentieth-century domination of women by men was not destroyed but was merely transferred from the home to the state. The state became the father or dominant male over women, dictating women's opportunities for employment, divorce, reproductive options, and family relations by using patriarchal principles to regulate women's activities in society.[38] Similarly, Diane Sainsbury notes that use of the breadwinner or family model for determining welfare policies means that women become entitled to welfare benefits only by virtue of their status as a wife or a mother, not by virtue of their status as an individual. This discriminates against women by imposing on them the necessity of a familial identity in order to be entitled to welfare assistance.[39]

Still others devote their attention to explaining why or why not nations develop a welfare state in general or particular types of welfare states. Some point to gender relations and motherhood roles as prime determinants.[40] Other influences include industrialization, working-class relations, national values, political traditions,[41] race,[42] state structures, legal institutions,[43] social movement activists, trade unionists, civil servants, political parties,[44] postindustrialism and globalization.[45]

Measuring Welfare Provision

Needless to say, scholarship on the welfare state is a thriving subfield of political science. I expand the analysis by drawing attention to the *constitutional standing of care-work* in combination with the degree to which a country *funds* welfare provision.

Constitutions. In the vast literature concerning the welfare state, a focus on the constitutions of such countries is usually missing. This is odd, because welfare provision is the prototypical form of social citizenship that T. H. Marshall refers to as defining the modern state. The question is not merely whether a country funds programs for those in need but also whether it conceives of the state as having an affirmative duty to do so.[46] The crucial point about government welfare provision is its normative as well as its practical dimension. Conceptualizing the modern, democratic state as an entity supposed not merely to guarantee law and order, national security, and individuals' civil and political rights, but also to guarantee the provision of welfare to meet people's basic economic needs is what is meant by social citizenship.

It is odd that constitutions are so often ignored in connection with the welfare state literature, because the study of constitutions is a growing scholarly enterprise. Recently more and more attention is being devoted to comparative analyses of constitutions, including the way they conceptualize the state to recognize and protect groups subordinated "because of" their race, class, sex, linguistic heritage, religion, and a host of other ascriptive characteristics. The constitutionalization of welfare provision as another measure of the welfare state, therefore, reflects not merely the practical, but also the normative dimension of government support for the needy. Constitutions are relatively more permanent than legislation and court decisions, and the inclusion of provisions in constitutions (or in the laws of the land that serve in lieu of a constitution), represent the most enduring values of a country.[47] As political scientist Vivian Hart notes, the American Constitution "specifies what government may do in pursuit of its definition of the public interest, and, within its guarantees of rights, prescribes a set of relationships among the state, the society, and the individual."[48] Thus, a constitution "is much more than a document that spells out a set of laws and lays out the design of government."[49] It also creates the very legal, social, economic, and cultural identity of the state as a carefully planned set of "meta-rules" for the political governance of a nation-state. Though not immutable, its system of laws is so fundamentally rooted that the "procedural order appears as given."[50]

Funding. In addition to whether a country's constitution affirms welfare provision as a duty of the state, so too is a country's funding for those in need relevant to its status as a welfare state. At issue is not merely the absolute amount of funds expended upon welfare provision from all private and public sources, but rather the proportion of funds expended on welfare that is specifically contributed by the state. One cross-national index of government-funded welfare provision comes from the proportion (percentage) of public funds spent on health care.[51] Health is so basic a need of all human beings that some people place it front and center as a core definition of human rights and citizenship.[52] Government-funded health care, therefore, is a good measure of welfare provision. I use this measure to assess a government's commitment to funding welfare needs. Specifically, I categorize countries by those that do and do not contribute at least 50% of the costs of health care for the people. Using the percentage of funds spent on health by the government as a measure of welfare provision, does not require that the recipients of health funding to be female. Rather, what associates government health care provision with women's maternal identities is that it is women rather than men who the public associates with the provision of health care. Initially health care was provided within the home, primarily by women in their roles as wives and mothers, as they nursed the sick and the needy. Later, health care roles shifted to include the market, as private providers become heath care workers. Still, women in the service sector of the health care field remain a dominant group, as shown by the percentages of nurses who are women and the percentages of women who work in health care related professions compared to men. Although at the levels of surgeons and highly trained medical professionals there is a greater percentage of men, in terms of the health care field as a whole, women dominate the field in the market, service sector.[53]

Constitutions and *funding.* It is the combination, therefore, of constitutional and funding guarantees for the public provision of health care that constitutes the measure of welfare provision used here. If a country affirms welfare provision in its constitution as an obligatory duty of the state, *and* the state contributes at least 50% of the funds spent on health care, then that country is one that maternalizes its state in the form of welfare provision. Of twenty-five democracies comparable to the United States in wealth and urbanization,[54] 80% constitutionalize maternal public policies by establishing that it is an affirmative duty of the state to provide for the basic welfare needs of the people, as table 2.1 indicates. Notably, the United States is not one of these countries. With the exception of the United States, all of the world's comparable democracies have government-spending levels that cover at least 50% of their health-care costs (see table 2.1). Some countries contribute at very high levels, such as the United Kingdom (82.2%), New Zealand (76.8%), and Luxembourg (89.9%), as well as the Nordic nations.

Table 2.1 Western democracies[a] and maternal public policies[b], 2006

	Welfare Provision[c]			Gender[d] Quotas	Hereditary[e] Monarchies
		% Gov funded	Constitutional Provision		
Yes	Australia	67.90	Yes	Australia	Australia
	Austria	69.30	Yes	Austria	Bahamas
	Belgium	71.70	Yes	Belgium	Belgium
	Canada	70.80	Yes	Canada	Canada
	Denmark	82.40	Yes	Denmark	Denmark
	Finland	75.60	Yes	Germany	Luxembourg
	Germany	74.90	Yes	Iceland	The Netherlands
	Greece	56.00	Yes	Ireland	New Zealand
	Iceland	82.90	Yes	Israel	Norway
	Ireland	76.00	Yes	Italy	Spain
	Italy	75.30	Yes	Luxembourg	Sweden
	Luxembourg	89.90	Yes	Netherlands	United Kingdom
	The Netherlands	63.30	Yes	Norway	
	New Zealand	76.80	Yes	Portugal	
	Norway	85.50	Yes	Spain	
	Portugal	69.00	Yes	Sweden	
	Spain	71.40	Yes	Switzerland	
	Sweden	85.20	Yes	United Kingdom	
	Switzerland	57.10	Yes		
	United Kingdom	82.20	Yes		
		80%[f]	(20)[g]	72% (18)	48% (12)
	The Bahamas	57.00	No	The Bahamas	Austria
	France	76.00	No	Finland	Finland
	Israel	69.20	No	France	France
	Japan	77.90	No	Greece	Germany
	United States	44.40	No	Japan	Greece
				New Zealand	Iceland
No				United States	Ireland
					Israel
					Italy
					Japan
					Portugal

Table 2.1   continued

	Maternal Public Policies			
	Welfare Provision[c]		Gender[d] Quotas	Hereditary[e] Monarchies
	% Gov funded	Constitutional Provision		
				Switzerland United States 52% (13)
	20% (5)		28% (7)	
Total	100% (25)		100% (25)	100% (25)

a) Western democracies: Democracies comparable to the United States: Have been a democracy since 1978 (coded as "free" on Freedom House scales, 1978 to the present), have a per capita income of $10,000 and above, and percent urban is 58% and above. Data on per capita income and urbanization is from World Bank: WDI Online; World Bank: World Development Report, World Economic Outlook Database, April 2004.

b) State maternalism: Defined by a public policy that represents social or biological maternal traits voters associate with women. Such public policies may, but need not, target women as recipients of benefits.

c) Welfare provision: Combination of 50% (not rounded-off) or more of the funds spent on health care are provided by the government and a constitutional provision or comparable information affirming that it is the state's duty to provide for people's welfare. Data on percent health care funds provided by the government are from the Organization for Economic Co-operation and Development (OECD), Social Expenditure Database, (2004). Data on constitutional provisions are based on the author's coding of constitutions, as of 2006; the constitutional provision can be a provision for specific assistance, such as the provision of education, health, or other such welfare services, or a statement about the provision of general welfare benefits to people. Constitutional provisions of pensions for government employees are not included.

d) Gender quotas: (1) Measured as a legislative quota above 15% in lower or upper house, (2) or a voluntary political party quota of 30% or more in at least two parties, (3) or a voluntary political party quota of 40% or more in at least one party and the political party is represented in the legislature in 1999, 2003, and (4) the justification for the gender quota is based on the sex difference between men and women. Political parties that are "women only," or "all women" are not included in this measure. Data for gender quotas are from the Global Database of Quotas for Women, Institute for Democracy and Electoral Assistance (IDEA), Stockholm University and from Mona Lena Krook and Diana O'Brien, "The Politics of Group Representation: Quotas for Women and Minorities Worldwide," paper presented at the Midwest Political Science Association, 2007.

e) Hereditary monarchies: Monarchies that do not restrict sovereignty to men, as indicated by national constitutions, as coded by the author.

f) Percent political systems in category.

g) Number of political systems in parentheses.

The United States government, however, contributes only 44.4% of the costs of health care, making it an outlier among the world's wealthy, urban democracies. In sum, 80% of the world's democracies comparable to the United States maternalize public policies by both their constitutional and funding commitment to provide for the welfare needs of their population.[55] The United States fails to make the grade, along with The Bahamas, France, Israel, and Japan.

Of course, it is not the case that the United States has no welfare policies at all. To the contrary, as political scientist Christopher Howard establishes, it has an extensive system of tax policies that are hidden from public view, amounting to about $400 billion in 1995, or almost half the outlay for direct social welfare payments.[56] While tax policies confer tremendous benefits to people, however, they are not only all but hidden, but also fail to address, much less solve, the glaring inequalities of wealth and economic well-being in American society.[57] This is because the U.S. welfare policies, so often disguised as tax policies, disproportionately benefit more affluent families, not the homeless or the working poor. Policies such as employer pensions, targeted jobs tax credit options, earned income tax credit write-offs, and deductions for mortgage interest payments assume that people are already in a bracket of employment and capital with the good fortune to have a job with a pension and to own their own home.[58]

What is more, it is not as if the United States is completely devoid of economic social provision to the needy or to the elderly. The country does seem committed to maintaining Medicaid and Medicare as basic policies addressing health needs of the American society. The point is rather that the United States does not have a heritage that views the government as having an affirmative duty to provide for the welfare needs of the disadvantaged, as shown by the silence of the American Constitution on this point and by the relatively low level of funding for health care compared to comparable democracies.[59] It is not as if there are no homeless or poor in the United States. To the contrary, the gap between the rich and the poor grows greater and greater with every passing decade. What is missing is a conceptualization and implementation of the state as the entity that is expected to solve the problem of those who are hungry, without shelter, and in need of education and a job when the family and the market fail as delivery systems.

Combining the constitutional provision of welfare with a threshold level of funding produces a new way of analyzing the delivery of economic services by the state to its population. It also frames some basic puzzles. As historian Susan Pedersen notes, it is odd that France developed a more comprehensive set of family policies than did Britain, even though Britain had the more vigorous feminist organizations and labor parties and the much earlier acquisition of women's voting rights.[60] The two constitutions, however, conceptualize the state differently. In Britain the state is viewed as an institution with an affirmative duty to provide for the welfare of the people.[61] The British Constitution, "Part 8, Social Rights, Section 24, General Social Rights," states that "Everyone, as a member of society, has the right to social security and is entitled to the realization, through national effort and international co-operation and in accordance with the organization and resources of each State, of the economic, social and cultural rights indispensable for his dignity and the free development of his personality." In addition, "Section 27" on the "Home," states:

> (1) Everyone has the right to a standard of living adequate for the health and well-being of himself and of his family, including food, clothing, housing and medical care and necessary social services, and the right to security in the event of unemployment, sickness, disability, widowhood, old age or other lack of livelihood in circumstances beyond his control. (2) Motherhood and childhood are entitled to special care and assistance. As children, whether born in or out of wedlock, shall enjoy the same social protection. (3) The National Health Service (NHS) provides comprehensive health care to all residents. Treatment is based on medical priority regardless of patients' income and is financed mainly out of general taxation. Patients pay charges for prescriptions although in practice some 75 percent are supplied free, since charges do not apply to people on low incomes, children, expectant mothers, pensioners and other groups.

By contrast, the French Constitution, Title XII, titled "The Community, Article 77," refers only to the "autonomy" of the members of the French community, not the affirmative duty of the state to provide for their welfare needs:

> (1) In the Community instituted under this Constitution, the States shall enjoy autonomy; they shall conduct their own administration and manage their own affairs democratically and freely, (2) There shall be only one citizenship of the Community, and (3) All citizens shall be equal before the law, regardless of their origin, race or religion. They shall have the same duties.

From a policy-feedback perspective, explaining how the state's adoption of maternal traits teaches the public that maternalism is associated with inclusion in the state, not exclusion. The British and the French states are distinguished not by the degree to which they fund welfare policies but by the degree to which they differ in conceptualizing that activity of the state, regarding it as an affirmative duty in the case of Britain versus a nonconstitutional mandate in the case of France. It is Britain, not France, that supplies the lesson to the public about the state's role as a guarantor of the social citizenship of its population. And not surprisingly, it is in Britain, not France, where women have been elected in greater percentages to the national legislature and as prime minister of the government.[62]

Gender Quotas

Female Sex Classification as Biological Maternalism

One of the traits defining biological maternalism is a classification as female, which is the sex the public views as having the capacity to be pregnant and to bear offspring. Such a public perception jibes with standard dictionary definitions of biological maternalism, as in the *OED*, which also defines maternalism as a *sex classification* that is female by virtue of being the sex that bears offspring.[63] This principle of biological maternalism is represented in the state by gender quotas. Gender quotas, which are really female sex quotas, are public policies that designate a minimum percentage of women to serve in national legislatures simply "because of" their sex classification as female, by means of either a constitutional amendment, a legislative statute, or a voluntary party quota. Thus, gender quotas in public policies define biological maternalism as a female sex classification.

The impact of gender quotas on women's political representation is a burgeoning field of study, most likely because nearly 90% of the world's nations have adopted some form of gender quota. What is not recognized, however, is that gender quotas are a form of state maternalism, similar in principle to welfare provision. Yet, if we start by first establishing what constitutes biological maternal traits, such as a female sex classification, and then ask how that definition can be represented by a public policy, we come to the conclusion that gender quotas are indeed a public policy representing a biological maternal trait, namely a female sex classification. By so doing, I study the impact on public attitudes toward women as political leaders of public policies representing not only *social* reproductive labor, such as welfare policies, but also the impact of public policies representing *biological* reproductive labor, such as gender quotas.

By now, most of the world's countries have some type of gender quota in place for promoting women's political representation. Twelve (6.3% of the world's nation-states) have *constitutionally mandated reserved seats* whereby a specified percentage of legislative seats are reserved for women. Three countries (1.6% of the world's nation-states) maintain *constitutionally regulated party lists*, requiring political parties to include a specified percentage of women on their list of candidates. Thirteen countries (6.8% of the world's nation-states) have *legislative statutes* designating a specified percentage of *legislative seats* to be filled by women. Eighteen (9.4% of the world's nation-states) have *legislative statutes* designating a percentage of women to be included on *party lists* as candidates. And sixty-six countries (34.4% of the world's nation-states) have at least one political party that has a *voluntary, party-based gender quota*, where "policy documents and practices," or sometimes simply the "goodwill" of the party's leadership, designate a specific quota for women's inclusion on candidate lists.

France is a special case in that it has constitutionally mandated gender quotas, and at least one political party has voluntary gender quotas. However, the meaning of gender quotas is quite different. Gender quotas—female sex classification quotas—in the view of most countries are public policies representing a biological maternal trait that refers to what is *different* in terms of women's and men's biological reproductive capacities. The reverse is true, however, in the way France sees constitutional gender quotas. Rather than serving as a marker of the biological maternal *difference* between men and women, gender quotas in France represent the universal *sameness* of men and women. The logic of the parité movement, as historian Joan Scott analyzes, is based on the idea that to be human requires that there be males and females in contrast to all other group distinctions. In the French view, male and female thus become universal signifiers of the human race. It is specifically because both men and women are human that it is necessary to include both men and women in a legislature, in order to have "human beings" represented as "human beings."[64] The universal precept behind parité in France is all but unique in the world. A few other countries have considered endorsing gender quotas on this basis, but only France as of now has done so. Since the representational logic of legally mandated gender quotas in France refers to the human sameness of men and women, rather than to women's biological maternal group difference from men, France is not coded here as having gender quotas.

Gender Quotas Do Not Guarantee Women's Election to Political Office

Research shows that gender quotas do enhance the election of women to national legislatures, as we would expect.[65] Nevertheless, the mere presence of gender quotas is no guarantee that women will be elected to national legislatures on a par with men. There are at least two reasons for this discrepancy: the use of sanctions to enforce gender quotas and the variability in the percentages designated for gender quotas. Of the countries with gender quotas, only 35% employ sanctions for violations of the quotas, and even when sanctions are specified, they often are not enforced. Of the thirty-one countries that have either legislative statutes designating gender quotas or voluntary legislative party quotas, only twelve impose sanctions to enforce them. Among the fifteen countries that have constitutional provisions establishing gender quotas, either by mandating seats or by regulating party lists, only two impose sanctions.

What is more, even when enforced, the sanctions imposed for violating gender quotas are often very mild. In 1999, for instance, France passed what is known as the "parité reform" bill, which amended its Constitution to specify that "the law favors the equal access of women and men to electoral mandates and elective functions" and that political parties are responsible for facilitating this access. In 2000 France passed a new election law that mandated a balance of 50% men and 50% women among candidates for each party in all national legislative elections and all elections using a proportional ballot. In addition, the 2000 election law included a financial penalty for parties or political groupings that failed to balance the number of women and men among their candidates. The penalty is a reduction in public funding as soon as a party deviates by as much as 2% from the 50-50 parity mandate. Such financial penalties, however, even if enforced, do not have a major impact on the larger political parties. Another reason gender quotas are not in and of themselves a guarantee of the election of more women to national legislatures is that in many countries the percentage required is very low. Some set no percentages at all, as in Croatia and Equatorial Guinea. Others set the quota for female representation to be under 10%, as in India, Jordan, Nepal, and Niger. In Kenya the constitutionally prescribed gender quota is as low as 2.68%.

There is tremendous variation, therefore, in types and percentage levels of gender quotas across countries. Assuming that a gender quota would need to be at a reasonably high level to be effective, I establish thresholds for assessing their effect on women's election to political office. To be counted as having gender quotas, therefore, the country must meet one of three criteria: it must have a constitutional or legislated gender quota that represents women's group difference from men above 15%, a voluntary party quota for at least two parties of more than 30%, or at least one voluntary party quota of more than 40%. In the case of political parties, they must have been represented in parliament as recently as 1999 and 2003, and the political party must have met its targets. "All women" political parties are not included in this measure.[66] Given these criteria, 72% of the world's comparable democracies have gender quotas, as is indicated in table 2.1. Again, the United States is not among them.

Hereditary Monarchies

Family-Kinship Networks as Biological Maternalism

Biological motherhood is more than just a female sex classification, of course. It also refers to women who actually have been pregnant and given birth. In regard to giving birth, needless to say, both men and women contribute to the birth of a child when they contribute their sperm and ova respectively as a necessary precondition to the conception of a fertilized ovum. However, over and above that biological parity, at least some individuals from the group of women must be pregnant and give birth, for which there is no male counterpart. Since no child can be born without a biological father and a biological mother, who in turn could not have been born without biological fathers and mothers, being a biological mother is coterminous with the generation of family-kinship networks.[67]

The state represents this definition of biological motherhood in its fusion with family-kinship networks in hereditary monarchies. If state welfare provision has escaped notice in terms of its impact on women's political representation, and if gender quotas have escaped notice as a form of biological state maternalism, it is safe to say that hereditary monarchies have escaped notice altogether. Occasionally there is recognition that the monarchies in the Middle East are the most stable and reliable Arab allies of the United States. Yet, taking monarchies seriously as a significant form of political governance that has connections, however symbolic, to democracy, much less to women's political representation, is anything but a thriving enterprise.[68] This is unfortunate because hereditary monarchies constitute the original way to make the personal political.

Historically the original way the family was fused with the state was in the political form of hereditary monarchies. Even though it is a fusion that entails only one family, the dynastic family, hereditary monarchies constitute the penultimate connection between the family as an institution and the state. To be eligible to be a political ruler requires that one be born into or marry into the dynastic family. Thus, a monarchy, as a hereditary institution,[69] is utterly dependent on women's biological reproductive labor capacities for their political viability. Women of the ruling family must be pregnant and give birth to replenish the pool of those eligible to be sovereigns.[70] When women of the dynastic family get married and give birth, they are doing *political work*. In this way a monarchical state is a form of government that fuses women's biological maternalism, defined in terms of women's generation of family-kinship networks, with the state's institutions of political rule.

Despite dependency upon women's biological reproductive labor, monarchies are usually associated with men, not with women, owing to the preference for men as sovereigns. However, the preference for male leaders in today's monarchies is less than the electoral preference for male leaders. Women have been elected in the twentieth century to be heads of state as prime minister, deputy prime minister, president, or vice president (which is as broadly as one can define electoral executive political leadership) in only 53% of the world's democracies. Yet, women have been chosen to be sovereigns in the twentieth century in 75% of the world's constitutional monarchies. Hence, if hereditary monarchies were to be eliminated on the grounds of their preference for men, electoral democracies would have to be eliminated as well.[71] Rather than eliminate monarchies, it is time to add them to our understanding of how the state's public policies teach voters about the political meaning of maternal traits attributed to women.

Point of Access for Women as Political Rulers

Anthropologists define the family as the institution created by societies to regulate the generation and care of children. What is more, it is women, rather than men, whom the public associates with the generation and social maintenance of the family. It is women's capacity to be pregnant and to give birth that generates children in the first place, and it is women in their roles as wives and mothers who disproportionately care for family members. Thus the public's association of women with biological and social maternal traits extends to associating women with the family as an institution.

As a political regime, a monarchical state represents the biological and social maternal traits voters associate with women and the family by virtue of fusing the family with the state. Although monarchies can be patriarchal,[72] their "dense kin networks" provide for the entry of women of the ruling family into court and into positions of informal and formal political power.[73] Consequently, as historian Antonia Fraser notes, monarchies typically had no clear distinction between private and public life.[74] Activities that are now considered to be personal, such as funerals and marriage, were political activities. The funeral arrangements for Charlemagne, for example, were considered to be political tasks.[75] Similarly, marriage was political because it had profound consequences for political alliances, landholding, and economic power.[76] Women, who were centrally involved with marriage decisions, exercised what can be termed *matrimonial diplomacy*.[77]

Thus, in a monarchical state, women's biological and social maternal roles become political roles. Even women rulers noted for their masculine strength, if not identity, such as Queen Elizabeth I, drew upon maternal imagery to define their relationship to the state. In a speech to her second Parliament, she identified herself as representing a "collective maternity,"[78] asserting, "I assure you all that though after my death you may have many stepdames, yet shall you never have any, a more naturall mother, than I mean to be unto you all."[79]

Of the many types of monarchies, those in which the sovereign has actual political power, such as Middle Eastern monarchies, generally receive the most attention.[80] Yet all monarchies are considered here to represent biological maternal traits that the public associates with women, namely women's capacity to be pregnant and to give birth. This biological reproductive capacity of women is considered by the public to be a necessary means for generating all families in general and the dynastic family in particular. In the case of the latter, it is a capacity that generates the state. However symbolic the monarchical state is in contemporary democracies, its presence nevertheless stands for connecting, not separating, the family and the state. Since women are associated with the family, hereditary monarchies stand for connecting women's familial identities with political rule of the state.[81] Of the world's most wealthy and urban democracies, 48% have hereditary monarchies open to women (see table 2.1). Again, the United States is not among them.

Women's Political Leadership and Maternal Public Policies: What Comes First?

A great deal of research has directed attention to how the presence of women in political office spurs the passage of women-friendly legislation, such as welfare provision. The public assumes that electing women to political office will improve the chances of passing legislation promoting the common interests of all people. A 1996 Gallup poll revealed that in twenty-one of twenty-two countries, respondents, both male and female, "thought things would improve" if more women were in political office. They attributed this to women's unique, relational leadership style, as well as being able to count on women to promote government programs supportive of "community health, public education, children, day care, families, and the elderly."[82]

These perceptions are not ill founded. Research shows that women legislators do consistently support welfare provision, such as educational, family-
leave, and health policies, more than men, irrespective of political party.[83]
Even in traditionally male environments women tend to resist socialization
pressures to become completely male in their political orientations. Women
elected to legislatures engulfed in patriarchal perspectives, as is Taiwan's,
nevertheless retain the "particular political views of women," thereby
avoiding the pitfall of simply mimicking men.[84]

This raises the question as to whether maternal public policies are the effect rather than the cause of women's election to political office. Of course,
these two views are not mutually exclusive. Maternal public policies presumably are strengthened by women's representation in legislatures, and so
too do maternal public policies bolster women's access to political leadership
by teaching the public that the maternal traits voters attribute to women
signify inclusion, not exclusion, in the public sphere of political governance.
That still leaves the question, however: What comes first?

In terms of welfare provision as a public policy representing maternal
traits, when its measurement includes constitutional provision, as it does
here, the answer is that maternal public policies come first. This is because
the constitutions of most countries predate the election of a sizable percentage of women to national legislatures. Norway's constitution, for example, dates back to 1814, Luxembourg's to 1868, and Australia's to 1900,
when there were no women at all in their respective legislatures. Even
more recently the percentage of women in legislatures at the time of the
adoption of their constitutions is low. The date for the Icelandic constitution is 1944, when there were only 3.3% women in the legislature; the date
for the Belgium constitution is 1970, when there were only 2.8% women
in the legislature; the date for Greece is 1975, when there were only 2%
women in the legislature; the date for Portugal is 1976, when there were
only 4.9% women in the legislature; and the date for Canada is 1982, when
there were only 5.8% women in the legislature. With some exceptions,
therefore, the general rule is that the date of adoption of the constitutions
used to measure whether a country conceptualizes the state as responsible
for providing welfare to people in need occurs far in advance of the election of a sizable percentage of women to its legislature. For this reason,
the presence of women cannot be the cause of adopting a constitution that
makes it an affirmative duty of the state to provide for the welfare needs
of people.

Similarly, in the case of gender quotas the whole point of adopting them
in the first place is to jump start women's election to national legislatures.
If there were already a sizeable percentage of women in a country's legis-

lature, there would be no need for a gender quota. The presence of gender quotas, therefore, assumes that women are not adequately represented in legislative office. Gender quotas are a catalyst for getting women into political office, not the result of their already being in political office. Finally, when we turn to hereditary monarchies as an example of a public policy representing maternal traits, it is obvious that they predate the arrival of women in a country's legislature, since hereditary monarchies predate the existence of democratically elected national legislatures in the first place.

State Maternalism

State maternalism is defined here as a political context generated when the state embodies maternal traits by adopting public policies such as welfare provision, gender quotas, and hereditary monarchies. It is similar and different from a number of related practices, including gendering the nation, gendering the government, state feminism, state paternalism, and the regulation of maternal behavior.

Gendering the Nation

The term *nation-state* has two components: the people who make up the nation; and the state that regulates the people. It is possible for people to identify with one another as a nation even in the absence of a state that governs them. The Jewish people are one example. Prior to the establishment of the state of Israel, many Jewish people had a national identity that linked them to one another even without yet having a state, that is, a government to represent them and even without a designated territory to call their own. It is possible, therefore, to have a nation without a state, but not a state without a nation.

As feminist scholars point out, it is common for governments to use gendered policies to establish national identities. In the Middle East, for example, government policies often regiment women's dress, behavior, and educational and professional opportunities as a way to define their own national identity as opposite to Western ones. Mohamad Tavakoli-Targhi notes, for example, that

> women of the West were often a displacement and a simulacrum for Iranian women. The focus and reflection on European women resulted in the production of the veil as a woman's uniform and as a marker of cultural, political, and religious difference and identity. What was perceived to be an

Islamic dress for women was a product of the cultural and political encounter with the West. These encounters transformed the notion of femininity (zananigi) from a polar opposite of masculinity (mardanigi) into a signifier of Western-meditated gender identity, a transformation which began with the Persian voyagers' curiosity about the exotic women of the West.[85]

The need to control women in postcolonial states has been equated with the need to find some area where control is possible. As Khawar Mumtaz notes, "In Pakistan, as in most other post-colonial states, the rapid transformation of the economic and social structures has resulted in a state of confusion and lack of control by men. In this shifting and bewildering reality the only area where control is possible is the domestic space. Hence the compelling need to exercise it over women."[86] That is, the state uses the "ideal of womanhood" both to symbolize the "ideal state" and "to control and manipulate individual conformity to state policy."[87]

In the American context gender has been employed by the state to define the "nation." Historian Nancy Cott analyzes how gender, embedded in the state regulation of marriage, served as a common denominator to hold together a vastly diverse national population. As she notes, "no modern nation-state can ignore marriage forms because of their direct impact on reproducing and composing the population. The laws of marriage must play a large part in forming 'the people.' They sculpt the body politic. In a . . . [culturally diverse] nation such as the United States, formed of immigrant groups, marriage becomes all the more important politically . . . marriage policy underlies national belonging and the cohesion of the whole."[88] Initially the American state had few ways to govern a population that was "strewn unevenly over a huge expanse of land."[89] One way, as Cott illuminates, was to use the gendered institution of marriage to promote national solidarity. By insisting, by means of state and national legal regulations, that all marriages must be monogamous and have male heads-of-households, the state used gender difference as institutionalized in marriage, particularly in the nineteenth century, to define a political citizen as being a man, who was married to one woman and who as head of household was actively employed in work that sustained his family.

State maternalism is distinguished from gendering the nation in that state maternalism refers to the identity of the government—the state—rather than to the people who make up the nation. It is not how the people are gendered by means of government policies that is the focus here. Rather, it is the way the state itself becomes gendered—or not—by adopting public policies representing the maternal traits that voters associate with women.

Gendering the Government

Feminist scholars also draw attention to the way government becomes gendered by the *presence* of women in government who are visible, proactive agents affecting the adoption of public policies. Political scientist Louise Chappell shows how feminists "cannot avoid the state" if they wish to be successful in establishing such policies as "equal pay, anti-domestic violence laws, or refuge or childcare centers." For feminists to implement their policy agenda, "they must engage with state institutions."[90] Using Australia and Canada as case studies, she powerfully shows how women can use political institutions to implement their feminist agenda.[91] Political scientist Mala Htun analyzes how public policies also focus on how women's relationship to the government influences their capacity to direct policy formulation in a political context defined by competing institutions, such as the state and the Catholic Church.[92]

In this project, gendering the government differs from state maternalism in the sense that the latter does not refer to the presence of women as activists in the state, but rather to the gendered identities of the state's public policies. State maternalism as used here refers to the maternal identities represented by the state's adoption of such policies as welfare provision, gender quotas, or hereditary monarchies. State maternalism differs from gendering the government, therefore, in that it refers to the maternal identities of the state's public policies rather than the feminist identities of the state's personnel. It is not so much whether women as activists are in or out of government as it is whether the government's policies represent maternal traits that teach voters the political meaning of having such traits.

State Feminism

Yet other scholars analyze what they term "state feminism," which refers to a study of how public policies foster greater equality between men and women in broad areas of society, such as employment and educational opportunities. Although a contested term, Joni Lovenduski defines "statefeminism" as "the advocacy of women's movement demands inside the state."[93] Political scientist Amy Mazur defines state feminism as the state's "responses to women's movements in Western post-industrial democracies."[94] She analyzes feminist public policies as the dependent variable that is the outcome of a myriad of institutional features and social movement activities.

State maternalism as used here differs from state feminism in the sense that the public policies defined here as embodying maternal traits are not necessarily targeted to the reduction of inequalities between men and women. Welfare provision in the form of publicly funded health care, for example, need not affect women's economic or social standing in society any more than men's, and hereditary monarchies certainly do not constitute an instrument for reducing sex-based inequities in society. Rather than directly reducing sex discrimination, state maternalism refers instead to policies that indirectly reduce sex discrimination by virtue of teaching voters that the maternal traits associated with women are also associated with the state. As a result of this lesson, voters learn that maternal traits signify a location in the state and that people who are presumed to have maternal traits—such as women—are suitable as leaders in the state. The result is the reduction in the gap between the percentages of men and women elected to political office.

State Paternalism

Yet another approach is state paternalism, which refers to public policies oriented toward the well-being of people, as are some policies classified as "state maternalism." Where the two approaches differ is in the way they impose on people without their consent. The idea behind state paternalism is that the state uses its coercive force to provide protections to people, whether those people wish to be protected or not. John Brueggerman, for example, defines state paternalism in the context of employment, as a public policy that links the employer to a segment of workers where the employer's "paternalistic treatment of employees is likely to foster their differential stance toward the employer."[95] Therefore, paternalism is associated with legitimizing inequality.[96] In addition, state paternalism "presumes that people are unable to understand their own best interest and require the protection of a benevolent state."[97] Making benevolent decisions coercively on behalf of people in order to provide for their own best interests is, according to Ronald Dworkin, privileging a person's "critical interests" over his/her "volitional interests," or what they should want versus what they actually want.[98]

State paternalism, therefore, is associated with coercion, inequality, and the protection of people, whether they consent or not. For this reason, for some it is a term of abuse because it is "illiberal, coercive, arrogant, and patronizing; it is thought to destroy autonomy and freedom, and to display a lack of respect for people."[99] Yet in some instances there is applause for paternal policies, such as those that seek to protect women from harmful practices. In India, there is much support for reformers who have sought "to counter the traditional gender-oppressive customs through wide-ranging legislation—from the abolition of widow immolation to raising the age at marriage, and from the introduction of maternity benefits to the banning of dowry and female foeticide after independence."[100]

In this project, state maternalism differs from state paternalism by reference to the coercive element. The particular public policies used to define state maternalism in this research do not include a necessarily coercive dimension. Welfare provision is not defined here in terms of coercive public policies that impose upon people without their consent; gender quotas do not entail coercing women as candidates to run as part of a gender-quota system; and hereditary monarchies do not require that people remain in the dynastic family if they do not so choose. Hence, the public policies used in this project that define state maternalism do not invoke the coercive element that many characterize state paternalism as having.

Regulation versus Representation

Finally, the term *state maternalism*, as it is used here, also differs from the policies that regulate maternalism. All countries regulate social and biological maternalism by means of marriage laws, family policies, and reproductive rights policies. In many cases women's reproductive labor becomes a direct target of political control by the state. As Nira Yuval-Davis notes, eugenic policies have been invoked by virtually all nations to control women's reproductive labor in relation to the nation when there are not enough children, too many children, or not enough of the "right" type of children.[101] It is women who bear the brunt of all of these policies, since is it women who disproportionately are involved in reproductive labor. When France after World War II suffered enormous population loss, the goal of the government was to establish naturalist policies that would encourage women to have more children, thereby reproducing the population in order to replenish the nation. The government in China, on the other hand, perceiving its national problem to be too many people, tries to reduce the population in order to protect the nation in terms of population size.

Still other governments seek to define the nation in terms of the type of children that are born, often by prohibiting the reproductive labor of subordinate groups. Such laws flourished in the United States in the early twentieth century, partly in response to the influx of millions of immigrants and to renewed racist attitudes. By 1905 twenty-six states prohibited marriage between blacks and whites, an additional six states barred marriage between whites and "Mongolians," and another four states outlawed marriage between whites and Native Americans.[102] Eugenic laws became the norm in many states during this period. By 1912 thirty-four states banned marriage between lunatics, a category that included epileptics. Forced sterilization of those deemed mentally retarded or otherwise mentally incompetent was adopted in as many as fifteen states between 1907 and 1912. Even progressive states engaged in aggressive eugenic practices, as when California sterilized one in every twelve mental patients between 1909 and 1927.[103] As a result, California performed 5,800 sterilizations by 1929, or four times more than had been performed in the entire world.[104] In other national contexts the government may mandate the reproductive labor of dominant groups. In Nazi Germany, the belief in a "master race" opened the door to extreme state control over women's choices of mates, sexual partners, and whether or not to have children. The wish to preserve racial purity was also the central element in defining some people as "non-human," preparing the way for their eventual murder."[105]

State maternalism differs from the regulation of maternal behavior by reference to the maternal identity of the state itself. State maternalism refers to policies that convey to the state a maternal identity parallel to the maternal identity voters attribute to women. As such, it is not the regulation of women's maternity that constitutes state maternalism, but rather the adoption by the state of policies representing the maternal traits voters assume women to have.

Individualism *and* Maternalism

All states must guarantee law and order within their own borders and also the security of their borders from external incursions, or they scarcely count as being a state at all. What is more, self-defense actions by the state are generally associated with men. In addition to self-defense, all democratic states necessarily must guarantee civil and political rights to individuals "in spite of" ascriptive group differences. Although individualism as a principle for public policies can be considered gender neutral, the principle of equal, autonomous individuals is often associated with men.[106]

When the state represents maternal traits associated with women, however, the liberal, democratic state—initially gendered as an individual, if not as male—becomes a hybrid state that represents traits associated with both men and women. Generally, the idea is that the characteristics that make a state hybrid conflict with one another, rendering such a state to be anything but ideal. Larry Diamond, for example, defines a hybrid regime as one that combines democratic and authoritarian elements, where the latter are clearly undesirable.[107] Diamond views hybrid elements that conflict with democratic characteristics as undermining the claim that a country is a democracy in the first place. As he describes such hybrid states, "For some years now, it has been apparent that a great many of the new regimes are not themselves democratic, or any longer in transition to democracy. Some of the countries that fall into the political gray zone . . . between full-fledged democracy and outright dictatorship are in fact electoral democracies, however feckless and poorly functioning, but many fall below the threshold of electoral democracy and are likely to remain there for a very long time."[108]

Others view hybrid regimes that combine democracy with nondemocratic elements to be little more than a sham. Examples are those countries that adopt some procedural principles of electoral governance but at the same time remain autocratic and unaccountable to the people of their country, such as Jordan under King Hussein and later King Abdullah. King Hussein signed a peace treaty with Israel, much to the consternation of his constituents, and King Abdullah acted arbitrarily by passing many decrees that gave unfair advantage to proregime candidates, by redistricting regions and by changing electoral methods to suit his own preferences. Although he did add six seats to the lower house reserved for women, he retains absolute authority to reverse any and all decisions made by the lower house. Hence, Jordan is an example of a hybrid regime that "has never been committed to meaningful political liberalization and has used the language and artifacts of democracy to legitimate its continued rule in a climate in which authoritarianism is increasingly rejected on an international as well as domestic level."[109]

In this study, the term *hybrid state* stands for the combination of policies that while representing opposite traits, nevertheless is a combination of positives policies, not negative and positive ones. Specifically, the policies that make-up the hybrid state considered here combine two positives: (1) liberal individualism, which guarantees the government will treat all people equally in spite of their ascriptive group differences, such as their race, class, or sex, thereby fulfilling the civil and political citizenship components of a democracy; and (2) maternalism, thereby fulfilling, in the case of welfare provision at least, the basic tenet of democracy, namely, social citizenship.

Among democracies comparable to the United States, most are hybrid states that combine liberal individualistic public policies, such as civil and political rights, with maternalist public policies representing traits that voters associate with women. Specifically, 80% of such democracies are hybrid states by virtue of adopting welfare provision, 72% by virtue of adopting gender quotas, and 48% by virtue of retaining their monarchies.

Table 2.2 Western democracies[a] and maternal public policies: Welfare provision, gender quotas, and hereditary monarchies

| Political System | Maternal State Action | | | Total: | |
	Welfare Provision[b]	Gender Quotas[c]	Hereditary Monarchy[d]	Maternal Public Policies	Percent
Australia	YES	YES	YES	3	40% (10)
Belgium	YES	YES	YES	3	
Canada	YES	YES	YES	3	
Denmark	YES	YES	YES	3	
Luxembourg	YES	YES	YES	3	
Norway	YES	YES	YES	3	
Spain	YES	YES	YES	3	
Sweden	YES	YES	YES	3	
The Netherlands	YES	YES	YES	3	
United Kingdom	YES	YES	YES	3	
Austria	YES	YES	no	2	24% (6)
Germany	YES	YES	no	2	
Iceland	YES	YES	no	2	
Ireland	YES	YES	no	2	
Italy	YES	YES	no	2	
Portugal	YES	YES	no	2	
Finland	YES	no	no	1	24% (6)
Greece	no	YES	no	1	
Israel	no	YES	no	1	
New Zealand	no	no	YES	1	
Switzerland	no	YES	no	1	
The Bahamas	no	no	YES	1	
France	no	no[b]	no	0	12% (3)
Japan	no	no	no	0	
United States	no	no	no	0	
				N = 25	
				All three: 40%	
				Two: 24%	
PERCENT				One: 24%	
YES	72%	76%	48%	None: 12%	

Table 2.2   continued

a) Democratic political systems with a per capita income of at least $10,000/year and at least 58% urban.
b) Welfare provision: There is a constitutional provision establishing that it is an affirmative obligation of the state to provide for the welfare needs of people and the government provides at least 50% of the funds spent on health care; health care funds are calculated on the basis of data provided by the World Health Organization for the year 2000. At www3.who.int/whosis/core/core_select_process.cfm?country.
c) Gender quotas: Measured as a constitutional or legislated gender quota that represents women's group difference from men of at least more than 15%; or a voluntary party quota for at least two parties of more than 30%; or at least one party for more than 40%. The political parties must be represented in parliament in 1999, 2003, and must have met its targets. "All women" political parties are not included in this measure. South Africa is included in this measure. France is not included in this measure because its legislated principle of gender quotas, parité, is premised on the universality of human beings, not their sex difference. See Joan Wallach Scott, *Parité!: Equality and the Crisis of French Universalism* (Chicago: University of Chicago Press, 2005).
d) Hereditary monarchy: Must be open to women to become sovereigns.

The United States is one of the few democracies that is not a hybrid state, as indicated in table 2.2.

Hybrid states that combine individualism and maternalism generate a political context that defines government as embodying traits voters associate with women's sameness with men and with women's maternal group difference from men. As such, hybrid states that represent both individual (or male), and female traits are valuable for normative and instrumental reasons. Normatively such a state delivers on the democratic goal of guaranteeing civil, political, and social rights to its people. While all democracies affirm civil and political citizenship, hybrid democracies as defined here also affirm social citizenship in the form of constitutional and fiscal guarantees for welfare provision. Instrumentally, a hybrid democracy bolsters women's access to political leadership positions by teaching voters that to have maternal traits—as women are presumed to have—signifies a connection to the public sphere, not a disconnection. The policy feedback effect is to increase public attitudes about women's suitability as political leaders and to increase the percentage of women elected to political office.

Generating Public Attitudes 3

The Policy Feedback Model

The relationship between public policies and democracy is usually discussed in terms of how public policies are established. As political scientist Paul Pierson notes, "active government is a central feature of modern life . . . [as] anywhere from 30 to 60 percent of GNP is filtered through government programs."[1] Public policies that consume such large financial resources are traditionally thought to come from citizens, as mediated by a chain of intervening processes that shape and direct the impact of voters. Social movements alert and mobilize voters to cast their ballots for or against particular candidates representing particular public policies; political parties gear candidate races in ways to capitalize on voter preferences; and interest groups representing segments of the voting population attempt to sway representatives once in office to support (or not) the passage of particular policies. In this view, citizen preferences are the "input" and public policies are the "output."[2]

Citizen-Centered

The traditional model of how public policies are generated, therefore, is *citizen-centered*.[3] Citizens' preferences generate public policies along several different tracks. One track follows the *sociological* features of the mass citizenry—how their social networks, racial divisions, and group interests constitute voting blocs that determine the fate of the acceptance or rejection of public policies.[4] The key to understanding the sociological perspective is to assess how group memberships and group interactions foster citizen policy preferences, which then translate into the passage (or not) of public policies.

Psychological characteristics offer another explanation for how citizens generate public policies. In this sense citizens' identities, beliefs, values, attitudes, and symbolic orientations account for their motivations, affect, and cognition.[5] As Torben Iversen notes, issues and public policies "represent symbols," and the responses that people have to these political symbols affect how people judge candidates.[6] The key issue is the subjective perceptions of individuals. Groups are viewed merely as the site where psychological processes take place. The feelings of citizens, particularly their sense of efficacy, trust in government, interest in politics, degree of partisanship, and sense of civic duty are what determine not only their policy preferences but also their general participation as voters in the country.[7]

Economic considerations are yet another way to evaluate how citizens generate public policies by means of their voting preferences. This perspective looks to the utilitarian dimensions of citizens' self-interest. That is, how can citizens best pursue their political goals based on rational choices designed to maximize their own, individual well-being. Political action becomes a goal-directed behavior, in which citizens act according to their "rational beliefs about the relationship between means and ends."[8] Although citizens as individuals may not perceive how best to maximize their own goals and may thereby generate difficulties, such as "rational ignorance," "rational abstention," and "free rider problems,"[9] the premise of the economic tradition is that citizens try to do so.

These three perspectives—the sociological, the psychological, and the economic—start with the belief that the citizen as an individual in society is the source for generating public policies. They may focus on the social relations of individuals, such as their group memberships and group locations, their psychological orientations, such as their attitudes and values, or their economic self-interest and instrumental actions.[10] What they have in common, however, is that they "treat mass opinion and behavior as a vox populi that emerges from sources that are not overtly political and that generate input for the country."[11] Public attitudes, as expressed or enhanced by social movements and as harnessed by political parties and interest groups, are converted into votes, which in turn transform candidates into political officeholders who support or oppose particular public policies.

The public's attitude about the accountability and continued responsiveness of their elected representatives determines whether or not political officeholders will stay in office. Thus, public attitudes of citizens, however mediated, are the source of public policies.

Public Policies Generate Public Attitudes: Feedback Effects

This cycle may also run in reverse. Once public policies are adopted in a country in response to initial grass-roots attitudes, those policies exert a feedback effect upon the very public attitudes responsible for their original enactment. In other words, to analyze the way public policies shape, determine, and generate public attitudes it is necessary to ask such questions as: How "do specific policy designs affect what individuals think, feel, and do as members of the polity?"[12] How do "public policies further or thwart democratic purposes?"[13] Why do "some policies draw citizens into public life and others induce passivity?"[14] How do "public policies shape mass opinion and behavior?"[15]

Asking how public policies affect public attitudes taps into a long-standing political tradition, which "explains mass opinion and behavior as products constructed through the interplay of state structures and institutions, political actions and communication flows, mobilization and demobilization, and the density and patterning of political organizations."[16] This perspective dates back to the work of E. E. Schattschneider, who argued over fifty years ago that "new policies create a new politics" and "Whoever decides what the game is about decides also who gets into the game."[17]

In developing the view that policies influence attitudes, political scientist Theodore Lowi argues that policies create citizen attitudes by two means: (1) the degree to which policies are coercive, where low coercion is defined by the distribution of benefits and high coercion by the distribution of costs; and (2) how specific or universal are the benefits of public policies, where specific refers to benefits received only by some people and universal to benefits received by all. Policies that are very coercive and benefit only select individuals are bound to create citizen attitudes and activities that are elitist in contrast to public policies that are low in coercion and more universal in their distribution of benefits.[18] Building upon Lowi's work, James Q. Wilson argued in a similar vein, though with a different typological schema.[19]

Political scientists Suzanne Mettler and Joe Soss focus on the "constructivist turn," which places a "greater emphasis on the ways mass responses get shaped by political actors, organizations, and information flows."[20] Similarly, as political scientists Anne Schneider and Helen Ingram explain:

"Policy teaches lessons about the type of groups people belong to, what they deserve from government, and what is expected of them. The messages indicate . . . what kind of game politics is . . . and who usually wins . . . what government is supposed to do . . . and what kinds of attitudes and participatory patterns are appropriate in a democratic society."[21]

Public policies can, therefore, *teach* citizens about government and about their relation to the public sphere of political governance. This is what political scientist Joe Soss refers to as the "political learning" model of policy analysis. It studies how policy designs and their implementation are "sites of political learning," which teach people firsthand about the nature of government and their relation to it. Even mundane experiences with the post office, for example, or with the Department of Motor Vehicles, not to mention the Police Department, are significant for the lessons they impart to people about their relative standing in the political order as equal citizens (or not) in relation to others.[22]

State-Centered

To view public policies, once established, as teaching people about government, thereby affecting the public attitudes that presumably generated public policies in the first place, adds a *state-centered* approach to the traditional *citizen-centered* approach to understanding the relationship between democracy and public policies. [23] It does not substitute a state-centered focus for a citizen-centered one, but rather it extends the relationship between public policies and democratic governance to include the way public policies—once in place and however they may have been generated—have an impact on public attitudes and political behavior. Public policies are best understood not only as the *effect* but also as the *cause* of political processes. Public policies affect public attitudes, political participation, trust in government, political efficacy, ideology, partisanship, and political mobilization.[24]

As Mettler demonstrates, public policies such as the GI Bill that reward those who have served in the military convey the message that the government, as well as the society that the government represents, values individuals who have engaged in such service to the country.[25] As Andrea Campbell further observes, policies such as Social Security and Medicare foster a political "group identity" among beneficiaries that enhances their propensity to engage in politics.[26] As a result, the "design of policies—what they do, to whom they are targeted, how generous they are, and how they are administered—*shapes attitudes toward fellow citizens* and the role of government, patterns of political participation, and partisan and ideological orientations."[27]

To focus on the state as the source of citizen attitudes, values, and ideological orientations is to argue that even though public attitudes are crucial for establishing public policies in the first place, once in place, those same public policies continue to have an impact on public attitudes and on political participation. From a *citizen-centered* perspective, a country with an egalitarian tradition that supports women's political equality would be more likely to have citizens that support public policies promoting gender equality, such as gender quotas, than would a country that does not have citizens with such public attitudes. A *state-centered* approach to the study of women's voting rights as a public policy, while also presuming that there must be some public support for establishing it in the first place, also presumes that such a policy teaches citizens that women are to be included in the governance of the state, at least as voters, and thus increases the degree to which the public views women as suitable political participants.

Public policies matter, therefore, because they define for the public who is either included or excluded from society in general and from political elites in particular.[28] Public policies are not only dependent variables, which *result from public attitudes* as expressed through political processes, but also independent variables that endogenously *affect public attitudes*. Among the ways that public policies affect the attitudes and behavior of both political elites[29] and the mass public[30] is their interpretive impact on public attitudes about women's suitability as political leaders.

The Interpretive Impact of Public Policies

The importance of public attitudes for explaining voting behavior is a precept of electoral politics. When it comes to women's election to political office, how the public views women's place in society is crucial. Political scientists Pippa Norris and Ronald Inglehart, for example, establish that countries in which the public embraces more egalitarian attitudes about women also elect more women to political office.[31] And as political scientists Pamela Paxton and Sheri Kunovich note, gender ideology, or the ideas and values that the public holds about women, dramatically affect women's prospects for election to political office.[32] Similarly, an Inter-Parliamentary Union (IPU) study found that a "negative" gender ideology posed the most potent obstacle to women's political representation. As one respondent in the study from Central Europe reported, ideology is more important than economic or political structures:

> In spite of a long tradition of active participation in the workforce by a vast majority of women, both women and men see motherhood in marriage as the most important goals of a woman's life. A common standpoint is that "politics is a man's business" . . . the reasons for this are not to be found in education, with women in [my country] being as educated as their male counterparts. It is simply because of the stereotyped and traditional structure of society.[33]

Gender ideology, or public attitudes about the suitability of women as political leaders, is critical to bolstering or hindering women's election to political leadership positions. In general government policies have an impact on public attitudes that affect people's view of the social and political realm, and in particular they have an *interpretive* influence on the capacity of citizens "to engage in political activity and the motivation to do so."[34] Pierson notes that public policies either facilitate or confer the ability to participate in a political process—that is, to be *included* in politics. As he emphasizes, the crucial *interpretive* effects that a public policy has upon its beneficiaries lead to greater political participation and inclusion. Public policies shape citizens' understanding of their status *as citizens*. Policies influence how people interpret their "place" in the country, help them estimate their value to government and civil society, and define their connection to or disconnection from the state, as well as their sense of whether or not they are politically included—all of which affect feelings of efficacy and self-worth.[35] From a *state-centered* perspective, therefore, public policies teach the public about who are suitable as participants in the political governance of the state.

When the government engages successfully in military activities, for example, we would expect such military public policies to define for the public that the people who are suitable as political leaders of government are men in general and military men in particular. When the government endorses liberal public policies that support the view that all individuals are equal "in spite of" their ascriptive characteristics, such as race, class, or sex, then we would expect such public policies to cue voters that people are suitable as political leaders of the state "in spite of" whatever might be their ascriptive group differences. Similarly, when the government engages in public policies that are associated with the public's view of women's social and biological maternal identities, these policies should have an interpretative impact on public attitudes that define women to be suitable as political

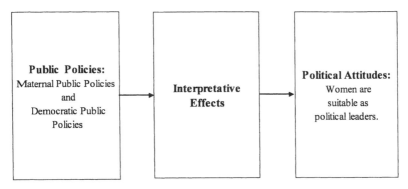

Figure 3.1: Policy feedback for mass publics: How public policies affect political attitudes. (Adapted from Mettler and Welch, 2004)

leaders. Adapting Mettler's model of the interpretative impact of public policies shows that the impact of maternal public policies, along with democratic ones, promotes public attitudes supportive of women's suitability as political leaders, as is shown in figure 3.1.

Welfare Provision: Interpretative Impact

When the government acts to affirm its role as the provider of health benefits, for example, there should be an *interpretive* impact influencing how the mass public views the political sphere and women's location in relation to that sphere. In other words, when the government endorses public policies that provide state benefits to people for their basic welfare, such as health, such maternal care-work provided by the state should cue the mass public that government is acting in a way associated with women's maternal identities as "care-workers."[36] The interpretive effect would be the public's view of women's "place," or women's identity, as coterminous with the state itself. Such a view, by connecting women to the public sphere of the state, should then translate into an increase in the public view of women as suitable for political office.

Gender Quotas: Interpretative Impact

The presence of gender quotas in a country also should have a crucial *interpretative* impact on public attitudes by defining women's "political place" in terms of their group difference from men, that is, their female sex classification. Countries that affirm gender quotas should generate public attitudes where the gender identity of women signifies *inclusion*, not exclusion, from the public sphere of political governance. Political scientist Miki Kittilson concurs that gender quotas, in addition to being instrumental mechanisms for "improving women's numerical representation," also "encourage new attitudes towards women in politics."[37] Kittilson notes how formal rules, such as gender quotas, can become norms that change public attitudes. Thus, even when there is resistance, once gender quotas are adopted, they can have the positive effect of "altering attitudes toward women's representation" by standing for the proposition that it is important in a democracy for women, simply by virtue of their sex classification, to be politically included.[38]

Hereditary Monarchies: Interpretative Impact

Monarchies, however symbolic or ceremonial they may be, are mechanisms that visibly include women in the state's political governance by fusing the family with the state. Currently, actual women are monarchical heads of state in eighteen nations, and monarchical rule is open to women in twenty-seven nations, or 14.1% of the world's nations. Of the world's democracies comparable to the United States, 48%, such as the Netherlands, Spain, Belgium, Sweden, Denmark, Norway, and the United Kingdom, have monarchies open to women.

Countries with monarchies open to women or ruled by women, in addition to conjoining women and political leadership, tend to have currency and coins that depict women political leaders, as in Canada and Australia. Depictions of women as monarchical heads of state on currency and coins remind people on an everyday basis that being a woman and being a political leader can and do go together. In the very first pilot episode, for example, of the TV series *Commander-in-Chief*, launched in 2005, a woman who was elected vice president assumes the role of president upon the death of the president. When discussing with her youngest daughter the prospects of assuming the office of the presidency, the mother is asked by the daughter, who is six to seven years old, "Will your picture be on dollar bills?" Even a child is therefore assumed to notice the sex of the political leaders honored by their portrayal on bills and coins. Surely at some level of public awareness it makes a difference, in terms of public associations of a person's sex with political authority, whether these leaders are all men, or also are sometimes women.

So, too, can women's assumption of political authority in hereditary monarchies generate more favorable public attitudes about women's role in politics. As Helen Irving notes, Australian states were federated around the time of the death of Queen Victoria. Although it is common to associate the Victorian period with the repression of women and of sexuality, there was another dimension to the queen's persona that served as an "important female symbol" and became a catalyst for the greater involvement of Australian women in politics. Victoria's reign, "was immensely useful to Australian women . . . [because] she symbolized the ability of women to occupy a position of power, and to exercise political judgment."[39] Significantly, she "represented the merging of the maternal and the political, something women of the time advocated and sought," as the female suffrage movement spread throughout the Australian colonies by the 1890s.[40]

In 1897, during the Australian Jubilee celebration, there was enormous public support for Queen Victoria. She exemplified, according to Irving, "feminine qualities," such as virtue, duty, philanthropy, and in general "womanliness." She was viewed as having a " 'woman's instinct' for peace, a woman's experience of sorrow, a woman's love of family. The Empire was a family. The Jubilee was a family gathering."[41] Queen Victoria's state performance was a maternal one, thereby imparting to the state maternal traits that its public associated with women. Australia exemplifies how the association of the state with maternal qualities by means of a monarchy in general and a female monarch in particular can bolster public support for women's inclusion as voters in the public sphere of government. The association of the queen with maternal traits, far from representing merely a metaphorical distinction between men and women, became in the hands of woman suffrage reformers a powerful representation of the political efficacy of enfranchising women for the good of the society. The Queen's "homely" political role offered to suffrage reformers a model for enlarging the public sphere of governance to include "those 'domestic' areas of primary female responsibility: welfare, education, health, hygiene, protection of children. . . . They argued for the vote not in order to become citizens, but on the grounds that they already were citizens, and they used their affinity to the model offered by the monarchy . . . to demonstrate this."[42]

The Impact of Public Policies on Public Attitudes

Individualism and Maternalism: Concepts and Definitions

Maternal public policies in combination with individualistic ones affect public attitudes about women's suitability as political leaders, particularly in contemporary democracies.[43] Democracy has both qualitative and quantitative meanings. Qualitatively, it refers to the core definition of citizenship, which is "inclusion." There are many ways to assess inclusion, but three of the most important are: civil citizenship, which refers to the government's guarantee that all individuals have basic rights to participate in a society's legal conventions, such as the right to marry, to form contracts, and to hold property; political citizenship, which refers to the government's guarantee that all individuals have the basic right to participate politically in a society, by voting, holding political office, and serving on juries; and social citizenship, which refers to the government's guarantee that the basic economic needs of individuals will be provided by the state, should the family or market fail as a delivery system.

The first two types of citizenship, civil and political, are premised upon treating all individuals the same "in spite of" their ascriptive group differences. For this reason these two types form the core of what is meant by liberal democracy, as both a theory and a practice, which is premised on the view that all individuals are born inherently free and equal in relation to each other and to the state. In the context of liberal democracy, the state guarantees negative individual rights, which in the case of civil rights means that the state will not interfere with the rights of individuals to marry, to sign contracts, or to buy property, and in the case of political rights, the state will not interfere with the rights of individuals to vote, to hold office, or to serve on juries. The term "democracy" as it is used here refers only to the government's guarantee of civil and political rights.

From a *quantitative* perspective, a country must guarantee negative individual rights to a sufficient percentage of its population in order to be scored as a liberal democracy. This need raises the issue of affirmative action policies adopted to promote greater inclusion of subordinate groups by giving them electoral preference, such as gender quotas. On the one hand, gender quotas can be seen to violate the liberal principle underlying civil and political rights in the sense that the government should treat all individuals the same in spite of their ascriptive group differences. On the other hand, when a country fails to include significant portions of its population in its representative institutions, thereby failing to meet quantitative standards for a democracy, arguments can be made that it is normatively and instrumentally permissible to increase the representation of those excluded by bolstering the probability of their election by means of quota policies.

The third type of citizenship, social citizenship, refers not to negative individual rights but rather to positive group rights. To receive welfare provision from the state, for example, a person must be in a status category that needs those benefits. Even when welfare benefits are available to everyone on a universal basis, such as health care, to receive that benefit requires that people need health care, thereby distinguishing themselves from people who do not. To put it another way, even when a benefit is "universal," meaning that everyone is potentially eligible to receive that benefit, the emphasis is on "potential." To make the claim that one deserves to be a recipient of even a universal benefit requires distinguishing oneself from others who do not. It is not until a person is sick and in need of a health benefit, say, that a person becomes eligible to receive that benefit, even if health benefits cover potentially everyone who could get sick. Thus, welfare provisions that target the ill, the elderly, children, mothers, parents, and the like, all invoke positive group rights, meaning that the government provides benefits, protections, and privileges "because of" people's group differences from one another, not "in spite of" those differences.

From a normative perspective a democracy that does not provide welfare to those in need, is by some *qualitative* standard, not a democracy at all. However, from the qualitative perspective used here a country is termed a democracy only on the basis of whether it guarantees *civil and political citizenship*, that is, whether it is a liberal democracy. Welfare provision, or *social citizenship*, is determined by whether a country adopts public policies that represent social maternal traits, defined as care-work. That is, welfare provision here denotes maternalism rather than liberal individualism. Thus, types of democracy are disaggregated into liberal democracy (civil and political rights) and social democracy (welfare rights), the former representing individualism and the latter representing maternalism. Although the measure of maternalism used here includes what many refer to as social democracy, it also includes more, because it encompasses public policies representing biological maternal traits that the public associates with women, such as a female sex classification and bearing children.[44]

Expanding the idea of maternalism to include not only social maternalism or welfare provision but also biological maternalism invites the prospect of expanding the language of democracy to go with the recognition of the latter. Thus, if social maternalism, welfare provision can be thought of as a form of *social citizenship*, then biological maternalism, gender quotas, and hereditary monarchies might be thought of as a form of *biological citizenship*. There is a growing literature on *sexual citizenship*, which refers to the government's need to guarantee people's inclusion in a democracy in spite of their sexual orientation or to deliver benefits to them on the basis of their transgender needs for health care, including surgical therapy.[45] As David Evans argues, there are "victimless consensual sexual behaviors which are not the law's business" but which nevertheless are prohibited by the legal system. To enhance citizenship rights requires the "extension of rights to sexual minorities."[46] Similarly, Brenda Cossman notes that because citizenship is defined as "practices of inclusion and membership," it is crucial to address the "contours of . . . sexual citizenship," which includes "rights to sexual expression and identity."[47] To view sexual minorities as "strange" or "different," much less as transgressing legal standards, is to deny them the rights of full citizenship.[48] In other words, "all citizenship is sexual citizenship" in the sense that inclusion in communities is predicated upon selected sexual practices. To reach everyone more completely requires expanding the range of accepted sexual practices to include "sexual minorities."[49]

The rights of the disabled also focus on physicality as a site of the government's responsibility to those in need of public services. The principle of biological citizenship follows analogously, referring to the use of biological categories for determining whether individuals receive benefits, protections, or privileges from the government. Two public policies that refer to biological categories are gender quotas that give preference to women's election to legislatures and monarchies that determine access to rule on the basis of family-kinship status as generated by women's biological capacity to bear children in the dynastic family. As such, biological citizenship is a concept that addresses the salience for democratic theory of people's biological identities, their physicality, or what political scientist Ruth O'Brien terms their "animality."[50] As she points out, it is incorrect to think of disability as an identity, because disability is a process that refers to the way the body does things.[51] This requires that society take into account what Oliver Sacks refers to as "our embodiment" or "our fleshy all too human selves." To say that the disabled have needs is really just to say that the needs of the disabled are more obvious and more pronounced than the needs of all human beings as organic, biological creatures. To be human, to be organically alive, is to be dependent on a host of resources, such as food, shelter, clothing, and health, if not education and employment. The disabled have additional needs, but because of the way their bodies work, the fact is that only those additional needs stand out, not that the disabled have needs and dependencies in contrast to other people, who do not.[52]

Democracy here refers to a country that is a liberal democracy guaranteeing negative individual rights, specifically civil and political citizenship. Maternal public policies refer to positive group rights, specifically policies representing social and biological traits that voters associate with women. The former is social citizenship and the latter could be termed biological citizenship. In sum, the analysis here of cross-national attitudinal and voting patterns employs a definition of political and civil citizenship as measures of public policies representing individual equality, and social and biological citizenship as measures of public policies representing the maternal difference from men that voters attribute to women.

Measuring Liberal Democracy

Freedom House scores serve as a measure of whether a country bases its public policies on civil rights and political rights premised on a principle of individualism. Freedom House also measures the quantitative extent to which a country guarantees the civil and political rights of individuals, namely, the degree to which all individuals are included in the guarantee of basic civil and political rights. Those countries that Freedom House evaluates as "free" are scored here as "democratic," that is, as guaranteeing civil and political rights broadly to everyone in society. Countries that Freedom House scores as "partly free" or "not free" are scored here as undemocratic. To be scored as a democracy comparable to the United States, a country must be "free" from at least 1978 to the present.

Measuring Maternal Public Policies

The public associates women with social and biological maternal traits that can be represented in public policies by welfare provision, gender quotas, and hereditary monarchies. Social maternal traits are defined by care-work, whether the recipients of care are men or women. When the government takes on the responsibility of caring for people by means of welfare provision, such public policies represent social maternal traits that voters associate with women. The government's provision of welfare to those in need is measured here as follows: (1) the constitutional affirmation that it is the responsibility of the government to provide for the welfare of people, in terms either of specific areas of care, such as health, education, and family benefits, or of welfare in general;[53] and (2) funding support such that at least 50% of the funds spent on health are contributed by the government.

Biological maternal traits include a sex classification as female and the actual bearing of children, the latter of which constitutes the generation of family-kinship networks. Government adoption of gender quotas—what are really female sex quotas—constitutes the adoption of a public policy representing biological maternalism defined as a female sex classification. In this research, the presence or absence of gender quotas is measured as follows: A legislative quota above 15% in lower or upper house or a voluntary political party quota of 30% or more in at least two parties or a voluntary political party quota of 40% or more in at least one party and the political party is represented in the legislature in 1999 and 2003. Data for gender quotas are from the Global Database of Quotas for Women,

Institute for Democracy and Electoral Assistance (IDEA), Stockholm University and from Mona Lena Krook and Diana O'Brien.[54]

The government's representation of biological maternalism defined by the generation of family-kinship networks is measured here as the adoption of a hereditary monarchy, an archetypical way to fuse the family with the state, albeit only one family, the dynastic family. This study measures the presence or absence of a hereditary monarchy in terms of the presence of a hereditary monarchy open to women.

Public Attitudes about Women as Political Leaders

To measure public attitudes toward women's suitability as political leaders, the World Values Survey (WVS) is a useful resource. It is a set of surveys investigating sociocultural and political change in more than eighty societies that encompass almost 85% of the world's population. This project uses the fourth wave of interviews conducted in 1999–2001 by an international network of social scientists that builds upon the European Values Surveys as initiated in 1981. The WVS project is coordinated by and data are available from the Institute for Social Research of the University of Michigan under the direction of Ronald Inglehart.[55] In addition to recording individuals' demographic characteristics (such as age, sex, and marital status), the WVS gathers information about people's attitudes about work, religion and morality, perceptions of life, family, national identity, the environment, and politics and society. The survey generally allows four different options for answering attitudinal questions: one can (1) strongly agree, (2) agree, (3) disagree, or (4) strongly disagree with the given statement.

For the purposes of this research, there is one question in the survey that is crucial for assessing the public's attitudes toward the relative political leadership capabilities of women and men. That question is: "Do you agree strongly, agree, disagree, or disagree strongly with the following statement: "Men make better political leaders than women do.""[56] A total of 68,498 respondents from forty-eight different countries answered this question. Among these, 10,401 people (15.6%) "disagree strongly" and 14,845 people (22.3%) "agree strongly." Thus, worldwide, the ratio of individuals who strongly view women as suited for political leadership compared to those who strongly believe the opposite is 0.701. That means for every 701 people in the world who strongly view women to be suitable political leaders, there are another 1,000 who strongly believe that women are less suited as political leaders.[57]

Once we begin comparing countries, however, we find that there is a great deal of variation in the support for women as political leaders. In Egypt,

Table 3.1   Support for women as political leaders: Ratio of people supporting women as
political leaders compared to those who do not, World Values Survey, 2000

Country	Ratio (n)	Country	Ratio (n)
Albania	0.915 (1,000)	Macedonia, Rep.	1.491 (1,055)
Algeria	0.005 (1,282)	Mexico	1.721 (1,535)
Armenia	0.065 (2,000)	Moldova, Rep.	0.467 (1,008)
Australia	5.371 (2,048)	Morocco	0.212 (2,264)
Bangladesh	0.311 (1,499)	New Zealand	3.540 (1,201)
Bosnia and Herzegovina	1.957 (1,200)	Nigeria	0.113 (2,022)
Brazil	1.164 (1,149)	Norway	12.700 (1,127)
Canada	6.386 (1,931)	Pakistan	0.585 (2,000)
Chile	1.518 (1,200)	Philippines	0.351 (1,200)
China	0.567 (1,000)	South Africa	1.233 (3,000)
Columbia	1.615 (6,025)	Spain	8.681 (2,409)
Dominican Republic	2.000 (417)	Sweden	12.286 (1,014)
Egypt	0.041 (3,000)	Taiwan	0.354 (780)
El Salvador	1.154 (1,254)	Tanzania, Rep.	1.138 (1,171)
Georgia	0.054 (2,008)	Turkey	0.528 (4,607)
India	0.569 (2,002)	Uganda	0.443 (1,002)
Indonesia	0.469 (1,004)	United States	4.204 (1,200)
Iran	0.342 (2,532)	Uruguay	1.022 (1,000)
Japan	1.608 (1,362)	Vietnam	0.231 (995)
Jordan	0.060 (1,223)	Venezuela	1.746 (1,200)
Korea, South	1.077 (1,200)	Zimbabwe	0.656 (1,002)

the ratio of strong support compared to strong opposition of women's political leadership capabilities is only 0.041, meaning that for every four
individuals who strongly view women as suited for political leadership,
there are 1,000 who adamantly do not. At the other end of the spectrum, in
Norway, the ratio is 12.7, meaning that for every 1,270 people who firmly
believe that women are as suited for political leadership as men, there are
only 100 people who strongly do not, as indicated in table 3.1.

The question of importance is what causes the variation among countries in the ratio of support versus opposition to women as political leaders
compared to men? There is no simple answer, since there are innumer-
able factors that undoubtedly influence public attitudes about women's
political leadership capabilities. We would presume, for example, the following to be important: the percentage of women already in political office as well as respondents' personal characteristics, such as their age, sex,

level of education, occupation, income, religious orientations, and beliefs about the equality of men and women. From the perspective of a policy feedback model of public attitudes, however, we would also presume that the state's public policies would be an important determinant of public attitudes about the suitability of women as political leaders. All governments must engage in actions associated with masculinity, such as maintaining law and order and training a military, so we can assume that the public starts off with the view that men in general and military men in particular are suited for political leadership. In addition, all democracies endorse public policies affirming individualism, that is, negative individual rights based on the individual equality of men and women. Hence, in democracies, to the degree that women can be considered individuals who are the same as men, people should be more inclined to view both men and women as suited for political office.

Some democracies, however, in addition to guaranteeing individualism, *also* have public policies based on positive group rights representing maternal traits that voters associate with women. When a democratic state not only acts like a man (as do all states) and acts like an individual (as do all democracies), but also acts like a woman vis-à-vis its public policies, then the interpretative, policy feedback effect of such a hybrid state should be to generate an increase in positive public attitudes about women's suitability for political leadership. When we take a look at the impact of such a hybrid state on public attitudes about women's suitability as political leaders, we find out that is exactly what happens.

Policy Feedback

Maternal Public Policies and Democracy

To ascertain the policy feedback effects on public attitudes of public policies based on individual equality and on maternal traits associated by voters with women, I incorporate into the World Value Surveys (WVS) data set information about whether the country has public policies representing individualism and maternalism. Specifically, in the case of the former, I add to the WVS data information about whether a country is scored by Freedom House as "free," and in the case of the latter, whether the country has welfare provision, gender quotas, or a hereditary monarchy. On the basis of this additional information, it is possible to assess the degree to which the state's public policies influence people's support for women as political leaders.

Democracy, defined as the guarantee of negative individual rights, namely civil and political rights, to individuals in spite of their group differences, is clearly a good thing for women, as table 3.2 shows. In nondemocratic countries the ratio of those supporting women as political leaders is only 0.641, but in democratic ones it is 3.739. In nondemocracies, therefore, for every 100 people who support women as political leaders, there are 641 people who do not. By contrast, in democratic countries, for every 3,739 people who support women as political leaders, there are only 1,000 who do not. Hence, countries that have public policies based on individualism, namely democracies, bolster public attitudes about women's suitability as political leaders.

It is also the case that countries with public policies based on social and biological maternal traits that the public associates with women boost public attitudes about the suitability of women as political leaders. In countries where there are no such public policies, the ratio of people supporting women as political leaders compared to those who do not is 0.544, meaning that for every 544 people in favor of women as political leaders there are 1,000 opposed, as indicated in table 3.2. Generally, as the number of maternal public policies increases, so, too, does the support for women as political leaders increase for both nondemocratic and democratic countries, though the latter consistently have higher ratios than the former. In nondemocratic countries that have only one type of maternal public policy, such as only welfare provision or only gender quotas, we find that the ratios are 1.084 and 1.079 respectively, but in democracies the ratio is higher, registering at 1.368.

In a country with two types of maternal public policies, support for women as political leaders continues to increase. In nondemocracies with welfare provision and gender quotas, the ratio is 1.627 (there are no democracies with only these two types of maternal public policies), and in democracies that have welfare provision and hereditary monarchies the ratio is 3.540 (there are no nondemocracies with only these two types of maternal public policies). Finally, in the countries, all of which are democracies, that adopt all three types of maternal public policies—welfare provision, gender quotas, and monarchies—the ratio soars to 8.326, as reported in table 3.2.

Individualism *and* Maternalism

It is neither individualism nor maternalism alone, therefore, that bolsters public attitudes about the suitability of women as political leaders, but

Table 3.2   Public attitudes and democracy: Support for women as political leaders, controlling for maternal public policies, World Values Survey, 2000

MATERNAL PUBLIC POLICIES	DEMOCRACY[a]		
	No	Yes	Total
No maternal public policies	0.260[b] (24,347)[c]	1.405 (8,018)	0.544 (32,365)
Welfare provision, only[d]	1.084 (11,634)	----	1.084 (11,634)
Gender quotas, only[e]	1.079 (4,375)	1.368 (8,502)	1.269 (12,877)
Hereditary monarchies, only[f]	----	----	----
Welfare provision and gender quotas	1.627 (2,255)	----	1.627 (2,255)
Welfare provision and hereditary monarchies	----	3.540 (1,201)	3.540 (1,201)
Gender quotas and hereditary monarchies	----	----	----
Welfare provision, gender quotas, and hereditary monarchies	----	8.326 (8,529)	8.326 (8,529)
Total	0.641 (42,612)	3.739 (26,249)	1.822 (68,861)

a) Democracy: Coded as "free" by Freedom House, 2004.

b) Ratio: The number of people strongly supporting women as political leaders/the number of people strongly not supporting women as political leaders.

c) n = total number of people included in the calculation of ratio in parentheses; number of respondents in category must be at least 1,000 to be reported.

d) Welfare provision: Combination of 55% or more of the funds spent on health care are provided by the government and a constitutional provision or comparable information affirming that it is the state's duty to provide for people's welfare. Data on percent health care funds provided by the government are from the Organization for Economic Co-Operation and Development (OECD), Social Expenditure Database, (2004). Data on constitutional provisions are based on the author's coding of constitutions, as of 2006; the constitutional provision can be a provision for specific assistance, such as the provision of education, health, or other such welfare services, or a statement about the provision of general welfare benefits to people. Constitutional provisions of pensions for government employees are not included.

e) Gender quotas: Measured as a legislative quota above 15% in lower or upper house or a voluntary political party quota of 30% or more in at least two parties or a voluntary political party quota of 40% or more in at least one party and the political party is represented in the legislature in 1999 and 2003. Data for gender quotas are from the Global Database of Quotas for Women, Institute for Democracy and Electoral Assistance (IDEA), Stockholm University, and from Mona Lena Krook and Diana O'Brien, "The Politics of Group Representation: Quotas for Women and Minorities Worldwide," paper presented at the Midwest Political Science Association, 2007.

f) Hereditary monarchies: Monarchies that do not restrict sovereignty to men, as indicated by national constitutions, as coded by the author.

rather *both*. The more maternal public policies there are, the more public attitudes about women as political leaders improve, and that improvement is greater for democratic countries than for nondemocratic ones. We can visualize the impact of a hybrid state representing both individualism and maternalism by looking at figure 3.2. The base line for a nondemocratic country with no maternal public policies is a ratio of 0.3 and for a democratic one, is 1.4. In a nondemocratic country with one type of maternal public policy, the ratio increases to 1.1, and in a nondemocratic country with two types of maternal public policies, the ratio increases to 1.6.

For democratic countries, however, there is a real jump from a country with only one maternal public policy, where the ratio is 1.4, to a country with two and three maternal public policies, where the ratios are 3.5 and 8.3 respectively, as can be seen in figure 3.2. Hence, maternal public policies, particularly when combined with public policies based on individual

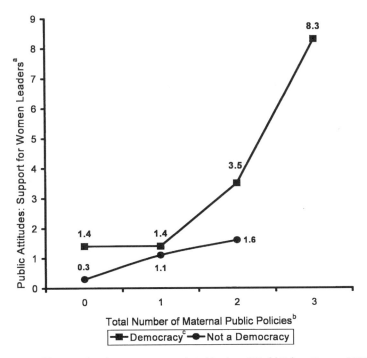

Figure 3.2: Public attitudes about women as political leaders. (World Values Survey, 2000)
    a) Ratio: number of respondents strongly supporting women as political leaders compared to number of people strongly opposed to women as political leaders, World Values Survey, 2000.
    b) Total number of maternal public policies: numerical tally of presence of welfare provision, gender quotas, and hereditary monarchies.
    c) Democracy: coded as "free" by Freedom House, 2004.

equality, have a profound impact on public attitudes about women's suitability as political leaders. When a democratic state adopts public policies representing social or biological maternal traits that the public associates with women, voters' attitudes about the suitability of women as political leaders dramatically increase. Policy feedback explains that increase as occurring because such public policies teach voters that the maternal traits attributed to women signify a location not only in the private sphere of the home or the service sector of the market, but also in the public sphere of the state.

Comparisons with Other Variables

There are other causes besides maternal public policies of public attitudes about women's suitability as political leaders in democracies, such as (1) the percentage of women already elected to a national legislature, (2) psychological orientations, (3) sociological attitudes about the proper roles for women, (4) economic status, (5) religious orientations, and (6) sex and age. We need to take these into account to find out how they augment or modify the impact of "what the state does" in terms of the feedback effect of its policies on political attitudes.

Percent Women Elected to National Legislatures

Even by just running for office, and becoming more visible as candidates, women increase female voters' engagement with politics and their likelihood to cast a ballot.[58] The greater political visibility women achieve when they are actually elected to political office should have a similarly positive effect on voters' perceptions of women as suitable leaders. Thus, when examining the policy feedback effects of maternal public policies on public attitudes about women as political leaders, I control for the percent of women already elected to a country's national legislature. The attitudinal question measuring attitudes about women as political leaders is in the 2000 survey wave, so I use the percentage of women in the lower house of the national legislature (or from the upper house in a unicameral legislature) for the year 1997, on the grounds that the full effect of women's visibility in national politics on public attitudes may not become evident until several years after they have assumed office. The percentages of women elected to national legislatures come from the Inter-Parliamentary Union, "Women in Parliaments."[59]

Psychological Orientations

The qualities cited most often as attributes of political leadership are those typically associated with masculinity, such as independent thinking and high self-esteem. One would expect people who themselves possess these attributes to be more likely to believe that others also do, including women. Such respondents would then be more likely to view women as suited for political leadership positions. To assess the psychological predisposition of respondents, I have chosen variables from the World Value Surveys that measure "perceptions of life" and "family." In particular, people were asked how important it is that "Children should be encouraged to be independent" and that "Children should be encouraged to be imaginative."[60] Those who believe that it is important for children to be independent and imaginative are presumed to be psychologically more predisposed to value individual self-esteem and efficacy than respondents who do not believe that it is important for children to be so inclined.

Sociological Roles

Sociological roles associated with gender have been shown to affect people's attitudes about the appropriateness of women's participation in nontraditional roles outside the home, such as political leadership. In order for a woman to become involved in the public arena of political leadership as an elected official, she must defy traditional expectations of women's domestic roles in favor of job independence. It seems reasonable, therefore, to assume that respondents who are favorably disposed to women assuming nontraditional roles outside the family will also be more likely to be favorably predisposed to women assuming nontraditional political roles in society. To assess the impact of sociological roles on public attitudes about women as political leaders, I use questions from the World Value Survey of 2000 that show the degree to which people affirm or deny the two statements: "The wife must obey her husband" and "Women should have the right to work outside the home."[61] People disagreeing with the former and agreeing with the latter are considered to have attitudes about sociological roles conducive to viewing women as political leaders.

Economic Status

Economic factors are considered crucial to explaining the extent of women's political participation as officeholders. There is general agreement[62] that women's election to office is promoted by a high percentage of women in the labor force, high education levels, high literacy rates (especially for women), high urbanization, and high GNP.[63] These characteristics affect attitudes toward women as political leaders. I assume that respondents who are employed in professional jobs rather than agricultural ones will have more positive attitudes about women as political leaders as will respondents who are highly educated, have high incomes, and live in urban areas. To measure these attributes of respondents, I use the following questions from the World Value Surveys: (1) Type of job, recoded as professional/managerial or not; (2) Education, recoded as low, middle, upper; and (3) Income, recoded as low, middle, upper.[64]

Religious Orientation

The World Value Survey of 2000 contains a long list of religious orientations (variable f025), which are grouped here as Protestant, Catholic, Muslim, Hindu, Jewish, and Other. A religious orientation of "none" is a residual category that is omitted from analysis. The degree of religious attendance comes from using the WVS, 2000, variable f038, which asks people how often they attend religious services. The answers are scored: (8) more than once a week, (7) once a week, (6) once a month, (5) only on special holy days (Christmas, Easter), (4) other specific holy days, (3) once a year, (2) less often, and (1) practically never. I measure religious orientation as a combination of religious affiliation and degree of religious service attendance.

Other Characteristics: Sex, Age, and Nordic Nation

Sex and age are likely to influence attitudes about the suitability of women as political leaders. Younger females are assumed to be more favorably disposed toward viewing women as suitable for political leadership positions than are older respondents, especially older males. In addition, the Nordic countries, composed of Sweden, Denmark, Norway, Finland, and Iceland, are often assumed to provide a more woman-friendly, positive context for promoting women's political leadership.

Putting It All Together

We are now ready to look at how maternal public policies affect public attitudes about women's suitability as political leaders in democracies and nondemocracies, while taking into consideration a host of additional variables that we also presume to be relevant. When we do so, we find that the impact of maternalism and individualism remain powerful. When we include in our analysis the percent of women already elected to the national legislature and whether the country is a Nordic country, for example, we find that all three public policies that represent women's social and biological traits continue to have a positive and strong impact on the public's view of the suitability of women as political leaders, as is reported in table 3.3.

When a country adopts welfare provision, for example, the ratio of people who strongly support women as political leaders increases by 4,370 people to every 1,000 who do not; when it adopts gender quotas, the number of people who strongly support women as political leaders increases by 1,520 people to every 1,000 who do not; and when the country retains a monarchy when democratizing, the number of people who strongly support women as political leaders increases to 4,502, compared to every 1,000 who do not. If a country adopts all three types of maternal public policies, the increase of people who strongly support women as political leaders increases to a whopping 5,091 for every 1,000 who do not. Hence, even when including the effects of a wide range of other variables, the power of maternal policies to sway the public in a positive direction remains crucial when it comes to determining public attitudes about the suitability of women as political leaders.

Public policies representing individualism also have a positive impact on public attitudes about women's suitability as political leaders, even when a host of variables are included in the analysis, such as percentage of women already elected to the national legislature and whether or not the country is a Nordic country. If a country is a democracy, the number of people strongly supporting women as political leaders increases by 5,950 for every 1,000 who do not. Clearly, individualism in the form of a liberal democratic state is a good thing for increasing women's political representation. However, it is not so powerful by itself. For what really does the trick when it comes to convincing the public that women belong in the public sphere of the state rather than at home cooking dinner or in jobs giving aid to those in need is a country that adopts public policies representing both individualism, namely women's sameness with men, and maternalism, namely women's group difference from men.

The interaction terms combine measures of both because the interaction terms for gender quotas and democracy and for hereditary monarchies and democracy drop out of the equation. In the case of the latter, most likely this is because there is no variability when it comes to the

Table 3.3 Public Attitudes: Regression analysis assessing the impact of maternal public policies on public attitudes about women as political leaders, controlling for other relevant variables, World Value Survey, 2000

	PUBLIC ATTITUDES: Support for Women as Political Leaders
	PERCENT SUPPORT [a]
MATERNAL PUBLIC POLICIES	
Welfare Provision[c]	0.437 (0.090) *** [b]
Gender Quotas[d]	0.152 (0.030) ***
Hereditary Monarchies[e]	4.502 (0.589) ***
DEMOCRACY[f]	0.595 (0.139) ***
MATERNAL PUBLIC POLICIES* DEMOCRACY	
Welfare Provision*Democracy	−0.000 (−0.066) ***
Gender Quotas*Democracy	---[s]
Hereditary Monarchies*Democracy	---[s]
PERCENT WOMEN ELECTED TO NATIONAL LEGISLATURE[g]	0.057 (0.188) ***
PSYCHOLOGICAL ORIENTATIONS	
Children's independence[h]	−0.012 (−0.003) **
Children's imagination[i]	0.004 (0.001)
SOCIOLOGICAL ROLES	
Wife's obedience[j]	0.007 (0.002)
Women having work outside the home[k]	0.006 (0.001)
ECONOMIC STATUS	
Professional Occupation[l]	−0.000 (−0.001)
Education[m]	0.086 (0.030) ***
Income[n]	−0.019 (−0.007)
RELIGIOUS ORIENTATION[o]	
Protestant	−0.078 (−0.073) ***
Catholic	0.016 (0.022) ***
Muslim	−0.030 (−0.032) ***
Hindu	−0.099 (−0.033) ***
Jewish	−0.000 (0.000)
Other	0.020 (0.014) ***
SEX[p]	0.013 (0.003) **
AGE[q]	0.056 (0.020) ***
NORDIC COUNTRY[r]	2.168 (0.211) ***
Constant	−0.044
R Squared	0.846

Table 3.3   continued

a) Ratio: Number of respondents strongly supporting women as political leaders compared to number of respondents strongly opposed to women as political leaders, as derived from World Values Survey, 2000, variable d059.

*** p = 0.000, ** p = 0.05, * p = 0.100

b) Unstandardized regression coefficients followed by standardized regression coefficient in parentheses.

c) Welfare provision: Combination of 55% or more of the funds spent on health care are provided by the government and a constitutional provision or comparable information affirming that it is the state's duty to provide for people's welfare. Data on percent health care funds provided by the government are from the Organization for Economic Co-Operation and Development (OECD), Social Expenditure Database, (2004). Data on constitutional provisions are based on the author's coding of constitutions, as of 2006; the constitutional provision can be a provision for specific assistance, such as the provision of education, health, or other such welfare services, or a statement about the provision of general welfare benefits to people. Constitutional provisions of pensions for government employees are not included.

d) Gender quotas: Measured as a legislative quota above 15% in lower or upper house or a voluntary political party quota of 30% or more in at least two parties or a voluntary political party quota of 40% or more in at least one party and the political party is represented in the legislature in 1999 and 2003. Data for gender quotas are from the Global Database of Quotas for Women, Institute for Democracy and Electoral Assistance (IDEA), Stockholm University and from Mona Lena Krook and Diana O'Brien, "The Politics of Group Representation: Quotas for Women and Minorities Worldwide," paper presented at the Midwest Political Science Association, 2007.

e) Hereditary monarchies: Monarchies that do not restrict sovereignty to men, as indicated by national constitutions, as coded by the author.

f) Democracy: Coded as "free" by Freedom House, 2004.

g) Percent women elected to national legislatures in 1997. The data about the percentage of women elected to national legislatures is from the Inter-Parliamentary Union, "Women in Parliaments." The percentage is for the Lower House. At www.iup.org/wmn-e/world.htm.

h) WVS, 2000, A029, The importance of children's independence: 0 = not mentioned, 1 = important.

i) WVS, 2000, A034, The importance of children's imagination: 0 = not mentioned, 1 = important.

j) WVS, 2000, D077, "Wife must obey," 1 = agree strongly, 2 = agree, 3 = neither agree nor disagree, 4 = disagree, and 5 = strongly disagree.

k) WVS, 2000, D073, "Woman having work outside the home," 1 = agree strongly, 2 = agree, 3 = neither agree nor disagree, 4 = disagree, 5 = strongly disagree.

l) WVS, 2000, X036, recoded as Professional/Managerial: 0 = no, 1 = yes.

m) WVS, 2000, X025R, recoded as Education: 1 = lower, 2 = middle, 3 = upper.

n) WVS, 2000, X047R, recoded as Income: 1 = lower, 2 = middle, 3 = upper.

o) WVS, 2000, Religious denominational affiliation (variable f025), recoded into categories measured as Protestant, Catholic, Muslim, Jew, Other, where each is combined with degree of religious service attendance (variable f028), rescored as follows: respondent attends religious services (1) never, practically never, (2) less than once a year, (3) once a year, (4) specific holy days other than Christmas, Easter, etc., (5) only on specific holy days/Christmas, Easter, (6) once a month, (7) once a week, (8) more than once a week. Those respondents answering "none" to religious affiliation question are omitted.

p) WVS, 2000, X001, recoded to Sex: 0 = male, 1 = female.

q) WVS, 2000, X003, recoded to Age: (1) = 15–29 years, (2) 30–49 years, (3) 50+.

r) Nordic countries, Denmark, Iceland, Finland, Norway, Sweden, dummy variable, 0 = no, 1 = yes.

s) Drops-out of regression equation.

combination of hereditary monarchies open to women and whether a country is a democracy. In addition, the interaction term combining welfare provision and democracy is minuscule in size, registering as an unstandardized regression coefficient of -0.000. To assess the impact of the combination of individualism with maternalism on public attitudes about women as political leaders, the best way is simply to add the effects of each to arrive at the total impact. For a country that adopts all three types of maternal public policies and is a democracy (and thus has public policies representing individualism), the increase in the number of people who strongly support women as political leaders is 5,686, compared to every 1,000 who do not.

There is also a positive impact on public attitudes about the suitability of women as political leaders in relation to the percentage of women already elected to the national legislature, as we would expect. For every 1 percent increase in the percentage of women elected to the national legislature, fifty-seven more people view women as suitable as political leaders, as is indicated in table 3.3. Psychological orientations of respondents, by contrast, have virtually no impact on public attitudes. Those who mentioned the importance of children's independence reduce ever so slightly, by only twelve people, the ratio of supporters to opponents of women as political leaders, as reported in table 3.3. Sociological role orientations appear not to have an impact.

When we turn to economic indices, we find that the most important and positive variable is education. As education increases, so, too, does the ratio of people supporting women as political leaders. At the lowest level of education, the ratio is 86 people who support women as political leaders, compared to every 100 who do not. Multiplying that number by 3, which is the value for people with a high education, shows that at the high educational level, the ratio of support for women as political leaders increases to 258 supporters for every 100 opponents.

Religious orientations when combined with degree of attendance do not produce more support for women as political leaders, with the exception of Catholic and "Other," which are positive, and Jewish, which is statistically insignificant. While it may be surprising to find a positive view of women's political leadership stemming from a Catholic religiosity, others have also found Catholic religions to have a positive impact on views about women's political equality.[65]

In addition, because of the exceptional way that the Nordic countries promote women's political representation, it is important to include whether a country is Nordic in the assessment of other impacts on political attitudes, so as to be sure that the findings do not reflect Nordic-specific patterns.

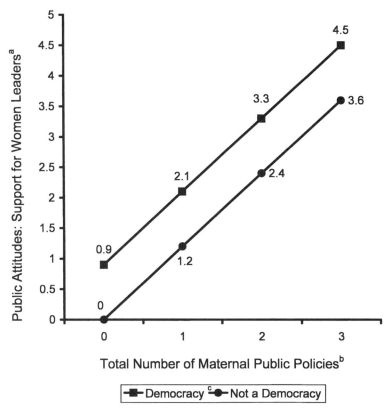

Figure 3.3: Public attitudes about women as political leaders, controlling for relevant variables. (World Values Survey, 2000)

a) Ratio: number of respondents strongly supporting women as political leaders compared to number of respondents strongly opposed to women as political leaders, World Values Survey, 2000.

b) Total number of maternal public policies: numerical tally of presence of welfare provision, gender quotas, and/or hereditary monarchies.

c) Democracy: coded as "free" by Freedom House, 2004.

Even when Nordic is included, however, the impact of public policies representing maternalism and individualism remain strong. However, so, too, does a Nordic political context itself have a powerful and positive impact on support for women as political leaders, as is indicated by the unstandardized regression coefficient of 2.168. This means that when people reside in a Nordic country, there is an increase of 2,168 people supporting women as political leaders, compared to every 1,000 who do not. Equally important, however, is that the public policies remain statistically significant and strong even when Nordic country is included. Finally, being female has a small but positive impact on support for women as political leaders, as is indicated by an increase in the ratio of support by thirteen people. Age also is positive, with a ratio increase of fifty-six people in support of women as political leaders.

What bolsters public attitudes about the suitability of women as political leaders is, therefore, a political context defined as a hybrid state, which represents in its public policies individualism, as all democracies do, and maternal traits associated with women, as some democracies do. The more maternal public policies the better. In a country that is a democracy with no maternal public policies, for example, the number of people who strongly support women as political leaders would be expected to increase by nine people for every 100 who do not, as indicated in figure 3.3. However, when that same democracy has even one maternal public policy, even when other relevant variables are included in the analysis, the number of people supporting women as political leaders increases to 210 for every 100 who oppose such leaders. The relationship, increases to 450 people supporting women as political leaders for every 100 who do not when a country is a democracy and adopts all three types of maternal public policies. The impact of maternal public policies on generating a political context fostering positive attitudes about women's suitability as political leaders is similar for nondemocracies, though the overall impact is less, given the missing positive impact of public policies representing individualism, or, women's sameness with men.

What the State Does Matters

There is ample reason to conclude that maternal public policies in democracies exert a powerful feedback impact on public attitudes about women's capabilities as political leaders. When democratic countries act like individuals by guaranteeing negative individual rights for all people, in spite of their ascriptive group difference, and *also* act like women by endorsing policies guaranteeing positive group rights associated with women's maternalism, the resulting hybrid state identity redefines the public sphere to include, rather than to exclude, women. The interpretive feedback effect of maternal public policies on the public influences the public's perceptions of who can be a political player. Hybrid states demonstrate that the political process is not just a man's game, nor is it only an arena for neutral, atomistic individuals whose ascriptive characteristics are irrelevant to political governance. To the contrary, when democratic countries combine public policies endorsing negative individual rights representing individualism with ones endorsing positive group rights representing maternalism, the percentage of the voting public that positively views women as potential candidates for public office increases. This is a necessary first step to electing greater numbers of women to national political office and improving women's political representation. Thus, rather than fearing maternalism, much less individualism, what benefits women is a state that represents both.

Electing Women Political Leaders 4

Gracie Allen for President

Among American women who have run campaigns to be president of the United States, the names that historically come to mind are Victoria Woodhull in the nineteenth century, Shirley Chisholm in the 1970s, Pat Schroeder in the 1980s, Elizabeth Dole in the 1990s, and in 2008 Hillary Rodham Clinton. Let us not forget, however, Gracie Allen in the 1940s.[1] When legendary comedian Gracie Allen tossed her hat in the presidential ring, literally and figuratively, she argued that "half the married people in the nation were women and they would all vote for her."[2] Although her campaign was a spoof, a diversion intended solely for her radio audience, she embarked on a barnstorming campaign via railroad from Los Angeles to Omaha, drawing crowds of up to 300,000 people at her many appearances. She was invited to be an honored guest at the National Women's Press Club's annual convention in Washington, DC by no less a personage than First Lady Eleanor Roosevelt.[3] Among the many gifts she received was a feathered headdress from the Omaha Indians, who inducted her into their tribe.[4] Harvard University students endorsed Gracie's candidacy; the Minnesota town of Menominee elected her mayor; and when the presidential election took place in November, Gracie received several thousand write-in votes.[5] Gracie's campaign illustrates an important truth about presidential campaigns. As she put it,

> Presidents are made, not born. That's a good thing to remember. It's silly to think that Presidents are born, because very few people are 35 years old at birth, and those who are won't admit it. So if you're only 16, don't be discouraged, because it's only a phase and there's nothing wrong with you that you won't outgrow.[6]

Gracie was right that leaders are made, not born. And what contributes to making leaders is the political context in which they live. In the case of contemporary women, they can get made into political leaders by a political context that combines policies representing individualism with those representing maternal traits that voters associate with women. Such a hybrid state teaches the public that the maternalism associated with women signifies not only a location in the private sphere of the home or the service sector of the market but also in the public sphere of political governance. The result is an increase in the public's view of women as suitable for political leadership and an increase in the percentage of women elected to political office. What "makes" women presidents and other political leaders, therefore, is a feedback mechanism generated by government policies that define the political significance of maternal traits to mean inclusion in the state.

Women's Political Representation Matters

Women's political representation matters for both normative and instrumental reasons. Normatively, representation is a core tenet of democracy. Originally in ancient Greece political power was restricted to those citizens who were deemed to have the leisure requisite to participate in the rule of a city-state. Qualified citizens did so directly, and thus the city-state of Athens was a *direct democracy*. In a direct democracy self-rule means that everyone who is eligible participates directly as an officeholder. In the case of ancient Athens, all of those eligible to be political rulers took turns as officeholders, rotating through their ranks.[7]

In a large contemporary democracy, however, such as the United States, it is not feasible for everyone to rule directly over everyone else. Rather what is needed is a *representative democracy* that allows individuals to vote to choose political leaders to represent them in office. Democracy as it is understood today, therefore, is a representative system of governance in which political candidates compete with one another for electoral support from citizens who choose who will hold political office. Political officeholders then become the representatives of their constituents, accountable to them for meeting their needs, if not their demands. The Congress of the United States epitomizes the meaning of representative democracy, to the point that House members are even referred to as *representatives*.

There are many ways of understanding representation in a contemporary democracy, but two of the most illuminating are *descriptive* and *substantive representation*. In a democracy descriptive representation refers to the idea that the legislature is "a microcosm of the entire population and can be readily substituted for a democratic convocation of the whole people."[8] A legislative body represents a citizenry descriptively when the relative proportion of significant group characteristics in the electorate and in the legislature is similar. Substantive representation, in contrast, occurs when officeholders represent the interests and goals of their constituencies, regardless of whether those in office share the group characteristics of their constituents.

In a direct democracy all people are directly involved in sharing political governance, while in a representative democracy the representatives have to take the place of all the people, and in that respect they should reflect the composition of the nation, mirroring the demographic characteristics of the population.[9] Questioning whether or not major groups, or even minor groups, are left out of the representative body is to question the political legitimacy of the body. Descriptive representation, therefore, is an important component of women's political representation. It is a fundamental goal in itself, which is central to the ethos of democracy. As Jane Mansbridge argues, it is intrinsically good that the demographic makeup of a population—its race, class, sex, religion, and language—be descriptively represented in national government, particularly in such representative institutions as the American Congress.[10] If women, for example, instead of men, comprised 84.9% of the American Congress, few would dispute that, since men make up about half of all Americans, something was wrong. It should be no less shocking or any less flawed the other way around. If a country, such as the United States, which is based on the premise of the inherent political equality of all individuals regardless of their group, evidences dramatic and systematic exclusion of a particular group over long stretches of time, it could be argued that the system fails to fulfill the most basic requirement of a liberal, representative democracy.[11]

Descriptive representation can also be an instrument to promote substantive representation. To achieve substantive representation, the key issue is not what sex a person is (a socially constructed, biological classifica-tion), but rather what gender a person is (a socially constructed, behavioral classification). Female gender roles are associated with issues such as sup-port for welfare provision and the promotion of peace; while male gender roles are associated with issues such as fiscal conservatism and national security. Yet since some male officeholders are substantively more sup-portive of welfare and world peace than some women, substantive repre-sentation of female issues can sometimes be best accomplished by electing a man, rather than a woman, to public office.[12]

Generally, however, there is a positive correlation between descriptive and substantive representation. Political scientist Kira Sanbonmatsu, for example, finds that descriptive representation increases the probabilities that issues important to women will get on the legislative agenda.[13] Politi-cal scientist David Canon has shown that African American officeholders are more likely to support interests held in common with most African Americans in at least some political contexts.[14] What is more, many scholars concerned with democracy as a process of deliberation stress the way de-scriptive representation is crucial for guaranteeing the presence of women and other minorities so that they can articulate for themselves their inter-ests.[15] Jane Mansbridge stresses how critical descriptive representation is for expressing the interests of groups that have not yet crystallized their agendas, are in situational contexts of mistrust, or are in political environ-ments that may not be aware of their perspectives.[16]

Although it is difficult to define what constitutes women's interests as a group, political scientists Susan Carroll and Michelle Swers find women in the general population, compared to men, to be "less militaristic on issues of war and peace, more opposed to the death penalty, more likely to favor gun control, more likely to favor measures to protect the environment, and more supportive of programs to help the economically disadvantaged," and these issue distinctions between men and women are replicated in the po-sitions taken by members of Congress.[17] Women legislators, regardless of party affiliation, are more likely than men to promote legislative attention to such public policy concerns as child care and domestic violence, con-cerns that transform what are often considered family issues in the private sphere into public issues in the political sphere. What is more, as Swers' research found, women have a distinctive impact on issues at all five stages of the passage of legislation, from bill sponsorship, to cosponsorship, com-mittee amendments, floor debate, and roll call voting.[18] Women members of Congress are also most active in the bill sponsorship stage of legislation, where women are less constrained by the demands of party loyalty, seniority, and committee membership. As Swers concludes, the "personal identities" of representatives, including their gender, "do have tangible policy consequences."[19]

Political scientist Debra Dobson also shows that increasing the presence of women in political offices "transforms the political agenda, with women officeholders giving greater attention than their male colleagues of the same party to women's rights as defined by the contemporary women's movement as well as to concerns reflecting women's roles as care-givers in the family and in society more generally."[20] Thus, the election of more women to national political office, a form of descriptive representation, is an effective means for increasing their substantive representation.[21] As Patricia Ireland, former president of the National Organization for Women, puts it, "if we are ever going to make a change on any of our issues—reproductive freedom, health, violence, workplace reform—we've got to change the faces [of Congress]. . . . if there was any object lesson out of [the] Clarence Thomas–Anita Hill [hearings], it was that we cannot rely on anybody else to represent us. We have to be there to represent ourselves. And it's got to be now."[22]

The connection between descriptive and substantive representation means that activists on behalf of women's rights define the former to be of fundamental importance to women's health and well-being. At the United Nations Fourth World Conference on Women (FWCW) in Beijing, China, in 1995, for example, participants adopted a "Platform for Action" that put the advancement of women into electoral positions of political decision making high on its agenda, stating emphatically:

> Achieving the goal of equal participation of women and men in [political] decision-making will provide a balance that more accurately reflects the composition of society and is needed in order to strengthen democracy and promote its proper functioning. Equality in political decision-making performs a leverage function without which it is highly unlikely that a real integration of the equality dimension in government policy-making is feasible. In this respect, women's equal participation in political life plays a pivotal role in the general process of the advancement of women. Women's equal participation in decision-making is not only a demand for simple justice or democracy but can also be seen as a necessary condition for women's interests to be taken into account. Without the active participation of women and the incorporation of women's perspective at all levels of decision-making, the goals of equality, development and peace cannot be achieved.[23]

In the wake of the Beijing conference, various efforts have been launched to increase women's representation in governments around the world.[24] Notable is the Women's Environment and Development Organization (WEDO),[25] a New York–based advocacy network that in 2000 kicked-off a "Get the Balance Right" campaign intended to promote women's equal representation in legislatures and cabinet ministries all around the world.[26]

Finally, descriptive representation matters as an instrument to promote women's identification with politics. Descriptive representation redefines the public sphere of political officeholding to be "an inclusive domain," open to women as well as men. As political scientists Nancy Burns, Kay Schlozman, and Sidney Verba show, when women's names are on the ballot, and much more so when women are elected, women voters become more engaged in the political process. Women become more knowledgeable about political issues and, as a consequence, are more likely to participate in politics as voters and as candidates.[27] The visibility of women's political campaigns provides them with a model of politics as a woman's game, not just a man's game.[28] Christina Wolbrecht and David Campbell confirm that women's visibility as role models in political office increases interest in and identification with politics among young women.[29] In short, descriptive representation in campaigns as well as in public office enhances women's identification with political rule of the state.

Political Leadership Matters

Political leadership can be considered in two ways. It can be something that one does as well as a position that one holds. Thus, leadership can be an action or a position. According to the *OED*, political leadership as an "action" refers to "leading a group of people or an organization." Political leadership as a "position" refers to "the state or position of being a leader," as, for example, "the leaders of . . . [a] country."[30]

Defining political leadership as both an action and as a position opens the door to diverse perspectives on women as political leaders. Studies of women's political leadership as action typically focus on the biographies of particular women leaders, or on the types of women leaders, or on the leadership styles of women compared to men, or on the policy consequences of women's political leadership.[31] Studies of women's political leadership as a position focus on what is termed women's *political recruitment*, by which is meant how women get into positions of political leadership in the first place, and what can be done to enhance that access.[32] This is not to say that women lead only from positions of formal political inclusion as voters and officeholders. To the contrary, women have influenced politics effectively from informal locations outside the electorate.[33] Yael Tamir describes the ways women exercise their power in the public realm, supplementary to established government structures "such as parliaments or congresses, parties, campaigns, and voting," by engaging in activities in the public sphere that have the intention of "influencing political institutions."[34] So, too, historian Pamela Radcliff finds that women's political power shifts from state-centered, "top-down constructions" to the "realm of civil society," where groups such as "housewife associations" combine the political and the private outside the domain of formal positions of political leadership.[35]

As political scientist Theda Skocpol establishes, although women in the United States in the early twentieth century did not have a national guarantee of the right to vote or to hold office, they nevertheless were major contributors to the legislative development of an innovative maternal welfare state.[36] Similarly, political scientist Mary Katzenstein makes the case that a feminist agenda can be conducted unobtrusively with mechanisms of informal as well as formal power even within the most patriarchal of institutions, such as the military or the Catholic Church.[37] Georgina Waylen and Maxine Molyneux also analyze how women implement democratization from their vantage point as social activists outside the arena of formal political office.[38]

Yet formal political inclusion as voters and officeholders remains a central interest and concern of democratic practice. As Virginia Sapiro argues, it does matter in a democracy whether women vote or not.[39] Similarly, Jane Mansbridge makes the case for the value of formal, descriptive representation.[40] Political scientist Barbara Burrell argues that women's election to positions in government provides a positive symbolic identification for all women; enhances the normative, democratic belief that politics is equally open to all, regardless of gender; and bolsters the passage of policies benefiting women, such as federal funding for child care, family and medical leave, and abortion rights.[41] Thus, increasing women's formal political representation as political officeholders promotes both normative and instrumental values central to democratic theory and practice.

Given the importance of women's formal inclusion in representative democracies, it is vital to consider what it is that promotes women's election to political office. The answer is the policy feedback effects of a hybrid state that, by adopting public policies representing both women's sameness with men and women's maternal group difference from men, teaches the public that women's maternal identities locate them inside the public sphere of political governance.

Election to Political Office: The Policy Feedback Model

Defining Democracy and Citizenship

Democracy refers to "rule by the people," and the core meaning of citizenship is "inclusion." Thus, citizenship stands in direct relation to all definitions of democracy, in terms of whether people are included in political rule. From a qualitative perspective, there are different components to the people being in charge of their own governance. For example, *civil citizenship* refers to the rights of people to engage in basic legal processes in society, such as to make contracts, marry, and purchase property. *Political citizenship* refers to the rights of people to engage in basic forms of political participation, such as to vote, to hold office, and to serve on juries. *Social citizenship* refers to the rights of people to have basic economic needs met by government in the event that the family and the market are insufficient. Social citizenship is included in the definition of democracy because without at least a minimum level of food, shelter, clothing, education, and health, if not of work, it is virtually impossible to activate civil and political citizenship rights.

Maternal public policies include social citizenship, but because they also encompass policies representing biological maternal traits, they also include what might be termed *biological citizenship*. Biological citizenship is analogous to *sexual citizenship*, in that it includes social practices and legal rights for those with transgendered sexual identities, same-sex sexual orientations, and other identities stemming from sexual practices and preferences.[42] Biological citizenship also includes disability as one of the sites requiring the integration of physically defined identities into political discourse and legal rights. Political scientist Ruth O'Brien defines the basic *animality* of human beings,[43] or the materiality of life that defines all human beings, to include their material, economic, and other dependency needs for physical assistance from others. People categorized as "disabled" are no different as a category from others who are "able," because all people at different points in their lives may be more accurately assessed in terms of the degree of their ableness. All human beings at the beginning of life as infants, for example, are severely "disabled" and hence severely dependent upon others for meeting their basic physical needs for food, shelter, and clothing. Throughout life ableness is a condition that for most people continues to ebb and flow. On the one hand, social democratic policies generally include social citizenship, such as welfare provision, which corresponds to social maternalism, but also include socialist policies designed to reduce class inequalities, which maternal public policies do not encompass. On the other hand, policies representing biological maternal traits, such as gender quotas and hereditary monarchies generally are missing from the agenda of social democrats.

In addition to qualitative types of citizenship, democracy is defined by its quantity, that is, the level of democracy operating in a country. Generally this is assessed by the percentage of people who are entitled to different types of citizenship rights. In terms of political citizenship, a country that guarantees voting rights only to men, is therefore a democracy in the qualitative sense of having an operating principle of political citizenship, but is not a democracy in the quantitative sense of having an electorate open to both men and women. Similarly in terms of social citizenship, a country such as the United States that guarantees some minimum types of health care assistance, such as Medicare and Medicaid, is a democracy in the qualitative sense of having a modicum of social citizenship rights, but in a quantitative sense it falls far short in comparison to other countries that provide a much higher level of economic resources for a much greater percentage of those in need. Maternal public policies measures encompass both qualitative and quantitative dimensions of social and biological citizenship.

The qualitative measure of democracy used here refers only to civil and political qualitative types of democracy. Both of these types are premised on the principle that all individuals are equal and should be treated by the government the same in spite of their group differences, such as their class, race, or sex. For this reason civil and political rights as founded upon individualism are measures of *liberalism* or *liberal democracy*. Freedom House scores are used here as a measure of whether a political system has public policies based on civil rights and political rights premised on a principle of individualism. From a quantitative perspective, Freedom House also measures the *degree* to which a country guarantees the civil and political rights of individuals, that is, the degree to which all individuals are included in the guarantee of basic civil and political rights. In the cross-national analysis of electoral patterns, countries are evaluated as "free" by Freedom House because they guarantee civil and political rights broadly to everyone in society. They are considered to be "democratic," meaning they are liberal democracies. Countries that receive a score of "partly free" or "not free" are scored as undemocratic. Freedom House must have scored a country as "free" from at least 1978 to the present to be regarded as a liberal democracy comparable to the United States.

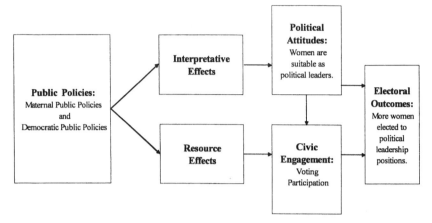

Figure 4.1: Policy feedback for mass publics: How policy affects political attitudes, civic engagement, and electoral outcomes. (Adapted from Mettler and Welch, 2004)

Liberal Individualism: Necessary but Not Sufficient

Liberal individualism is not bad for women and does not fail women. In fact, democracies based on liberal individualism create a political context that fosters acceptance of women as political leaders when compared to nondemocratic countries. Yet, democracy defined as liberal individualistic public policies is not enough to promote fully the public's endorsement of women as political leaders. What also is necessary is a political context that represents the maternal traits voters associate with women. What promotes women's acceptance by the public as political leaders, therefore, is a hybrid state representing women's dual identities as both individuals who are the same as men and maternalists who differ from men. In their effect on the political participation of voters, hybrid public policies turn out to have an interpretative impact on public attitudes, and also a positive impact on the election of women to political office by means of their instrumental impact on the civic capacity of voters, as is diagrammed in figure 4.1.

Civic Capacities: The Resource Impact of Public Policies

Some public policies affect civic capacity by influencing how much voters trust government, how much they view their vote as really counting and making a difference, how much they identify with the government as an entity, and how much they feel they have a civic duty to vote. Public policies that convey to people that the government cares about them, that the government is responsive to their needs, and that the government is a "good" entity that seeks their input and deserves their attention are also public policies that serve to increase the civic capacity of voters by increasing the likelihood that people will vote.

The impact of public policies on voting participation differs from the impact of private, individual, or group membership. Individuals with greater educational attainment, higher income, and higher occupational status participate in the electorate more than others who lack such benefits. Individuals who belong to or identify with mobilized groups, such as unions, activist religions, or social movements, are also more likely to turn out to vote. In addition to such individual-level impacts, the government's public policies have an impact on how people feel about political participation and how people actually do participate in elections. Public policies influence how people view their relationship to the state and consequently how people will participate in elections that determine who are the leaders of that state. In terms of resources, as political scientist Andrea Campbell observes, programs such as Social Security enable older Americans to retire from employment, thereby providing them with more time to participate and be included in politics.[44] Partly because of this instrumental effect of Social Security policy on elderly Americans, their interests are exceptionally well represented at the state and national level.[45] Public policies that affirmatively target disadvantaged groups are thus mechanisms for providing resources, such as economic or social benefits in the case of the GI Bill or Social Security, that influence the civic capacity of people to participate in elections.

Maternal Public Policies and Civic Capacities

Public policies associated with the maternal traits attributed by the public to women have instrumental impacts upon people's civic capacity to engage in political participation. Welfare policies in particular generate resources that enhance the public's participation in politics. Health care, for example, enables people to live longer, with fewer impediments burdening their everyday lives, including their ability to vote, campaign, and run for political office.

Political scientists Frances Rosenbluth, Rob Salmond, and Michael Thies explain that women are underrepresented around the world in national legislatures owing to a lack of welfare policies. Welfare policies are crucial for women's political empowerment, because they stimulate a chain of events that predisposes political parties to compete for women's votes, which has the effect of increasing women's presence in legislative bodies.[46] The process by which welfare policies promote political participation is fourfold. First, welfare provision enables women to enter the labor market more easily, thereby giving it a greater percentage of women than in a country without welfare. The provision of welfare then creates a public labor niche that is especially desirable for many women, who enter that service sector and thereby also increase women's presence in the labor market. Once women are in the labor market, their political interests then change, producing an ideological gender gap between men and women. Finally, the ideological gender gap prompts political parties to be receptive to the issue needs of women as distinguished from men, thereby resulting in partisan attention both to women's issues and to women's entry into politics as political candidates and elected officeholders.[47] Thus, democratic maternal public policies bolster not only the political participation of the public in general but also women's participation as voters and as candidates.

Gender quotas also enhance the civic capacities of voters. From the standpoint of descriptive representation, such quotas affirm that gender is a significant attribute of the state's population that should be used to make sure that the state's legislature, as a representative body, reflects the gender component of society. The national legislature thus descriptively "looks like" the composition of society. A national legislature composed entirely of men, when half the people in a society are women, is flawed, because such a legislature looks vastly different from the population of the state. It is not proportional. From the standpoint of substantive representation in a state, gender quotas also imply that there are substantive issues that may vary systematically by gender. The best way to ensure that the interests of both men and women are substantively represented is to be sure that the national legislature is composed of both men and women. One way to do this is to specify a threshold quota of genders that guarantees that the subordinate group, women, will be included in the national legislature, at least at the quota level.[48]

What is more, the significant characteristic of women's difference from men is that what benefits women benefits everyone. Legislation that is in the interest of women, such as health care and family leave, is in the interest of the general welfare. Including women in national legislative bodies is crucial, not just to represent and achieve legislation beneficial to women, but also to represent and achieve legislation beneficial to everyone.[49] Specifically, women enhance the general welfare by enhancing the economic development of a nation-state. As Bo Asplund, resident representative of the United Nations Development Programme (UNDP) in Indonesia, explains it: "Women's participation [in government] is about ensuring development policies and programs addressing the concerns, needs and experiences of both men and women. The presence of women in Government contributes to better governance. A recent World Bank study, for example, indicates that there is a correlation between an increase in women's representation in parliaments and a decrease in corruption in Government."[50] Less corruption enhances economic development.

Gender quotas are a way, therefore, to provide what political scientist Lisa Baldez refers to as an "exogenous shock," one that can, "loosen the hold of longtime norms associating politics with men."[51] In Latin America, gender quotas have been adopted to facilitate women's entry into politics as an antidote for the baseline corruption and lack of civic responsibility currently characterizing the male domination of politics. In this respect, while gender quotas represent women's biological maternalism, or their sex classification as a female, such policies also represent women's social maternalism, defined as women's greater tendency than men's to be altruistic and to be oriented toward the needs of others, rather than to be governed by their own self-interest narrowly defined by self-aggrandizing activities.[52] During the Argentine crisis in 2001, for example, the phrase *que se vayan todos* (kick them all out), referring to the entrenched male politicians, was accompanied by renewed support for getting women into politics by means of gender quotas, as captured in the phrase *que se entran ellas* (let the women in).[53]

Although the third type of state maternalism, hereditary monarchy, does have a positive impact on public attitudes about the suitability of women for political leadership positions, some may find it difficult to imagine why it would increase people's civic capacity to vote. Monarchies open to women today, which are all constitutional democracies, have only symbolic political authority, with little actual political authority to make the populace wealthy, healthy, or wise, and thereby increase people's civic capacity of people to vote. Monarchies are potent political symbols that teach voters to associate familial identities with the public sphere of the state. Voters learn from monarchical symbolism that to have the familial, maternal identity attributed to women signifies a suitable location in the state, thereby increasing the support for women as public leaders. Many might question, however, whether this impact translates into a greater civic capacity to vote. Hence, in the following analysis of conditions that influence women's chances of election to public office, I limit my consideration of the resource capacity of maternalist policies to welfare provision and gender quotas.

Women's Election to National Legislatures

Liberal democracies that embrace public policies treating individuals the same in spite of their group differences are in general a good thing for women's election to national legislatures, as shown by looking at the world's countries as a whole. The average percentage of women elected is 15.4%, as indicated in table 4.1. For countries that are not democracies, the average percentage of women elected is 12.9%, while for democracies it is 18.1%. There are additional instrumental payoffs when democracies, which by definition embrace public policies based on a principle of negative individual rights or individualism, *also* endorse public policies based on positive group rights representing maternal traits, such as welfare provision and gender quotas. In *democratic* countries that provide neither welfare nor gender quotas, for example, the average percentage of women elected to national legislatures is only 9.9%. However, in democratic countries that have at least one maternal public policy, the average representation of women in national legislatures increases. Political *democracies* that provide only welfare elect an average of 17.6% women to their national legislatures, and democracies that provide only gender quotas elect an average of 17.2%. In democratic countries that provide *both* welfare and gender quotas, the average percentage of women elected to national legislatures increases dramatically to 27.5%, as table 4.1 reports.[54]

Two of the most salient influences on women's political recruitment or on women's chances of winning election to national public office are political structures and economic status. Women, for example, are more likely to be elected in multimember districts than in single-member districts, in states with proportional representation electoral systems than in states with plurality voting systems, and in highly competitive elections where multiple parties are running candidates for office. Women's campaigns are often more successful in parliamentary systems than in presidential systems, where there is a clearer delineation between the legislative and executive branches of government.[55] Political structures consistently stand out as extremely potent influences on women's chances of electoral success.

The recognition that structural factors have significant power to enhance or diminish women's access to political office has led many countries to institute changes, including the adoption of gender quotas. Quotas are in place at the legislative or party level in Sweden, Taiwan, India, Venezuela, France, Norway, Denmark, Iceland, Germany, Luxembourg, Portugal, Italy, the Netherlands, and Britain. Even though quotas may create a glass ceiling by setting a limit to the percentage of women to be elected,[56] which ultimately hinders gender parity in national office, quotas clearly benefit women's access to national office.[57]

Gender quotas differ from other political structures, such as electoral systems and configurations of executive branch power, which have no reference to gender identity. By contrast, a gender quota is a public policy

Table 4.1   Percent women elected to national legislatures, controlling for individualism (democracy) and maternalism (maternal public policies), 2006

MATERNALISM:	INDIVIDUALISM: Democracy[a]		
Welfare Provision[b]	No	Yes	
Gender Quotas[c]	(Not Free)	(Free)	Total
No maternalism	9.9%[d] (54)[e]	10.2% (31)	10.0% (85)
Welfare provision only	13.4% (28)	17.6% (23)	15.3% (51)
Gender quotas only	22% (11)	17.2% (8)	20% (19)
Welfare provision and gender quotas	19.4% (7)	27.5% (27)	25.8% (34)
Total	12.9% (100)	18.0% (89)	15.3% (189)

a) Democracy: Coded as "free" by Freedom House, 2006.
b) Welfare provision: Combination of 55% or more of the funds spent on health care are provided by the government and a constitutional provision or comparable information affirming that it is the state's duty to provide for people's welfare. Data on percent health care funds provided by the government are from the Organization for Economic Co-Operation and Development (OECD), Social Expenditure Database (2004). Data on constitutional provisions are based on the author's coding of constitutions, as of 2006; the constitutional provision can be a provision for specific assistance, such as the provision of education, health, or other such welfare services, or a statement about the provision of general welfare benefits to people. Constitutional provisions of pensions for government employees are not included.
c) Gender quotas: Measured as a legislative quota above 15% in lower or upper house or a voluntary political party quota of 30% or more in at least two parties or a voluntary political party quota of 40% or more in at least one party and the political party is represented in the legislature in 1999 and 2003. Data for gender quotas are from the Global Database of Quotas for Women, Institute for Democracy and Electoral Assistance (IDEA), Stockholm University, and from Mona Lena Krook and Diana O'Brien, "The Politics of Group Representation: Quotas for Women and Minorities Worldwide," paper presented at the Midwest Political Science Association, 2007.
d) Percent.
e) Number of cases.

that explicitly represents biological maternalism as defined by a sex classification as female. It is a type of political structure that has a gender-specific content in that it represents a maternal trait. Hence gender quotas are categorized as the state's performance of maternalism, rather than as a gender-neutral political structure, for the purpose of assessing the relative impact of different variables on women's election to national legislatures. Hence, gender quotas are political structures having interpretative and instrumental feedback on how the public views the suitability of women as political leaders. The category of political structures includes proportional representation, multiparty electoral systems, and parliamentary or presidential systems.

Economic factors are another crucial influence on women's political citizenship as officeholders. Women's election to office is promoted by a high percentage of women in the labor force, high education levels, high literacy rates (especially for women), high urbanization, and high GNP.[58] Thus, the economic characteristics of countries must be considered when assessing impacts on women's election to national legislatures.

Putting It All Together

A hybrid state that represents both individualism and maternalism vis-à-vis its public policies, namely a state that is both democratic and maternal, affects women's election to national legislatures quite apart from other important factors, specifically political structure and economic status. Political attitudes have a more positive impact on voting decisions about women candidates when a greater proportion of the public do view women as suitable political leaders than do not. As the ratio increases, the percentage of women elected to national legislatures increases by 3.047%.[59]

Among the variety of political structures, closed proportional representation,[60] parliamentary, presidential, and multiparty systems all have positive impacts on the election of women to national legislatures, as is shown in table 4.2. In countries with closed proportional representation, women's election to national legislatures is boosted by 7.7%; in states with a parliament, women's election is boosted by 8.3%; and with a multiparty system, it is boosted another 3.5% if party lists are used by an average district size of fewer than five seats, or if a combination of party list and candidate voting is used, or if voters choose among individual candidates but in a multimember district. The percentage increases to 7.1% if voters choose among party lists in a multimember district that averages five or more seats. Thus, political structures do in fact matter for women's election to national political office. Presidential systems also have a positive impact on women's election to national legislatures, though to a lesser degree than do parliamentary systems, increasing the percentage of women elected by only 5.9%.[61]

The economic characteristics of countries also matter. States with a higher GDP per person and a higher percentage of women in the labor force elect more women to their national legislatures.[62]

Maternal public policies in a democratic state also have a positive impact on the election of women to national legislatures. The sole fact of a country being a liberal democracy has no relative impact on the election of women to national legislative political office. Gender quotas, in contrast, do have a positive impact on women's election to national legislatures, regardless of whether a country is a democracy. In other words, when gender quotas are in effect, the predicted increase in women's election to national legislatures is 9.7%, whether or not the country is a democracy. The state's provision of welfare alone has no positive impact on women's election to national legislatures. However, there is a positive impact on women's election to national legislatures when the country is democratic *and* maternalist, in the sense of providing welfare. Democratic countries that also provide welfare benefits increase the election of women by 5.956%, as indicated in table 4.2.[63]

Democracy and State Maternalism

When political structures, economic characteristics, maternal public policies, and democracy are all included in the analysis, we see the power of state maternalism in democracies for increasing the percentage of women elected to national legislatures. *Public attitudes* remain positive, increasing women's election to national legislatures by 2.074%, as indicated in Model V, table 4.3.[64] *Political structure* remains important in terms of closed proportional representation, where the predicted percentage of women elected to national legislatures increases by 4.422%, a parliamentary system remains positive, increasing the percentage of women elected by 6.248%. Other political structures and economic variables are not statistically significant. Average GDP remains slightly positive, and urbanization becomes a somewhat negative influence on women's election to national legislatures.

Liberal democracy alone does not have a statistically significant impact, on women's election to national legislatures. Nor does welfare provision alone. Only gender quotas alone increase women's election to national legislatures, by 8.892%. However, when a *democratic* country provides for welfare, the percentage of women elected to national legislatures increases by 9.875%, as is reported in Model V, table 4.3. In the case of the United States, therefore, if the American state were to adopt welfare provision, the number of women elected to the House of Representatives would be expected to increase by 9.875%, for an addition of more than forty-three women.[65] If the United States were to adopt gender quotas, an additional thirty-nine women would be expected to be elected to the House.[66]

When controlling for whether a country is Nordic, the same patterns hold. Yes, there is the whopping impact of simply being Nordic, which increases the percentage of women elected by 11.355%, along with the continuing positive impact of democratic maternal state action. Political

Table 4.2 Percent women elected to national legislatures: Regression analysis of the percent women elected to national legislatures as predicted by political structures, economic characteristics, and democratic maternal state action, 2006

	Model I	Model II	Model III	Model IV
	Percent Women Elected	Percent Women Elected	Percent Women Elected	Percent Women Elected
POLITICAL ATTITUDES[a]				
Support women as political leaders	3.047 (0.602)[k] ***			
POLITICAL STRUCTURES				
Closed PR[b]		7.678 (0.365)**		
Plurality[c]		2.311 (0.114)		
Parliamentary system[d]		8.291 (0.410)***		
Presidential system[e]		5.908 (0.262)**		
Electoral system[f]		3.537 (0.281)**		
ECONOMIC CHARACTERISTICS[g]				
Population			−0.000 (−0.045)	
Manufacturing			0.151 (0.115)	
Urbanization			0.020 (0.048)	
Average GDP			0.000 (0.278)**	
Labor force, percent women			0.291 (.0198)**	
DEMOCRACY—MATERNAL PUBLIC POLICIES				
Democracy[h]				−0.542 (−0.027)
Welfare provision[i]				2.352 (0.115)
Gender quotas[j]				9.748 (0.430)***
Welfare provision x Democracy				5.956 (0.258)**

Gender quotas x Democracy			−0.829 (−0.032)
CONSTANT	13.220 ***	3.834	10.33 ***
R SQUARED	0.362	0.356	0.342

*** p = 0.001, ** p = 0.05, * p = 0.100

a) Ratio: Predicted average by country of number of respondents strongly supporting women as political leaders compared to number of respondents strongly opposed to women as political leaders, as derived from World Values Survey, 2000, variable d059, and regression analysis, chapter 3.

b) Closed-list proportional representation (PR) system, dummy variable, party leaders rank candidates and voters only cast votes for parties, from Jana Kunicová and Susan Rose-Ackerman, "Electoral rules and Constitutional Structures as Constraints on Corruption," *British Journal of Political Science* 35 (2005): 573–606.

c) Plurality, dummy variable, plurality/majoritarian system with single-member districts, from Jana Kunicová and Susan Rose-Ackerman, "Electoral rules and Constitutional Structures as Constraints on Corruption," *British Journal of Political Science* 35 (2005): 573–606.

d) Parliamentary system: Dummy variable, coded by author, based on Arthur S. Banks, ed., *Political Handbook of the World* (Binghamton: State University of New York, 1991).

e) Presidential system: Dummy variable, coded by author, based on Arthur S. Banks, ed., *Political Handbook of the World* (Binghamton: State University of New York, 1991).

f) Electoral system: Structure of the electoral system. Coded 2 if voters choose among party lists in multimember districts that average five or more seats per district; 1 if party lists are used by district size averages of fewer than five seats, or a combination of party list and candidate voting is used, or voters choose among individual candidates in multimember districts; 0 if voters choose among individual candidates in single-member districts; −1 if no party system at all. Adapted from Lane Kenworthy and Melissa Malami, "Gender Inequality in Political Representation: A Worldwide Comparative Analysis," *Social Forces* 78, no. 1 (1991): 235–68.

g) Economic characteristics: Population 2003, Percent Manufacturing 2002, Percent Urban 2003, Average GDP 2002 = GDP2002/Population 2003, Labor Force Percent Women 2003 from World Bank, World Economic Outlook Database, April 2004.

h) Democracy: Coded as "free" by Freedom House, 2004.

l) Welfare provision: Combination of 55% or more of the funds spent on health care are provided by the government and a constitutional provision or comparable information affirming that it is the state's duty to provide for people's welfare. Data on percent health-care funds provided by the government are from the Organization for Economic Co-Operation and Development (OECD), Social Expenditure Database (2004). Data on constitutional provisions are based on the author's coding of constitutions, as of 2006; the constitutional provision can be a provision for specific assistance, such as the provision of education, health, or other such welfare services, or a statement about the provision of general welfare benefits to people. Constitutional provisions of pensions for government employees are not included.

j) Gender quotas: Measured as a legislative quota above 15% in lower or upper house or a voluntary political party quota of 30% or more in at least two parties or a voluntary political party quota of 40% or more in at least one party and the political party is represented in the legislature in 1999 and 2003. Data for gender quotas are from the Global Database of Quotas for Women, Institute for Democracy and Electoral Assistance (IDEA), Stockholm University, and from Mona Lena Krook and Diana O'Brien, "The Politics of Group Representation: Quotas for Women and Minorities Worldwide," paper presented at the Midwest Political Science Association, 2007.

k) Unstandardized regression coefficients followed by standardized regression coefficient in parentheses.

Table 4.3   Percent women elected to national legislatures: Regression analysis of the percent women elected to national legislatures, controlling for political attitudes, political structures, economic characteristics, and democratic maternal state action, 2006

	Model V Percent Women Elected	Model VI Percent Women Elected Control for Nordic Nations[l]
PUBLIC ATTITUDES[a]		
Support for women as political leaders	2.074 (0.275)[k] **	1.448 (0.869)+
POLITICAL STRUCTURES		
Closed PR[b]	7.422 (0.379)**	8.261 (0.422)**
Plurality[c]	5.120 (0.267)	6.181 (0.322)
Parliamentary system[d]	6.248 (0.329)*	7.232 (0.381)**
Presidential system[e]	4.956 (0.250)	5.153 (0.260)
Electoral system[f]	3.062 (0.240)	2.136 (0.167)
ECONOMIC CHARACTERISTICS[g]		
Population	−0.000 (−0.124)	−0.000 (−0.168)
Manufacturing	−0.294 (−0.156)	−0.276 (−0.146)
Urbanization	−0.159 (−0.314)	−0.151 (−0.299)**
Average GDP	0.000 (0.257)*	0.000 (0.132)
Labor force, percent women	0.123 (0.074)	0.038 (0.023)
DEMOCRATIC MATERNAL STATE ACTION		
Democracy[h]	0.839 (0.039)	3.362 (0.158)
Welfare provision[i]	−6.666 (−0.341)	−5.510 (−0.282)
Gender quotas[j]	8.982 (0.476)*	9.364 (0.496)**
Welfare provision x Democracy	9.875 (0.523)*	8.880 (0.471)*
Gender quotas x Democracy	−4.637 (−0.243)	−5.317 (−0.279)
NORDIC	- - -	11.355 (0.281)**
CONSTANT	7.235	9.542
R SQUARED	0.670	0.721

*** $p = 0.001$, **$p = 0.05$, *$p = 0.100$

a) Ratio: Predicted average by country of number of respondents strongly supporting women as political leaders compared to number of respondents strongly opposed to women as political leaders, as derived from World Values Survey, 2000, variable d059, and regression analysis, chapter 3.

b) Closed-list proportional representation (PR) system, dummy variable, party leaders rank candidates and voters only cast votes for parties, from Jana Kunicová and Susan Rose-Ackerman, "Electoral rules and Constitutional Structures as Constraints on Corruption," *British Journal of Political Science* 35 (2005): 573–606.

c) Plurality, dummy variable, plurality/majoritarian system with single-member districts, from Jana Kunicová and Susan Rose-Ackerman, "Electoral rules and Constitutional Structures as Constraints on Corruption," *British Journal of Political Science* 35 (2005): 573–606.

d) Parliamentary system: Dummy variable, coded by author, based on Arthur S. Banks, ed., *Political Handbook of the World* (Binghamton: State University of New York, 1991).

attitudes also still have a positive impact, increasing the election of women to national legislatures by 1.488%. Welfare provision, when combined with democracy, is a positive influence, increasing the percentage of women elected to national legislatures by over 8.88%, as reported in Model VI, table 4.3. Gender quotas remain a positive influence as well, increasing the percentage of women elected by 9.364%.

These findings confirm and extend the connection between hybrid public policies and women's political representation. When public policies correspond to women's dual identities, both as individuals who are the same as men and as maternalists who are different from men, democratic state maternalism becomes for the public a crucial *interpretative* and *instrumental* mechanism for locating women's "place" in the public sphere of the state itself. Such policies enhance women's access to political rule by giving women access to national legislative officeholding. The question remains whether these results hold as well for women's executive political leadership.

---

e) Presidential system: Dummy variable, coded by author, based on Arthur S. Banks, ed., *Political Handbook of the World* (Binghamton: State University of New York, 1991).

f) Electoral system: Structure of the electoral system. Coded 2 if voters choose among party lists in multimember districts that average five or more seats per district; 1 if party lists are used by district size averages of fewer than five seats, or a combination of party list and candidate voting is used, or voters choose among individual candidates but in multimember districts; 0 if voters choose among individual candidates in single-member districts; –1 if no party system at all. Adapted from Lane Kenworthy and Melissa Malami, "Gender Inequality in Political Representation: A Worldwide Comparative Analysis," *Social Forces* 78, no. 1 (1991): 235–68.

g) Economic characteristics. Population 2003, Percent Manufacturing 2002, Percent Urban, 2003, Average GDP 2002 = GDP2002/Population 2003, Labor Force Percent Women 2003 from World Bank, World Economic Outlook Database, April 2004.

h) Democracy: Coded as "free" by Freedom House, 2004.

i) Welfare provision: Combination of 55% or more of the funds spent on health care are provided by the government and a constitutional provision or comparable information affirming that it is the state's duty to provide for people's welfare. Data on percent health care funds provided by the government are from the Organization for Economic Co-Operation and Development (OECD), Social Expenditure Database, (2004). Data on constitutional provisions are based on the author's coding of constitutions, as of 2006; the constitutional provision can be a provision for specific assistance, such as the provision of education, health, or other such welfare services, or a statement about the provision of general welfare benefits to people. Constitutional provisions of pensions for government employees are not included.

j) Gender quotas: Measured as a legislative quota above 15% in lower or upper house or a voluntary political party quota of 30% or more in at least two parties or a voluntary political party quota of 40% or more in at least one party and the political party is represented in the legislature in 1999 and 2003. Data for gender quotas are from the Global Database of Quotas for Women, Institute for Democracy and Electoral Assistance (IDEA), Stockholm University, and from Mona Lena Krook and Diana O'Brien, "The Politics of Group Representation: Quotas for Women and Minorities Worldwide," paper presented at the Midwest Political Science Association, 2007.

k) Unstandardized regression coefficients followed by standardized regression coefficient in parentheses.

l) Nordic countries, Denmark, Iceland, Finland, Norway, Sweden, dummy variable, 0 = no, 1 = yes.

Women's Election to Executive Leadership

Leadership Style

At this time in American history, given the United States' stature in the world as a major economic and military power, the president's role as commander-in-chief is seen as central to the office. The president's duties as commander-in-chief are associated with the president's role as a protector, with the ability to use military force. Women running for the presidency must find a way to project a commander-in-chief persona, even though Congress did not permit women to attend the nation's major military academies until the 1970s and army regulations have yet to include women fully in combat. As recently as 1997, for example, the state of Virginia continued to view all women as unacceptable students in its Military Institute, a policy that took a Supreme Court decision to overturn.[67]

Actual combat experience is, of course, not necessary to serve as an effective commander-in-chief, as the presidency of President Franklin Delano Roosevelt exemplifies. However, the play-acting of President George W. Bush on the flight deck of the USS *Abraham Lincoln*, regardless of the shimmering layers of fantasy and stagecraft behind it, testifies to the impact of public perceptions about the military components of the office of chief executive. The question is how a woman can project the competence to command the military, given that women have only recently even been allowed to obtain the training and education necessary to qualify as officers in the Army, Navy, and Air Force. What is more, how can a woman project a leadership style that is consonant with the aggressiveness the public expects from the executive role, when women's maternal identities not only are associated with opposing characteristics, such as nurturing and care, but also are socially constructed as ontologically necessary for the very survival of society and the state.

Small wonder that Laura Liswood, director of the Women's Leadership Project, discovered that women leaders shared a common problem. Interviews with fifteen existing or former female heads of state—ranging from leaders of major global players, such as Margaret Thatcher, former prime minister of the United Kingdom, to leaders of smaller countries, such as Maria Liberia-Peters, prime minister of the Netherlands Antilles—found that most placed special emphasis on political style. Most believed that women executive leaders had a different leadership style than men did. Mary Robinson, president of Ireland, observed that "women [are] instinctively less hierarchical," whether they are in charge of grassroots organizations, voluntary associations, or the nation-state itself.[68] Nearly all the women executive leaders had experienced the public as applying a different set of standards and a different degree of scrutiny to them as women leaders compared to men, focusing on small issues of public interest. As a result the media scrutinized their clothes, on the one hand, and their ability to make military decisions on the other.[69]

Hybrid Candidates

In order for a woman to be a successful candidate for executive political office, it is therefore imperative that she present a personal style that is consistent with public expectations of executive leadership. Yet this equation has as much to do with the state's policy-making style as it does with the leadership style of each individual woman who runs for office. That is to say, women's chances of holding executive elected office in contemporary democracies increase when the style of the state—how it performs individualism and maternalism in its public policies—aligns with the public perception of women's dual identities as individuals who are the same as men and as maternalists who are different from men.

Hybrid States

Different policy contexts have different feedback effects on public attitudes about women's suitability as political leaders and women's election to national positions of political leadership. Specifically, a political context generated by public policies representing both individualism and maternalism has an interpretive impact on public attitudes, which generates more favorable views of women's capabilities as political leaders. So, too, does this mixed policy style have an instrumental effect on civic capacities promoting women's election to positions of legislative leadership. America's failure to maternalize the state explains its laggard status when it comes to electing women to legislative positions of leadership. The question is whether the "motherless" status of American democracy also explains its failure to elect a woman as president.

Since 1789, when the United States was the first nation to hold elections to determine who would serve as chief executive of the country, most of the other nations of the world have followed suit. It was not until 1954, however, that the first woman was elected to a national executive political leadership position, when Sühbaataryn Yanjmaa took over as acting head of state in Mongolia.[70] Since that time, eighty-five countries have elected forty-eight women to serve as prime minister and fifty-four women to be president of their countries (see table 4.4).[71] In addition, six women have been elected deputy prime minister, and thirty women have been elected

Table 4.4 Women prime ministers and presidents

Political System	Prime Minister Deputy Prime Minister*	President Vice President*
Antigua and Barbuda	Millicent Percival,* 1994	
Argentina		Maria Estella Martínez Cartas de Isabel Perón, 1974–76
Austria		Barbara Prammer,* 2006–
Azerbaijan	Elmira Makail-Kyzy Kafarova, 1989–90	S.M. Mamedaliyeva,* 1963 Sukina Alas-Kyzy Alievna,* 1966–90
Bahamas, The	Cynthia A. Pratt,* 2002, 2005	
Bangladesh	Begum Khaleda Zia, 1991–96, 2001– Hasina Wajed, 1996–2001	
Belarus		Nadezhda Grigoryevna Grek,* 1938 Zinaida Mikhaylovna Bychkovskaya,* 1975–78
Bolivia		Lydia Gueiler Tejada,** 1979–80
Bosnia-Herzegovina	Biljana Plavsic, 1996–98	
Bulgaria	Renata Ivanova Indzhova,** 1994–95	Blaga Nikolova Dimitrova,* 1992–93
Burundi	Sylvie Kinigi, 1993–94	Sylvie Kinigi,**1993–94
Canada	Kim Campbell, 1993	
Central African Republic	Élisabeth Domitién, 1975–76	
Chile		Michelle Bachelet Jeria, 2006
China		Song Qingling,* 1976–78; 1976–78
The People's Republic of China		

Costa Rica		Lineth Saborío Chaverri,** 2002, 2003
		Elizabeth Odio Benito,* 1998–2002
		Astrid Fischel Volio,* 1998–2000
		Rebecca Grynspan Mayfis,* 1994–98
		Victoria Garron de Doyan,* 1986–90
Croatia	Savka Dabcevic-Kucar, 1967–69	Ema Derossi-Bjelajac, 1986
Djibouti	Kadidja Abeba,* 1992–	
Dominica	Mary Eugenia Charles, 1980–95	
Dominican Republic		Milagros Ortiz Bosch,* 2000–2004
El Salvador		Ana Vilma de Escobar,* 2004
Ecuador		Rosalia Arteaga Serrano de Fernández de Córdova,** 1997
Estonia		Meta Jangolenko-Vannas,** 1978
Finland	Annelli Jäätteenmäki, 2003	Tarja Halonen, 2000–
France	Edith Cresson, 1991–92	
Georgia		Nino Burjanadze,** 2003–4
Germany	Angela Merkel, 2005–	
Germany		
German Democratic Republic (East Germany)		Sabine Bergmann-Pohl, 1990
Greece		Anna Psarouda-Benaki,** 2004
Guinea Bissau		Carmen Pereira,** 1984
Guyana	Janet Jagan, 1997	Janet Jagan, 1997–99
		Viola Harper Burnham,* 1985–91

Table 4.4 continued

Political System	Prime Minister Deputy Prime Minister*	President Vice President*
Haiti	Claudette Werleigh, 1995–96	Ertha Pascal-Trouillot,** 1990–91
Hungary	Szili Katalin,* 2002–	
Iceland		Vigdís Finnbogadóttir, 1980–96
India, Republic of	Indira Gandhi, 1966–77	
Indonesia		Megawati Sukarnoputri, 2001–4
Irish Republic	Mary Harney,* 1997–2006	Mary Robinson, 1990–97
		Mary McAleese, 1997–
Israel	Golda Meir, 1969–74	
Jamaica	Portia Simpson-Miller, 2006–	
Kazakhstan	Kapitolina Nikolaevna Kryukova, 1960–62	
	V. V. Sidorova, 1988–89	
Korea, South	Chang Sang,** 2002	
	Han Myung-Sook, 2006	
Kyrgyzstan		Kalima Amankulova,** 1938
		Maryam Tugambayeva** 1937
Latvia		Vaira Viķe-Freiberga, 1999–
Liberia		Ruth Sando Perry, 1996–97
		Ellen Johnson-Sirleaf, 2006
		Elizabeth Brook-Randolph,** 1958

Lithuania	Kazimiera-Daniute Prunskienė, 1990–91
	Irena Degutienė,** 1999
Macedonia	Radmila Šekerinska,** 2004
Malta	Agatha Barbara, 1982–87
Mexico	Maria de Los Angeles Moreno Uriegas,* 1999–2000
Moldova	Ing. Eugenia Ostapciuc,* 2001–5
Mongolia	Sühbaataryn Yanjmaa,** 1953–54
	Tuyaa Nyam-Osoryn,** 1999
Mozambique	Luísa Días Diogo, 2004
New Zealand	Jenny Shipley, 1997–99
	Helen Clark, 1999–
Nicaragua	Violeta Barrios de Chamorro, 1990–97
	Julia de la Cruz Mena Rivera,* 1995–97
Norway	Gro Harlem Brundtland, 1981, 1986–89, 1990–96
	Anne Enger Lahnstein,** 1998
Pakistan	Benazir Bhutto, 1988–90, 1993–96
Panama	Mireya Moscoso Rodríguez, 1999–2004
Peru	Beatriz Merino Lucero, 2003
Philippines	Maria Corazón Sumulong Cojuangco Aquino, 1986–92
	Gloria Macapagal-Arroyo, 2001–
Poland	Hanna Suchocka, 1992–93
Portugal	Maria de Lourdes Ruivo da Silva Pintasilgo, 1979–80

Table 4.4 continued

Political System	Prime Minister Deputy Prime Minister*	President Vice President*
Romania		Magdalena Ionescu,** 1989
		Eugenia Iorga,** 1989
		Ana Blandiana,** 1989
		Cristina Ciontu,** 1989–90
		Doina Corena,** 1989
		Maria Ghitulici,* 1985–89
		Maria Ciocan,* 1980–85
		Constanta Craciun,* 1966–70
		Maria Paretti,* 1961–66
Rwanda	Agathe Uwillingiyimana, 1994	
Saint Christopher and Nevis	Constance V. Mitcham,** 1994–95	
San Marino		Maria Lea Pedini-Angelini, 1981
		Gloriana Ranocchini, 1984, 1989–90
		Edda Ceccoli, 1991–92
		Patrizia Busignani, 1993
		Rosa Zafferani, 1999
		Maria Domenica Michelotti, 2000
		Valeria Ciavatta, 2003
		Fausta Simona Morganti, 2005
São Tome and Principe	Maria das Neves Ceita Batista de Sousa, 2002–3	
	Maria do Carmo Silverira, 2005	

Senegal	Mame Madior Boye, 2001–2
Serbia Montenegro	Natasa Micic,** 2002–04
Sierra Leone	Elizabeth Alpha Lavalie,** 2004
South Africa	Phumzile Mlambo-Ngcuka,* 2005–8
Sri Lanka	Sirimavo Ratwatte Dias Bandaranaike, 1960–65; Chandrika Bandaranaike Kumaratunga, 1994; Chandrika Bandaranaike Kumaratunga, 1994–2005
Swaziland	Seneleleni Ndwandwe, 1975–81
Sweden	Ulla Lindstrom,** 1958
Switzerland	Ruth Dreifuss, 1999; Elisabeth Kopp,* 1989; Ruth Metzler-Arnold,* 2003; Designate Federal President, 2004
Taiwan	Annette Lü Hsiu-Lien,* 2000–
Tajikistan	N. Zaripova,** 1984
Trinidad and Tobago	Linda Baboolal,** 2002
Turkey	Tansu Çiller, 1993–96
Turkmenistan	Roza Atamuradovna Bazarova, 1988–90
Uganda	Wandira Speciosa Kagibwe,* 1994–2003
Ukraine	Evheniya Bohdanivna Bosch,** 1917–18; Yuliya Tymoshenko, 2005; Valentina Semenovna Seveenko, 1985–90
United Kingdom	Margaret Thatcher, 1979–90
Uzbekistan	Yadar Sadykovna Nasriddinova, 1959–70; U. Ibadulayeva,* 1959–63; P. Yezhanova,* 1963–70

Table 4.4 continued

Political System	Prime Minister Deputy Prime Minister*	President Vice President*
Venezuela		Adina Mercedes Bastidas Castillo,* 2000–2002
Vietnam		Nguên Thi-Binh,* 1987–2002
		Truong My Hoa,* 2002–
Yugoslavia	Milka Planinc, 1982–86	
Totals = 85 nations	Prime Ministers = 48 women	Presidents = 54 women
	Deputy Prime Minister = 6 women	Vice Presidents = 30 women

*Deputy Head of State (Vice Prime Minister) or Vice President, **Acting Head of State (Prime Minister or President)

I am indebted to president of Ireland, Mary Robinson, for her advice about the construction of this table, which I followed to some degree. Information about women world leaders is available at country-specific Web sites and at The Council of Women World Leaders, http://www.womenworldleaders.org, last accessed 11-25-08.

vice president. All told, since 1954, nearly half the world's contemporary countries, or 44%, have elected a total of 138 women to executive positions of political leadership.[72] The United States regrettably is not among them.

A cross-national analysis of the countries that have elected a woman as executive political leader reveals the same pattern as found with women's election to national legislative office.[73] Let us examine women's executive leadership patterns worldwide in four types of countries: those that perform neither maternalism nor individualism, those that perform only maternalism, those that perform only individualism, and those that are mixed or *hybrid*, meaning that they adopt public policies based on a principle of individualism but *also* maternalism, as defined by welfare provision, gender quotas, or hereditary monarchies. The hybrid group is the one that includes not only all of the Nordic countries but also the largest proportion of states that have elected a woman to be head of state as shown in table 4.5.

Comparing Democracies

One example of how democratic state action can enhance women's access to executive political leadership comes from no farther away than Canada. Not only is Canada a neighbor, but it is also similar to the United States in a variety of ways. Both countries are democracies that perform individualism by guaranteeing equal individual rights. Demographically both countries are wealthy industrialized democracies with high literacy rates, large percentages of women high school and college graduates, and significant numbers of women professionals. The similarities end, however, with maternalism, which Canada performs, and the United States does not. Canada performs all three modes of maternalism by means of gender quotas, welfare provision, and a hereditary monarchy. The New Democratic Party and the Liberal Party of Canada, two of the four main political parties, institute gender quotas. The state recognizes its affirmative duty to provide welfare, as expressed in the Canadian Constitution and carried out by substantial public funding. And Queen Elizabeth II is the hereditary monarchical head of state. In these respects Canada is more like Sweden than the United States. Canada also has a higher percentage of women in its legislature than does the United States and has elected a woman as prime minister, Kim Campbell, making it a country more like Germany and Norway than like its English-speaking neighbor.

Comparisons of the United States with other wealthy industrial democracies, such as Australia, Germany, and the United Kingdom, tell the same

Table 4.5 Typology of public policies representing maternalism and democracy (individualism): Elected women executive leaders,[a] since twentieth century

	MATERNAL PUBLIC POLICIES			
DEMOCRACY	No Maternalism		Yes Maternalism	
No Individualism	Armenia	Maldives	Afghanistan	Laos
	Bangladesh+	Moldova	Albania	Liberia+
	Brunei	Morocco	Algeria	Libya
	Burma (Myan.)	Nepal	Angola	Macedonia+
	Cambodia	Nicaragua+#	Azerbaijan+	Madagascar
	Cameroon	Niger	Bahrain	Malaysia
	Comoros	Nigeria	Belarus+	Mauritania
	Congo (Dem. Rep.)	Pakistan+^	Bhutan	Mozambique+^
		Paraguay	Bolivia+#	North Korea
	Cote d'Ivorie	Philippines+#	Bosnia-Herz+	Oman
	Djibouti+#	Singapore	Burkina Faso	Papua New Guinea
	Egypt	Somalia	Burundi^	
	Ethiopia	Sri Lanka+^	Cnt Afr. Rep.+#	Qatar
	Gabon	Sudan	Chad	Russia
	Gambia	Swaziland	China+	Rwanda+^
	Georgia+#	Syria	Colombia	Saudi Arabia
	Guatemala	Tajikistan+	Congo (Dem. Rep.)	Seychelles
	Iran	Togo	Cuba	Sierra Leone+
	Jordan	Tunisia	Ecuador+#	Solomon Islands
	Kenya	Vietnam#	Equatorial Guinea	Tanzania
	Kyrgyzstan+	Yemen	Eritrea	Thailand
	Lebanon	Zimbabwe	Fiji	Timor Leste
	Malawi		Guinea	Tonga
			Haiti+^	Turkey+^
			Honduras	Turkmenistan+
			Iraq	Uganda#
			Kazakhstan+	United Arab Rep.
			Kuwait	Uzbekistan+
				Venezuela#
				Zambia
	(n = 44)		(n = 57)	
	Percent political systems in this quadrant with women elected executive leaders = 25% (% = 11/44)		Percent political systems in this quadrant with women elected executive leaders = 35% (% = 20/57)	

Table 4.5   continued

DEMOCRACY	MATERNAL PUBLIC POLICIES		
	No Maternalism	Yes Maternalism	
Yes Individualism	Benin	Andorra	Malta+
	Botswana	Antigua#	Marshall Islands
	Chile+	Argentina+#	Mexico#
	Cyprus#	Australia#	Micronesia
	El Salvador#	Austria+	Monaco
	France^^	The Bahamas^	Mongolia+^
	India^	Barbados	Namibia
	Israel^#	*Belgium*	*The Netherlands*
	Japan	Belize	New Zealand+^
	Kiribati	Brazil	Norway*^
	Mali	Bulgaria^#	Palau
	Mauritius	Canada^	Panama+
	Nauru	Cape Verde	Peru+
	Samoa West	Costa Rica+#	Poland^
	Trinidad Tobago+#	Croatia+	Portugal^
	United States	Czech Rep.^	Romania+#
	Uruguay	Denmark*#	St. Kitts Nevis^
	Vanuatu	Dominica^#	St. Lucia
		Dominican Rep.#	St. Vincent
		Estonia+#	San Marino+#
		Finland*+#	São Tomé^
		Germany+	Senegal+
		Ghana	Serbia Montenegro
		Greece+#	Slovakia
		Grenada+	Slovenia
		Guinea Bissau+	South Africa+#
		Guyana^#	South Korea^
		Hungary#	*Spain*
		Iceland*+	Suriname
		Indonesia+#	Sweden*^
		Ireland+	*Switzerland+#*
		Italy	Taiwan#
		Jamaica^	Tuvalu

Table 4.5   continued

DEMOCRACY	MATERNAL PUBLIC POLICIES		
	No Maternalism	Yes Maternalism	
		Latvia+#	Ukraine+
		Lesotho	United
		Liechtenstein	Kingdom^
		Lithuania^	Serbia
		Luxembourg	Montenegro
			*Nordic nations omitted = 64%
	(n = 18)	(n = 74)	(% = 44/69)
	Percent political systems in this quadrant with women elected executive leaders = 39% (% = 7/18)	Percent political systems in this quadrant with women elected executive leaders = 65% (% = 49/74)	

*Nordic nation
~ elected but never took office
+ president, acting president
^ prime minister, acting prime minister
^^ appointed prime minister in a presidential system
# vice president, deputy prime minister
comparable democracies in italics ($10,000 per capita income and 50% urban)

story. Among contemporary democracies there are twenty-five countries with the highest level of urbanization and wealth, as indicated in table 4.6. As democracies, these states by definition act like individuals, performing public policies based on negative individual rights. Where they differ is in also performing public policies based on a principle of positive group rights associated with women, or, maternalism. With the exceptions of Japan, France, and the United States, all other comparable democracies perform both individualist and maternalist public policies. Thus, the Nordic countries are not unusual when it comes to the performance of maternalism and individualism. Rather, the United States is the odd nation out by being one of the few wealthy urban democracies that performs only individualism but not maternalism.

France has had a woman serve in a position of executive political leadership, Édith Cresson, but she was not elected to that office. Rather, she was appointed by President Mitterrand in 1991, a position she left after less than a year. In France, since the prime minister is appointed by the president rather than elected by the public, the duties of this office are more like that of a cabinet position, akin to an American secretary of state. It is not a political position signifying chief control over the executive branch of the government and not comparable to serving as prime minister in Canada or as president of the United States. In 2007, Ségolène Royal ran unsuccessfully as the Socialist Party candidate for president of France, stressing her support for maternalist public policies. Yet her campaign was unfurled in the context of a country that, despite its generous funding of welfare benefits, does not constitutionalize social maternalism, nor does it affirm gender quotas as positive group rights, choosing instead to base them on universalistic claims about the sameness of men and women as human beings rather than their sex difference. France destroyed its monarchical heritage by means of a violent revolution. Hence, France lacks a political context that defines the meaning of maternal traits attributed to women as signifying a location in the public sphere. Consequently, French voters are less likely to vote for women candidates. Royal's defeat is therefore not surprising. It fits the pattern. Namely, women's prospects for inclusion in electoral political rule, both as legislators and as executives, increases or decreases in relation to the presence or absence respectively of a *political context* generated by the adoption of hybrid public policies representing both women's individual sameness with men and women's maternal group difference from men.

Women candidates representing hybrid traits are not enough. It takes a state. Take the examples of two-time prime minister of India, Indira Gandhi, related by blood and marriage to two important political families, the Nehrus and the Gandhis, and of her daughter-in-law, Sonia Gandhi, who was married to assassinated prime minister Rajiv Gandhi and served as president of the Indian National Congress Party, despite the fact that she was born in Italy. Not only do family ties in India matter as cultural norms and values, but, "family ties" or, maternalist policies are built into the country by means of constitutional gender quotas. Consequently, there are two views of family ties in India: first as a cultural family-kinship group, and second as an institutionalized family-kinship group by means of state-sponsored gender quotas.

Along the same lines it is common to consider the Nordic countries as unusually woman friendly, to be virtual paradigms of democratic political equality when it comes to women's representation in positions of political leadership. The most important characteristic of these countries, however, is the way they *combine* individualism and maternalism in public policies. Sweden, Denmark, and Norway perform all three forms of maternalism—

Table 4.6 Western democracies[a] and maternal public policies: Welfare provision, gender quotas, and hereditary monarchies

Political System	Maternal Public Policies			Total: Maternal State Action Policies	Percent Women in Nat'l Legis	Has had a Woman as Exec. Leader
	Welfare Provision[b]	Gender Quotas[c]	Hereditary Monarchy[d]			
Australia	YES	YES	YES	3	25%	no
Belgium	YES	YES	YES	3	35%	no
Canada	YES	YES	YES	3	21%	YES
Denmark	YES	YES	YES	3	37%	no
Luxembourg	YES	YES	YES	3	23%	no
Norway	YES	YES	YES	3	38%	YES
Spain	YES	YES	YES	3	36%	no
Sweden	YES	YES	YES	3	45%	YES
The Netherlands	YES	YES	YES	3	37%	no
United Kingdom	YES	YES	YES	3	20%	YES
Austria	YES	YES	no	2	34%	YES
Germany	YES	YES	no	2	32%	YES
Iceland	YES	YES	no	2	33%	YES
Ireland	YES	YES	no	2	13%	YES
Italy	YES	YES	no	2	17%	no
Portugal	YES	YES	no	2	21%	YES
Finland	YES	no	no	1	38%	YES
Greece	no	YES	no	1	13%	YES
Israel	no	YES	no	1	14%	YES

New Zealand	no	no	YES	1	YES	32%
Switzerland	no	YES	no	1	YES	25%
The Bahamas	no	no	YES	1	YES	20%
France	no	no[b]	no	0	YES*	12%
Japan	no	no	no	0	no	9%
United States	no	no	no	0	no	15%
PERCENT "YES"	72%	76%	48%	N = 25	64%	

All three: 40%

Two: 24%

One: 24%

None: 12%

a) Democratic political systems with a per capita income of at least $11,000/year and at least 60% urban.

b) Welfare provision: There is a constitutional provision establishing that it is an affirmative obligation of the state to provide for the welfare needs of people and the government provides at least 50% of the funds spent on health care; health care funds are calculated on the basis of data provided by the World Health Organization for the year 2000. At www3.who.int/whosis/core/core_select_process.cfm?country.

c) Gender quotas: Measured as a constitutional or legislated gender quota that represents women's group difference from men of at least more than 15%; or a voluntary party quota for at least two parties of more than 30%; or at least one party for more than 40%. The political parties must be represented in parliament in 1999, 2003 and must have met its targets. "All women" political parties are not included in this measure. South Africa is included in this measure. France is not included in this measure because its legislated principle of gender quotas, parité, is premised on the universality of human beings, not their sex difference. See Joan Scott (*).

d) Hereditary monarchy: Must be open to women to become sovereigns.

* Appointed prime minister in a presidential system.

gender quotas, welfare provision, and monarchies; Iceland performs two—welfare provision and gender quotas; and Finland performs one—welfare provision.

Political Families Are Not Enough

The American state exemplifies the liberal principles invented in the 1600s by theorists such as Thomas Hobbes and John Locke. According to these principles, the basic unit of society is the individual, all individuals are equal, and the legitimacy of government rests upon the consent of the people, as expressed regularly in elections that choose leaders from among the people themselves. In this liberal, American concept of the state, the public sphere of political governance is separated from the private sphere of the family. No one can inherit the right to rule as a political leader because of membership in a family-kinship group, as is the case in monarchies. Rather, all individuals are equally eligible to be political leaders, regardless of who constitutes their family.

Relegating the family to a sphere separate from the state in principle does not play out necessarily in practice. Americans are proud of a revolutionary heritage that destroyed hereditary status as a marker of access to political rule, but just one look at the then and now of the American state proves how powerful family connections remain for access to political leadership. Right from the founding of the American state, family dynasties are evident. Take the Lee family of Virginia. Two Lees signed the Declaration of Independence, three served as governors, two were elected senators, nine became members of the House, and four fought in the Civil War as Southern generals, including Robert E. Lee himself.[74] Although the Frelinghuysens may not be a household name, they constitute an important family dynasty in New Jersey, starting in the 1700s when Frederick (born in 1753) served as a delegate to the Continental Congress and later as a senator in the U.S. Congress. The family is still represented in Congress by Rodney (born in 1946).[75]

While the first president of the United States, George Washington, considered it a positive attribute to be childless and hence to have no family heir to promote in politics, the same cannot be said for the second president of the United States, John Adams (1797–1801). His son, John Quincy Adams, in 1825, became the sixth president of the United States. Other family members followed in the presidential footsteps of their relatives, including William Henry Harrison, the ninth president, who was followed by his grandson, Benjamin Harrison, as the twenty-third president; Theodore Roosevelt, the twenty-sixth president, who was followed by his fifth cousin, Franklin Delano Roosevelt as the thirty-second president; and most recently, George W. Bush the forty-third president who is the son of George H. W. Bush, the forty-first president.[76]

For women in the United States, familial ties have provided a point of entry to political office. As of 2007 there have been 244 women elected to the House and Senate. Of these, 23%, or fifty-eight women, gained office on the basis of succeeding their husbands or fathers.[77] In the case of their husbands, that succession most often was as a widow. In the United States, replacing a deceased husband, or the "widow effect," is sometimes considered "the single most important method of entrance into Congress for women."[78] In 1922 Edna Mae Nolan (R-CA) illustrated this point of access to the House by replacing her husband upon his death. Hattie Caraway (D-AK) demonstrated that the widow effect could also work for access to the Senate when she replaced her husband there in 1931 after his death, staying on for over fourteen years.[79] This historical phenomenon is far from antiquated, as shown by the succession of Jean Carnahan (D-MO), who after the demise of her husband in 2000 replaced him as a candidate for the Senate.

Women benefiting from the widow effect who gain access to political office do so on the basis of characteristics associated with their husbands, such as his seniority in office, his leadership position in Congress, and the competitiveness of his district.[80] In addition, widows benefit from the name recognition of their husbands, assuming that a wife has taken her husband's surname in the first place. When a party official was asked, for example, why Edna Mae Nolan (R-CA) was chosen as its candidate for the House, given that she was shy, quiet, and unlikely to generate much enthusiasm among voters, he replied, "The Nolan name means victory."[81]

When it comes to family politics and name recognition, the presidential primaries of 2008 stand out for the candidacy of Hillary Rodham Clinton. Twenty-eight years earlier, in 1980, when her husband, Bill, lost his bid for reelection as governor of Arkansas, some voters, apparently resented the fact that Hillary had not taken his surname. She did so in time for his next bid as governor, which was successful, and it is that name that propels her forward in her own quest for political office. As Michelle Goldberg notes, Senator Clinton can readily depend on the contributors and supporters her husband courted and won over years ago. For others, her name is a problem. It puts her at an advantage, but the advantage is "tainted." Her candidacy appears to be a way around term limits, because she is "offering a third Clinton term, a return to the golden days of the 1990s," back to when "we"—she and former president Clinton—were in office.[82] For this reason she almost needs an asterisk next to her name to explain how she got a leg up in the field from her husband's popularity.[83]

Terry Golway believes that "our political campaigns have become so dependent on massive amounts of private funds that candidates with name recognition have a huge advantage over their lesser known competitors. Contributors are more likely to give to candidates whose names they know because of family accomplishments regardless of the products' merits or drawbacks."[84] Thus, if Clinton could have won in 2008, much less been reelected, it would mean that the Clinton and Bush families would have run the country for a span of twenty-eight years, a testimony to little more than how political families constitute a "political class," complete with all the elitist connotations that term implies.[85]

A woman running for president on the basis of family ties, while new in the United States, is not so unusual when it comes to executive political office worldwide. Benazir Bhutto of Pakistan, Indira Gandhi of India, Violeta Chamorro of Nicaragua, Corazón Aquino of the Philippines, Megawati Sukarnoputri of Indonesia, and Khaleda Zia and Sheikh Hasina Wazed of Bangladesh all did so successfully. Family politics merges with electoral politics, notwithstanding their separation in liberal theory. And when family politics merges with electoral politics, it can produce access to political leadership for women, even in democracies based on individualism where that normatively should not happen. To the extent that women are associated with political families, therefore, family politics can privilege women fortunate enough to have such an asset in ways that also privilege men.

Yet the *patterns* characterizing women's election to political office, either to the legislature or to the office of president or prime minister, are less dependent on their own personal family heritage than on the heritage of the *political context* in which they reside. A more effective way to fuse family with the state is therefore to turn the maternal traits already associated with women and the family into an integral component of the state vis-à-vis public policies. Countries can do this through public policies that represent social and biological maternalism, such as welfare provision, gender quotas, and hereditary monarchies. When a democratic state that by definition represents individual equality also represents social and biological traits associated with women, the state becomes a political context that predisposes voters to view women as suitable political leaders and to vote for them as members of legislatures, if not also as chief executives. For women to succeed as political leaders in the realm of electoral politics, therefore, family politics is not enough. What is really needed is a hybrid state that represents women's dual, hybrid identities both as individuals who are the same as men and as maternalists who are different from men.

Solving the Puzzle

It is now possible to solve the puzzle of why the United States is such an outlier when it comes to electing women to political office, vis-à-vis comparable democracies. The reason is that while most democracies similar to America have adopted one, if not more, public policies representing maternal traits, the United States has adopted none. The United States is in that sense a "motherless," lopsided country, which guarantees only that the government will treat people the same in spite of their ascriptive group differences, such as race, class, or sex, without the orthogonal complement that the state will also guarantee to groups positive rights representing maternal traits.

It is no small feat for a country to guarantee individual rights. Still today the United States has a long way to go, even on the individualism dimension. Same-sex marriage laws, for example, as of November 2008 exist only in the states of Massachusetts and Connecticut, rather than being the norm across states, much less being federally guaranteed. This is in contrast to most democracies comparable to the United States (56%) that do have guarantees in place for same-sex marriage rights at the national level, such as Belgium, Canada, Denmark, Finland, France, Germany, Iceland, Luxembourg, the Netherlands, New Zealand, Norway, Spain, Sweden, and the United Kingdom (see Appendix 2).

Furthermore, the United States has yet to pass an Equal Rights Amendment (ERA) guaranteeing that the federal government will treat individuals the same in spite of their sex differences. The Supreme Court in 1971 did rule in *Reed v. Reed* that the Equal Protection Clause of the Fourteenth Amendment could be used to challenge and strike down discriminatory policies targeting women. Yet, the ERA that was introduced into Congress in 1923 and was passed by a two-thirds majority in Congress in 1972 failed to be ratified by the required three-fourths of the states. In contrast, most other comparable democracies not only have an ERA in place to protect against sex discrimination, but also have many other ERAs in place to guard against discrimination on the basis of race, economic status, nationality,

Table 4.7 Constitutional guarantees of individual rights in contemporary democracies, ERA Constitutional Provisions, 2002

Political System	Sex	Race	Economic	Nationality	Political Group	Religion	Language	Disable/Age	Marriage
Australia									
Austria	yes			yes		yes			
The Bahamas	yes	yes		yes	yes	yes			
Belgium			yes		yes			yes^	#
Canada	yes	yes		yes		yes		yes#	#
Denmark		yes	yes						#
Finland	yes			yes	yes	yes	yes	yes#^	#
France		yes		yes		yes			#
Germany	yes	yes		yes	yes	yes	yes	yes	#
Greece+	yes								
Iceland									#
Ireland+	yes+								
Israel									

Italy	yes	yes	yes			yes			yes
Japan	yes	yes	yes			yes			#
Luxembourg+	yes+			yes		yes			#
The Netherlands	yes	yes			yes	yes			#
New Zealand	yes	yes		yes	yes	yes			yes
Norway									#
Portugal	yes	yes	yes	yes		yes			
Spain	yes	yes	yes	yes	yes	yes			#
Sweden	yes	yes	yes	yes					#
Switzerland	yes	yes	yes	yes	yes	yes	yes	yes#^	
United Kingdom	yes	yes	yes	yes	yes	yes	yes		#
United States									
Total Percent	68%	56%	32%	52%	40%	60%	9%	20%	56% [a]
Yes	(17)	(14)	(8)	(13)	(10)	(15)	(5)	(5)	(14)

a) Includes ERA guarantee plus national-level guarantees of same-sex marriage rights and/or civil union rights.

#Democracies guaranteeing at the national level same-sex marriage rights, which includes civil union rights. See appendix 2 for elaboration; +Democracies with a general ERA; ^age, #disability.

Table 4.8 Degrees of individualism and maternalism, occurring in contemporary democracies, 2006

Individualism Public Policies

Maternalism Public Policies:	No ERA Guaranteeing Sex Equality	Only ERA for Sex Equality	Only Same-Sex Marriage Rights	ERA and Same-Sex Marriage Rights	Total Percentage
No maternalism	United States	Japan		France	12% (3)
Only Welfare Provision		Greece		Finland	8% (2)
Only Gender Quotas	Israel				4% (1)
Only Hereditary Monarchies		The Bahamas			4% (1)
Two Types of Maternalism	Australia	Austria Ireland Italy Portugal Switzerland	Iceland	Germany New Zealand	36% (9)
All Three Types of Maternalism				Norway Belgium Canada Denmark Luxembourg The Netherlands Spain Sweden United Kingdom	36% (9)
Total Percentage	12% (3)	32% (8)	4% (1)	52% (13)	

n = 25

political status, religion, language, disability, age, or marital status (see table 4.7).

The United States, therefore, though one of the world's most wealthy and urbanized democracies, barely passes the individualism test. And when it comes to maternalism, though the American state has some modicum of welfare provision, such as Medicare and Medicaid, it falls short of the threshold necessary for being a state that affirms in principle and practice the affirmative duty of government to provide economic assistance to those in need. Yet, it is precisely this combination of policies representing individualism and maternalism that boosts public attitudes about the suitability of women as political leaders and the election of women to political office.

Far from being in oppositional tension, policies representing individualism and maternalism go together in most of the world's comparable democracies. Thus, countries that adopt more public policies based on negative individual rights, that is, individualism, also are more likely to adopt policies based on positive group rights, that is, maternalism. Of the thirteen countries, for example, that guarantee ERA constitutional protection to both women and men that they will be treated the same in spite of their sex, 69% also endorse all three forms of maternalism, namely welfare provision, gender quotas, and hereditary monarchies (see table 4.8). At the other extreme of the three countries that do not specifically guarantee either sex equality by means of an ERA to their constitutions or same-sex marriage at the national level, two of these countries also endorse no form of maternalism whatsoever.

More individualism and more maternalism, therefore, go together in most democracies comparable to the United States. Specifically, a high degree of individualism combines with a high degree of maternalism as a basis for public policies. What is more, on average it is the highly individualized as well as highly maternalized countries that have the highest percentage of women elected to national legislatures. In countries that have a higher level of individualism, with at least an ERA, and two forms of state maternalism, for example, the average percentage of women elected to national legislatures is 22%. And countries that are both the most individualized and the most maternalized produce the highest percentage of women elected to national legislatures, namely, an average of 32.4%, as reported in table 4.9. In contrast, the average percentage of women elected to national legislatures in countries where there is a low level of individualism (no ERA and no same-sex marriage guarantee) and no maternalism is only 15%, as indicated in table 4.9.

Table 4.9 Percent women elected to national legislatures, controlling for degrees of individualism and maternalism, 2006

Maternalism Public Policies:	Individualism Public Policies:				
	No ERA Guaranteeing Sex Equality	Only ERA for Sex Equality	Only Same-Sex Marriage Rights	ERA and Same-Sex Marriage Rights	Total Average Percentages
No Maternalism	15% United States (15%)	9% Japan (9%)		12% France (12%)	*Ave % =* 12% (3)
Only Welfare Provision		13% Greece (13%)		38% Finland (38%)	*Ave % =* 25.5% (2)
Only Gender Quotas	14% Israel (14%)				14% (1)
Only Hereditary Monarchies		20% The Bahamas (20%)			20% (1)

					Ave % = 25.8% (9)
Two Types of Maternal Public Policies	25% Australia (25%)	Ave % = 22% Austria (34%) Ireland (13%) Italy (17%) Portugal (21%) Switzerland (25%)	33% Iceland (33%)	Ave % = 32% Germany (32%) New Zealand (32%)	
All Three Types of Maternal Public Policies				Ave % = 32.4% Norway (38%) Belgium (35%) Canada (21%) Denmark (37%) Luxembourg (23%) The Netherlands (37%) Spain (36%) Sweden (45%) United Kingdom (20%)	Ave % = 32.4% (9)
Total Average Percentages	Ave % = 18% (3)	Ave % = 19% (8)	33% 33% (1)	Ave % = 31.2% (13)	n = 25

What the State Does Matters

Over historical time and political place and on into the foreseeable future, the public will continue to associate women both socially and biologically with maternal identities. When seeking the key to political empowerment, therefore, it is not enough for women to neutralize their maternal identities in order to claim sameness and equality with men, nor are family politics enough, nor is it enough simply to be a hybrid candidate who represents individualism and maternalism in her persona. Rather, what is necessary is for the democratic *state* to embody maternal traits, thereby assigning a meaning to maternalism that signifies its inclusion, not exclusion, in political rule. Thus, it takes a state—a hybrid state representing both individualism and maternalism—to enhance women's access to political leadership. The laggard status of the American state compared to other democracies when it comes to women's political representation is therefore explained by its failure, beginning with its very founding, to institute such a state.

The Laggard American State **5**

Hereditary Monarchies

Most democracies comparable to the United States are hybrid states, meaning that in addition to public policies representing individual equality, they also have policies representing maternal traits, such as welfare provision, gender quotas, or hereditary monarchies. When a democratic government has maternal characteristics vis-à-vis its public policies, voters learn that women's maternal identities signify inclusion in the public sphere of state, and higher percentages of women are elected to political office. When democratic governments fail to affirm maternal traits as characterizing the state, voters fail to learn that lesson, and lower percentages of women are elected to political office. To achieve women's political inclusion, therefore, entails developing a state that incorporates maternalism into the government vis-à-vis such public policies as welfare provision, gender quotas, or hereditary monarchies. It is the failure of the American state to adopt any of these policies that explains why it lags so far behind most comparable democracies when it comes to electing women to political office. This is a failure that starts with its very founding as premised on the ideological and institutional destruction of historically the first type of state maternalism: hereditary monarchies. Although it is common to view the American Revolution through a heroic lens, from the standpoint of developing a state that incorporates maternalism into its public policies, this was a very bad start.

Journalist Nicholas Kristof argues that it is easier for women to rise to the top of political leadership in monarchies than in democracies because in monarchies they can do so by dealing with only a small elite of contenders for office rather than the mass public, which is prejudiced against women when it comes to political leadership capabilities.[1] When people are asked to evaluate a speech, supposedly written by a man, they rate it higher than when they think it was written by a woman. The public is also generally turned off when women highlight their own accomplishments, whereas for men this strategy proves to be helpful for achieving their political goals. As business professor Rosabeth Moss Kanter puts it, "It's an uphill struggle, to be judged both a good woman and good leader."[2] Thus, Kristof proposes that democracies do not necessarily enhance women's access to positions of political leadership while nondemocratic monarchies do.

We can augment Kristof's observations about how monarchies give access to women as political leaders by pointing to the way monarchies not only provide women with access to political rule as sovereigns, but also to the ways monarchies bolster women's election to political office in democracies. Monarchies fuse the family with the state, thereby representing maternal traits that voters associate with women. As such monarchies have a direct, positive impact on public attitudes about the suitability of women as political leaders. For example, if the United States had retained its link to its monarchy, as did other comparable English-speaking colonies, such as Canada, Australia, and New Zealand, right now it would be using currency and coins with the image of a woman ruler, Queen Elizabeth II, rather than of men, such as Andrew Jackson and Abraham Lincoln. It would have a woman head of state, Queen Elizabeth II, rather than a man, however symbolic that position may be. In short, Americans would have examples of how government includes women in positions of political power rather than excludes them.

In addition, when we look at historical patterns, it is the countries that retained their monarchies when democratizing, thereby becoming hybrid states, that are the ones more likely to have extended the hybrid principle by adopting additional policies that represent maternal traits, such as welfare provision and gender quotas, which also enhance the public's acceptance of women as political leaders. Perhaps this is because monarchies, welfare provision, and gender quotas are all based on the positive group rights principle that the government will give benefits, privileges, and protections to people because of their ascriptive statuses, such as their family-kinship network, need for care, or female sex classification. Retaining one type of positive group rights policy, such as a monarchy, when democratizing, most likely makes it subsequently easier to accept other types of positive group rights policies, such as welfare provision and gender quotas. Similarly, destroying the legitimacy of a principle of positive group rights as a basis for government policies by destroying the legitimacy of monarchies undoubtedly makes it more difficult to bring that principle back in to the state in other forms, as embodied in welfare provision or gender quotas.

The positive group rights principle underlying monarchies epitomizes relationships between people, and between people and their government, that are based on dependencies defined by their statuses and obligations. This is because monarchies are founded upon the antiquated feudal principle that people are born into a static status. Once born a peasant, always a peasant; once born an aristocrat, always an aristocrat; and once born into the dynastic family, always a member of that family. By implication, if a person is a peasant or otherwise poor, that status or condition is the result of an accident of birth, not the result of a person's character of lack thereof. To be dependent on others is therefore not a sign of moral weakness or a lack of character, but rather the simple result of one's parentage, over which one has no control. Consequently, feudal relationships are ones of status, dependency, and obligation, not contract, autonomy, and rights. Those whose accidents of birth put them in the privileged category are morally, if not politically, obligated to help those less fortunate, as exemplified by the ethic of noblesse oblige.[3]

As a result, monarchies often used public resources to effect changes designed to benefit the cultural and economic well-being of the people. State patronage in this sense fulfilled the *obligation* of a sovereign to take care of her or his "subjects," that is, the people. Historian Frank Prochaska notes that monarchical social welfare policies have been an overlooked area of research.[4] He makes the case that royal philanthropy is a central occupation of monarchies, yesterday and today. In the case of the British monarchy there is a long tradition of charity. The Royal Maundy ceremony, symbolizes the responsibility of the monarchy for the poor. It is an annual event dating back to the twelfth or thirteenth century, which is still celebrated by the Crown. The word *Maundy* derives from the Latin word *mandatum*, which means *commandment*, referring to the commandment Jesus gave to his disciples at the Last Supper to "love one another."[5] The ceremony takes place the day before Good Friday. Until 1830 it entailed the sovereign literally washing the feet of her or his subjects, harking back to the Last Supper when Jesus washed the feet of his disciples, thereby reminding "rulers that they are here to serve their subjects."[6] Traditionally, the sovereign also distributes money to the poor, which in contemporary times includes elderly citizens recommended by their clergy on the basis of contributions they have made to the church and community.[7]

Royal philanthropy served the purpose of transforming the idea of nobility to increase the political authority of the British monarchy. It made clients dependent on the Crown and served to develop an image of the sovereign as the "servant" of the people. The result was a maternalism in which the sovereign's involvement in charity set a standard for national morality.[8] The monarchical rule of Elizabeth I, for example, initiated in 1536 what is considered to be the first form of state welfare, the Poor Laws. This legislation required each parish to collect voluntary contributions from its members "to assist the 'impotent' poor," those who were not able-bodied adults. Parliament adopted additional measures in 1597–98 and 1601 to meet the economic needs of the destitute by establishing a "compulsory system of poor relief" administered and financed at the local parish level, which was the basic unit of local government.[9]

Historian E. P. Thompson similarly depicts the feudal relationships between the nobility and laborers as ones that necessarily included maternal care. The noble, in the course of running his estate among other tasks, "was a welfare agency: he took care of the sick, the aged, the orphans."[10] The major point is that this was not in principle a discretionary philanthropic activity undertaken because of a promise that a new building would be named for the benefactor or some other such ploy to trigger the ego of the rich in order to get them to share their economic surplus with those less fortunate. Rather it was the *duty* of the privileged to assist those in need. Granted, that the maternalism of the privileged did little to ameliorate the systemic inequalities between the rich and the poor, and the assistance they provided to the poor simply made their subservience more palatable and habituated them to their "irrevocable station" in life.[11] However, the principle that it is the *job* of those with political power to provide for the welfare of the less fortunate is a valuable legacy, one that presumably fosters adoption of other positive group rights policies, such as state welfare provision and gender quotas, later on down the historical trajectory.

This feudal legacy is totally lost, however, when a monarchy is violently destroyed. Demolishing the principle of a monarchy by means of a violent revolution de-legitimizes the idea that fixed statuses are relevant to the state and, concomitantly, that dependency needs stemming from statuses over which people have no control are the responsibility of the government. As historian Joan Gundersen notes, "before the American Revolution, British citizenship was a vague concept since the relationship of an individual to the state was that of a subject . . . to the crown . . . it was impossible to relinquish subject-ship since status as a subject was a permanent birthright.... All men and women thus occupied the dependent position of a subject."[12] For this reason, throughout the British Empire "people did not equate dependency with abject powerlessness but, rather, thought it a relationship in which rights and duties accrued to both parties."[13]

When liberal theory and practice *totally* replace and discredit a monarchical system, principles of dependence are replaced by independence, principles of coercive status are replaced by voluntary contract, and principles of duty and obligations are replaced by rights. Although there are many advantages to these switches, when the switch becomes too absolute, the result is that dependency needs related to the procurement of food, shelter, and health become a personal failing rather than an accident of birth. As feminist theorists Nancy Fraser and Linda Gordon put it, in modern, industrial societies, in contrast to older, feudal ones, "dependency" becomes an "ideological term . . . [that] carries strong emotive and visual associations and a powerful pejorative charge." The dependent status of people is attributed to them as a character fault rather than as a product of economic structure.[14]

No surprise, therefore, that in the aftermath of the American Revolution, "dependence" came to signify a characteristic that rendered a person ineligible for participation in the public sphere of the state rather than a person whom the state was obligated to assist. One of the major groups that suffered political exclusion because of being identified as dependent on others was women. Women's roles were considered to be naturally dependent on family relationships, but now "the association of women with dependency" served to disqualify them as voters.[15]

When the liberal presumption that everyone is born equal prevails too completely, fostering the idea that "anyone" can be president or be Bill Gates if they just work hard enough, the accidents of birth do not disappear.[16] To the contrary, the disparities between the rich and the poor persist in developed capitalist systems, such as the United States. As Gosta Esping-Andersen notes, "the impact of social inheritance is as strong today as in the past—in particular with regard to cognitive development and educational attainment."[17] Although he views current welfare states as equalizing living conditions to some degree, he argues that it has "failed to deliver on its promise of disconnecting opportunities from social origins and inherited handicaps."[18] Destroying the idea that inherited statuses should be connected to the government, as is part and parcel of destroying a monarchy, destroys not only the way that principle privileges elites but also the way that principle can be used to muster state support for the disadvantaged. When status differences are deemed irrelevant to the state, however, what disappears is not economic inequality, but the idea that government is responsible for the care of those in need on the basis of their status.

Historical Legacies Matter

As political scientist John Gerring et al. note, a "country's regime history" has a powerful impact on the adoption of current policies. For this reason, it is best to think about regimes as "historically informed phenomena rather than as contemporary variables." History matters because the "accumulated effect of . . . historical legacies . . . [explains] a variety of current outcomes—social, cultural, political, or economic."[19] Or as Georgina Waylen argues, it is important to focus on the "nature of institutions" and their "role in the consolidation of democracy," by which democracy becomes "the only game in town."[20] As for the American revolutionary heritage, once the principle of connecting the state to the welfare needs of people based on their group's dependency is destroyed in the course of demolishing a monarchical heritage, as in the American state, subsequent policy patterns show how difficult it is to bring that principle back in to the state to meet the welfare needs of contemporary people. Thus, if the United States had not destroyed its monarchical heritage, passing positive group rights policies, such as welfare legislation to assist those in need and gender quotas to boost women's political representation, would be easier today on the grounds that the state meeting the dependency needs of people would not be so alien as it currently is to many Americans.[21]

As political scientist Robert Putnam argues, historical legacies have an enduring impact on contemporary policies. In Italy, for example, the influence of a civic community heritage dating back 1,000 years to medieval centuries could still be discerned in the civic involvement patterns of the twentieth century. Those regions that had horizontal community organizations, such as choral societies, fostered the norms of reciprocity, trust, and the development of social capital, and these regions were the ones more likely to be currently characterized by citizens' support for political equality and public policies promoting civic community.[22] Similarly, Steven Roper and Florin Fesnic show that historical legacies in Eastern European countries persist as influences on contemporary voting patterns, supporting the contention of those who study regime transitions, or "transitologists," that the mode of transition from one regime to another as well as other legacy factors can have enduring relevance.[23]

These lessons about the long-term impacts of political heritages on contemporary public policies make it probable that if a country retains, or at least does not destroy, a monarchical heritage, thereby retaining the principle that group status is a legitimate principle for organizing the sphere of the state, the idea of gender quotas, for example, would be easier to accept in the twentieth and twenty-first centuries. That is, by not destroying the legitimacy of group status as a point of access to political authority, it would presumably be easier to adopt a public policy that uses the group status of belonging to the female sex as a qualification for being a legislator. Gender quotas would also be more acceptable in the United States were it not for our revolutionary legacy, which by destroying the legitimacy of a monarchy also destroyed the principle of group status as a qualification for political office.[24] Monarchies are indeed elitist (as if capitalist democracies are not), but, retaining them symbolically rather than destroying them outright during democratization can have positive effects for women's political representation, as shown by the patterns of women's acquisition of voting rights; the patterns of adopting contemporary public policies representing maternal traits; and the legacy of women who ruled as sovereigns that illustrates the power of fusing the family with the state for providing access to political rule for women.

An Orthogonal Imperative?

Most comparable democracies, including the United States, started off with a monarchical heritage, which represents social and biological maternal traits by fusing family with state. In so doing, monarchies assume that (1) the basic unit of the state is the family; (2) families are inherently unequal, such that one family, the dynastic family, has an inherent, God-given right to rule over all others; and (3) the government is legitimized when members of the dynastic family choose from among their own members who will be the sovereign. Hereditary monarchies are elitist, with access to political rule being open only to the very small number of people constituting the dynastic family, who reign without fear of being voted out of office by their "subjects."

In order to open up political rule to more people, in the 1600s liberal theorists such as Thomas Hobbes and John Locke came up with a different justification for government, one based on individualism rather than on the social and biological maternal traits associated with women. In direct opposition to the premises of a hereditary monarchy, they asserted that (1) the basic unit of the state is the autonomous individual; (2) all individuals are born inherently equal; and (3) government is legitimized by the consent of the governed in elections, where equal individuals choose from among themselves who will be their political leaders. From the perspective of liberal theory and practice, the principle of equal individualism underlying the liberal, democratic state stands in opposition to the fusion of family with state in hereditary monarchies. Its power is its promise to open up access to political rule to many more people and to make elected political leaders accountable to their constituents, who are "citizens."

Given the orthogonal relationship of liberal principles to monarchical ones, it would seem imperative for a political system to abandon, if not destroy, its monarchical heritage when instituting liberal principles as the basis of the state. In the case of the United States that is certainly what happened. We demolished our monarchical heritage when democratizing in the 1700s. What is more, most Americans proudly celebrate that destructive legacy. When Americans celebrate the Fourth of July as Independence Day, fireworks stand in for the bombs and gunfire of the bloody war we initiated to rid ourselves of any trace of a hereditary monarchy, which necessarily included destroying any trace of the fusion of family with state. Similarly, every time Americans stand, hand on heart, to sing "The Star-Spangled Banner," they affirm pride in the battles fought to disconnect ourselves from our original monarchical ties. The American Constitution reflects that commitment, in Article I, Section 9, which states: "No Title of Nobility shall be granted by the United States: And no Person holding any Office of Profit or Trust under them, shall, without the consent of the Congress, accept of any present, Emolument, Office, or Title, of any kind whatever, from any King, Prince, or foreign State." In addition, many state constitutions contain exactly the same type of prohibitions.

The centrality to the War for Independence of eradicating the monarchical heritage and hence the fusion of family with state is shown by the Founders' choice of the first president of the United States, General George Washington. He was a war hero, celebrated for distancing himself from associating the family with the state. He was proud of being childless on the grounds that no offspring of his could be viewed as next in line to the presidency, even on an electoral rather than an inheritance principle. However proud Americans may be of the destructive heritage that demolished their past, obliterating a monarchy, and concomitantly the social and maternal traits associated with women as a component of government, it failed to promote the basic promise of democracy to expand access to political rule for those previously excluded because of race, class, sex, or familial status. One of the most important markers of political inclusion in an electoral democracy is voting rights. Yet the expansion of suffrage in the United States, as well as in comparable democracies, gives evidence that although monarchial destruction works at least to some extent for men subordinated because of their class or race, it is an utter failure at increasing political access for women.

The United States and Women's Voting Rights:
A Historical Laggard

The United States is in many ways a pioneer of liberal democracy. Americans are for the most part proud to belong to the first country to overthrow an established political regime defined by the sovereignty of monarchs, who inherit the right to rule because of their family-kinship dynastic status. In its stead, American founders established a republic—a political regime in which sovereignty was located in the people, who have the right to decide who will be the political rulers by means of elections. Although far from egalitarian at its founding, the American state is nevertheless a historical trailblazer in terms of overthrowing the principle of aristocracy, based on a birth-right for inclusion in political rule. Other countries—France, Argentina, and Chile—modeled themselves on the American example when overthrowing monarchy in favor of an electoral system of political rule.

In the early nineteenth century the American state continued to be a pioneer, becoming the first political system to remove property ownership as a qualification for voting for any portion of its population. One by one, states opened up their electorates to unpropertied white males. Yet, the United States allowed slavery to exist as an institution well into the nineteenth century, eventually fighting a civil war to eradicate it long after other political systems had already abolished slavery without bloodshed.[25] In regard to slavery as an institution, therefore, the United States was not the first to abolish it. When it comes to voting rights, however, the United States was the first and only state to enfranchise newly freed slaves immediately concurrent with their emancipation. As the Fifteenth Amendment states, "The right of citizens of the United States to vote shall not be denied or abridged by the United States or by any State on account of race, color, or previous condition of servitude." Its passage in conjunction with the Thirteenth Amendment, which abolished and prohibits slavery, is unique.[26]

When it comes to women's political rights, however, the United States did anything but break new ground. At the founding of the American state, the Constitution conferred upon the original thirteen states the authority to establish voting qualifications, and all states invoked group differences to bar people from their electorates. Six states prohibited blacks from voting (see table 5.1). Every state invoked property qualifications for the right to vote. Yet the most absolute criterion used to restrict state level electorates was not race or class, but sex. Racial barriers were far from universally used by all states, and property qualifications could be satisfied by an unusually diverse array of methods. In Connecticut, for example, the property requirement of holding land could alternatively be met by having served in the military or by paying taxes. Other states that allowed the payment of taxes to substitute for landholding were Delaware, Georgia, Massachusetts, New York, New Hampshire, North Carolina, Pennsylvania, Rhode Island, and South Carolina. States such as New York, Rhode Island, and Virginia also allowed the payment of rent to substitute for the holding of land. In one state, Georgia, being in a "mechanic trade" could satisfy the property qualification for the right to vote.

When it came to sex, however, not only was it all but universally invoked by the states as a voting qualification, but there were no substitute ways to override or get around it, whatever the class or race or marital status of a woman. Initially, all states but New Jersey categorically restricted their electorates to males only. In 1776 New Jersey adopted a constitution that defined voters as adult inhabitants who were worth "fifty pounds."[27] At this time, the colonies and later the United States adopted English common law, which defined marriage in terms of the husband and wife becoming one, and that one was the husband, as codified by William Blackstone in his *Commentaries on the Laws of England*, published in 1753:

> By marriage the husband and wife are one person in law: that is, the very being or legal existence of the woman is suspended during the marriage, or at least incorporated and consolidated into that of the husband: under whose wing, protection, and *cover* she performs everything; and is therefore called in our law-French a *feme-covert* . . . or under the protection and influence of her husband, her *baron*, or lord; and her condition during her marriage is called her *coverture*.[28]

The married couple was therefore one legal entity, and the will of that one entity was to be expressed through the husband. Wives were "civilly dead" and, as such, could not in their own right sue or be sued, make contracts, draft wills, or buy or sell property. Since all the property and earnings of married women legally belonged to their husbands, married women had no right to their own property, their own earnings from their own employment, or even their own inheritance from their parents. In addition, under coverture marriage, a husband could beat his wife to discipline her, although "with a stick no bigger than a judge's thumb" and "the children of the marriage fell entirely within the custody of the father."[29]

The inability of married women to own their own property rendered them voteless, since they could not meet the "fifty pounds" qualification. However, single women and widows who did meet the property requirement routinely participated in New Jersey's electoral process. What is more, between 1797 and 1807 women's votes began to have an impact on the two competing political parties of that time, the Federalists and the Republicans. Federalists sought to widen their political base by appealing to women's political participation, emphasizing the "suitability and desirability" of women's involvement in politics.[30] All this changed in 1807 when the competition between political parties prompted the Republicans to view women's votes as a threat that needed to be contained. Political deals were struck among the players, with the result that by 1808 the state legislature had abruptly changed New Jersey's constitution to exclude all women from voting.[31]

By the early years of the nineteenth century there was no state in the country where women could even cast a ballot, much less run for political office. Although states began to drop property requirements for white men in the early nineteenth century, no state that once barred women from the right to vote ever reversed its decision. The use of sex as a qualification for voting rights to bar women from the electorate even became constitutionally sanctioned in the late nineteenth century, when the Fifteenth Amendment was ratified after the Civil War. Notably, it prohibited states from using race as a qualification for voting. However, despite the pleas of woman suffrage reformers, members of Congress refused to prohibit states from using *sex* as a qualification for voting rights in this crucial piece of legislation, thereby allowing states to continue to exclude women from voting. The word *male* was also introduced into the American Constitution for the first time with the addition of the Fourteenth Amendment, in the context of establishing citizenship rights, thereby making sex discrimination in relation to political rights explicitly permissible and constitutional.

By the end of the nineteenth century, four new Western states were added to the Union that did not use sex as a qualification for voting, and hence women had these very limited state-level guarantees of the right to vote.[32] In percentage terms, however, the addition of these four new states did not change the overall proportion of states where women could and could not vote from the founding of the American state to the end of the nineteenth century. At both points in time, women had no right to vote in 90% of the states. By contrast, the voting rights of racially or economically

Table 5.1 Electoral qualifications in post-Revolutionary American state constitutions

	Property/Alternative[a]	Race	Sex
Connecticut, 1787	Land, Military Service, or Taxes: Freehold of $7/year, or having done or been excused from military duty for the year preceding the election, or paid state tax in year preceding the election	White	Male
Delaware, 1792	Taxes: Paid state or county tax assessed at least six months before election	White	Male
Georgia, 1777	Property, Taxes, Occupation: Ten pounds in property and liable to pay taxes, or being of any mechanic trade	White	Male
Maryland, 1776	Land, Property: Freehold of 50 acres in county of election, or property amounting to more than thirty pounds	Not specified	Male
Massachusetts, 1778	Taxes: To vote for Representative: must have paid taxes in town where resident; to vote for Governor, Lt-Governor, or Senator: above plus sixty pounds	No Negroes No Indians No Mulattos	Male
New Jersey, 1776	Wealth: 50 pounds' proclamation money	Not specified	Not specified[b]
New York, 1777	Land, Rent, Taxes: Freeholder of 20 pounds, or rented tenement of 40 shillings/yr; and paid state taxes	Not Mentioned	Male

State, Year	Qualification	Race	Sex
New Hampshire, 1779	Taxes: Paid taxes	Not Specified	Male
North Carolina, 1776	Land, Taxes: To vote for Senator, 50-acre freehold in county of election for six months preceding election; To vote for county House of Commons, paid public taxes for town; to vote for representative in House of Commons, paid public taxes	Not specified	Male (although section on town representatives refers to "all *persons* possessed of a freehold")
Pennsylvania, 1776	Taxes: Paid public taxes	Not mentioned	Male
Rhode Island, 1842	Taxes, Real Estate, Rent: Total of $1 in taxes and fees and real estate worth $134, or $7/year in rent	No Narragansett Indians	Male
South Carolina, 1778	Land, Taxes: Own 50-acre freehold, or town lot, for six months preceding election, or paid tax in last/present year (at least six months before election) of an amount equivalent to the tax on a 50-acre freehold	White	Male
Virginia, 1776	Land, Property, Rent: Shall remain "as exercised at present"; i.e., Freeholders having 50 acres, or 25 acres and house 12x12 (1762); or to vote for assemblyman, tenants for life or lives	White	Male

a) See Chilton Williamson, *American Suffrage from Property to Democracy, 1760–1860* (Princeton, NJ: Princeton University Press, 1960), 30. The Virginia constitution merely specified that voting qualification shall remain "as exercised at present," which refers to colonial qualifications for suffrage, as cited by Williamson. The reference to "white male" explicitly appears in the 1830 Virginia constitution, Article 3, Section 14.

b) Changed by 1808 to be "male only."

disadvantaged men improved dramatically over the course of this century, women's voting rights stagnated, as indicated in figure 5.1.

Women in the United States eventually gained the right to vote in 1920, with the ratification of the Nineteenth Amendment, but in the context of the American state the amendment came late. America had expanded the right to vote to unpropertied white men in the early nineteenth century and to previously enslaved African American men in the late nineteenth century.[33] Granting women the right to vote in 1920 hardly marks the United States as a front-runner in enfranchising women when compared to other countries. Whereas the United States was the first to enfranchise people without a property qualification and was the quickest to enfranchise previously enslaved African American men, it was the belated twenty-sixth nation to entitle women to vote, as indicated in table 5.2.

In an electoral political system the very first step in women's acquisition of political equality with men is to acquire voting rights on the same basis.

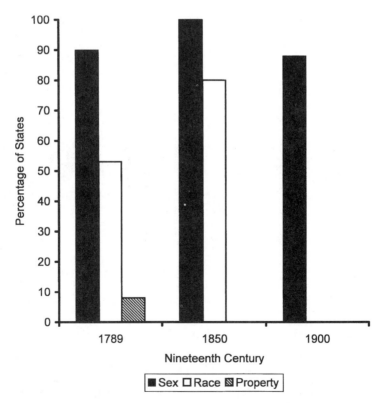

Figure 5.1: Percent states using sex, race, or property as voting qualifications in the nineteenth century.

Table 5.2   Year of woman suffrage[a]

Rank	Political System	Year of Woman Suffrage
1st	New Zealand	1893
2nd	Australia	1902
3rd	Finland	1906
4th	Norway	1913
5th	Denmark	1915
5th	Iceland	1915
7th	Canada	1917
7th	The Netherlands	1917
9th	Austria	1918
9th	Estonia	1918
9th	Georgia	1918
9th	Germany	1918
9th	Hungary	1918
9th	Ireland	1918
9th	Kyrgyzstan	1918
9th	Latvia	1918
9th	Lithuania	1918
9th	Poland	1918
9th	Russian Federation	1918
9th	United Kingdom	1918
21st	Belarus	1919
21st	Belgium	1919
21st	Luxembourg	1919
21st	Sweden	1919
21st	Ukraine	1919
26th	United States	1920

a) Adapted from "A World Chronology of the Recognition of Women's Rights to Vote and to Stand for Election," IPU, www.ipu.org/wmn-e/suffrage.htm (9/28/06).

Individualism alone, however, proves insufficient for promoting women's political inclusion in electoral democracies as a comparative look at women's acquisition of voting rights across countries shows. Rather it is the combination of hereditary monarchies, the original form of state maternalism, and individualism as represented by a democratizing state that go hand in hand with women's inclusion in the electorate. Democratic countries based on a principle of individual equality that also retained their monarchies as a form of state maternalism include women in the electorate more quickly than democratic countries that do not, as is evident in the history of women's voting rights in twenty-five democracies comparable in wealth and industrialization to the United States.[34] The first democracy to extend voting rights to women is New Zealand, which did so in 1893. Fourteen other democracies followed suit prior to the United States in 1920. When we examine what these pioneer countries have in common we find that it is the retention of their monarchies—or at least not their ideological and institutional destruction—that promotes the early extension of voting to women. [35]

Constitutional Monarchies

The failure of the United States to maternalize its state starts with its founding, initiated by a violent revolution that demolished its original form of state maternalism, the hereditary monarchy. This alone is an unusual beginning, when compared to most other comparable democracies, which did anything but demolish their monarchies upon adopting an electoral system of political rule based on a principle of individual equality (see table 5.3). New Zealand, Australia, Norway, Denmark, Canada, the United Kingdom, Belgium, Luxembourg, the Netherlands, Sweden, Spain,[36] and The Bahamas, or 48% of the world's comparable democracies, not only retained their monarchies at the outset but also continue to retain them to this day. Four other political systems—Austria, Germany, Italy, and Greece—retained their hereditary monarchies into the twentieth century and then let them go only by using the most peaceful of means, such as allowing them to slip away or consensually voting them out of existence.[37]

Four democracies—Iceland, Israel, Finland, and Ireland—never had an indigenous monarchy of their own, constituted by family-kinship networks corresponding to their own religious, ethnic, and linguistic identity. In contrast, the American colonies had an indigenous monarchy in the sense that monarchical England corresponded to the colonists' English identities in terms of ethnicity and language, if not religion. The British Crown sponsored the American colonists' settlements. Thus the colonists were themselves British. Although the headquarters of their monarchy was located across the Atlantic, it was "theirs," not that of a foreign country. Not so with countries that were dominated, even occupied, by foreign monarchies that represented alien linguistic, religious, and ethnic groups, such as Ireland's domination by the British monarchy or Finland's domination by Sweden and the Russian Empire. Because these democracies never had a monarchy of their own, so to speak, they avoided even the possibil-

Table 5.3   Status of hereditary monarchies in contemporary democracies, 2007

Retain Monarchy	STATUS OF HEREDITARY MONARCHY			Total
	Fade Away Monarchy	No Indigenous Monarchy	Demolish Monarchy	
Australia	Austria	Finland	France	
The Bahamas	Germany	Iceland	Japan	
Belgium	Greece	Ireland	Portugal	
Canada	Italy	Israel	United States	
Denmark		Switzerland		
Luxembourg				
The Netherlands				
New Zealand				
Norway				
Spain				
Sweden				
United Kingdom				
48% (12)[a]	16.7% (4)	20% (5)	16.7% (4)	100% (n = 25)

a) number of political systems in parentheses

ity of discrediting maternalism by the violent eradication of hereditary monarchies.[38]

Out of the entire group of comparable contemporary democracies only four actually destroyed the original form of state maternalism, their hereditary monarchies: the United States, Portugal, France, and Japan. The history of the destruction of monarchies in the United States and France is well known. In the case of Japan, although its hereditary monarchy is still in place, the monarchy was de-maternalized in the late nineteenth century by a new stipulation that only men could be sovereigns, which flew in the face of a long heritage of women empresses. In so doing, Japan destroyed the fusion of the family with the state that signifies women's inclusion in political rule. In Portugal the monarchy was destroyed when Manuel II succeeded to the throne after the assassination of his father and brother, but then barely escaped death when a socialist government took power. Although he never abdicated, he was essentially the victim of a violent overthrow of the government.

Those countries that retained hereditary monarchies, the first form of state maternalism, disproportionately were the first to grant women the right to vote as individuals equal to men. Of the twelve democracies that retained their monarchies upon establishing an electoral political system, ten of them, or 83.3% granted women the right to vote prior to 1920, compared to the 16.7% that did not (see table 5.4). Of the four democracies that retained their monarchies into the twentieth century and then let them quietly fade away, two of the four (or 50%) enfranchised women before the United States. Of the four democracies that never had a monarchy in the first place, and hence avoided demolishing it, three (or 75%) included women in the electorate on the same basis as men before the United States did so.[39] And of those four countries that destroyed ideologically and institutionally their monarchical heritage, all of them (100%) enfranchised women in 1920 or later. The pattern is clear. Women did better in gaining access to voting rights in political systems that retained their monarchies or never had an indigenous monarchy in the first place.

Even given the patriarchal preference for male sovereigns in hereditary monarchies, women could still be political leaders wielding the same political power as men. If women could be *sovereigns* in a hereditary system of political rule—the chief executive of the entire political system—then why on earth shouldn't women *at least* be *voters*, if not officeholders, in an electoral system of political rule? Why not, indeed. Women took over political systems as chief executives precisely "because of" their location within a hereditary system that defined their social and biological maternalism as signifying inclusion, not exclusion, in political rule. This heritage is wiped out when monarchies are wiped out. Since the key to women's access to political leadership is not their social and biological maternal identities per se, which are virtually constant across historical time and political place, but rather the *political meaning* assigned to those identities, wiping out an institution such as a monarchy that signifies women's inclusion in political rule is a regressive developmental move. Rather than fulfilling the democratic promise of including more women in political rule, it portends just the opposite of excluding more women from political rule. In the case of the United States, while some women lost the right to be queens, after 1808 and for virtually the entire extant of the nineteenth century, no women gained the right to be voters.

Voting rights are just the first step, not the last step, toward women's acquisition of political equality. Also crucial is the access women have to officeholding, such as their election to national legislatures. Considering the percentage of women elected to national legislatures in relation to the way a democratic country dealt with the state maternalism of a hereditary monarchy shows a strong, positive correlation between *retaining* hereditary monarchies and women's election to national legislatures (see table 5.5). The average percentage of women elected to national legislatures among

Table 5.4 Woman suffrage and monarchical status in contemporary democracies

Political System	Retained Monarchy % (n)[a]	Fade Away Monarchy % (n)	Never Had Monarchy* % (n)	Demolish Monarchy % (n)	Totals % (n)
Woman Suffrage prior to 1920	83.3% (10) Australia Belgium Canada Denmark Luxembourg The Netherlands New Zealand Norway Sweden United Kingdom	50% (2) Austria Germany	75% (3) Finland Iceland Ireland	0% (0)	62.5% (15)
Woman Suffrage 1920 or later	16.7% (2) The Bahamas Spain	50% (2) Greece Italy	25% (1) Switzerland	100% (4) France Japan Portugal United States	37.5% (9)
Total Percent	48% (12)	20% (4)	20% (4)	12% (4)	100% (n = 24)

a) number of cases in parentheses
*Table does not include Israel, which did not exist prior to 1948.

Table 5.5 Percent women elected to national legislatures in contemporary democracies, controlling for monarchical status, 2006

	Monarchical Status in Contemporary Democracies		
Retained Monarchy	Fade Away Monarchy	Never Had Monarchy	Demolish Monarchy
Average Percent Women Elected to National Legislature: 29.2%	*Average Percent Women Elected to National Legislature:* 24%	*Average Percent Women Elected to National Legislature:* 24.6%	*Average Percent Women Elected to National Legislature:* 14.3%
Australia 25%	Austria 34%	Finland 38%	France 12%
The Bahamas 20%	Germany 32%	Iceland 33%	Japan 9%
Belgium 35%	Greece 13%	Ireland 13%	Portugal 21%
Canada 21%	Italy 17%	Israel 14%	United States 15%
Denmark 37%		Switzerland 25%	
Luxembourg 23%			
The Netherlands 37%			
New Zealand 32%			
Norway 38%			
Spain 36%			
Sweden 45%			
United Kingdom 20%			

the group of democracies that still retain their monarchies is 29.2%; the percentage among those democracies that simply allowed their monarchies to fade away is 24%; the percentage among those democracies that never had a monarchy and hence no option to retain, relinquish, or demolish one is 24.6%; the percentage for those democracies that demolished their monarchies is by far the lowest—at only 14.3%.

Adopting Welfare Provision and Gender Quotas

In addition to monarchies, there are other public policies that represent social and biological maternal traits voters associate with women, such as welfare provision and gender quotas. These public policies, in combination with those representing individualism bolster public attitudes about the suitability of women as political leaders. When the government acts vis-à-vis its public policies in maternal ways that voters associate with women, voters learn that to have the maternal traits attributed to women signifies inclusion in the public sphere of the state not exclusion to the realm of the private sphere of the family or the service sector of the market. The result is an increase in the public's view of the suitability of women as political leaders. In addition, maternal public policies increase the civic capacity of voters to participate in electoral processes, and when this capacity is combined with more favorable attitudes about the suitability of women as political leaders, the result is more women elected to political office. It is important for women's political inclusion, therefore, for a democratic state that has public policies representing individualism to also adopt public policies representing maternalism. This is easier to do if a country does not initially destroy the first type of state maternalism, hereditary monarchies.

The ways a democracy dealt with its monarchical heritage correspond to the way subsequent forms of state maternalism, such as welfare provision and gender quotas, are adopted. Of those democracies that to this day retain their monarchies, all but one has added at least one new type of maternal public policy: New Zealand added welfare provision and Australia added gender quotas, while 75% added both types. Only one political system that retained its hereditary monarchy, The Bahamas, failed to add a new form of maternal public policy (see table 5.6). Of those democracies that simply allowed their monarchies to fade away, 75% have subsequently added *both* new forms of maternal public policies, welfare provision and gender quotas. Only one democracy, Greece, added welfare provision alone. Of the democracies that never had a monarchical heritage, 40% added welfare provision as a new type of maternal public policy, and the remaining 60%

Table 5.6 Status of hereditary monarchies and subsequent adoption of welfare provision and gender quotas, 2006

ADOPTION OF NEW TYPES OF MATERNAL PUBLIC POLICIES: WELFARE PROVISION AND GENDER QUOTAS	STATUS OF HEREDITARY MONARCHY: AN OLD TYPE OF MATERNAL PUBLIC POLICY				
	Retain Monarchy	Fade Away Monarchy	No Indigenous Monarchy	Demolish Monarchy	Total
No new state maternalism	8% (1)[a] The Bahamas	----		75% (3) France Japan United States	16% (4)
Welfare only	8% (1) New Zealand	25% (1) Greece	40% (2) Finland Israel		16% (4)
Quota only	8% (1) Australia				4% (1)
Welfare and Quota	75% (9) Belgium Canada Denmark Luxembourg The Netherlands Norway Spain Sweden United Kingdom	75% (4) Austria Germany Italy	60% (3) Iceland Ireland Switzerland	25% (1) Portugal	68% (17)
Total	(12)	(5)	(5)	(4)	n = 25

a) number of countries in parentheses

added welfare provision and gender quotas. By contrast, in democracies that ideologically and institutionally destroyed not only their actual monarchies but also the very principle of monarchical rule as a form of state maternalism, we find a dearth of new forms of state maternalism. Only one, Portugal, added new forms of maternal public policies, while the other three have added nothing to replace the original type of maternal public policy, the hereditary monarchy, which was destroyed.

The long-term impact of demolishing a monarchial heritage on contemporary public policies can be explained by what political scientist Paul Pierson refers to as the asymmetric relationship between establishing versus dismantling public policies. As difficult as it may be to establish public policies, it is often easier than dismantling them. In this sense, retrenchment or the dismantling of established policies is "in no sense a simple mirror image of . . . [their] expansion."[40] The dismantling of political principles comes at a critical juncture in the process of democratizing, when "triggering events" occur, "which set development along a particular path."[41] Although the path is not absolutely locked down, a critical juncture in political development means that there are self-reinforcing processes, "increasing returns," that result in persisting "organizational and institutional practices." As Pierson explains, "change continues, but it is bounded change—until something erodes or swamps the mechanisms of reproduction that generate continuity."[42] As James Mahoney adds, "critical junctures are characterized by the adoption of a particular institutional arrangement from among two or more alternatives. These junctures are 'critical' because once a particular option is selected it becomes progressively more difficult to return to the initial point when multiple alternatives were still available."[43]

The problem with demolishing a monarchical heritage, from the perspective of *prospectively* establishing new, contemporary forms of state maternalism, is that part and parcel of its destruction is the destruction of the principle of infusing positive group rights into the state and of using fixed statuses as a legitimate premise upon which government is to dispense protections, benefits, and privileges to people. Yet without acceptance of these principles, it is all but impossible to institute newer and more contemporary types of state maternalism, such as welfare provision and gender quotas. If, for example, a democracy retains (or at least never violently destroys) its monarchy, however symbolically, in so doing it retains the principle that the accidents of birth, such as one's family-kinship status, are a legitimate basis for access to special political privileges. Given acceptance of that view, it is then easier to accept the idea that a group, such as women, should have privileged access to political representation simply because of a fixed status, namely, their sex classification as female. The result is the adoption of gender quotas. In a democracy that has violently destroyed that principle in the course of violently destroying its monarchy, however the very principle itself becomes discredited as universal individualism absolutely prevails. The result is that even when gender quotas are adopted, as in France, their meaning is contorted to stand for what men and women have in common rather than their sex difference. Such a rendition of gender quotas obviates the incorporation of maternal difference into the state, and fails to produce the requisite public attitudes supportive of women as political leaders, much less women's election to political office.

Similarly, retention of a monarchy when democratizing—or at least avoiding the violent destruction of one—leaves in place the idea that the government is based on more than a liberal social contract between autonomous individuals who need nothing more from the state than protection of their persons and property from nonconsensual intrusion by others. Rather a monarchy stands for the inclusion of the family in the state and for a set of obligations and duties between the state and the populace based on familial relationships defined by fixed statuses, such as parent and child, ruler and subject. Given the retention of this view of the state, it becomes easier for a contemporary democracy to adopt public policies, such as welfare provision, that extend the services traditionally located in the family to the state itself, since the latter institution already has a familial identity as represented symbolically by its monarchy. Those democracies, therefore, that never destroyed their monarchical heritage are more open in contemporary times to expanding principles of state maternalism to include both the adoption of gender quotas and welfare provision. The result is more women elected to political office.

Throw-Away Queens—Not

Monarchies are elitist forms of government that are electorally unaccountable to the people. The monarch is sovereign, and the people are his or her "subjects." For this reason, a monarchy is the antithesis of both a "republic," where the people are sovereign, and a liberal democracy, where all individuals have equal access to political rule as voters and officeholders. The elitist and antiquated character of monarchies places them outside most political science scholarship on democracy and feminist scholarship on women's political leadership. In terms of the latter, it is as if women who ruled as queens were "thrown-away" on the grounds that their reign was based on an illegitimate governmental form, according to the norms of a liberal democratic republic. This is a mistake, however, because hereditary monarchies illustrate the power of the state to give a political meaning to women's maternal identities as wives and mothers. Women's association with maternalism is a virtual constant over historical time and political place. What changes is the political context, specifically, whether a political context defines maternalism as signifying inclusion in political rule of the state. From the point of view of understanding women's political leadership, hereditary monarchies are a powerful illustration of how *political context* determines women's access to political rule.

Familial Paths to Political Rule

The political point about monarchies in relation to women's access to political leadership is that systems of hereditary political rule, by fusing the family with the state, give a positive political meaning to the maternal identities people attribute to women. The political meaning of women's maternalism in hereditary systems of political rule signifies that women, at least those in the ruling family-kinship group, are *included* in the pool of those eligible to rule. Thus, women's disproportionate contributions to generating families by means of their biological capacities to be pregnant and to give birth, not to mention their disproportionate tendency to care for people once they are born, are fused with the state, thereby giving women a point of access to political rule.

Over the course of human history, thousands of such women have ruled over empires, territorial nation-states, provinces, and tribes. The great names of women associated with hereditary executive political leadership are familiar, such as Elizabeth I, Catherine the Great, Mary Queen of Scots, Cleopatra, Queen Isabella of Spain, and Queen Victoria. Much less familiar are the legions of other women who ruled on the basis of a hereditary principle. I have identified 4,180 who have served as executive rulers of their political systems.[44] Of these, only 180 (4.3%) were elected to their political office, compared to 3,527 women (84.4%) who became leaders on the basis of a hereditary principle. The remaining 472 women (11.3%) acquired executive positions by other means, such as being a de facto leader, holding a titular position, gaining leadership as a consequence of military conquest, or being appointed as governor general in a monarchical political system. Thus, more than 3,500 women gained access to executive political rule on anything but a principle of election to office. For a list of the women who ruled as sovereigns in the twentieth century alone, see appendix 3.

Among the thousands of women who ruled in hereditary political systems, their familial relationships provide access to three main types of

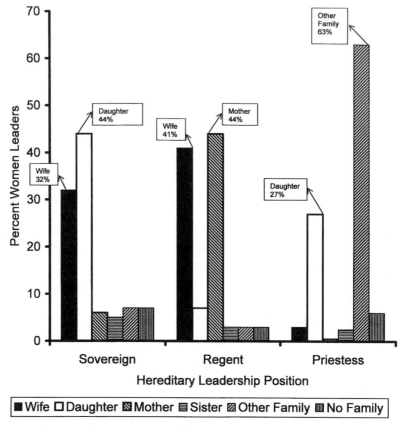

Figure 5.2: Women's hereditary leadership in relation to family-kinship networks.

leadership: hereditary sovereigns, who rule in their own right; regents who rule on behalf of another sovereign; and religious sovereigns who rule from a position within a religious institution. Of the women leaders who ruled as hereditary sovereign authorities in their own right, almost half (44%) gained sovereignty by virtue of being the daughter of a member of a ruling family-kinship group (see figure 5.2). After daughters, the second most exercised familial path to sovereignty was being the wife of a sovereign (32%). Only 6% of the women who were sovereigns in their own right achieved that status by virtue of being a mother. In short, to become a sovereign authority directly was most open to the daughters and wives of ruling family-kinship group members.

What is more, over historical time the most frequent position by far held by women as executive rulers of their political system is the hereditary sovereign. Of these 2,099 women, fifty-seven ruled as empresses (1.4%);

867 ruled as queens (24.6%); 960 ruled as sovereigns of provinces, such as duchesses, countesses, or sultanas (27.2%); and 215 ruled as tribal chiefs (6.1%). Thus, over and above Catherine the Great, fifty-six other women ruled as empresses over vast territories. Although built into the idea of being a "king" is the idea of being a "queen," which is a must if the ruling dynasty is to continue, hereditary political systems also included over 800 women who ruled as political sovereigns in their own right. Women's inclusion in political rule in a hereditary political system is characteristic of regions throughout the world, including regions today noted for policies designed to keep women out of politics.

The Middle East, with the exception of Israel, is considered a backward region in today's world when it comes to women's political leadership. There are restrictions on women's right to vote or even to succeed to monarchical positions in countries such as Saudi Arabia, Morocco, and Jordan. Historically, however, the Middle East, Mesopotamia, and North Africa were regions where women first served as hereditary executive leaders. The first woman hereditary sovereign who appears on the historical record is Queen Eyleuka of Ethiopia, who ruled for forty-five years sometime between 4530 and 3240 BCE. One of the few Antediluvian leaders on record, she assumed her reign after the death of her husband, King Borsa. Although Iraq today can hardly be viewed as a bastion of women's rights, in 3000 BCE Shagshag ruled as Queen in Mesopotamia. And women pharaohs of Egypt include Queen Nefertiti, who is believed to have ruled as pharaoh after the death of her husband, Akhenaten, in about 1336 BCE; Hatshepsut, who ruled a hundred years earlier; and Cleopatra, the last pharaoh of Egypt.[45]

Over time, women hereditary sovereigns are spread out over the basic historical eras, namely the Ancient Period (5000 BCE to 449 BCE), the Classical Period (500 BCE to 449 CE), the Postclassical Period (450 to 1499 CE), the Early Modern Period (1500 to 1788 CE), the Modern Period (1789 to 1899 CE), and the Contemporary Period (since 1900), as illustrated in figure 5.3. While most women hereditary executives might be expected to have reigned during ancient periods, clearly that is not the case. The highest percentage is in the most recent, contemporary period.

Regents, the Vice Presidents of Monarchies

The second most frequent type of executive rule exercised by women over historical time is hereditary regent. A regent is a person who rules for another due to a temporary incapacity on the part of the person chosen to be the monarch. Typically, a regent would rule in the stead of a young child

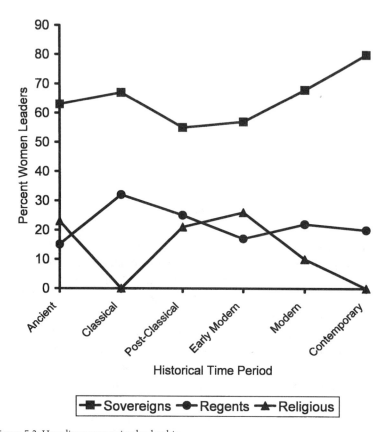

Figure 5.3: Hereditary executive leadership.

who had been chosen to be the monarch but who lacked the maturity to take control of the government. The designated regent would rule until the heir to the throne was able to assume political responsibilities. Women also served as regents when their husbands were away at war. Even in monarchies that prohibited women from being sovereign in their own right, women became political rulers as regents. A case in point is France, which in the early fourteenth century, had become the first male-only monarchy in Western Europe by invoking what is known as "Salic Law."[46] The wife of Henry II, Catherine de' Medici, however, became a regent with political authority on two separate occasions when her husband was on military campaigns, the first time in 1552. When he died in 1559, she successfully launched a political career that included recognition of her leadership as a regent for her son. A royal council issued an edict in 1560 that ordered "all governors, crown officials, and military officers" to report to her, and "all information regarding matters of justice, royal finances, and the organization of the realm was to be directed" to her and to be "read by her first."[47]

Women who ruled as regents generally possessed the political authority and responsibilities of the chosen rulers themselves. They were like vice presidents in a presidential political system, taking on roles that were anything but passive. They were actively involved in domestic policy, foreign affairs, and military enterprises. In some cases they became the legitimate ruler of the kingdom. In the late 790s, for example, an Athenian noblewoman, Irene, who had married Emperor Leo IV, became regent of the Byzantine Empire when her husband died and their son, Constantine IV, who was only nine years old, lacked the capacity to take control of the throne. Irene was a ruthless regent, who succeeded in eliminating other contenders to the throne, such as Constantine's five half brothers. When Constantine finally took over as ruler and proved to be a disaster, Irene's supporters moved to arrest and incapacitate her son in order to put Irene back on the throne. In 797 Irene took the title of Emperor (not Empress), and ruled alone for five years.

Similarly, Queen Margaret I of Denmark (1387–1412) started as a regent for her son Olaf. She engaged in complicated diplomatic negotiations to expand the land holdings of Denmark, "no doubt that . . . [she] was the soul of Danish politics."[48] When Olaf died, Margaret took over as Queen of Denmark and succeeded in becoming Queen of Norway and Sweden as well.[49] Although the European medieval concept of power was highly masculinized and physical and moral frailties such as "capriciousness, physical weakness, lust, instability, lack of intelligence, irrationality, and a tendency toward duplicity" were attributed to the female sex,[50] women characteristically took over political governance once men were gone to war. Noble women were expected to perform as managers and defenders of their family estates while their husbands were away for long periods of time fighting or crusading in distant lands.

It was also the expectation of the times that noble and royal women would participate in political councils and routine governmental matters.[51] The advice offered by Bernard to Melisende, a royal wife, after the death of her husband typifies the way women, supposedly the weaker sex, were considered to be able to adopt the attributes of men when the situation called for women's leadership: "Now that your husband the king is dead, and the young king as yet unfit to discharge the affairs of state and fulfill the duty of a king, the eyes of all will be on your hand to great things and, although a woman, you must act as a man by doing everything you have to do 'in a spirit prudent and strong.'"[52] All told, over a fifth (21%) of the women who have ruled as hereditary executives have done so on the basis of their regency. In the Classical Period more than 30% of the women who ruled as hereditary sovereigns did so on the basis of their regency. After that time period, the average percentage of women who were hereditary sovereigns on the basis of their regency is closer to 20%.

Wife and mother stand out as the familial relations that most often propel women into regency leadership. Of the 748 women who ruled as regents, 41% did so on the basis of being the wife of a sovereign who was unable to rule due to illness, absence, or some other incapacitating problem, and 44% did so on the basis of being the mother of a reigning sovereign who could not rule due to age, illness, absence, or some other incapacitation. A case in point is the Roman Empire, noted for its patriarchal heritage. During the initial years of the Empire (14 BCE to 284 CE), four women were sovereigns on the basis of their regency over their children. In addition, during this period, Ulipia Serverina was a regent sovereign by virtue of being the wife of the male ruler. Hence, even in the most patriarchal of hereditary political systems, the Roman Empire at its peak, women retained access to political rule by virtue of their familial relationship within the ruling family-kinship class.

In the case of regency authority, although there is no comparative data to show whether women were chosen to be regents more often than men, there is reason to speculate that being a woman in the status of a wife or mother of a reigning sovereign may actually have given women a political advantage compared to men. The requirement that marriages be heterosexual limits the choice of male sovereigns when choosing a spouse to females only. In addition, to the degree that being the spouse of a male sovereign imparts a positive familial status in terms of eligibility to replace that male sovereign, women have an advantage over men. Men would also gain this familial spousal status when married to women who were sovereign authorities, but assuming that there initially are more male sovereigns than female sovereigns, more wives will be boosted into the leadership hierarchy by virtue of marriage to a sovereign than will husbands. Although fathers could also be chosen as regents for their children, mothers were the more likely choice, since women are initially more likely to be in charge of the care of children. Thus, a mother of a child who becomes the designated sovereign but cannot exercise that authority due to age or incapacity, holds an advantage over the child's father when it comes to choosing a regent for that child. This was an avenue for many mothers to claim the throne as sovereign authority.

Religious Sovereigns

Today, some religious theologies can scarcely be viewed as women-friendly, making it odd to think of religious institutions as an avenue for women to gain political authority. Catholicism, for example, prohibits women from being priests, much less pope; evangelical Christian sects view women's roles as restricted to the domestic sphere; the Old Testament's Adam and Eve heritage designates women to be the cause of mankind's downfall; and Islam assumes women's inherent inferiority in relation to men. Historically, however, this has not always been the case. In ancient as well as more modern times women exercised political authority by virtue of their religious standing as priests and as abbesses.

According to anthropologists, the first political authorities were derived from divine authorities. The first religious deity may have been one goddess, which later proliferated in a multitude of goddesses, then a multitude of goddesses and gods, then a multitude of gods, and finally, with the advent of Egyptian monotheism and Judaism, one male god. In many political systems the vestigial association of women with divine authority is retained in the form of women having positions of religious authority with political ramifications. Beginning around 2400 BCE, for example, women served as high priestesses in religious temples in Ur (Iraq), especially the Moon Temple, where High Priestesses Lipusha, Enheduanna, Emmenanna, among many others, held sway. These women were the daughters, granddaughters, or other family members of the ruling kings of the period.

Starting around 1388 BCE, Egyptian pharaohs also commonly depicted themselves as the result of a union between their mother and God. The ruler's mother then attained the title of God's Wife, signifying a formal office that derived its political authority from God. Queen Tiaa of Egypt, for example, held the title God's Wife, throughout her son's rule and had to relinquish it afterward. In later times, the position of God's Wife entailed rule over territorial areas. For example, High Priestess and God's Wife of Amon Schepenupet I of Thebes (Egypt) was given rule over Upper Egypt from 754 to 714 BCE.[53]

In early modern times (1500–1788) women in Europe similarly gained access to political authority by means of religious appointments as abbesses. María Pérez of the Monastery of Santa Maria la Real de las Huelgas in Burgos (Spain), for example, was the reigning abbess-general from 1230 to 1238 CE. As such, she "exercised unlimited secular authority over more than fifty villages, held her own courts, granted letters . . . for ordination, and issued licenses authorizing priests, within the limits of her abbatial jurisdiction, to hear confessions, to preach, and to engage in the cure of souls. She was privileged also to confirm Abbesses, to impose censures, and to convoke synods."[54]

All told, over historical time nearly a fifth (19%) of women exercised executive political authority by virtue of their positions as religious sovereigns. Yet, when it comes to women's sovereign leadership in the context of religious authority, there is more variability by historical time period than in other forms of hereditary leadership. In the Classical Period, there is no record of any women serving as sovereign leaders in religious capacities, nor have there been any such women since 1900. In other historical eras, however, such as the Early Modern Period, as many as 25% of sovereigns in the context of religious authorities are women. In terms of the familial path to being a religious sovereign, such as a priestess, wife of God, or abbess, other family memberships were important, such as being an aunt, grandmother, cousin, or niece of a member of a ruling kinship group. Of the 666 women who so ruled, 63% did so on the basis of such a family relation. The next highest number (27%) ruled on the basis of being the daughter of a ruling kinship member.

The Monarchical Lesson

Today Americans seem worried that a woman elected to be head of our government and state might lack the skills, courage, temperament, or just plain ability to be the chief executive of our political system, particularly in her role as commander-in-chief of the military. The thousands of women who ruled in the past on the basis of a hereditary principle are relevant to contemporary women's executive leadership because they demonstrate how women obtain more freedom to act as leaders when their class trumps their gender. When women become sovereign on the basis of their dynastic familial status, it is their class that is their most salient identity, not their sex. As such, they are free to act like men in terms of military ventures without fear of violating gender norms deeming such behavior to be "unfeminine." As full-fledged members of the ruling political family, it is their job to be the sovereign, and it is only incidental to that job that their persona includes being female.

In contrast, when women in a democracy run for political office, it is their gender, not their class, that is most important in the eyes of the public when it comes to women's capabilities as a political leader. For elected women leaders, this is a Catch 22, because to be a political leader, they must be as tough as men are presumed to be, yet not lose the primary feminine and maternal attributes ascribed to them by the public. The result is that the public, if not women leaders themselves, fear the "Thatcher factor," namely, that a woman leader will lose her feminine and maternal identity in the course of doing her job as a political leader. When Margaret Thatcher was prime minister of Great Britain, she did some characteristically unfeminine and unmaternal things. She attempted to dismantle the British welfare state, thereby acting in a decidedly unmaternal way. In addition, the "Iron Lady" launched a war with Argentina over proprietorship of the Falkland Islands, and she took an ostentatiously aggressive stance on the struggle in Northern Ireland, parading through buildings presumably bombed by the IRA, seemingly oblivious to the potential danger. To this day, whenever anyone has the temerity to suggest that women might be more oriented to the welfare needs of others as well as to peace, all an opponent need do is to raise the red flag of Margaret Thatcher . . . who was anything but.

Aside from the fact that women's political association with welfare and peace is a norm, not a perfect correlation, the telling aspect about women's political leadership in today's electoral systems is that women must assume such positions in a way that reflects their dual identities as women who are maternally different from men and as individuals who are the same as men. In hereditary political systems, the same dynamic does not hold. To the contrary, the entire system of hereditary rule is based on a recognition of the political relevance of male and female maternal group difference, without which there would be no dynastic group, because no children would be born to continue the ruling dynasty. Thus, women's maternal identities in a hereditary monarchy are a reproductive labor identity that has to do with the work they do by being pregnant and giving birth to new members of the ruling family, if not for the care of those new members after they are born. Thus, it is not women's femininity per se—how they behave and how they dress—that is their most important contribution to hereditary monarchies as an institution, but rather their maternal work, that is, whether they bear children or not.

Similarly, once a woman is chosen to be a sovereign, regent, or religious authority, what counts is how she acts to preserve and protect the dynasty and its subjects, not her femininity in terms of her sex role behavior or manners. Granted, there is always interest in such aspects of people, but once women are in charge of the state on a hereditary principle, the assumption is that they will assume and exercise the full range of political leadership roles, including military ones without worry about whether such activities are perceived as being "feminine" or not. One of the earliest examples is Queen and Admiral Artemisia I of Cara-Harlikarnassos and Kos in present-day Turkey, who ruled around 480 BCE. Artemisia ruled over a region that was a vassal of Persia. When Xerxes, King of Persia, decided to invade Greece, he commanded Artemisia to assist him by recruiting troops. She not only recruited soldiers, but became one herself, taking on the job of admiral in charge of five ships. Of all of Xerxes commanders, she alone tried to dissuade him from invading Greece. However, he ignored her recommendations, listening instead to his male advisors. Consequently, Xerxes met the Greeks in September of 480 BCE in the sea channel of Salamis. The Persians succeeded in taking the offensive, in large part due to Artemisia's naval skill in battle. Although she had lost all but one of her five ships, she was able to use this one to disable a key ship of the opposing forces.

When Xerxes' commanders met in council after the war, Artemisia was extremely vocal in her opposition to the war, despite her courageous contributions to it. Xerxes finally acknowledged her wisdom, as the war was draining the resources of all engaged in it. When Xerxes returned home to the kingdom, leaving his two sons in the care of Artemisia, he was met by rebellious revolutionaries who sought to overthrow him. Artemisia's kingdom, by contrast, prospered.[55] Notably, while Xerxes is indexed in major historical encyclopedias of world history along with other military leaders of classical times, Artemesia is missing from those same indexes.[56]

Artemesia was not the only woman during the Classical Period to assume a position as political leader. After her husband, Ashoka, died in 233 BCE, Rani Padmavati ruled the Maurya Empire, India's "first really large and powerful centralised state."[57] In her one-year reign she was noted for creating an unusually well-governed and efficient administration. When a Greek ambassador, visited her, for example, he expressed extreme admiration for her leadership skills, mentioning the prosperity and stability generated by her regime. Although the top of her administration was autocratic, at the lower city and village levels she implemented a principle of democratic rule by the people. Other women, such as Queen Zabibe of Qedar (Arabia), who ruled around 738 BCE, also were in command of armies that included large numbers of women.[58]

So, too, are women leaders notable for their military accomplishments if not for their battle prowess. Hōjō Masa-Ko of Japan seized power over the shogunate in 1199 CE after the death of her husband, who had been the first shōgun. When the shogunate was threatened in 1221 by opposing forces, she was the one who galvanized the shogunate army to crush the challengers. Her military success ensured for the next century and a half the rule of the Hōjōs. For this reason she is often referred to as Mother Shōgun and as the founder of the shogunate.[59] Other women were primarily military leaders, without formal political power, but their achievements are impressive. In Arabia in about 600 CE, for example, two women, Kahula and Safeira, who were commanders of armies, joined forces, and together were successful in turning back the Greek army. Another notable case is the military leader Hau Ma-Lan, who lived in China around 50 CE and was one of its most famous warriors. For twelve years she disguised herself as a man in order to take her father's place in battle. Her military skills were so impressive that her commanding officer called her his greatest warrior. So impressed was he, that, thinking she was a man, he offered his daughter to her in marriage.[60]

The ease with which many women sovereigns take on military leadership roles illustrates that the most important characteristic of executive leadership based on hereditary family-kinship is the leader's membership in that group, not other attributes, such as the person's age, race, ethnicity, religion, or social construction as feminine or masculine. Although many characteristics are considered when deciding who will be the next in line to inherit the throne, the most powerful attribute is membership in the ruling kinship group. Hence, when it comes to women's leadership identity, dynastic family status trumps all else. What is important is not their hairstyles, their hobbies, or even their marital status, but rather their placement in the ruling kinship group. Given that this group has absolute political power, it is assumed that when a woman hereditary executive exercises political power, including military power, she does so as a member of the powerful ruling kinship group on behalf of the political system she rules, rather than as a member of the "female" as opposed to the "male" sex. Thus, even in hereditary contexts though "women" might be viewed as physically and mentally inferior to "men" as a "sex," a woman's membership in the dominant kinship group trumps sex as the most important characteristic of who she "is," overriding her socially constructed inferiority based on her sex classification.

Maternal Political Environments for Democracies

Electoral environments have a powerful impact on women's success as candidates.[61] Specifically, as political scientist Kathleen Dolan found, women's prospects for inclusion in electoral politics are improved by "the amount of gendered information that is available to voters," specifically the amount of media attention directed to "women candidates, their sex, and the issues on which they campaign."[62] A gendered electoral environment must also include policies representing maternal traits associated by the public with women as an ongoing presence in the lives of voters—especially in democracies that by definition embrace public policies representing individualism.

Understanding women's maternal group difference from men as signifying a location not only in the private sphere of the home or the service sector of the market but also in the public sphere of the state opens up new ways to think about the American state. Prior to the invention of individualism and democratic liberal theory in the 1600s, maternalism was the foundation of the monarchical state. Although men were usually preferred as sovereigns, that preference generally did not exclude women. Even in the most patriarchal of monarchies, such as the Roman Empire, women ruled at least as regents. In the course of time, a principle of hereditary political rule served to give thousands of women access to the authority of the state, not only as regents but also as sovereigns and religious leaders.

Because hereditary monarchies are elitist and unaccountable to their "subjects," from a contemporary perspective, in terms of democratic norms they are "bad" forms of government. However, they nevertheless contain a "good" principle in that they assign to women's socially and biologically maternal identities a political meaning of inclusion, not exclusion, from the public sphere of the state. The liberal invention of separate spheres for the family and for the state cuts off those familial paths to political rule provided by a monarchy to women. Today, according to the principles underlying a liberal democracy, women's social and maternal identities are irrelevant to their place in the public sphere of the state, because those identities now signify only their suitability as wives and mothers in the private sphere of the family or the service sector of the state. This means that when theorists invented a liberal theory of the state and when founders of the American state implemented those ideas in establishing the United States, women did not lose their maternal identities, at least in the mind of the public. To the contrary, the public associates women to this day with social and maternal traits, whether individual women care to affirm those identities or not. It just means that women's maternal identities in a liberal construction of the state no longer signify inclusion in the public sphere of political governance.

The key to bolstering the public's view of women's suitability as political leaders is therefore to find a way to bring maternal traits back in to the state itself, that is, to regender the state as maternal, not just as individual, much less just as male. When the state either maintains its ties with maternalism by never severing in a violent way its connection with a historical monarchy in the first place or reintegrates itself with maternalism by adopting contemporary public policies representing such maternal traits as welfare provision or gender quotas, the public learns once again that to be identified as maternal is to be located not only in the private sphere of the home or the service sector of the market, but also in the public sphere of the state. The result is the election of more women to political office. The key to women's political inclusion in democracies is therefore a hybrid state that combines public policies based on individualism and on maternalism.

The significance of such a hybrid state for producing a gendered political environment inclusive of women is evident not only in women's acquisition of voting rights and women's track record as hereditary sovereigns, but also in the one brief period of American history, the early decades of the twentieth century, when public policies combined principles of individual equality with principles of women's social and biological maternalism. As testimony to the power of a hybrid state to increase women's political inclusion, it was in precisely this brief era that American women finally obtained the right to vote.

6

Maternalizing American Government, Briefly

Women as Political Leaders

Marie Wilson, president of The White House Project, an organization with the ultimate goal of seeing a woman in the Oval Office, views television as far more than mere entertainment. Rather,
TV affects people's attitudes and perceptions about the world they
live in, and so "the most important part of our work at The White
House Project is the perception piece."[1] Before Americans will be
ready to elect a woman president, they "have to be able to envision a woman effectively running the country . . . and pop-culture
images can do what thousands of hours of speeches, educational
campaigns and campaign ads can't. . . . They capture imagina-
tions."[2] Thus, for eight years Wilson tried to interest major television studios in a series depicting a woman as president of the
United States.[3] "We offered a prize, we offered to pay for a script.
Yet they still didn't think it would interest people," Wilson la-
mented.[4] Finally, in the fall of 2005, ABC took the plunge, launching a new series, *Commander in Chief*, starring Geena Davis as
the first female president of the United States. Davis, who won an
Academy Award for her role in *The Accidental Tourist*, becomes
an "accidental president" when the elected president dies after a
stroke. Serving as vice president when this happens, her character,

Mackenzie Allen, has to decide whether to take over the office of the White House or step down, as virtually everyone advises her to do.

In the pilot episode, there were two big questions for Vice President Allen to resolve. First, *could* she do the job of president?[5] This question is easy. When discussing it with her family, her three children and her husband, Allen confidently proclaims, "I can do this job." The second, more complicated question, in her mind and others, is: *Should* she? The "should" refers to the public's view of appropriate roles for women, particularly of nontraditional political roles that might portend destruction of the societal and familial order. Although prepared to resign in order to let a more seasoned politician assume the position of president, Allen changes her mind upon encountering the blatant sexism of those resistant to the idea that she could—or should—do the job. In the end, she tears up her letter of resignation and takes the Oath of Office, thereby becoming, on TV, the first female president of the United States.

This fictional account of women's political leadership makes an astute diagnosis of the quandary that American women face when seeking higher office: namely, before any woman can convince people that she will be a good (or even a competent) president, she first has to become president. The "could she?" and "should she?" questions haunt women candidates in particular who seek any national political office, much less the presidency itself. While a particular man who aspires to political office might be quizzed on his qualifications as an *individual* as to whether he "should" or "could" be president—that is, whether he's "the right man for the job"— those two questions of competence and suitability are demanded of women as a *group*. People are as likely to ask themselves and each other, "Can a *woman* do this job—and should she?" as they are to ask, "Can this *candidate* do this job—and should she?"

These questions plagued American women even when seeking the right to vote. People asked whether women "could" exercise voting rights responsibly, and whether women "should" be allowed to participate as voters in our democracy. Many emphatically answered "no" to both questions. In terms of "could," Orestes Brownson, a writer, editor, and labor activist, proclaimed in 1873:

> We do not believe women . . . are fit to have their own head. The most degraded of the savage tribes are those in which women rule, and descent is reckoned from the mother instead of the father. Revelation asserts, and universal experience proves that the man is the head of the woman . . . his greatest error, as well as the primal curse of society is that he abdicates his headship, and allows himself to be governed . . . by woman. It was through

the seductions of the woman, herself seduced by the serpent, that man fell, and brought sin and all our woe into the world . . . without masculine direction or control, she [woman] is out of her element, and a social anomaly, sometimes a hideous monster, which men seldom are, except through a woman's influence.[6]

In terms of "should," the answer was also "no" even at the minimum level of voting, for sanctioning women's formal entry into the male sphere of politics promised to many people nothing more than the destruction of the family and concomitantly of society and the nation. As Brownson had argued earlier in 1869,

> The conclusive objection to the political enfranchisement of women is that it would weaken and finally break up and destroy the Christian family. The social unit is the family, not the individual; and the greatest danger to American society is that we are rapidly becoming a nation of isolated individuals, without family ties or affections. . . . Extend now to women suffrage and eligibility; give them the political right to vote, and to be voted for; render it feasible for them to enter the arena of political strife, to become canvassers in elections and candidates for office, and what remains of family union will soon be dissolved . . . and when the family goes, the nation goes too.[7]

Or as Senator George Williams, Republican of Oregon, said in 1866: "When the women . . . love to be jostled . . . [in] trade and business; when they love the treachery and turmoil of politics; when they love the . . . blood of battle better than they love the affections . . . of home and family, then it will be time to talk about . . . women voters." In other words, those who opposed woman suffrage did not believe that women had valuable skills to offer the republic. What women "could" do is maternalism, which they "should" do in the private sphere of the home. For many of those who opposed suffrage, maternal duties and duties of civic governance were ineluctably separate and mutually exclusive.

Historically, the most effective way for women to silence "could" and "should" questions about their capacities for political leadership is simply "to do" it.[8] While *Commander in Chief* is fiction that did not last long on TV, its message, nevertheless, is clear and enduring: once women are given the chance to be political leaders, they can do a very good job. The trick is getting in the door in the first place.[9] In the case of electoral democracies, to "get in the door" means women must first have the right to vote. American women did not receive a national guarantee of their voting rights, the Nineteenth Amendment, until as late as 1920, despite a woman suffrage campaign launched by reformers as early as 1848. As such, worldwide, American women's voting rights lagged behind that of women in comparable democracies. New Zealand, for example, the first country to include women in its electorate, did so as early as 1893. And within the United States, women's acquisition of voting rights lagged far behind that of unpropertied white males, who were enfranchised at the state level in the early nineteenth century, and African American males, who were enfranchised by means of the Fifteenth Amendment that was added to the Constitution in 1870.

What caused American society to change in the early twentieth century, to accept the claim of woman suffrage reformers by ratifying the Nineteenth Amendment? The answer is that the American state for the first time endorsed public policies that provided for economically disadvantaged civilians, thereby representing maternalism as well as individualism. By so doing, the American state became a hybrid political context with policies representing both women's sameness with men and women's maternal group difference from men. In the case of the latter, government took on the job of caring for people, a task the public associates with women as social maternalists who do more care-work than men. The Progressive Era thus retained the American liberal individualist heritage even while becoming a maternalist era. As such, American government became maternal not necessarily because the beneficiaries of its economic policies were women, but rather because it became identified as a legitimate instrument for caring for people, whether the recipients of that care were men or women, adults or children, American citizens or newly arrived immigrants.

The Individualism Heritage

The American state was decidedly liberal at its inception in the eighteenth century and continued to be so through the nineteenth century. In principle, all individuals were politically equal in spite of their group differences, such as race, class, or sex, but in practice they were not so. At the origin of America, states used race, class, and sex qualifications to restrict voting rights. All states invoked some reference to a property requirement as a qualification for voting, though many states allowed substitutions. In Connecticut military service or the payment of taxes could serve in lieu of property ownership; Delaware, Georgia, Maryland, Massachusetts, New Hampshire, North Carolina, Pennsylvania, Rhode Island, and South Carolina all allowed the payment of taxes to substitute for owning property; Georgia allowed people to substitute an occupational status in a mechanical trade for property ownership to meet the qualifications for joining the electorate; and New York, Rhode Island, and Virginia permitted the payment of rent to substitute for property. Turning to race, only six states barred African Americans from voting and one state barred Native Americans from voting. Every state but New Jersey, however, absolutely prohibited women from voting, and by 1808, New Jersey also required that a person be "male" as a requisite for inclusion in the electorate.

It took major efforts over centuries to remove these state-level property, race, and sex restrictions on voting rights, but of all the restrictions, "sex" as a qualification for voting would prove the most intractable. In the early to mid-nineteenth century, for example, reformers successfully invoked individual equality to rid state constitutions of property requirements for the right to vote. As a result, America was a pioneer, the first nation in the world to grant any portion of its citizenry the right to vote without a class-based criterion. When women tried to employ the same argument in the mid-nineteenth century, they completely failed.

Women's organized efforts to obtain the right to vote began with the meeting at Seneca Falls in 1848, which is generally considered the first women's rights conference. The language employed by early woman suffrage leaders, such as Elizabeth Cady Stanton, was decidedly based on liberal individualism. Those attending the conference, for example, drafted a Declaration of Sentiments to enumerate the way law and tradition prohibited women not only from voting but also from access to higher education, employment opportunities, and equal legal status with husbands in marriage. This document explicitly paralleled the language of the American Declaration of Independence, with the crucial modification of identifying men as the oppressor of women instead of King George as the oppressor of American colonists.

Whereas arguments based on liberal, individual equality had worked to gain voting rights for men subordinated because of their class, the same arguments did not work for women, whatever their class. No state dropped sex as a qualification for voting in the nineteenth century.[10] Furthermore, although liberal individualistic arguments succeeded in gaining newly freed African American men the right to vote after the Civil War, those same arguments continued to fail to do the trick for women. Northern women had been active in the abolition movement leading up to the war and in the war itself, so they fully expected to be included in the reconstruction of the American state after the Union victory. Congress, however, balked at including sex along with race in the Fifteenth Amendment on the grounds that to do so would be too revolutionary. Men would not support women's voting rights, and states would never ratify an amendment guaranteeing blacks a right to vote if such an amendment included women's right to vote. The consequence would be that the Fifteenth Amendment would fail and that neither blacks nor women would gain the vote. Thus, the Fifteenth Amendment prohibited states only from using race as a qualification for voting, thereby constitutionally allowing states to continue to bar women from the electorate. When the Fifteenth Amendment was added to the Constitution in 1870, every state in the country prohibited women from voting.

Although women in the nineteenth century did employ the instrument of liberal protest to challenge their exclusion from the public sphere of political governance, they failed to gain entry to the electorate at either the state or national levels. Liberal individualism alone was clearly insufficient for achieving women's political inclusion as voters. Women did not gain a constitutional guarantee of the right to vote until the addition of the Nineteenth Amendment to the Constitution in 1920. This achievement is significant not just for its timing but also for the political context in which it was accomplished, namely, one marked by a hybrid combination of public policies representing individual equality and maternal traits associated with women.

The Hybrid State in the Progressive Era

The liberal heritage of the American state in some ways stalled if not regressed in the Progressive era when it came to the political and civil rights of subordinate groups. It is in this period that Southern states adopted voting regulations that had the effect of disenfranchising African American men and poor whites. Although African American men had gained the constitutional right to vote with the addition of the Fifteenth Amendment to the Constitution, that right was undermined at this time with the passage of state-level legislation establishing requirements such as literacy tests, poll taxes, and registration standards that made it virtually impossible for blacks or poor whites in the South to exercise the right to vote.[11] Immigrants also fared badly in terms of their civil rights. Literacy tests were invoked at the national level as a qualification for immigrant entry into the United States. So, too, did Northern states at this time adopt voting procedures such as registration and ballot formats that had the effect of making it more difficult for the masses of urban, illiterate immigrants to vote. In addition, during the Progressive Era, state-level eugenic policies flourished in such practices as forced sterilization, thereby seriously compromising the civil rights of those most vulnerable.[12] It is also possible to interpret support for prohibition in the early twentieth century, which eventually culminated in a constitutional amendment, as a mechanism used by native born, white, Protestants to control the life-style choices of "alien," newly arrived peoples from parts of the world whose consumption of alcohol, particularly beer and wine, signaled nothing more than unwanted diversity in America.

Despite these serious flaws, in other ways the Progressive Era remained a period when liberal individualism thrived. In fact, some of the individualism that was institutionalized at the state level even seems extreme. Take the case of *Lochner v. New York*,[13] a 1905 Supreme Court decision involving bakers in New York who were all but coerced to work extremely long hours, or face losing their livelihood. The state of New York, wishing to protect workers from this sort of exploitation, passed legislation restricting employers from requiring such long hours without overtime compensation. The Supreme Court overturned the law on the grounds that workers, as individuals, enjoyed the freedom of contract to consent or not to consent to the conditions of their employment. Far be it for the state to interfere with the workers' freedom of contract, for to do so would violate workers' rights as individuals to make contractual choices as protected by the Due Process Clause of the Fourteenth Amendment. While such a reading of the Constitution may appall us today, the decision testifies to the strength in the Progressive Era of the liberal principles of individualism, consensual contract, and the negative individual rights of people to be free from government interference in their lives. Liberal individualism, therefore, while compromised by race and class bias, nevertheless remained as a constitutional and legislative precept for shaping the laws of the land.

What is significant about the Progressive Era, however, is that it is a time that also marks the fledgling adoption at both state and federal levels of maternal policies providing for the economic needs of people suffering the effects of the rapidly industrializing American state.[14] Political scientist Theda Skocpol describes the early decades of the twentieth century as a time when America pioneered a new form of welfare state, which she terms "maternalistic."[15] The model of maternal care that is ordinarily associated with women's motherhood roles in the private, domestic sphere of the home shifted at least slightly to the public sphere of the state. These policies often specifically benefited women, but that does not make them maternal. What makes them maternal is the government's engagement in the type of work that the public associates with women. One innovation was the extensive statewide policy of mothers' pension legislation, which authorized state governments to provide monetary benefits to women who were stranded without economic support due to the absence of their husbands and the fathers of their children. The passage of this legislation spread like wildfire as state after state took up the cause of protecting women and children from the ravages of what was, at that time, a brutal and relatively unregulated phase of industrial economic development.

Class and race biases, however, also affected the implementation of maternal public policies. As historian Joanne Goodwin and legal scholar Dorothy Roberts note, states implemented such policies as mothers' pensions unfairly by failing to include African American mothers. In addition, to be eligible, recipients were required to meet moral standards set in place by those more advantaged. Aid was withheld from deserted families and from unwed mothers.[16] As political scientist Gwendolyn Mink puts it, such policies are a form of "sticky racial liberalism that conditioned equality on similarity."[17] In addition to excluding people on the basis of race, these policies excluded people on the basis of nontraditional family structures.

Nevertheless, reframing maternalism to locate it inside the state was a potent new component of American government, and it created new ways for social movement activists to marshal the public on behalf of women's voting rights.[18] Welfare policies, for example, not only provided women with resources that increased their opportunities to mobilize and be active in politics,[19] welfare provision also defined the public sphere as an arena of mothering activity. And who would be best suited for participation in such an arena but mothers—women—themselves. Using this new frame, woman suffrage reformers could then claim—and did—that women should have the right to vote not only because they were individuals who were the same as men but also because they were maternalists who were different from men.

Social Citizenship in the Progressive Era

Social citizenship refers to the government's guarantee that people will have at least their minimum economic needs met, such as food, health, clothing, shelter, and education. Many scholars date the Progressive Era as the first instance in the United States of the government's guarantee of social citizenship, referred to by historian Philip Ethington as the "birthplace" of the American welfare state.[20] At the time the damages wrought by rampant industrialization on people's health and welfare were highly visible and horrifyingly severe. The urban poverty, anonymity, and misery created by unregulated industrialization were unlike anything Americans had ever seen before. Many strove to improve the working conditions of children and adults caught literally and figuratively within the gears of a factory system that was dangerous to their health and well-being. Private and religious charities until then had assumed the leading role of providing for the indigent and those unable to care for themselves. Reformers in the Progressive Era argued that it now required the action of government to provide for people's welfare.

Political sociologist Elisabeth Clemens establishes the power of people's lobbies to bring the state into play when dealing with the welfare needs accompanying breakneck industrialization. During the Progressive Era, women, farmers, and labor organized to change how the state would act, not only at the state level but also at the national level.[21] According to Clemens, it was the power of these people, not the legislation emanating from a privileged middle class, that effected political remedies by using the resources of government. In addition to federated women's organizations getting mothers' pension legislation passed in states, a wide array of grass-roots actors and organizations were involved.

The welfare domain, broadly defined, resulted from the expansion at the time of the American state in at least two major areas of economic policies. First, reformers invented the term *poverty*, thereby shifting responsibility for social and economic problems from individuals to market forces, and hence shifting the needs of the disadvantaged "from charity to entitlement."[22] Second, redefining the causes of social problems expanded the jurisdiction of state power to encompass regulation of at least the most egregious effects of a capitalist economic system upon people.

Some reformers in the Progressive Era, such as Muckrakers, attempted to stimulate the adoption of welfare legislation simply by documenting the severity of the effects of immigration, urbanization, and industrialization.[23] Typical of these compelling descriptions of urban economic distress is one by William Dean Howells:

> to be in it [New York poverty], and not have the distance, is to inhale the stenches of the neglected street, and to catch yet fouler and dreadfuller poverty-smell which breathes from the open doorways. It is to see the children quarreling in their games, and beating each other in the face, and rolling each other in the gutter, like the little savage outlaws they are. It is to see the work-worn look of mothers, the squalor of the babes.[24]

By inventing the word *poverty* to define economic distress and its causes, Progressive Era reformers signified that market forces were responsible for an individual's economic deprivation in contrast to the earlier term, *pauperism*, that had implied a person's character or lack of will caused economic deprivation.[25] As Samuel Mencher notes, there was a "gradual shift from individual to social causation [of economic misery] at the beginning of the twentieth century" as the preoccupation with "unique individual characteristics" accounting for economic suffering gave way to consideration of "the social and economic conditions affecting the general well-being."[26] Or as Robert Fogel puts it, the Progressive Era was distinctive for replacing the notion that "sin causes economic ills" with the notion that "economic ills cause sin."[27]

Assigning social and economic problems to forces beyond the individual's control had been an obvious rationale for state intervention when economic distress was associated with a major force such as war, which was clearly beyond the control of any one individual. Consequently, the very first economic assistance provided by the federal government to individuals for income security was veterans' pensions in the aftermath of the Civil War. Extending this principle of causation to the processes of laissez-faire capitalism, however, represented a profound departure from long-dominant premises in American liberal culture that stressed just the opposite.[28] This departure underlies what John Buenker considers the "launching" of the American welfare state.[29]

In the Progressive Era, those disadvantaged by the market system came more and more to be seen as the victims of forces beyond their control, and the use of governmental power to intervene on their behalf became more legitimate.[30] As James Weinstein puts it, one of the major changes that took place in the liberal state in the Progressive Era is the "replacement of the ideological concepts of laissez faire" with an "ideal of a responsible social order in which all classes could look forward to some form of recognition and sharing in the benefits of an ever-expanding economy."[31] As a result, millions of middle-class citizens as well as officeholders came to believe that the adverse effects of industrial capitalism could be humanized through regulatory legislation that set limits to business and purified politics. In Richard Hofstadter's view, the Progressive era is unique in America history as a time when reformers were successful for the first time in establishing the premise that government is responsible for the welfare of citizens, particularly those who are poor and the most powerless.[32] A key characteristic of economic and welfare policies at the time was, therefore, their legitimation of state regulation as a means of setting limits to the damaging effects of uncontrolled industrial capitalism.[33] With rare exceptions, legislation stopped short of monetary provision or social insurance.[34] Nonetheless, these policies were innovative by virtue of reformulating the scope and authority of the American state to include regulatory intervention in what hitherto had been sacrosanct laissez-faire relationships between employers and laborers and between consumers and business. If only for this reason, the early twentieth century was an era of major institution building and reform.[35]

At the top of the policy agenda were antitrust legislation; social justice measures, such as workmen's compensation, minimum wage and hours, vocational educational legislation; urban housing codes; and child welfare legislation, such as child-labor laws, educational programs, mothers' pensions, and maternal health services.[36] Eugene Tobin identifies the dual combination of a "concern for positive government intervention and a sensitivity for reform" as the distinguishing feature linking the Progressive Era with subsequent achievements in the New Deal.[37] Prior to 1900, for example, fifteen states, spanning a regional cross-section, passed laws for railroad and streetcar workers and after the turn of the century another sixteen states added similar statutes. Railroad regulation reached the national level as early as 1907, when Congress passed a law specifying that train men must have ten hours of rest after sixteen consecutive hours of work and that train dispatchers must have a nine-hour working day.[38] By 1920 all but five states had enacted workmen's compensation legislation,[39] and major bills, passed at the national level in 1909 and 1916, eventually covered "about one-fourth of the civilian employees of the United States.[40] At the state level, fourteen states enacted the more controversial minimum wage legislation between 1912 and 1923.

Child labor legislation also succeeded at both the state and national levels. By 1914 all but one state had a minimum age (usually fourteen), and some restrictions for the employment of children in dangerous occupations and nighttime work.[41] The regulation of child labor was successfully passed in Congress in 1916, only to be overturned by the Supreme Court, and a constitutional amendment passed Congress in 1924, only to fail the ratification process.[42] Passage of mothers' pensions was achieved in all but two states[43] between 1913 and 1931.[44]

Establishing the government's involvement in welfare provision was important to women's right to vote because it cast the state as a careworker, whether the beneficiaries are women or not. The assumption of care-work roles by the government, corresponding to the roles the public attributes to women, then predisposes the public and political officeholders to view women as more connected to government, hence as more suitable to be voters, and eventually to be political officeholders. What is more, in periods of change requiring social movements to achieve political equality for women, a political environment in which the state "acts like a woman," enhances the ability of activists to claim that women as a group, long associated with social maternalism through their care-work, belong "in" the state, at least as voters, not "outside" the state.

Hybrid Arguments for Woman Suffrage

The government's *hybrid* performance of social maternalism along with traditional individualism in the Progressive Era led to hybrid arguments for woman suffrage. The term *woman* itself, rather than *women*, was used more often by suffrage leaders when advocating women's voting rights. Although *woman* suffrage may sound funny to modern ears, it was thought to be a more appropriate term because of its parallel with the term *manhood* suffrage, which had been the focus of nineteenth-century reform efforts. For this reason references to women's activism in the Progressive Era to secure voting rights for women generally refer to the *woman* suffrage movement.

It was not as if the Progressive Era was the first time people happened to notice that those who become pregnant and bear children are women, not men, or that women, instead of men, are the ones who do most of the care-work in society. Since the founding of the American state (if not before), patriots had celebrated women's special maternal duties as wives and mothers. They honored and enforced the concept of what Linda Kerber terms "Republican Motherhood," the notion that the health and future of the republic depends on women's contributions in the private sphere of the family as child-bearers and child-rearers who provide care and nurturance to produce good citizens.[45]

The provision of care-work had never been considered a public duty that fell within the scope of the state's responsibilities to its citizens, and women's performance of their maternal duties had always been circumscribed by legal, social, and cultural forces within the private, domestic sphere. During the Progressive Era the American state for the first time took on maternal roles via public policies that corresponded to women's maternal identities as people who differed from men. In this way the state's performance of maternalism made nonsense of Republican Motherhood arguments for the disenfranchisement of women, such as Orestes Brownson's fulminating in the previous century that if one were to, "give [women] the right to vote . . . what remains of family union will soon be dissolved . . . and when the family goes, the nation goes too."[46]

It became extremely difficult to argue that women should be kept from participating in governance as voters because of their maternal duties to the family, when the state itself was undertaking those same duties in its public policies. The maternalization of the state in the Progressive Era demolished the separation of private, familial responsibilities from civic, political responsibilities. By bringing the family back in to the state, Progressive Era reformers reinstituted the principle Founders had destroyed when they delegitimized the fusion of the family with the state by means of a violent revolution that demolished the American monarchical heritage. The state's performance of maternal duties in the Progressive Era once again conferred to maternalism a political meaning as a signifier and attribute of the public sphere of the state, not just an attribute of the private sphere of the family.

It did not take woman suffrage reformers long to argue that the state could perform its new maternalistic policies even better if members of the group associated with maternalism—women—were allowed to vote. Given the tenacity of the American individualist liberal heritage, arguing in favor of a subordinate group's political citizenship because of their group difference, rather than in spite of it was—and still is—a novelty, to say the least. That argument had never been advanced in the case of race or class inequalities. And although it had been included as a sidebar to liberal arguments by woman suffrage reformers in the late nineteenth century, it had by no means held equal footing with liberal rationales for women's political citizenship. The emphasis on maternalism arguments for woman suffrage in the Progressive Era along with individualistic ones, therefore, was all but unprecedented.

Suffrage reformers' claim that women should be added to the electorate because of their maternal group difference became such a dominant rhetorical mechanism, according to Aileen Kraditor, as to all but replace the liberal individualist arguments of the nineteenth-century.[47] Women's group difference, according to Alexander Keyssar, was transformed from a reason to be politically excluded to a reason to be politically included.[48] Views that women would elevate the tone of politics by putting an end to "scoundrelism and ruffianism," particularly in urban areas, were embraced by many male politicians, who seemed more comfortable stressing women's unique virtues rather than their similarity to men. And men after all were the ones with the power to vote for woman suffrage in Congress or to defeat it. The idea that enfranchising women would "tend to impart integrity and honesty to politics, and to control the tricks of those who make politics their trade," became a "difference" argument easily accepted by both political office-holders and the public at large.[49]

Despite the new emphasis on women's maternal difference, liberal arguments about individual equality did not disappear from suffrage rhetoric. To the contrary, arguments that women should have the right to vote in spite of their sex difference from men *also* continued to flourish in the Progressive Era. The continuation and development of these sameness arguments may have tipped the balance for the success and ratification of the Nineteenth Amendment, according to Ellen Carol DuBois, who traces how Elizabeth Cady Stanton's nineteenth-century liberal legacy continued into the Progressive Era via her own daughter, Harriot Stanton Blatch, a noted woman suffrage activist in the state of New York.[50]

The use in the Progressive Era of two different sets of arguments for woman suffrage corresponds to the fledgling hybrid character of American public policies. Just as the American state continued to embody liberal principles even as it added maternalist principles to them, so was women's acquisition of the right to vote in the Progressive Era founded on a combination of individualism and maternalism. This conjunction of maternalism and individualism served as a foundation for women's access to formal political representation as voters in two arenas: reform organizations and Congress.

Hybrid Reform Rhetoric

Mainstream suffrage organizations, such as the National American Woman Suffrage Association (NAWSA), are most often identified as using maternal difference arguments. However, their rhetoric typically combined both maternal difference arguments and individual equality arguments.

The basic outlines of the maternalist, difference rationale for woman suffrage were stated by NAWSA president Anna Howard Shaw:

> The problems of our government are constructive: How shall we house, feed and rear our people? How are we to erect our tenements with light and with air, how to equip them with proper fire protection; how shall we make our streets clean, how shall we banish contagious and preventable diseases; how shall we stop the smoke nuisance; how shall we stop sweated business in the homes of the poor; how shall little children's lives be spared from avaricious business which contaminates food and drink. How to stop child labor and the traffic in girlhood? These are the problems of the Government today which come home to the lives of women and which women understand and feel more keenly than men.[51]

Such difference arguments would be expected from a representative of a mainstream woman suffrage organization. Less well known is the way social feminist leaders characteristically combined maternal group difference with the equality of individuals. Both Anna Howard Shaw, who became president of NAWSA in 1905, and Carrie Chapman Catt, who took over leadership in 1916 and saw the Suffrage Amendment through to the end, consistently used both types of arguments in their own campaigns for women's right to vote. That both Shaw and Catt used difference arguments to advance the suffrage cause is well known, but their advance of sameness, individual equality, arguments on behalf of woman suffrage is often overlooked. Their writings illustrate the hybrid maternalism-individualism combination at work within a suffrage organization.

As Shaw stated, "all humanity was created equal and women are human. All human rights are equal, all human rights are inalienable, all human rights are indestructible, without reference to sex, or color, or race, or creed. . . . these [are] fundamental principles [of] the constitution of the United States."[52] In later years Shaw not only restated these equality arguments but also began to discredit difference arguments, objecting that they tended to cancel out individual equality: "the trouble with people is that they are not able to forget for a moment when they discuss the political position of women that women are human beings. Most men think of them in terms of mother, or wife, or sister, etc. Men are tolerably reasonable when they discuss problems of justice, freedom and right in regard to men, but the moment that the question arises in regard to women, they seem to lose their heads and go off on a tangent."[53]

Shaw went so far as to speculate that it might be a mistake to think that women would vote differently from men or be counted on, to vote to change society. "I dislike to discuss the subject from that standpoint [that women vote for social policies] not because there are not sufficient proofs in the country . . . but because I prefer to discuss it, woman suffrage, on the fundamental basis of a republican form of government."[54]

Carrie Chapman Catt believed women's difference from men manifested itself in a variety of ways, including differences in character, conscience, and capabilities. She held firmly that "men must climb up and that women must always refuse to go down."[55] To Catt, women's policy priorities differed from those of men so fundamentally that by excluding women from the ballot box, the government "continues to make and to enforce laws not only without regard to the wishes or opinions of its women citizens, but often in direct opposition to the known views of the majority of them."[56] She also ascribed different abilities to women and men, saying that women are used to taking "half a loaf" and doing much more with it than men.[57] She declared that "the virtues of women are assets worth having in a government," implying not only that women's virtues differ from men's but also that they are absent from government.[58]

For Catt, these differences between women and men meant a pragmatic and observable difference in behavior, whether with or without the vote. Excluded from suffrage, "the best types of [rich] women . . . have engaged their activities in good works. The land is covered with the institutions which such women have built and are maintaining. Along a thousand avenues their hands are outstretched to uplift the fallen, to guide the erring, to help the weak, to strengthen our entire social machinery."[59] Without the right to vote, women's efforts were limited in scope to the domestic and eleemosynary. As voters, women would be able to effect fundamental change in the societal conditions that left so many in need. Catt considered the vote "a tool with which to build a better nation,"[60] giving women the leverage to enact humane and decent legislation that would help women and children and clean up corruption. She claimed that, "From that moment they seek the vote, not only as a right denied them, but as a duty that they may aid the reclamation of democracy from the degradation to which in too many localities it has been allowed to sink."[61]

Some might argue that Shaw's reliance on individual equality and sameness is understandable, given that she was born in the nineteenth century, when this type of argument for suffrage was dominant. Yet Catt, a leader from the following generation, made use of individual equality arguments as well. Echoing the 1848 Seneca Falls Declaration of Sentiments, she equates woman suffrage with the Declaration of Independence: "woman suffrage became an assured fact when the Declaration of Independence was written . . . woman suffrage rests exactly upon the same basis as man suffrage. Women ask for it because it is the right of a citizen of a Republic to express a ballot's share in the making of the law the citizen is expected to obey."[62]

If anything, the advent of World War I intensified Catt's reliance on the equality of all citizens as a basis for suffrage. In fact, she referred to sameness twice as often as to difference arguments. Thus, even within NAWSA, a mainstream organization that exemplified the maternalist argument in the Progressive Era, suffrage leaders characteristically combined it with the sameness argument.

Hybrid Congressional Rhetoric

Congressional debates around woman suffrage, also display the fusion of maternalist and individual equality arguments. Those arguing on behalf of woman suffrage paradoxically reason that women should have the right to vote both because of and in spite of their group difference from men. Representative Philip Campbell, Republican of Kansas, articulated the difference argument by stating, "woman has been equal to every duty that has been imposed upon her and to every responsibility she has assumed. The franchise will give her opportunities to do good in the republic. . . . Women will raise the standard in politics, as she raised and maintained the standard in every relation she sustains in life."[63] In a similar vein, Representative Melville Clyde Kelly, a Progressive Party member from Pennsylvania, noted, "I go further and maintain the Nation needs the vote of its womanhood fully as much as the women need the ballot. This Nation needs intelligent, educated voters and more girls than boys are being graduated from our high schools and colleges every year . . . it needs law-abiding voters and women form the minority of all criminal and vicious classes, . . . Is women's place in the home? Then she must have the vote to protect her home."[64] Representative Victor Murdock, another Kansas Republican, joined the chorus of difference advocates by stating, "Woman does not need suffrage so much as suffrage needs woman and the impress of her high, uncompromising and ennobling instinct and capacity for civic decency."[65]

Often, the very same legislators who proposed that women's difference from men was the reason they should be granted suffrage argued that women should have the right to vote precisely in spite of that difference. The same Representative Kelly who reasoned that women's natural integrity and lack of criminality should gain them the vote also advanced the classic liberal individualist argument that,

> woman suffrage is a natural evolution in that democracy which has traversed the centuries, gaining new victories with every conflict. The ballot has always been regarded as the symbol of human liberty and it has been secured by larger groups in every forward movement . . . I believe in woman's suffrage because I believe in democracy . . . Women are citizens, they are part of the people and they have the right to help elect those who shall represent them and to help make the laws under which they shall live and to which they must render obedience.[66]

Similarly, Kansas Representative Murdock who in arguing for suffrage had championed women's "high, uncompromising, and ennobling" instincts which made them inherently different from men, also professed his liberal belief in women's equality:

> I hold that this [woman suffrage] is the next step in the development of the democracy, for democracy can best be developed through more democracy, the moving up of the individual closer to the process of his Government—

local, State, and National. And, the movement cannot be complete or ef-
ficacious if one-half of the social fabric only is affected . . . the women of
America are equal in intellect and capacity and in the law, [and women]
must move up with him [men].[67]

The congressional record, therefore, reveals the hybrid combination of
both women's group difference from men and women's equality with men
as justifications for woman suffrage. A combination made possible by the
hybrid character of the American state itself at this time.

The Briefly Maternalized American State

Social reformers advocating on behalf of women's voting rights in the
United States in the Progressive Era capitalized on the government's
adoption of policies based on individualism and maternalism by means of
a new rhetoric that corresponded to the hybrid political context generated by such policies. Consequently, women became the first group in the
United States to be included politically not only because of their individual
sameness with others, but also because of their group difference. This political achievement, however, stalled after women's voting rights were obtained, rather than continuing to advance in the form of women's election
in sizeable percentages to political office. The reason is because the hybrid
phase of the American state in the Progressive Era was as remarkable as
it was brief. Within a few years of women obtaining a national, constitutional guarantee of the right to vote, Congress rescinded and the Supreme
Court repealed policies representing maternal traits, such as the Sheppard-
Towner Act and protective labor legislation for women, respectively.

The Sheppard-Towner Act, passed in 1921, was a remarkable piece of
legislation in the context of American political development. It was the
first national law to allocate federal funds for the provision of health care,
in this case to pregnant women and infants. To say that this legislation
challenged the American liberal heritage of individual equality is a severe
understatement, as is dramatically evident in the debates it provoked in
Congress prior to its passage. As historian J. Stanley Lemons notes, the
Sheppard-Towner Act was the "first venture of the federal government
into social security legislation."[68] And it was sorely needed. In 1918 the
United States ranked seventeenth among the world's nations for maternal
mortality and eleventh for infant mortality. The U.S. Children's Bureau had
investigated and conclusively documented the correlation between poverty
and mortality rates. For families in the lowest income group, those earning

less than $450 annually, one out of six babies died before reaching their first birthday; that figure dropped to one in ten for families earning slightly more, or $650–$850 annually; and for families earning about $1,250 annually the mortality rate fell further, to one in sixteen.[69]

Nations with a program of care for mothers and infants had significantly lower mortality rates. In New Zealand, for example, the infant mortality rate for families earning the equivalent of $1,250 annually was one in twenty-one, or less than 5%.[70] Armed with this evidence, some members of Congress wanted to implement a similar program in the United States. Representative Jeannette Rankin, a Montana Republican, was the first woman to serve as a member of Congress and an early advocate of such legislation. She had been able to be elected because women in Montana had state-level voting rights prior to the adoption in 1920 of the Nineteenth Amendment, which gave all women voting rights on the basis of a national guarantee. In 1918, the year after she was elected, she introduced a bill to provide federal funds for the protection of mothers and infants. It did not pass. In the following (66th) Congress, Texas Democratic Senator Morris Sheppard and Iowa Republican Congressman Horace Towner reintroduced Rankin's bill as the Sheppard-Towner Act.

Again the bill went nowhere, until the Nineteenth Amendment was added to the Constitution in 1920.[71] After its ratification, the NAWSA reconstituted itself as the League of Women Voters and assisted in the creation of the Women's Joint Congressional Committee (WJCC). This organization's purpose was to coordinate lobbying activities in Washington for nearly twenty-four national women's organizations, said to represent 20 million members.[72] Now that members of Congress were accountable to their female constituents, they feared the power of the woman's vote. Women had promised—or threatened, as the case may be—to support welfare legislation that would help people. Implementing protective legislation for mothers and infants was an obvious choice, and it became the first goal of the major women's organizations in the aftermath of the woman suffrage success.[73]

Lobbying on behalf of the Sheppard-Towner Act was intense, "one of the strongest lobbies" that had ever been seen in Washington, according to contemporary accounts. Wielding the massive power of 20 million women's votes, the WJCC explicitly told congressmen that if they did not support passage of the Sheppard-Towner Act, they could expect every woman in their district to vote against them in the next election.[74]

The gambit worked, and the Sheppard-Towner Act passed with a margin of 279 to 39.[75] Although groundbreaking in its legislative intent, the act was modest in its provision for mothers and children. It authorized an appropriation of $1,480,000 for fiscal years 1921–22, and another $1,240,000 for each of the next five years, until June 30, 1927. In distributing these funds, the act specified that each state would get $5,000 outright; that if states could provide matching funds, each state would get another $5,000; and that the remaining funds would be allocated on the basis of population and matching funds. The act set a limit of $50,000 for its administration, and the Children's Bureau was designated as the administrator. In order for a state to be eligible to receive funds, the act required that the state must first pass enabling legislation, then provide a satisfactory plan for implementation, and, finally, come up with the required matching funds. The act specified that neither the state nor the federal government could enter a home or take custody of a child without a judicial order. Its goal was to provide instruction in maternal hygiene and infant care by means of child-care conferences, public health and visiting nurses, consultation centers, and the distribution of informational literature.[76]

Even with matching state funds, the total each state would have for the provision of maternal and infant health instruction was about $10,000 in most cases. Such a budget was ridiculously puny. In contrast, the governor of New York signed a legislative bill that appropriated $125,000 for the construction of a single hog barn at the State Fair in 1922; he signed an identical bill in 1923.[77] Despite the modest scale of the Sheppard-Towner Act, those against it were all but hysterical in their opposition to this "dangerous" piece of legislation. Organizations like the American Medical Association (AMA) denounced it as being hostile and contradictory to the liberal tradition of the American state. Others went so far as to call the law a "Bolshevik conspiracy" designed to destroy the American state.

For these critics, maternalist policies were so illiberal as to be associated with an entirely different political system, the Soviet Union, whose values were seen to be in direct conflict with those of the United States. Some of the most vocal opponents of the act were also opponents of another example of state maternalism: woman suffrage. For instance, the Woman Patriots organization, which described the Sheppard-Towner Act as a "feminist-socialist-communist plot" to undermine the very character of the American state, had previously been known as the National Association Opposed to Woman Suffrage. As Mary Kilbreth, a leading antisuffragist, stated, "there are many loyal American men and women . . . who believe that this bill [the Sheppard-Towner Act], [is] inspired by foreign experiments in Communism . . . [and that it] strikes at the heart of our American civilization."[78] Suffrage and civil rights leader Florence Kelley's efforts supporting the act earned her the appellation "the ablest legislative general Communism has produced."[79]

Others characterized the legislation as an improper intrusion of the federal government into the realm of states' rights. Even more vehement opposition came from medical doctors and health practitioners themselves. Although the Medical Woman's National Association supported the Sheppard-Towner Act, the AMA intensely opposed the legislation on grounds that it was the beginning of "state medicine."[80] The AMA had taken progressive stances in the early twentieth century on some health legislation, such as pure food and drug regulation, professionalization of medical care, and the establishment of the federal Department of Health. The AMA had failed, however, to support legislation designed to deal with major problems of a rapidly industrializing American state, such as child labor, women's poor working conditions, factory hazards in general, and the egregious conditions prevailing in slums and tenements. In the case of the Sheppard-Towner Act, the AMA did much more than merely exhibit benign neglect. It actively condemned the involvement of the state in any form of health insurance or health care in general and in the Sheppard-Towner Act in particular, labeling that act as an "imported socialist scheme."[81] State medical societies led the attack on the Sheppard-Towner Act. As an official of the Illinois State Medical Society declared, "today Washington, D.C., is a hotbed of Bolshevism . . . where will it all end? We know where it ended in ruined Russia. . . . Can the people of America set up Bureaucratic Autocracy in Washington without a resulting industrial slavery?"[82]

Opponents nevertheless failed to prevent the initial passage of this pioneering act, which succeeded in reducing infant mortality rates by providing needed infant and maternal health assistance. Prior to passage of the Sheppard-Towner Act, a mere forty-two organizations located in only thirty cities had provided assistance to promote infant health.[83] While the act was in effect, nearly 3,000 centers were established to promote child health, maternity hygiene, or both. What is more, these were permanent centers. By 1928, with states providing about 55% of the funds, the total money expended for child and maternity health was over $2 million.[84] In the seven years during which the act was implemented, the Children's Bureau reported that it made possible more than 3 million home visits, distributed in excess of 22 million pieces of literature, reached more than 4 million infants and 700,000 expectant mothers, and organized over 183,000 health conferences. As a result, the infant death rate dropped from 75 per thousand live births to 64 per thousand, and the maternal death rate dropped from over 67 per thousand to 62.3 per thousand.[85]

Regardless of the lives saved by the legislation, congressmen and politicians gradually lost concern about a women's voting bloc. In the elections of 1922, 1924, and 1926 women failed to demonstrate their power at the polls. Women did not turn out to vote in the percentages expected and did not exhibit partisan loyalties, leaving an open field for opponents of the Sheppard-Towner Act to make their case without fear of it resulting in their electoral defeat. This brief attempt to institutionalize social maternalism as a component of the federal government's policies came to an end in 1929, when Congress failed to renew the act.

State maternalism in the form of protective labor legislation for women was also short-lived, confined to the early decades of the twentieth century. In 1923 the Supreme Court reversed its ruling in *Muller* and declared it unconstitutional to treat women differently in employment contexts because of their maternal capacities and roles. The case in question, *Adkins v. Children's Hospital,* involved a District of Columbia law that established minimum wages for women but not for men.[86] In a five-to-three majority opinion, the Court decreed that "we cannot accept the doctrine that women of mature age, *sui juris*, require or may be subjected to restrictions upon their liberty of contract which could not lawfully be imposed in the case of men under similar circumstances."[87] Woman suffrage itself was advanced on the liberal doctrine of women's individual equality with men, who should be treated the same in all contexts in spite of their sex group difference. Although the success of the Nineteenth Amendment rested on a combination of maternalism and individualism, the language of the amendment itself was purely the language of individualism. As Congress and courts began to prune back the maternalist foothold gained in the Progressive Era, all that was left was individualism, leaving the American state much like when it was founded.

In the wake of a return to individualism alone as a principle for establishing public policies, however, some women reformers, such as Florence Kelley, continued to work toward an expanded institutionalization of maternalism by seeking to nationalize labor legislative policies that gave special benefits, protections, and privileges to women. Kelley, a lawyer,[88] did not explicitly reference women's maternal group difference from men in her arguments for protective labor legislation for women.[89] Instead, she attempted to redefine state action in the context of the American liberal, individualistic heritage so as to include an obligation to "the new social relations and responsibilities of industrial life."[90] To this end, she sought to use the inherent regulatory power of the state "to pass laws that protect the health, safety, and welfare of its citizens—to enact laws that serve the interests of working people, and women and children in particular."[91] Hers was a visionary version of the welfare state, where state maternalism meant that the needs for the nurturance of people, particularly of children and mothers, would be met by the government. Fundamentally Kelley was developing social citizenship, a set of social rights that government was obliged to recognize.

Kelley's attempt to incorporate maternalism into America's public policies, however, ultimately failed. In this battle over political inclusion, only the liberal arguments succeeded. A case in point is Alice Paul, a suffrage leader who while considering variations of the Equal Rights Amendment, was pressured to include exceptions for women's protective labor legislation. In the end, however, the version that she finally submitted to Congress was individualistically liberal to its core. Her ERA stated, "no distinction between the rights of the sexes shall exist within the United States or any place subject to its jurisdiction."[92] In a similar vein, the liberty of contract principle established in *Adkins* was adopted by the National Woman's Party as the foundation of their "ambitious vision of women's complete equality with men in all social and legal relations."[93] In the end, the principles behind the ERA triumphed, not maternal principles underlying Kelley's protections for people in need of care.

The failure of the American state to sustain the inclusion of social maternalism as a component of basic public policies continued with the New Deal. Some call the New Deal revolutionary because it created a novel kind of "liberal regime" at the federal level.[94] Instead of defining welfare provision as a form of maternalist "care-work," Franklin Delano Roosevelt cast the social service policies of the New Deal in the classic liberal vocabulary of rights and contracts. In 1932, for example, Roosevelt explained his rationale: "Government is a relation of give and take, a contract. . . . The task of statesmanship has always been the redefinition of these [contractual] rights in terms of a changing and growing social order. New conditions [such as an economic Depression] impose new requirements upon Government and those who conduct Government," including new policies to provide support for those in need.[95]

The New Deal legislative policies were oriented primarily toward providing care for paid, productive workers. To the extent that women fell into the productive labor categories recognized by the New Deal, they were "included in the same manner as similarly situated men."[96] In practice, given that women were generally excluded from the realm of productive labor in the 1930s, most New Deal policies did not include women, except to the extent that women were married to paid, productive laboring men.[97] Old-age insurance policies of the New Deal, for instance, were available only to full-time workers in the paid labor force, a category that included only 25% of women in the United States.[98]

What is more, women who may initially have been eligible for New Deal social services as full-time members of the paid labor force immediately

lost that eligibility if they left the work force in order to engage in reproductive labor, whether in its biological aspect of being pregnant and giving
birth or in its social aspect of providing care to dependents. By 1945 at least
eleven states considered that women's relinquishment of productive labor
in the workforce in favor of reproductive labor through either pregnancy
or family obligations was grounds to disqualify them from unemployment
benefits.[99]

As political scientist Suzanne Mettler notes, "Ironically, the major route
through which women did gain access to the national realm [of social pro-
vision] . . . in the New Deal was through incorporation on a distinctly
nonliberal basis."[100] That is, women gained access to economic provision
for care-work by means of their maternal roles as wives, widows, or mothers. In 1939, New Deal policies added the provision that wives and widows
of men who qualified for the Old Age Insurance program would also be
included in the benefits.[101]

The extent of women's exclusion from these policies is seen in the one
case where the New Deal did attempt to adopt policies representing maternalism, namely, in legislation creating Aid to Dependent Children (ADC).
Modeled after the mothers' pension legislation of the Progressive Era,
ADC was intended to provide economic support to mothers and children
who lacked the support of a male productive laborer.[102] Essentially ADC
was meant to require the government to pay for the social reproductive
labor activities of mothers. However, as the legislation was going through
drafts, "mothers" significantly disappeared from the wording of the law,
which ended up referring only to the needs of children,[103] the recipients of
reproductive labor, not the reproductive laborers themselves.

Furthermore, the reproductive labor foundation of the ADC made it difficult for the public to accept. The problem was the potential disconnection
of ADC from productive labor. A child in need of care may or may not be
in a family context with a connection to a productive laborer. The child of
an unmarried, unemployed mother, for instance, has no legal connection to
a paid, productive laborer. Such children were continually excluded in the
allocation and administration of ADC benefits. In 1938, 75,000 children
were born out of wedlock; yet only 2% of the children who received ADC
funds were born out of wedlock.[104]

Thus, even in a legislative program designed to make government funds
available for the provision of care-work, productive labor norms were in-
fused into the provision of funds for reproductive labor. In subsequent re-
visions of ADC, the word *need* was added to the legislation, making it clear
that recipients were unproductive workers, who were to be identified solely
on the basis of what they lacked in terms of economic funds, that is, on

the basis of a means test. There is nothing inherently stigmatizing about "needing" economic assistance. What stigmatizes the need for economic assistance from the government is a political context, as exemplified by the American liberal heritage, which defines society as composed of independent, autonomous individuals who need nothing from the government other than the protection of their persons and property from nonconsensual intrusion by others. Given that standard, lacking property or the means of subsistence becomes a stigmatizing identification.

The adoption of maternalism as a basic national policy that began with ADC is still with us in the form of welfare. Significantly, many Americans view it as an alien governmental activity that may be temporarily necessary, but should ultimately be tied to productive labor. Contemporary welfare legislation, formally called Temporary Assistance to Needy Families (TANF), has been reformulated to require that mothers who are the recipients of government welfare funds take action to become members of the paid work force.[105] From "welfare to work" has become a political watchword enjoying middle-class approval in the United States, thereby undermining the very idea that reproductive labor is not only valuable in and of itself but also deserves to be represented in national government policies. In the end, as progressive as the 1935 Social Security Act of the New Deal was in providing government support for potentially productive laborers, it failed to institutionalize support for reproductive labor, that is, for maternalism.

The Family Medical and Leave Act of 1993 (FMLA) also is a perfect example of how the United States continues to fail to represent maternal group difference in its welfare policies. The FMLA legislation was also passed with excruciating difficulty. It took twenty years of highly contested debate and compromise between those who sought relief from conflicting claims of work and family and those who resisted "federal regulation of the workplace or of the family."[106] President George H. W. Bush vetoed this legislation twice, in 1990 and again in 1992, and it was not until Bill Clinton took office that it could become law, albeit in the most modest of formulations.[107]

The stated purpose of the FMLA is "to balance the demands of the workplace with the needs of families, to promote the stability and economic security of families, and to promote national interests in preserving family integrity."[108] Yet remarkably, the FMLA makes only limited provision for reproductive labor. It does not provide for paid leave, only for unpaid leave,[109] and it covers only employers who employ at least fifty workers. Thus, it is a far cry from the family leave policies of other countries that provide workers with paid leave from productive labor so that they can provide family members with reproductive labor. In addition, the FMLA targets employed workers as its direct beneficiaries. It is not a benefit targeted at those in need of care, namely the family members who would be the recipients of care, so much as it is a benefit for those who have shown themselves to be deserving members of the productive workforce. Nor does it advance the use of maternalism as a foundation for what the government itself "does." The FMLA deliberately rejects the idea that the government itself should act directly to provide for the reproductive labor needs of those in society who are dependent, owing either to their family status as mothers, fathers, children, or to their need status as the ill, the elderly, or the disabled. The FMLA instead attempts to make it easier for productive workers to engage in reproductive labor as well as in wage-earning labor. This type of welfare policy does not associate the state with maternal traits in such a way as to teach the public that to have maternal traits is to be located inside, not outside, the public sphere of political governance.

The United States differs from most other comparable democracies, therefore, in its failure to sustain public policies representing maternalism. Most other countries comparable to the American state embrace at least one type of maternal public policy, such as welfare provision, gender quotas, or hereditary monarchies. While the American state today provides a modicum of welfare, it does not do so at levels comparable to other Western-oriented democracies. The United States has never adopted gender quotas, it long ago destroyed its monarchical heritage, and it failed to sustain the maternal impetus marking the Progressive Era. Thus, while the impact of state maternalism continues to be a positive benefit for women seeking political inclusion as elected officeholders in most other democracies, not so here. This missing maternalism in the American state explains its laggard status in electing women to positions of political rule. The question is whether anything can be done to fix the American state.

Fixing the State 7

The Fallacy of the Single Cause

In a memorable episode of *The Simpsons*, an illegal immigrant from India, Apu, is in a panic because of the proposed passage in California of Proposition 24, which would have him deported.[1] Lisa, a character who is fond of Apu, seeks to solve the problem of how he can stay in the United States if Prop 24 passes. She discovers that if Apu can pass a U.S. citizenship test, he will not be deported. Apu, who is bright and able, having graduated from Calcutta Technical Institute and learned computer science in the United States, studies diligently for his citizenship exam. When the day for the test arrives, Apu is more than ready. He has mastered all the intricacies of American political history, including the multiple causes of the Civil War. During the questioning by the examining proctor, this is what happens:

> *Proctor:* All right, here's your last question. What was the cause of the Civil War?
> *Apu:* Actually, there were numerous causes. Aside from the obvious schism between the abolitionists and the anti-abolitionists, there were economic factors, both domestic and inter . . .
> *Proctor:* Wait, wait . . . just say slavery.
> *Apu:* Slavery it is, sir.

This anecdote illustrates the fallacy of reducing the causes of anything, much less complex political processes, to "one" cause. Despite the emphasis on maternalism and individualism in this book, its goal is not to reduce women's political inclusion in the American state to a single cause: the state's hybrid representation of both in its public policies. Political structures are important, as are economic indices and the sociological and psychological dynamics that influence women's access to electoral political leaders. To these, however, we must add the power of democratic political contexts to define the political meaning of the maternal traits voters attribute to women as signifying inclusion in the public sphere. It is this hybrid construction of the state representing individualism and maternalism that improves public attitudes about the suitability of women as political leaders and women's election to political office.

The problem with the United States is that although hybrid symbolism is evident in the political campaigns of candidates, the state itself is deficient in this regard. Hybrid symbolism appeared in the context of race, for example, in the 2008 presidential primaries, when Democratic candidate Barack Obama represented himself as a hybrid embodiment of how race can bring about unity, not division, in American politics. As he pointed out, his mother was white and his father was black. Hence, his mixed race background showed that a union of different races at the micro-level in one person can represent harmony not only for that person, but as a principle that could also work at the macrolevel of American society.[2]

A hybrid symbolism that works for race has also worked for decades for sex, as women seeking access to political office assure voters they can be "male" while still being "female." Although by virtue of their parents, all human beings are necessarily a hybrid mixture derived from a male father and a female mother, from the moment of birth, if not before, most human beings become rigidly categorized as either male or female, despite their "mixed sex" parentage. While there is some latitude for fluidity in sex classification, sex stereotypes persist, and the best that most people can do is to change the stereotypes at their edges by integrating nontraditional roles and behaviors with traditional ones. This is what women do as political candidates. They try to establish their male credentials as people who are the "same" as men, who will be leaders able to guarantee domestic law and order and meet the needs of national security, even while maintaining their traditional roles as women who exemplify social and biological maternal traits.

For women to succeed as political candidates, however, it is not enough to locate hybridity in the candidate herself. What is also necessary is for the state to reflect sex hybridity by adopting public policies representing both individualism (women's sameness with men) and maternalism (women's difference from men).[3] The laggard status of the United States with respect to women's political inclusion as compared to other democracies comes not from its public policies based on liberal individualism, but rather from its lack of public policies representing maternal traits. Liberal individualism is not bad or wrong for women. It is just not enough. The failure of the liberal state based on individualism alone to increase women's political representation, however, leads some feminists to question whether liberal democracy can be thought of as a progressive form of governance in the first place.

Is Liberal Democracy Progress for Women?

A strong tradition among feminists holds that liberalism is the problem, not the solution, to women's lack of access to political rule. The liberal view that society is composed of abstract, autonomous individuals promotes less, not more, political inclusion for women.[4] Liberal democratic states are not the only ones to evidence gender discrimination. In fact, except for rare historical cases, gender discrimination is a feature of all political systems.[5] Yet some feminists contend that gender as a category of political exclusion becomes stronger, not weaker, in the liberal democratic state. From both historical and theoretical perspectives, when liberalism "wins," women do not necessarily "win" in terms of their greater political incorporation into the state on an equal basis with men. To the contrary, liberalism can exacerbate, rather than mitigate, political exclusion based on sex and gender, raising the question of whether the modern, liberal state produces political progress for women at all.[6]

The Renaissance

One of the first to ask whether democratization means progress for women was the historian Joan Kelly, who argues that although the Renaissance is generally acknowledged to represent "progress" and "improvement" in social and political relationships for human beings, it in fact constituted a *loss* of political and social stature for women, in terms of the regulation of women's sexuality and of their economic and political roles.[7] Before the Renaissance, sexual equality prevailed among the nobility in the form of "courtly love," a relationship marked by a mutuality of consent between male and female lovers and by a separation from the utilitarian, economic institution of marriage. In the feudal structure, where "everyone was somebody's 'man,' the right to freely enter a relation of service characterized aristocratic bonds."[8] Thus, "mutuality entered the notion of heterosexual relations along with the idea of freedom." "A lady must honor her lover as a friend, not as a master," wrote a female troubadour.[9] Women and men were both idealized as objects of spiritual passion and of physical love, and the sexuality that was involved in the relationship between a loving man and woman was exalted. These relations between men and women of the nobility took place outside of the context of both the family and the Church.[10]

The distinctive features of the noble class were both its freedom from "work," that is, from any utilitarian task or any kind of labor that might be necessary for the ongoing aspects of reproductive or productive life, and its use of leisure to define essentially a new relationship between men and women. Men and women of the upper noble class were defined by their equality to one another. The key principle typifying relationships within the nobility was consent. In courtly love relationships between men and women, the idea that a nobleman would sexually impose himself on a noblewoman just because of his greater strength was unthinkable. Nor were women coerced into courtly love relations because of demands for utilitarian reproduction of the species, that is, bearing children. While women in the context of marriage were required and expected to bear children, women in the context of courtly love were freed not only from the necessity of bearing children but even from the advisability of bearing children. Courtly love was the prototype of a completely free, consensual relationship.[11]

In feudal society economic power also accrued to women in the noble class. Women "could hold both ordinary fiefs and vast collections of counties—and exercise in their own right the seigniorial powers that went with them."[12] In the absence of their warrior husbands, women also exercised complete power over courts, estates, and vassal services. The social reality of women's economic and political power was reflected in the "retention of matronymics in medieval society."[13] Husbands needed the support of their wives to acquire property, since a wife's property remained her own upon marriage. Women's inheritance thus became an important leverage, along with women's ongoing position as large landowners and managers of great estates. For this reason, within the institution of marriage, a wife was valued not just for her utilitarian, reproductive services but also for her economic power.[14]

An immediate political consequence of these feudal norms was that kinship identity could serve as an entry point for women's ascendancy to heads-of-state positions as queens. The use of the private sphere for access to the public sphere in a feudal system is precisely what is lost in liberal formulations that separate the private sphere of kinship ties from the public sphere of political rule. As Kelly notes, the advent of the Renaissance in Italy was an advance for "human beings," since the breakdown of the rigid feudal caste system allowed more people to acquire more political power and economic resources. The "more people," however, were all "men." The Renaissance was *not* an important advance for women, because it was founded upon separating the private and public spheres, thereby transforming the private sphere of the home into the property of men. Consequently, women became socially and legally the property of their fathers and their husbands. The idea that a wife was owned, in a sense, by her husband, originated at this time. Her reproductive capacities were his property, exemplified by her taking his surname for herself and their children. In feudal times, by contrast, maternal lines were as important as paternal ones, and women with economic resources had more equal access to their property, inheritance, and even political rule. In the Renaissance, however, when women became the property of their husbands, they lost any independent existence or identity outside of that status.[15]

Relationships between men and women within the bourgeoisie class in the Renaissance also evidenced much greater inequality than had been the case in feudal times. Even if there was less vertical inequality between classes, namely more opportunity for upward mobility and the acquisition of economic resources, this upward mobility existed only for some men. The only way women could achieve economic resources was through marriage, and marriage entailed a loss of their own economic personage and a dependency on their husband for their economic existence. Marriage concomitantly signified women's loss of access to the public sphere as voters or officeholders.

The French Revolution

Historian Joan Landes concludes that women also failed to benefit from the democratizing processes of the French Revolution. The patriarchy of the Old Regime did not prohibit participation in politics on the basis of gender.[16] Political rights were not universal, and many characteristics other than gender figured into their determination. As Stephen Hause notes, prior to the Revolution, the church and throne acknowledged women's right to vote. Under the monarchies of Philip V (1318) to Louis XIV (1661), noble women had the right both to vote and to sit in parliament. One's class power was more significant for political authority than one's sex, and women privileged by class bore arms and governed jurisdictions.[17] In addition, women of the 1st, 2nd, and 3rd estates had the right to vote until the 1790s, as did women who were widows, or unmarried, who served as heads of a family, or whose husbands were absent.[18] In the thirteenth century Pope Innocent IV recognized the right of all people over fourteen years of age to vote, whether they were male or female, married or unmarried, or belonged to any particular class.[19]

After the French Revolution, however, women lost formal and informal political rights. Not only were women denied the right to vote, but in October 1793 the government decreed all women's clubs and associations to be illegal.[20] Thus, Landes argues, women did not benefit from the "shift from the iconic imagery of the Old Regime to the symbolic structure of bourgeois representation," nor from the shift from a monarchy to a republic. To the contrary, "from the standpoint of women and their interests, [the] enlightenment looks suspiciously like counterenlightenment, and [the] revolution like counterrevolution."[21]

Theoretical Critique

Some feminist theorists also view liberal democracy as a cause of the gender deficit in political representation. Jean Bethke Elshtain, for example, faults liberalism for disconnecting the public sphere of political rule from the private sphere of family relations. In doing so, liberalism loses sight of the value of the family as the "linchpin" of society. It introduced instead unstable, if not dangerous, ideologies based solely on utilitarian principles that fail to recognize the family as the site of identity formation and socialization.[22] Political theorist Anne Phillips equates liberal theory solely with formal rights, such as voting and office-holding. In her view, women in particular are not served well by this aspect of liberalism because the focus on formal equality ignores economic and social inequalities that prevent many women from securing their formal rights.[23]

American Political Development

On the other hand, many scholars of American political development see liberalism as the most effective weapon for eradicating nefarious inequalities in the American state. Political scientists Karen Orren and Stephen Skowronek define political development as a "durable shift in governing authority,"[24] which entails "*re*arrangement, *re*direction, *re*construction," which become the focal point for "changing definitions of citizenship and civil rights."[25] In the wake of numerous examples in American history of the use of group identity to deny political rights to people, the problem has seemed to be the existence of identifiable groups in the first place. It is the prevailing assumption that public policies affirming the relevance of group differences are "bad" for subordinate groups in contrast to public polices based on individual equality that are "good." It is as if there is thought to be a zero-sum game between policies based on feudal-like group differences and policies based on liberal individual equality. The more feudalism, the less liberalism, and vice versa. In order to expand political inclusion to everyone, therefore, the goal is to get rid of feudal-like traits altogether.

Behind this view of American political development is the idea that the country is marked by a positive liberal tradition, which eschews any connection with feudal ideology or institutions, such as monarchies. Society is, rather, composed of atomistic individuals, all of whom are born equal, according to the "master assumption of American political thought."[26] Feudalism is absent in American political history even in the context of slavery in the South. As Louis Hartz argues, all Americans, even Southerners, agreed that slavery did not fit any categories of liberal thought. What is more, when Southerners sought for a defense of slavery, they discovered that slavery did not fit any categories of Western political thought, including Greek political thought. Greek political philosophers, such as Aristotle, had never made the claim that slaves lack human attributes.[27]

Although Aristotle, had defined the slave as a "living tool," he also conceded that slaves had a capacity for "friendship," where friendship is the basic capacity upon which the human community is built.[28] Consequently, once the human attributes of slaves are affirmed, any rationale for their enslavement breaks down. The most that Southerners could claim was the legal construct that slaves were property, but this legal artifact did not justify "why" a human being should be property, especially given the liberal heritage of the American state that presumes all individuals are born free and equal.[29] As Hartz argues, therefore, slavery in the South, rather than being a holdover, feudal institution from the past, was instead an anomaly that was recognized by Northerners and Southerners alike as incongruous with the principles of the American state. Consequently, it was necessary not so much to repudiate slavery as to purge the American state of slavery—that is, to purge the state of an anomaly that no one could justify in the first place.[30]

Other theorists, such as Alexis de Tocqueville, Gunnar Myrdal, and Samuel Huntington,[31] depict liberal principles in the United States as hegemonic. There may be anomalies, such as slavery, and it may take considerable historical time to include all subordinate groups in the electorate, but these anomalies are simply ad hoc incongruities that just happened to be present without any roots in American institutions. They are like weeds in a garden. Unplanned and unwanted, they do nothing but distract from the overall landscape design. Political change occurs by weeding the garden to get rid of the anomalies, which just happen to be there and for which there is no rationale or justification in the garden's master, or liberal, plan. In the view of Huntington, weeding the garden, or getting rid of nonliberal elements in the American state and society, is simply the process of bringing greater correspondence between theory and practice to American liberal democracy during successive periods of political reform.[32]

Others illuminate, however, that it is not correct to assume that feudalism is absent in the American political context. The American state may indeed have ideologically and institutionally rejected monarchies, but feudal principles remained in other areas of ideological and institutional life. As Karen Orren establishes, one of the most resilient areas to retain feudal principles is labor relations as adjudicated by courts using common law precepts. Courts have interpreted labor policies on the basis not of individual equality, but of a master-servant relationship.[33] In so doing, courts undermine the liberal conception of labor as the "capacity to . . . will one's body and hands to work," or an intentional activity that, "cannot be surrendered to another without violating natural law."[34] Resolving labor disputes within the common law court system meant that instead of courts "arbitrating between two parties [employer and employee] who had entered, *de novo* as in contract theory, into an agreement," judges used longstanding common law assumptions about the dominance-subordination structure of the relationship between employer and employee, adapted from the relationship between master and servant.[35]

According to Orren, a worker in nineteenth-century America was viewed by the courts as being in a "status relation" with an employer, not a "contractual relation."[36] Status refers "to an established position in society conferred upon an individual that does not arise from any specific action or from a contract but from the individual's personal characteristics."[37] The status of worker was imposed upon able-bodied men who had no means other than employment to support themselves. Every jurisdiction in the United States criminalized able-bodied men without any means of support for not working. Thus, "American law conferred the *status* of being one who committed a crime by not working or by not seeking work."[38]

Another example of the application of feudal principles via common law adjudication in American courts to disadvantaged workers was the provision against enticements, derived from the law of master and servant. English law "provided for both civil and criminal proceedings against any person who knowingly enticed or persuaded a servant away from his employment by another master."[39] This provision was accepted by American courts in suits brought by employers against strikes organized by workers. Employers claimed that the workers instigating employee strikes were intentionally interfering with the employer-employee relationship so as to entice the worker away from the employer. Courts agreed that inducing employees to stop work "constituted the wrongdoing of enticement."[40]

As Orren shows, the residual feudalism located in the common law precedents used by courts to adjudicate labor disputes between employer and employees was challenged by legislative bodies, where principles of worker volition, contractual rights, and the legality of collective action were used to give employees more comparable leverage in labor negotiations with employers. However, the liberal impulse lodged in the legislature, despite conflict and competition with the remnants of feudalism lodged in the courts, did not prevail until the Supreme Court's decision of 1937 in *N.L.R.B. v. Jones & Laughlin*.[41] In this landmark case the Supreme Court for the first time established the supremacy of the legislature, namely Congress, to regulate on the basis of the Commerce Clause the nation's economy, which included in part the regulation of relationships between employers and employees.[42] Here at last, as Orren puts it, "the remnant of feudalism that was labor relations gave way to liberal government."[43] As a consequence, in the United States the liberal formula of separating society from the state, distinguished from the feudal formula of fusing society and state, was finally implemented.[44] This separation of society and state resulted in good policies, specifically the protection of workers from the disproportionate power of employers in labor relations.

Rogers Smith, rather than viewing feudalism as simply a remnant left over from a distant past, also considers feudalism—or, as he terms it, ascriptivism—to be as much a founding component of the American state as was liberalism. Rather than locating feudalism within only one institution, the courts, he sees it as diffused throughout all the institutions of society and government. The ascriptivist tradition is therefore as indigenous and "American" as is the liberal tradition.[45] According to Smith, American political development, defined in terms of expanding citizenship rights to previously excluded groups, occurs when liberalism prevails over ascriptivism. In his view, therefore, the Enlightenment idea of the equality of a rights-bearing individual, when dominant, fosters institutional guarantees of greater political equality and produces greater political inclusivity of marginal groups. The "logic of Enlightenment liberalism," reflected in such documents as the Declaration of Independence and John Locke's writings, makes "a prima facie case that all those capable of developing powers of rational self-guidance should be treated as bearers of fairly robust individual rights." Because liberal ideology serves as the basis for evaluating "legal systems that automatically subordinate women, blacks, Native

Americans, homosexuals, and non-Christians" as invalid, it is an important mechanism for establishing alternative institutional structures and public policies to achieve greater political inclusivity.[46]

When turning to gender as a component of American political development, political scientist Gretchen Ritter argues that the goal for women in the United States was to switch from a civic status based on identity in the private sphere defined by marriage, family relations, and economic dependency, to a status based on an identity in the public sphere defined by liberal individualism and legal personhood. That this shift has not been made completely accounts for women having not yet attained equal political status with men in America.[47] As she puts it, "So long as gender remains relevant to a woman's civic membership . . . it is a signal of inequality, and of her failure to be fully absorbed into the ideal of liberal, individuated civic membership. The cost of equality, for women, then, is the cost of their gender." Since there is no way women can fully divest themselves of their sex difference, "women have never readily fit into the liberal ideal of citizenship . . . grounded on individualism," and women probably never will.[48]

A cross-national analysis of women's political leadership patterns, however, gives us a different way to think about the feudal or ascriptive tradition versus the liberal one in American political development. Rather than women's political inclusion depending upon the replacement of their ascriptive identities as mothers with their acquisition of identities as individuals who are the same as men, what works best is when the identity of the state itself constitutes a combination of both. It is not women's ascriptive, maternal attributes, as defined by their relationship in marriage, their care-and-nurture of others, or their role as biological mothers upon whom the very propagation of society depends, that block access to political leadership positions. Rather it is the failure of the liberal state to define the meaning of those identities to be a location inside the public sphere. What stands in the way of women's political inclusion, therefore, are not women's maternal identities but rather a democratic state's failure to embody those identities in its public policies. When a democracy, such as the United States, fails to adopt public policies representing the social and biological traits that the public attributes to women, voters fail to learn that the *political meaning of maternal identities* is to be located inside the public sphere of the state. On the other hand, when democracies do adopt a hybrid set of public policies based on both individual equality and maternal differences, voters learn that women are suitable as political leaders inside the state because of their individual sameness with men and because of their maternal group difference from men. The result is a higher percentage of women elected to political office.

An over-reliance on liberal ideology and institutions can blind one to the limits of liberalism for producing an inclusive political society, particularly when it comes to women.[49] Both the historical record and cross-national patterns of women's election to political office illustrate that when it comes to women's political representation, what matters is a state that combines individualism and maternalism in its public policies. The question for the American state then becomes how to fix it so that it, like most other comparable democracies, represents both individualism and maternalism in its public policies. Specifically, the United States has three choices: to adopt welfare provision, gender quotas, or, least likely of all, a hereditary monarchy. Let us start with the least likely first on the grounds that for most Americans it is also the least familiar.

Hereditary Monarchy

At first glance, it might seem strange even to think about adding a monarchy to the American state. After all, the American Constitution prohibits the association of hereditary status with the acquisition of public office. Thus, to establish a monarchy would presumably require a constitutional amendment. Nevertheless, the United States has a monarchist society, the Monarchist Society of America, which is "dedicated to the dissemination of information and ideas relating to monarchy and the monarchic form of government . . . as a superior alternative to other forms of government, and to encourage the discussion and support of these ideas in national and international forums of intellectual and political discourse."[50] The Monarchist Society does not advocate absolute monarchy but rather constitutional monarchy, and it does not advocate the "overthrow of any regime in order to achieve restoration or creation of a monarchic system." It exists simply to distribute and illuminate the "ideals of Monarchism and the defense of Monarchy as a viable political system in today's world and in the future."[51]

As the official Web site of the Monarchist Society states, "the Crown in law is a common law institution that derived from ancient and primaeval traditions," and for that reason "it can never be abolished." According to this view, the common law tradition entails recognizing that the "kingship never dies," even if individual kings and queens die and even if, for what are presumably temporary periods of time, monarchical institutions are replaced by other forms of government. The idea that the kingship never dies stems from the view that the monarchical heritage in the form of the monarchical family can always be "restored."[52] As those advocating a restoration of the American monarchy declare, the current American "republic is run by a charter that was composed by some businessmen in secret, who intended to use it [to] preserve their wealth. . . . The king [on the other hand] in law evolved as a common law institution. It did not suddenly appear among men after a select few had a secretive meeting, where they invented the office . . . of the Presidency of the United States . . . the monarchy represents a government that originates in a family, the royal family, which by extension becomes the focal point of the national family. The presidency has attempted to fulfill this mythic need of a country in its pursuit of an identity, with the usage of terms like First Family, and First Lady, but the political baggage of the presidency has made it unfit to represent the American Nation."[53]

According to those who would restore a monarchy in America, the "American Crown was made vacant by the overthrow of George III by the [American] Revolution. The inauguration of a republic did not abolish the monarchy, which is a common law institution, which cannot be abolished . . . instead . . . The monarchy went into a state of interregnum," from which it can be restored. Those proposing to do so state,

> the movement to restore the Crown of America is not a violent social
> movement, but a movement of enlightenment. It is based solely around
> correcting the mistakes of history. . . . The Restoration of the Crown of
> America is not so much a political movement as a social movement with
> political implications. For those who believe that America is *one* family,
> the Crown embodies that family, and gives life to the vision of the nation
> as an extended national family . . . a unified national culture . . . [inclusive
> of] White Americans . . . African Americans, Hispanic Americans, Asian
> Americans, Native Americans, Polynesian Americans, and any other members of the human race who are American Nationals.[54]

When it comes to "whom" or "what family" would constitute an American monarchy, there is always Great Britain, with whom we could reunite, or there are active legions of loyalists nearby, descendants of Americans who fled to Canada in the wake of the American Revolution. The United Empire Loyalists, a Canadian organization that keeps track of refugees fleeing from revolutions, estimates that 100,000 colonists loyal to the Crown were driven into exile by those fighting the American Revolution, 60,000 of whom fled to Canada. The loyalists claim that this influx saved Canada from a subsequent takeover by the United States when, in 1812, the United States declared war on Great Britain. At that time, four-fifths of the population of upper Canada was American born, according to estimates by the

Loyalists, and it was their resistance, combined with that of other Canadians and Great Britain, that succeeded in thwarting the American invasion of Canada's eastern provinces, thereby ensuring the development of Canada as a country.[55] From their ranks, which are still numerous and strong, at least one family most likely exists that would be pleased to return to America to reinstate a monarchical heritage.

Movements to restore monarchies exist not only in the United States but also in other contemporary political systems. There are movements to institute or to reinstate monarchies in such nations as Albania, Austria, Afghanistan, Bulgaria, the Czech Republic, Georgia, Estonia, Iran, Iraq, Israel, Italy, Romania, Russia, Serbia, Uganda, and Yugoslavia. In 2004 Leka Zog, a pretender to the Albanian throne, launched a political platform to restore a monarchy in Albania, calling it the Movement for National Development.[56] Included in its platform were goals of restoring the people's lost confidence in politicians, establishing a rule of law, and developing democratic practices.[57] The common feeling was that reinstating the monarchy would restore a symbolic nationalism and trust in the national government.[58]

Monarchical rule is no longer viewed as the threat to the American state that it was at its founding. Twentieth-century American foreign policy advisors worried about Communism in the Soviet Union, but not about the return of the Russian monarchy. If anything, the reliance of the Russian monarchy on such traditional values as private property and religion would have most likely been viewed by Americans as positive buffers to the ideology of the Communist Soviet regime, which appeared to be so alien. An alliance between democracy and monarchy is not a contradiction. As Prince Ermias Sahle Selassie of Ethiopia, the grandson of Emperor Haile Selassie, observed, a constitutional monarchy "can be an institution that will not prevent democracy but can enhance it."[59] As Neil Conan noted, the monarchy in Spain "played a vital role in that country's restoration of democracy after the end of the Franco dictatorship."[60]

For many political analysts of the twentieth century, monarchies are in disrepute.[61] The American writer Austin O'Malley considers monarchies to be "useless when quiet" and necessary to remove "when obtrusive."[62] British Marxist Mark Kirby views the English monarchy and its royal family as standing at the pinnacle of an unethical class system based on the wealth and well-being of a few at the expense of the poverty and suffering of the many.[63] Antimonarchists consider the Crown to be little more than a symbol of centuries of "class domination, social injustice, and imperialism, a wasteful frippery at best and a malignant atavism at worst."[64] Yet in a study of twenty-seven Western societies, political scientists Jeremy

D. Mayer and Lee Sigelman find that monarchies have positive affects on the successful operation of a democratic political system: "Other factors being equal, in monarchies, public support for revolution was significantly less widespread, interpersonal trust was significantly higher, per capita wealth was significantly greater, income was significantly less concentrated, and the political system had been significantly more democratic during the 1970s."[65] As the authors wryly observe: "Political scientists, whose learned treatises on the requisites of societal well-being and good government have been responsible for felling millions of trees, have heretofore sacrificed remarkably little wood to advance the study of monarchy or, for that matter, to advance monarchy itself. However, to judge from . . . [our] results, both monarchy and the study thereof are causes well worth advancing."[66]

Despite the existence of those few who wish to reinstate America's monarchical heritage, however, we can assume it is not going to happen. That leaves the possibility of adding to government the other two forms of maternal public policy, welfare provision and gender quotas.

Welfare Provision

It may be that the U.S. government will step up to the plate by establishing, at long last, a public health care program, but when it comes to welfare provision, it is not merely the money the government redistributes but also the way the state assumes the affirmative duty of caring for the needy. This is what T. H. Marshall defines as social citizenship. The idea that government has a fundamental responsibility to care for those who lack the resources to provide for themselves is at the heart of welfare provision. To imagine that the American Congress would pass with a two-thirds majority, and then that three-fourths of the states would ratify an amendment to the American Constitution asserting that the provision of welfare to those in need is a fundamental obligation of government is, in my estimation, no more likely than that America will reinstate a monarchy. Hence, I do not place my bet for fixing the American state on constitutionalized and legislated welfare provision. So let us consider the third option, gender quotas.

Gender Quotas

The third way a liberal democracy can associate itself with women's maternalism is by implementing gender quotas, However, as political scientist Lisa Baldez notes, "*Quota* is a bad word in the United States."[67] Even if the term were to be semantically disguised by calling quotas "positive discrimination," that linguistic turn would still not do enough to make Americans favor the adoption of quotas.[68] Despite the fact that the Republican administration of the United States all but imposed gender quotas as a mechanism for advancing women's rights recently in Afghanistan and Iraq, as well as the fact that the Republican Party was a trendsetter in the 1920s when it adopted an "equal division rule" to assure parity in the representation of men and women at its national convention, it is highly unlikely that proposals for national gender quotas will be forthcoming from current Republican leaders or even Democrats contending for the election to the presidency.

Yet, commensurate with its very founding the United States had already endorsed the suspicious, if not hated, format of quotas by instituting geographic, territorial quotas for determining political representation. James Madison and other founders of the American republic looked to Enlightenment thinkers, such as John Locke, Montesquieu,[69] and David Hume,[70] for guidance. These philosophers viewed the construction of the state as a product of universal principles, rational planning, and a realistic assessment of what was possible. In opposition to contemporary conservatives, such as Edmund Burke, they did not view government and constitutions as a product of slow evolution over time or organic historical growth. Nor did they believe that the state was founded on the particularities of specific national identities.[71] The goal of the Founders was to find practical mechanisms for institutionalizing universal, abstract principles.

Among the liberal ideas endorsed by many of the Founders was a principle of natural rights: the premise that people are born free and equal. It follows that the purpose of political institutions is to "liberate people, not confine them, and to give them the substance and the spirit to stand firm before the forces that would restrict them."[72] Since the Founders believed that social status was not relevant to the construction of the state, political institutions should not be based on social status, that is, on such group characteristics as class. In other words, "no public office or function was legally a prerogative of birth."[73] A corollary of this principle, emphasized by the Federalists, is that it is not the institutions of government but the people themselves who are sovereign. Locating sovereignty in the people was not a new concept. The idea had been asserted as a component of Whig theory as far back as the English Civil War in the seventeenth century.[74] What was novel was meaningful institutionalization of popular sovereignty by the fledgling American states.

The Federalists believed that the idea of popular sovereignty would be best served by a stronger, more centralized federal government. This was a contentious issue, because the Anti-Federalists believed that sovereignty was located in the states. Thus, a centralized federal government would constitute an infringement of liberty. In the view of the Anti-Federalists, unless the states, as units of sovereign government, consented to the transfer of sovereignty—either to the people or to the federal government—the states, not the federal government, remained the sovereign units of the American republic. Indeed, Anti-Federalists rejected as invalid the federal Constitution drafted during the Constitutional Convention, because it co-opted the sovereignty of the states, without the consent of those states, by "illegally circumventing the [earlier] Articles of Confederation, no part of which could be amended except by unanimous consent of the state governments."[75] The Federalists countered that sovereignty had never resided in state governments, nor could it, any more than sovereignty could reside in rulers, magistrates, or governments of any kind. Rather, sovereignty resides "in the whole body of the people, who can never allow it to be taken anywhere else."[76]

From the very founding of the American state, therefore, there have been two opposing views about what constitutes the sovereign component of the American republic, the *people* or the *states*.[77] Both were crucial to the construction of the bicameral Congress. And regardless of which component was considered sovereign, the question remained as to how representatives would adequately represent the interests of their constituents. The idea behind republican representation is that representatives should have in mind the public good as a whole rather than the interests of particular sectors of society.[78] The question is how to disentangle the public good from competing specific interests. According to one view, what matters is not that a lawmaker implements the direct wishes of those who are being represented, but that a representative shares with his or her constituents "a mutuality of interests and sympathy of sentiments."[79] The representative in such a "virtual" system, as Edmund Burke explained, serves as a guide for his constituents, not the other way around. In this conception of government it matters little whether the representative is directly elected.[80]

Although the American colonies had been prohibited from sending representatives to Parliament, British members of Parliament were speaking on their behalf. That is, they had virtual representation in the British Parliament.[81] The American Revolution was proof that the colonists considered this form of representation insufficient. And so it became important to the Founders to establish a system of actual representation, whereby representatives would be chosen by their constituents. They regarded voting rights and actual representation as the mechanisms of government by which a sovereign people could express their consent to be governed.[82]

According to the theory of actual representation, elected representatives mirror the interests of their constituents. As Theophilus Parson expressed this view in 1778, "representatives should have the same views, in interest with the people at large. They should think, feel, and act like them, and . . . should be an exact miniature of their constituents."[83] Or as John Adams wrote, the representative assembly "should be in miniature an exact portrait of the people at large."[84]

The problem remained of how to establish the *unit of representation*. Presumably each individual is a unit whose interests are to be represented in national governance. Yet when Congress was created, the basic unit of representation was a person's state of domicile, where that person lived. Due to the size of the American republic, it was not possible at the founding to allow every homogenous community of interest to send a representative to the national government. It became necessary to aggregate communities into congressional districts. The Founders viewed the congressional district to be little more than a mechanism for aggregating votes for the selection of House members.[85] Although each congressional district would inevitably contain heterogeneous interests, the Founders speculated that the large size of the districts would "neutralize particular interests"[86] to better represent the interests of the people as a whole.

According to Article I, Section 2, of the Constitution, congressional districts were determined by population, as constrained by the territorial boundaries of the states. Each state, however, is guaranteed at least one representative, regardless of population.[87] The Constitution also stipulated that an elected representative of a state be an inhabitant of that state. The founders did not intend for congressional district lines to extend across states.[88] This system has perhaps grown so familiar to us that its arbitrariness fails to be visible. For example, even if the people of Kansas City, Kansas, share more closely in the interests and concerns of their counterparts in Kansas City, Missouri, than those in more rural parts of their own state, territorial districts dictate that they cannot be represented by the same member of Congress.

Because it was assumed that states were an "association of men" coterminous with a set of political interests, the Founders designated the states to be the basic representative units for the Senate.[89] As a result, in the Senate there is an even greater reliance upon territory for the principle of electing representatives to Congress. According to Article I, Section 3 of the Constitution, each state was to have two senators chosen by the state legislature of that state, which was later amended to provide for the direct election of senators by the people of a state. Whether elected indirectly or directly, the crucial characteristic about senators is that they represent states, not people. Thus, the unit of representation for the Senate is completely territorial.

As political scientist Andrew Rehfeld argues, the selection of territory as the unit of representation and the allocation of quotas of representatives to units of territory, namely the states and congressional districts, rather than to units of people or to the people as a whole, was an instrumental decision by the Founders, chosen as a means to achieve other democratic aims. Congressional districts were never viewed by the Founders as a mechanism for transferring issue positions from the smallest unit of the town or county to the larger unit of the congressional district.[90] Nor did the authors of the Constitution decide upon territorial districts as the unit of representation for the House because of constituents' attachment to their district, nor because congressional districts were an efficient way to ensure the protection of property, nor because there was a historical tradition of using an aggregation of inhabitants, bounded by an arbitrary territory, as a basis for representation.[91] Pragmatic, logistical considerations alone were at the heart of the Founders' selection. Territorial units for representation had no theoretical significance in and of themselves and did not rely on historical tradition. Their only virtue was that they facilitated the other democratic ends of deliberation and consent. The Founders believed that territorial units allowed constituents to gather together easily to deliberate national policy and, by voting together, to express their consent in symbolic and tangible ways.[92]

In terms of the executive branch of government, another way quotas figure into the construction of American political institutions is in the Electoral College for the selection of the president. The Founders set up this structure to ensure that states would have a set quota of representation when choosing the president and vice president of the United States. Each state has a specific number of electors, determined by the number of House members the state has plus the number of its Senators.[93] Thus, people voting in a presidential election are not voting directly for their candidate but are voting for electors to represent them at the Electoral College. While it is all but unthinkable that state electors would vote for any other presidential and vice presidential candidates than the ones who received the majority vote in their state, only three states actually require their electors cast their vote with the popular vote.

Quotas are therefore at the very heart of the American representative legislature and the American executive branch of government. Lest one think that the effect of these territorial quotas is neutral, one need only recall the controversy surrounding the 2000 election. As it happened, the presidential and vice presidential candidates who won the popular vote lost the Electoral College vote, violating the principle that each individual's vote is of equal value. Because of the Electoral College system and the concept of territorial quotas that lies at its heart, individuals in some states may effectively have more voting power than individuals in other states. The controversies over redistricting and gerrymandering prove that where territorial lines are drawn matters, to the extent that redistricting can tip the balance of power in state and national legislatures without any corresponding change in the electorate. Partisan redistricting can dilute the voice and vote of some communities while increasing the power of others. The ongoing dispute over these practices is proof enough of the power of territorial quotas.

The adoption of territorial quotas at the founding of the American state resulted from concerns about how to generate a representative body, the Congress, that would be descriptively representative of the country, defined in terms of its territorial units, the states. Today it could well be argued that a more important descriptive representation than where a person lives is their sex, race, class, or other demographic characteristic. Hence, the use of quotas by the Founders to guarantee the representation of the states on the basis of a territorial principle could be altered to base representation on a *different* demographic characteristic of the American people, such as sex. If states were the candidates for such special treatment at the founding of the United States, that privilege could be extended today to women, if not to other underrepresented groups in American society, such as African Americans, Native Americans, Asian Americans, the disabled, and those economically disadvantaged. To do so would be to update the quota system already in place, so as to give representation in Congress to contemporary groups in American society, over and above how territorial groups, the states, achieve representation.

It Takes a State

It should be clear by now that liberal individualism per se does not hinder women's access to political rule in the United States or elsewhere. Liberal, individual equality is *not* at all bad for women, nor has it failed women.[94] On the contrary, liberal individual equality is a good thing for women. As Alan Wolfe and Jytte Klausen show, a state's failure to support women's rights as individuals equal to men risks policies that demand stereotypical behavior from women.[95] In such states, policies ostensibly honoring cultural difference can end up perpetuating women's oppression. Women fleeing countries that require them to wear a veil or to undergo genital surgeries without their consent can often be refused political asylum on the grounds that such policies simply represent cultural differences that must be respected, rather than political practices from which women as individuals have a right to exit and to receive protection.[96] Liberal individualism, however, powerfully counters that without consent, cultural practices constitute harm to women and entitle them to political asylum. Political scientists Yael Tamir, John Rawls, and Ronald Dworkin agree that liberalism's emphasis on the equality of all individuals in the context of democratization is a good thing for subordinated groups.[97]

The problem is that liberal ideology, while necessary, is not sufficient for achieving the political inclusion of historically subordinated groups in general or women in particular. The goal for contemporary nation-states, therefore, should not be to discard liberalism, but rather to rework it, so that a liberal state recognizes the politics of difference along with the rights of individuals. Exponents of multiculturalism, such as Amy Gutmann and the late Iris Marion Young, agree that the "good state" is one where citizens are free individuals whose equality is legally recognized, but where, at the same time institutionalized mechanisms provide for the "explicit recognition and representation of oppressed or disadvantaged groups."[98] Applying that precept to women's political representation means that women's access to political leadership requires a political context that embodies a "sameness" principle when the state acts like an individual and a "difference" principle when the state acts like a woman.[99]

Many advocate for the complementary combination of autonomy and difference at the level of the individual, As legal scholar Martha Minow notes, to say that someone is "different" due to deafness, for example, is not to describe a characteristic of that person, but rather to describe a relationship between that person and others, where the former differs in some respect when compared to the latter. Difference as defined by boundaries and categories necessarily implies relational connections rather than embedded traits in one person.[100] Similarly, law scholar Jennifer Nedelsky challenges the idea of boundaries between people as separating and protecting a "self" from others. To conceive of personal autonomy as a form of "protection from the intrusion of the collective" is misguided[101] because "what actually makes human autonomy possible is not isolation, but relationships, first with parents, then teachers, friends, and, potentially, agents of the state," such as providers of welfare. Interdependence and even dependence are not the enemies of autonomy. Rather, they in fact foster autonomy.[102] When it comes to the body an apt metaphor for it is not a container, whose surrounding skin separates the person from the rest of the world. To the contrary, as Catherine Keller notes, "Our skin does not separate—it connects us to the world through a wondrous network of sensory awareness. . . . Through my senses I go into the world, and the world comes into me."[103]

The hybrid principle of autonomy and connectedness needs to be applied not only to people but also to the state itself. Rather than separating maternal traits from the state, it is important to bring those traits in to public policies as an orthogonal complement to individual equality. Individualism and maternalism can mutually reinforce each other as foundations for public policy. And it is their combination that opens up political rule to women, which a state built on individualism alone does not do. That their combination also bolsters human rights in general, both in the realm of civil and political rights and in the realm of social economic rights, is another, ethical benefit of their adoption. Some maternal policies, such as welfare provision, directly meet the needs of the disadvantaged, thereby fulfilling the intrinsic democratic guarantee of equal opportunities and outcomes for more, if not all. In addition, many of the political issues disproportionately associated with women's political leadership, such as health care, world peace, and the redistribution of economic resources, promote the well-being not only of women but also of people in general.

On instrumental and normative grounds, therefore, electing more women to positions of political leadership is fundamental to fulfilling the promise of democracy. And it is time to recognize that to achieve that goal takes more than a candidate, a family, a village, or even a nation.[104] It takes a state.

Concerning Maternalism

This book focuses on the maternal identities the public associates with women. Whatever the ontological status of those identities, it is reasonable to presume they are here to stay for the foreseeable future. For this reason, what becomes important for women running for political office is whether the state itself represents those traits in its public policies. When the state does so, voters learn that to have maternal traits is to be in the public sphere, which improves their attitudes about women's suitability as political leaders improve and their electoral support for women candidates. Attributing to any group, much less to women or the state, a specific identity, never mind a maternal one, can raise issues about the consequences of such identification. For some, for example, to discuss the attribution to women of maternal identities constitutes harmful reductionism.

Reductionism

Identifying women as biological, if not social, maternalists can take many negative forms. One pernicious form is reductionism, as evidenced in Norman Mailer's emphasis on women's biological reproductive capacities as defining their identities. Mailer writes,

"through history . . . to conceive or not to conceive . . . was finally an expression of the character of the woman, perhaps the deepest expression of
her character . . . the prime responsibility of a woman is probably to be on
earth long enough to find the best mate possible for herself, and conceive
children who will improve the species."[1]

Joyce Carol Oates counters that once women's identities are reduced to
being instruments for reproducing the species, it won't "if we protest that
sexual identities are the least significant aspect of our lives . . . if we hope,
not absurdly in this era, that technology might make our lives less physical and more spiritual," because established views of women won't change.
Rather, as Oates points out, age-old limitations on women will prevail,

> throughout human history women have been machines for the production
> of babies. It was not possible for them to live imaginative, electoral, fully
> human life at all, if indeed they survive for very long. They live longer
> than men to find a mate, to have a number of children, many of whom
> would not survive . . . but it was the process of matter, the blind, anony-
> mous reproductive process that gave these women their identities . . . to
> be mechanically operated, to have one's body moving along in the process
> the Spirit cannot control, to have the spirit trapped in a chosen physical
> predicament—this is a kind of death. It is life for the species, perhaps, but
> death for the individual.[2]

Thus, as Oates concludes, "the mechanical fact of possessing a certain body
must no longer determine the role of the spirit, the personality. If Wom-
en's Liberation accomplishes no more than this it will have accomplished
apparently everything."[3] That is to say, it is crucial to refrain from reducing women to identities derivative of biological and social maternalism
alone.[4]

Judith Butler agrees. She cautions that it is dangerous for any theory of
women's rights to take "an easy return to the *materiality* of the body."[5] To
use the body as a reference point is to confer upon its materiality a "sign"
of sexual difference. This in turn is to "re-ensnare woman in her natural-
ized, materialized, 'womanhood.' In doing so, we re-essentialize she whom
we have struggled so long to free from her essential bindings."[6] Those
concerned about reducing women to their biological maternal capacities
find evidence that their concerns are valid by such attitudes and policies
as those advocated in Japan. The growing percentage of women adopting
Western, feminist attitudes includes for many Japanese women the rejection of traditional roles as wives and mothers, by delaying marriage until

their thirties or by not getting married at all. This trend prompted former Prime Minister Yoshiro Mori to assert that "women who don't bear children are unworthy and ought to be denied public pensions." By this he meant that public pensions for women were a way for the government "to thank them for their hard [maternal] work . . . [and that] it is wrong for women who haven't had a single child to ask for taxpayer money when they get old, after having enjoyed their freedom and had fun."[7] Similarly, as Sherilyn MacGregor notes, "there are political risks in celebrating women's association with caring, as both an ethic and a practice . . . the positive identification of women with caring ought to be treated cautiously for it obscures some of the negative implications of feminized care and narrows our understanding of women as political actors."[8]

To associate women with biological, if not social, maternalism, however, need not reduce them to those identities alone. On the contrary, to ignore the connection between maternalism and not only women, but all people is to ignore the "animality" in all of us as human beings. As philosopher Martha Nussbaum cautions, such neglect "leads us to slight aspects of our own lives that have worth," such as childbearing and caring for the material and emotional needs of others. Denying the biological dimension of our existence as animals also

> makes us think of the core of ourselves as self-sufficient, not in need of the gifts of fortune; in so thinking we greatly distort the nature of our own morality and rationality, which are thoroughly material and animal themselves; we learn to ignore the fact that disease, old age, and accident can impede the moral and rational functions . . . [and] makes us think of ourselves as a-temporal . . . [thereby forgetting] that the usual human life cycle brings with it periods of extreme dependency, in which our functioning is very similar to that enjoyed by the mentally or physically handicapped throughout their lives.[9]

Rather than ignore the attribution by the public of biological maternalism to women, focusing on women's biological as well as social reproductive identities confronts head-on the continuing salience of these traits as a *subset of sex difference identities*. While we wait for a transformation in public attitudes to shift the attribution of social and biological maternal traits from women to men, or even to equalize their attribution to both sexes, it is important to take into account how the government itself is associated or not with maternal traits and the impact this has for women running for political office.

Essentialism

Another pernicious form of identifying women as maternalists is essentialism, whereby one specific characteristic is used to characterize all women. As political scientist Jane Mansbridge notes, it is very human to make essentialist claims because "human cognitive capacities tend automatically toward some forms of essentializing."[10] This cognitive tendency is reinforced by a host of social conventions, including the way societies regulate the behavior of men and women, thereby producing difference between the groups; social interactions that regularly include jokes about the differences between men and women; linguistic conventions that impose gendering formats as a component of speech, such as male/female nouns, pronouns, and such;[11] and familial, socializing experiences that in most cultures skew infancy and early childhood relations as ones defined by relations with women, if not specifically with mothers in contrast to adult relations, which include being dominated by males in general, if not specifically with fathers.

Given what appears to be the human cognitive need to generalize upon experience, people tend to perceive their in-group as more alike than it really is and to view out-groups as more different than in reality they are,[12] thereby reifying different groups as if they were essentially—naturally or ontologically—different from one another. Identifying any characteristic as associated only with women, therefore, runs the risk of essentializing women. Or as political scientist Sherry Martin puts it, "Why does 'acting like a woman' mean maternalism? Does this re-establish biological difference, or reify it, when 'mothering' is so strongly associated with what it means to be fully adult; i.e., an essential part of the life course? Are women who are not mothers still excluded?"[13] Or, as political scientist Cynthia Daniels asks, don't you need to distinguish between "women's interests, maternalism, and gender equality ('feminist interests')?"[14] Or, as another states, "I am sure I am not the first to point out that this construction . . . the idea that . . . women's biological difference and roles as mothers . . . [is a valid premise for analyzing women's access to political leadership] is deeply essentialist."[15]

To mitigate these essentializing tendencies, it is crucial to recognize diversity within as well as between groups.[16] Within the group women and the group men there is great diversity on most measures, and that diversity is an important activist agenda item so ensure that individuals within those groups do not fall victim to stereotyping.[17] Yet while we wait for the transformation of those identities to occur in the public, such that voters no longer impose on women maternal traits, life and political campaigns must go on. Instrumentally, therefore, what boosts women's access to political office are public policies that represent maternal traits. And in the case of welfare provision, such a state also normatively promotes democracy by guaranteeing social citizenship for its populace.

Intersectionality

Another issue of concern is intersectionality, that is, the way any one ascriptive group difference, such as sex, is inextricably mixed with a myriad of other ascriptive group identities. There is no way to isolate one ascriptive characteristic from the many that intersect to define each human being. All of us are a combination of characteristics acquired coercively at birth, such as race, class, sex, religious background, nationality, and linguistic heritage. It is a mistake to single out any one ascriptive characteristic in isolation from all others to explain an individual's identity.[18] As political scientist Ange-Marie Hancock stresses, "more than one category" is required to explain political institutions or political actors because of "the tremendous variation *within* [such] categories as "Blackness" or "womanhood.""[19]

As legal scholar Kimberlé Crenshaw notes, this does not mean that intersectionality is "some new, totalizing theory of identity."[20] It simply means that there are "multiple grounds of identity when considering how the social world is constructed."[21] What is more, as Hancock observes, the intersectional approach "has yet to gain a firm foothold in the domain of political science," in favor of compartmentalizing citizens "according to a singular 'politically relevant characteristic,'" which then leads "only to an additive rather than multiplicative approach."[22] As a result, much analysis of gender, race, and class is seriously flawed. As Crenshaw puts it:

> Black women are sometimes excluded from feminist theory and antiracist policy discourse because both are predicated on a discrete set of experiences that often does not accurately reflect the interaction of race and gender. The problem of exclusion cannot be solved simply by including Black women within an already established analytical structure. Because the intersectional experience is greater than the sum of racism and sexism, any analysis that does not take intersectionality into account cannot sufficiently address the particular manner in which Black women are subordinated.[23]

Political scientist Jane Junn also warns about the danger of thinking about any one category such as race, class, or sex, as a static rather than a dynamic component of experience and political context. So doing, she cautions, can lead one to look at the independent effects of one category, such as gender, on another, such as race, because both are "moving targets" that defy such fixed analyses.[24] What is more, the diversity within a single category, such as race, for example, in which contestation occurs between the Latino and Hispanic populations in the United States, renders race as a static classifications useless, if not misleading.[25]

While it is true that all ascriptive characteristics—such as race, class, sex, religion, language, ethnicity, and nationality, and so on—intersect in every human being, it is not true that all other ascriptive characteristics are as necessary for the survival of society and for the survival of the state as is biological sex difference. Despite the fluidity of sex classifications, binary sex group difference is the foundation of a type of labor—biological reproductive labor—upon which all societies and all states depend for their survival. What is more, biological reproduction, or biological maternalism, has been socially constructed to be associated with women rather than with men since the very beginnings of human civilization and is likely to remain so in the foreseeable future.

When it comes to women's identities, therefore, integrating race, class, religion, and other ascriptive identities with the attribution of maternalism to women has the effect of modifying but not substituting women's basic identities as biological maternalists, if not also social ones. These modifications are crucial to recognize and to analyze, but so, too, is it important to realize how as modifications of a common denominator they do not substitute women's identities as maternalists for something else. For example, as Dorothy Roberts shows, race and class layer onto the public perception of women's social and maternalist identities, attributing positive value to white, middle-class women's maternalism and negative value to black, welfare women's maternalism. The result can be criminalizing the behavior of women who give birth to infants who test positive for drugs, most of whom are poor and black, thereby exemplifying the way race, class, and sex intersect to pose all but insurmountable problems for some women. She traces the disproportionate prosecution of poor, black women to a long history in the United States of devaluing black women as mothers.[26] She argues that this policy orientation stems from the legacy of racialized slavery in the United States, from which derives the preponderance of social policies premised on the assumption that "Black people's poverty is caused by their reproduction"[27] and that black mothers are "bad" mothers whose reproductive irresponsibility warrants curbing means government "encouragement" (read "coercion") of dangerous contraceptives, such as Norplant and Depo-Provera.[28] She extends her analysis to that of the child welfare system, pointing to the disproportionate number of black children in foster homes compared to whites, on the assumption that black family members are incapable of caring for their own children. Rather than a black mother, grandmother, or aunt, Roberts contends that social workers assume child care competency resides somewhere among white caretakers, thereby destroying black families in the process.[29]

The point is, however, that even if the reproductive activities of white women and black women are hierarchically valued by the public, as they are, nevertheless, both are associated with reproductive labor, maternalism. The particular value assigned to women's maternalism on the basis of their race and class modifies those identities by stratifying their value, but those modifications do not entail the substitution of maternal identifies for something else. Hence, Roberts is not arguing that the public fails to assign reproductive identities to black women compared to white women (or vice versa), but rather that the *value* of those identities is racially inscribed such that the public views one as more valuable to society than the other. This project presumes, therefore, that the public attributes maternal identities to all women, whatever their race, class, or other ascriptive identities. When analyzing women's relationship to the state, therefore, what is crucial is the way the state associates itself with maternal identities by means of adopting public policies representing social and biological maternal traits.[30]

Fear of Individualism

While for some feminists it is dangerous to attribute a maternal identity to women or to the state, for others it is just the opposite. They fear that the basic concept of the state is male as is attributing individualism to people or to the state, both of which undermine women's prospects for political inclusion. The concept of the state as male derives from Max Weber's classic definition of the modern state as the institution that has a monopoly on the legitimate use of coercive force, even the use of violence.[31] All governments must provide, usually by means of the use of force or the threat of the use of force, at least a modicum of law and order within their own territories and a modicum of defense from nonconsensual intrusion of their territories from other states. States do this by means of a domestic police force and military branches of government.

Inasmuch as the public associates men with law, order, and military defense, while associating women with nurturing policies, such as education, health, peace, and welfare, the state itself is gendered. What the state "does" in its most theoretical and practical sense is what the public associates with men. This does not mean that voters and others assume that all men, compared to all women, have been in the past or are today more involved in law and order or military activities. Rather, the public's association of men as a group with police forces and military defense stems from its observation that a far greater percentage of men have been from time immemorial in police and military units.

A 2004 study by Jennifer Lawless, for example, assesses the impact on women's electoral prospects of the renewed military focus and martial atmosphere of the U.S. government after the terrorist attacks of September 11, 2001. She finds that despite "scores of studies" that reveal that "female candidates fare as well as their male counterparts," in the two years since the attacks on the World Trade Center, "the percentage of citizens willing to support a woman presidential party nominee has significantly decreased." Basing her analysis on the results of a *Knowledge Networks* random national sample survey to examine the manner in which the atmosphere of war might affect women candidates' electoral prospects, Lawless discovers that "citizens prefer men's leadership traits and characteristics, deem men more competent at legislating around issues of national security and military crises, and contend that men are superior to women at addressing the new obstacles generated by the events of September 11, 2001. As a result of this gender stereotyping, levels of willingness to support a qualified woman presidential candidate are lower than they have been for decades." Lawless concludes that in order for women to fare as well as men, the political climate must be dominated by issues that play to women's stereotypical strengths, and concomitantly, when "men's issues" dominate the political agenda, women are disadvantaged.[32]

In addition to the legitimate use of coercive force, democratic states by definition guarantee individual rights, both civil and political. Civil rights refer to state guarantees that individuals have the right, for example, to sign contracts and be married "in spite of" their ascriptive group characteristics, such as race, class, or sex. Political rights refer to state guarantees that individuals have the right to participate in political governance, as by voting, holding office, or serving on jury duty, again regardless of their ascriptive characteristics. British sociologist T. H. Marshall viewed civil and political rights as necessary ones for a political system to be considered a democracy.[33]

The idea of individual equality as a basis for public policies stems from liberal theorists such as John Locke, who assert that all individuals are born free and equal to one another. What makes government legitimate is individuals' consent to be governed as expressed by electing political leaders from among themselves. Though a democracy based on individual equality as theory and practice imagines society as composed of individuals void of demographic markers, such as race, class, or sex, many feminist political theorists believe that liberal political systems not only are really masculine in character but also for that reason serve women's interests badly.

One of the most forceful critics of the liberal state is law scholar Catharine MacKinnon, who analyzes the liberal state as a male apparatus, in which the right of privacy to be free from interference by the government means little more when it comes to women than their right to be free of government assistance in defending themselves against male violence. As she puts it, "the state is a male institution not only demographically but [also] socially and politically—its structures and actions [are] driven by an ideology predicated on an epistemic angle of vision with concomitant values, attitudes, and behaviors based on the status location of the male sex in society, members of which . . . occupy a superior position in gender hierarchy, resulting in a sexual politics."[34] As she points out, equality theory as the cornerstone of the liberal state, which demands equal treatment of people who are alike, has little to offer in the way of correcting basic inequalities among people in the first place. Thus, defining discrimination as treating someone who has the same rank, status, or qualities as others in a group holds out no promise of protection for a person who lacks membership in the group in the first place. Title VII, for example, requires that all employees be treated alike "in spite of" their sex or race, and it is discriminatory to refuse to hire a woman simply because she is female. Once on the job, however, formal equality theory requires no attention to inequalities that exist between men and women when it comes to women's generally greater involvement in pregnancy, birth, and care of the young or elderly family members, all of which impinge upon women's capacities to earn as much or to advance as far on the job compared to men. As MacKinnon notes, "rather than being a means of ending hierarchal arrangements based on group rank, formal equality can be a way to maintain unequal status. Indeed, its success can be inconsistent with substantive equality, which may require social change."[35]

The presumption of universalism that underlies the democratic, liberal idea of the individual all too often falls short of providing a level playing field for all members of society. Rather than substantiating its promise of equal opportunity for all, liberal practice has failed to recognize equality within diverse societies. As political theorist Uday Mehta demonstrates, during the expansion of the British Empire it was not the liberals, such as James Mill, who opposed colonial expansion and the paternalistic subjugation of nonwhite peoples in India, but rather, the conservatives, such as Edmund Burke.[36]

Liberalism's scrupulous determination to "ignore" ascriptive differ-ence—to create "race-blind," "gender-blind" policies—can thus have the effect of whitewashing over diversity and difference as meaningful components of human life and social experience. As philosopher Will Kymlicka notes, frequently one's ascriptive identity—even when that identity signifies subordinate group status, such as being a woman, a person of color, or a member of the working class—can nevertheless be extremely meaningful and an "important and constitutive element of personal identity."[37]

The Hybrid State

Just as maternalism as a basis for public policies need not harm women, so, too, individualism as a basis for public policies need not harm women The extension of individual rights to women based on their sameness with men is not the problem when it comes to women's political inclusion in a liberal, democratic state. Rather, what promotes women's election as political leaders is the combination of individualism and maternalism as a basis for public policies. Even one of the most effective critics of the liberal state, Catharine MacKinnon, uses its guarantee of individual equality to advance women's rights. The case in point is sexual harassment. MacKinnon pioneered the successful legal argument that sexual harassment in employment contexts is a form of sex discrimination that violates Title VII of the Civil Rights Act of 1964.[38] This breakthrough achievement disproportionately advantages women, given that 85% of the sexual harassment cases involve women suffering in relation to men who are harassing them in the work force. It is a prototypical example of using the principle of individual equality, that men and women are the same, to promote women's rights and interests. The liberal state may fall short when it comes to equalizing class inequalities stemming from differences between jobs resulting from differences in educational opportunities or other market forces. However, the liberal state as exemplified by the American state, nevertheless, can do a good job when it comes to equalizing the treatment of men and women within any specific job context by making it a federal crime to discriminate on the basis of sex when hiring, promoting, or retaining personnel and when engaging in the harmful practice of sexual harassment.

Rather than failing women, therefore, a more accurate assessment of liberal individualism is that it is simply not enough to secure women's equality with men in society. In the context of a work environment, not only to women need equal access to employment and freedom from sexual harassment, but they also need pregnancy leave, child-care support, and flexible work schedules disproportionately to the needs of men. This means that women need more than Title VII alone to meet their familial roles as the people who disproportionately deliver more care to others compared to men. It is not that Title VII is a failure—it is just that it is not enough.

Similarly, critiques of liberalism from cross-national, historical perspectives need to be careful when extolling the virtues of conservatism as an *alternative* to individual equality. National liberation movements, including those in India, have founded their claims on individual equality, demanding that liberal states follow through on that promise rather than subverting it by colonial domination. Praise by some conservatives, such as Burke, of the bonds of community and the virtues of a colonized people with reference to their ascriptive identities does not work as a substitute for individual equality, only as a supplement. Mehta, for example, gives no indication that Burke also supported the liberation of colonized populations or viewed colonized Indians as equal in their capacities for self-rule compared to their British conquerors. To the contrary, one of Burke's main contributions to political theory was his support for systems of representative government based on a trustee principle,[39] where representatives make policy as they see fit,[40] on the presumption that the mass public cannot be trusted to know their own best interests. Far from supporting the actual representation of members of various groups in legislatures, he developed instead what is known as *virtual* representation in which the interests of a group can be represented by people other than members of the group. As Burke contended, "since it is interests which are represented and not people, it is not necessary that each district or group of people choose a member of parliament; it is sufficient that their interest be represented, even if it is done by a representative chosen from some other geographical location."[41]

Today, although we recognize that the substantive representation of group interests can be achieved by others than the members of the group itself, it would be hard to find advocates for coercive representative designs that prohibit direct, descriptive representation on the grounds that the group in question could not, or should not, represent itself. The goal is now to recognize group difference in conjunction with civil and political guarantees of individual equality. Thus, liberal individualism is not the enemy of subordinate groups. It is just not sufficient for achieving their greater equality with others. In the case of women, liberal individualism has not "failed" them, as some contend. Rather, liberal individualism, while a necessary condition for women's political inclusion in contemporary democracies, is simply not a sufficient condition.[42] What also is necessary to bolster women's election to national political office is a political context in which the government represents the maternal traits that voters associate with women. What promotes women's access to political leadership positions, therefore, is a hybrid state that is associated not only with being male or being an individual but also with being female, and hence being maternal. And the failure of the American state today to be such a hybrid explains its failure to elect women to political office at levels comparable to other democracies.

Political Systems with Same-Sex Union Rights[a]

Political System	Year	Marriage	Civil Unions	Notes
Andorra	2005		Yes	
Argentina	2003		Yes	In July 2003, the first gay civil union took place, giving legal rights similar to those for heterosexual couples, but excluding adoption and inheritance rights. Argentina is the first country in Latin America to allow such unions.
Belgium*	2003	Yes		Gay marriages were allowed in 2003.
Canada*	2005		Yes	In July 2005, a bill to legalize same-sex marriage became law. Gay marriage was already legal in eight of ten provinces and one of Canada's three territories.
Croatia	2003		Yes	Civil partnerships for same-sex couples since 2003.
Czech Republic	2006		Yes	On March 15, 2006, the parliament of the Czech Republic voted to override a presidential veto and allow same-sex partnerships to be recognized by law, effective July 1, 2006, granting registered couples inheritance and health-care rights similar to married couples, but not granting adoption rights. The parliament had previously rejected similar legislation four times.
Denmark*	1989		Yes	The first country to institute legislation granting registered same-sex partners the same rights as married couples. Church weddings are not allowed.
Finland*	2002		Yes	Registered partnership, which allows two members of the same sex to register their partnership and gain much of the same rights and duties as married couples. Adoption was not included.
France*	1999		Yes	In 1999 introduced a civil contract called the Pacs, which gives some rights to co-habiting couples, regardless of sex. These do not include the full rights of marriage, notably over taxes, inheritance, and adoption. In 2004, a mayor conducted the country's first gay marriage, but it was later nullified by a court.
Germany*	2001		Yes	Has allowed same-sex couples to register for "life partnerships" since 2001. The law only gives couples the same inheritance and tenants' rights as heterosexual married couples.

Country	Year			Description
Great Britain*	2005		Yes	Legislation came into force in December 2005 giving same-sex couples in registered partnerships similar rights to married couples, in areas such as pensions, property, social security, and housing.
Iceland*	1996		Yes	Registered partnership, which allows two members of the same sex to register their partnership and gain much of the same rights and duties as married couples. Adoption was not included.
Luxembourg*	2004		Yes	A law on civil partnerships largely inspired by the French model was introduced in 2004.
The Netherlands*	2001	Yes		Became the first country to offer full civil-marriage rights to gay couples in 2001.
New Zealand*	2004		Yes	In December 2004, New Zealand's parliament passed controversial legislation to recognize civil unions between gay couples.
Norway*	1996		Yes	Civil unions are offered, permitting most of the benefits and obligations of marriage. The second cabinet Stoltenberg announced a common, unified marriage act as part of its foundation document, the Soria Moria statement. A public hearing was opened on May 16, 2007, and the final act is likely to be treated by the parliament in 2008.
Portugal*	2001		Yes	Same-sex partners have the same rights as opposite-sex partners in common law marriage.
Slovenia	2006		Yes	Currently recognizes unions, giving same-sex partners access to each other's pensions and property.
South Africa	2005	Yes		The post-apartheid constitution includes a clause making discrimination based on sexual identity illegal. Homosexual couples are allowed to adopt. In December 2005, South Africa's high court said it was unconstitutional to deny gay people the right to marry, and instructed parliament to amend marriage laws to include same-sex unions within a year.

Political System	Year	Marriage	Civil Unions	Notes
Spain*	2005	Yes		Legalized full marriage for gay couples in June 2005, despite fierce opposition from the Roman Catholic Church. Gay married couples can also adopt children.
Sweden*	1996		Yes	Registered partnership was granted in Sweden in 1995. Sweden was the third country to legalize same-sex unions, after Denmark and Norway. The Registered Partnership Act grants full range of protections, responsibilities, and benefits as marriage, including adoption and arrangements for the breakdown of the relationship. Only available to same-sex couples. Same-sex registered partners can adopt jointly. In vitro fertilization for lesbian couples was allowed in 2005.
Switzerland*	2007		Yes	Limited legal benefits granted via civil recognition.

a) Information is taken virtually verbatim from "Gay Marriage around the lobe," BBC News, http://newsvote.bbc.co.uk/mpapps/pagetools/print/news.bbc.co.uk/2/hi/americas/4081999.stm; "Where Is Gay Marriage Legal?" http://gaylife.about.com/od/samesexmarriage/a/legalgaymariage.htm, accessed August 8, 2007.
* Comparable democracies. See Table 4.3.

Women Hereditary Executives
since the Twentieth Century[a]

Political System	Sovereigns and Regents*
Antigua and Barbuda	Queen Elizabeth II, 1981
Australia	Queen Elizabeth II, 1952
The Bahamas	Queen Elizabeth II, 1952
Barbados	Queen Elizabeth II, 1952
Belize	Queen Elizabeth II, 1952
Bénin	Kpojito Kanai, 1894–1990
	Kpojito Adonon, 1972
	Kpojito Hwanjile, 1972
Bhutan	Regent Queen Ashi Kesang-la Choden, 1972
Botswana	Acting [Regent] Paramount Chieftess the Queen Mother Gagoangwe Sechele of the BaNgwaktse, 1923–24
	Acting [Regent] Paramount Chieftess the Queen Sister Ntebogang a Bathoen of the BaNgwaktse, 1924–28
	Acting [Regent] Paramount Chieftess the Queen Mother Dulano Seeco Elizabeth Pulane Moremi of the BaTwana, 1946–56
	Kgôsi Rebecca Banika of Chobe District, 2000
	Paramount Chiefess Kgôsi Mosadi Seboko a Mokgôsi of the Balete in Bagamalete, 2001
	Designate Regent Princess Kealebile of Batwana, 2003
Brazil	Regent Princess-Imperial Isabel da Brangança e Borabon, 1889–1921
Burundi	Umugabekazi *(Queen Mother)* Nyiaranauugo III Kankazi, 1931
	Regent The Queen Mother Mugabekazi Nidi Ririkumutima, 1908–17
Cambodia	Queen Sisovath Monivong Kossomak Nearieath Serey Cathana, 1960–70
Cameroon	Queen Mother of Babete, 1999
Canada	Queen Victoria, 1837–1901
	Queen Elizabeth II, 1952–
Central African Republic	Natélégé, Queen of the Mzalara, 1855–1900
China	De-facto Co-Regent H.I.H Dowager Empress Xiao Ding Jing Long Yu Huagtaihou, 1908–12
	Huang Tai Hu, Empress Regent, 1881–1908
	Xiao Ding Jing Long Hu huagtaihou Cixi, Empress-Regent, 1911–12
Cyprus	Queen Elizabeth II, 1952–60

Political System	Sovereigns and Regents*
Denmark	Temporary Rigsforstander HRH Princess, Benedikte, 1965– Queen Margrethe II, 1972– Queen Ingrid of Sweden, Co-Deputy Head of State, 1972–2000
Egypt	Valida Sultana Emine Hanim, 1892–1914
Ethiopia	H.I.H. Negista Nagast Empress, Titular Ruler Zawdute Menilek, 1916–30 Itegé Taytu Betul, Regent Empress, 1906–10
Fiji	Queen Elizabeth II, 1970–87
	Paramount Chieftess of Rewa Ro Adi Lady Litia Cakobau Lalabalavu Kaloafutoga, 1974–2004
	Paramount Chieftess Bulou Eta Kacalini Vosailagi of Na-droga Navosa, 1977–2001
	Samanunu Cakobau Talakuli, High Chiefess of Tailevu, 1989
	Paramount Chief Kuini Teimumu Vuikaba Speed of Na-vosa, 1998–2004 (also listed as Prime Minister)
	Adi Sainimili Cagilaba, the Marama Tui Ba, around 1999 Paramount Chiefess Adi Laite Kotomaiwasa of the Vanua Nawaiviluri, 2005–
Gambia, The	Queen Yvonne Pryor of the Madingo, 1995– Mama Adame, Mansa Ruler, Gambia, 20th c
Germany	Guardian Dowager Princess Marie von Gemmingen-Hornberg of Sayn-Wittgenstin-Berleburg, 1889–1900
Ghana	Queen Elizabeth II, 1957–60
	12th Asantehemaa Nana Ama Sewaa Nyaako of Asante, 1944–77
	11th Asantehemaa Kwaadu Yaadom II of Asante, 1917–44
	Yaa Asantewaa, Asante Edweso Tribe, Queen Mother of Asante Tribe, 1900–1901
	10th Asantehemaa Nana Yaa Akyeaa of Asante, 1994–17
	Regent of Edweso, Edwesohemaa Nana Yaa Asantewaa, 1896–1900
	Chieftainess Nana Ekua Bri II of Apraponso, 2004
Greece	Regent Dowager Queen Olga Konstatinovna Romanova, 1920

Political System	Sovereigns and Regents*
Grenada (became an associated state with the United Kingdom in 1967 and independent [Kingdom] in 1974)	Queen Elizabeth II, 1974
Guyana	Queen Elizabeth II, 1966–70
India	Rani Mariyumma Adi-raja Bibi of Cannanore, 1946–47
	Regent H.H. Shrimant Akhand Soubhagyavati Maharani Pramula Bai Maharaj Sahib of Dewas, 1941–43 and 1947–48
	Regent The Maharani of Mudhol Nanasaheb, 1937–47
	H.H. Rani Shrimant Akhand Soubhagyavati Parvati Bai Raje Sahib Bhonsle of Savantwadi, 1937–47
	President of the Council of Regency H.H. Shrimant Akhand Soubhagyavati Maharani Gajra Bai Raje Sahib Scindia of Gwalior, 1931–36
	Regent Dowager Maharani Kumari Shri Tejkunuerba of Barwani, 1930–40
	Shrimant Sitabaisaheb Bhalchandrarao Patwardhan of Kurandvad, 1927–69
	Titular Head of the Royal Family Princess Bamba Sophia Jingan of Punjab, 1926–57
	Regent H.H. Shrimant Akhand Soubhagyavati Maharani Lakshmi Devi Bai Sahiba of Dhar, 1926–31
	Tamil Nadu Jayaram Jayalalitha, Chief of the Tamil Nadu State, 1995–96
	Regent Rajmata Krishna Kumari of Marwar and Jodhpur, 1947–49
	Regent The Dowager Maharani Kanchanpura Devi of Tripura, 1947
	Regent H.H. Shrimant Akhand Soubhagyavati Maharani Chinku Bai Raje Sahib Scindia of Gwalior, 1925–31
	Regent Dowager H.H Rani Shrimant Akhand Soubhagyavati Tara Bai Raje Sahib Bhonsle of Akalot, 1923–36
	Rani Profulla Kumari Devi of Bastar, 1922–36

Political System	Sovereigns and Regents*
India cont'd	Regent and President Maharani Indra Devi Sahiba of Cooch-Behar, 1932–36
	Regent and President of the State Council Maharani Siniti Devi of Cooch-Behar, 1922–32
	Regent Dowager Rani Saida of Badalpur, 1921–?
	Rani Ayisha Adi-Raja Bibi of Cannanore, 1921–31
	Regent Dowager Rani Soubhagyavati Gajara Bai Raje Sahib Bhonsle of Savantwadi, 1913–24
	Rani Imbichi Adi-Raja Bibi of Cannanore, 1907–11
	Head of the Princely Family H.H. Sikander Saulat Iftikhar ul-Mulk Haji Nawab Mehr Tai Sajida Sultan Begum Sahiba, Nawab Begum of Bhopal, 1960–95
Indonesia	Datuk I Suji of Suppa, 1950–59
	Maradia Regnant of Balan(g)nipa, 1947–57
	Regent Datuk I Pateka Tana of Tanette, 1926–27
	Ranrang Toewa Andi Ninong of Wajo, 1925–46
	Ratu Donna Maria da Costa of Djeniloe, from 1923
	Adatuwant I Ba Eda of Sawito, 1922–40
	Datuk I Pancaitana Aru Pancana of Tanette, 1910–26
	Aru Kabe af Alla, until before 1909
	Princess I We Tanri of Rapang, 1908–42
	Regent-Ratu/Magau I Tondai of Biromaru, 1906–15
	Regent-Ratu/Magau Yahasia of Biromaru, 1906–15
	Aru I Samatana, 1906–17
	Makole I Raja of Tojo Indo di Salaso, 1905–15
	Ratu Petronella da Costa of Lidak, 1900–13
	H.H. Sikander Saulat, Iftikhar ul-Mulk, Nawab Sultan Kaikhusrau Jahan Begum Sahiba, Nawab Begum of Bhopal, 1901–26
	Senior Rani H.H. Sri Patmanabha Sevini, Vanchi Dharma Vardhini, Raja Rajeshwari, *Rani* Setu Lakshmi Bai Maharaja of Attingal 1901–85; Regent of Travancore, 1924–31
	Junior Rani H.H. Maharani Setu Parvati Bal of Attingal, 1901–83

Political System	Sovereigns and Regents*
Indonesia cont'd	Maradi Kavea Ta Saïnta of Sausu, 1898–1905
	Payung e-ri Luwu Andi We Kambo Opu Daeng Risompa of Luwu, 1898–1935
	Aru I Buabara of Kassa, 1897–1936
	The Aru I Coma of Batulapa, 1890–1933
	Adatuwang We Tan-ri Paaderang Bau Jella of Alitta, 1861–1902
	Queen Tjoet Njak Dien in Aceh, 1873–1901
	Aru I Batari toja of Barru, 1875–1908
	Princess Regnant Anna Elisabeth of Aunoni of Amfoan, 1880–1902
	Datuk I-Madellung Karaeng Kajuwara, *Datu* of Supa, 1881–1902 [11122]
	Sultan Aisya of Indragiri, 1885–1902 [11132]
	Soledatu Siti Saenabe Aru Lapajung of Soppeng, 1895–1940 [11174]
	Princess I Njilitimo Aru Baranti of Rapang, 1905–8
	Adatuwang Regnant Bau Rukiah of Sawito, 1951
	Acting Head of the Princely Family Rjamata Krishna Kumari of Jodhpur, 1952–69
	Titular Ratu Tambu Rambu Queen of Sumba Yuliana of Rende, 1992–2003
	Regent Princess Siti Hajjah Maryam Salahuddin of Bima, 2001
Iraq	Joint Regent Lady Surma d'Mar Shimun of Assyrian Nation, 1918–27
Ireland	Queen Victoria, 1837–1901
Jamaica	Queen Elizabeth II, 1962–
Kenya	Queen Elizabeth II, 1963–64
	Assistant Chief Neima Kimojino of the Embulul Sub-Location Ngong Division of the Kajiado District, 2002
Kongo (Angola)	Queen Dowager Dona Isabel Maqria da Gama of Kongo, 1957–62
Lebanon	Al-Sitt Nazira Jumblatt of the Druze, 1921–39

Political System	Sovereigns and Regents*
Leshoto	Regent Queen 'MaMohato Thabita 'II Masente Lerotholi Mojela (Queen Mother Mamohato II), 1970, 1990, 1996
	Regent Queen Karabo Mohato Bereng Seeiso, 2001
	Acting Paramount Chief The Mofumahali 'MaNtsebo Amalia 'Matsaba Sempe, 1941–60
	Chieftainess Mamatheola Matela, chief of Ngoajani, 2000
	Senior Chieftainess Mboanjikana of Libonda, 2000
Luxembourg	Lieutenant-Representant HRH Grande Duchesse Mari-Anna d' Braganca 1908–12
	Grand Duchess Maria-Adélheïde zu Nassau-Weiburg, 1912–19
	Grande-Duchesse Charlotte zu Nassau-Weiburg, 1919–64; leader of the government in exile, 1940–44
Malaysia	Regent Princess Sharifah Leng binti al-Marhum Yang di-Pertuan Muda Syed Abdul Hamid of Tampin, before 1944
	Queen Elizabeth II, 1952–56
Marshall Islands	Leirojlaplap Libinnirok of Mejit, 1900s
	Leirojlaplap Atama Zedkeia of the Majuro Atoll, 2001
	Hereditary Leiroij Elma Kenny of the Majuro Atoll, 2000s
Mauritius	Queen Elizabeth II, 1968–1992
Namibia	Queen Maria Mwengere of Shambyu, 1947–87
	Queen Mother Mutaleni ka Mpingana of Ondonga, 1941
	Queen Kanuni I of Uukwangali, 1926–41, 1958–71
	Anna Katrina Christian of Bondelswart, Captain, 1977 (she is 17th in the recorded genealogy of these captains)
	Ohamba Nekoto (royal ruler), 1891–1908
	Chief Constance Letang Kgosiemang, 1979–92
	Queen Hompa Angelina Matumbo Ribebe of Shambyu, 1989–
Native North American Tribal Chiefs	Chiefess, Alice Brown Davis of the Seminole Nation of Oklahoma (USA), 1922–35 [11240]
	Jumper, Betty Mae, Chief of Seminole Nation, 1960s
	Ywahoo, Dhyani, Cherokee Nation Clan Chief, 1969
	Mankiller, Wilma T., Chief of Cherokee Nation, 1985–95

Political System	Sovereigns and Regents*
Native North American Tribal Chiefs, cont'd	Gloria Yazzie, Chairperson, Las Vegas Paiute Tribe, 1978–88 [elected]
	Margaret Henry, Chairperson, Las Vegas Paiute Tribe, 1988–90 [elected]
	Alfreda Mitre, Chairperson, Las Vegas Paiute Tribe, 1990–93, 1994–98 [elected]
	Chief Darlene Bernard, Lennox Island, 2001
	Vivian Juan Sanders, Chairperson, Arizon Tohono O'odham Nation, 2004 [elected]
	Pearl E. Casias, Acting Chairperson, Southern Ute Indian Tribe, 2004 [elected]
	Herminia Frias, Chairperson of the Pascua Yaqui Tribal Council Arizona (USA), 2004
	Cecelia Fire Thunder, Chairperson, Pine Ridge Indian Reservation, 2005– [elected]
	Alphonsine Lafond, Chief of Muskeg Lake, 1960–62 [elected]
	Mary Louise Bernard, Chief of Lennox-Island Confederacy of Indian Nations in Nova Scotia, 1960–62
Nepal	Regent H.H. Svasti Sri Sri Sri Sri Sri Sriman Mahara-jadhiraja Patta Rajninam Bada Maharani Revati Raman Rajya Lakshmi Devi Shahamam Sada Sabhajnabtinam of Nepal, 1911
The Netherlands	Queen Wilhelmina, 1890–1948
	Queen Juliana, 1948–80
	Queen Beatrix, 1980–
New Zealand	Maori Leader Princess Te Kirihaehae Te Puea Hērangi, 192?–52
	Queen Elizabeth II, 1952–
	Chieftainess Ena Te Papatahi from Ngati Whatua and Ngati Paoa, 1902
	Chieftainess Te Aitu Te Irikau, 1922
	Te Arikinui Dame Te Atairangikaahu Ariki Nui of the Tainui & Arki Hui (Paramount chief), Queen/Kuini of the Maori, 1966–

Political System	Sovereigns and Regents*
Nigeria	Iyoba Iha II of Uselu in Benin, 1888–1914 [11144]
	Regent Princess Teramade Adetule of Erijiyan-Ekiti, 1978–80
	Regent Princess Abigail Adegoke of Ido Ekiti, Acting Village Chieftainess, 1983–2000
	Regent Princess Adeboyoe Aladeyelu of the Igabara Odo-Ekiti, Acting Village Chieftainess, 1995
	Regent Princess Victoria Fasan of Agede Ogbese, 1996
	Erelu Oba Princess (Chief) Abimbola Dosumu-Shitta of Saki, 1999
	Chief Rita Lori-Ogbebor (in the Warri Kingdom), 2000–
	The Deji Princess Adeyinka Adesia of Akureland, 2000–2001
	Regent Princess Adenike Adebomi of Ise-Ekiti, Acting Village Chieftainess in the Ekiti State, 2000–
	Regent Princess Arinade Olayisade of Ido Ekiti, Acting Village chieftainess in the Ekiti State, 2000–
	Regent Princess Adegolarin Adeyeye of Ire Ekiti, Acting Village Chieftainess in the Ekiti, 2000
	Regent Princess Fehintola Omoleewo of Ayegabjau Ekiti, Acting Village Chieftainess in the Ekiti State, 2000–
	Regent Princess Adetola Opeymi of Iyin Ekiti, Acting Village Chieftainess in the Ekiti State, 2000–
Palau	Acting Ibedul (Huge Chief) Gloria Gibbon Salii of Koror, 1972–73; Bilung, 1975
	Ebilrekai Uma Basilius, Chiefess in the Babeldaob region, before 1996
	Lucy Orrukem, Matriarch of the second-ranking clan in Koror, until 1999
Panama	Queen Rufina Santana of the Nasos (elected queen within designated family), 1982–88
Papua New Guinea	Queen Elizabeth II, 1952–75
Philippines	Regent Rajah Putri of Maguindanao, 1888–1906
Russia	
Rwanda	Regent Umugabekazi Nyiraj V Kanjogera, 1916, 1922–27
	Reigning Umugabekazi Nyirauhi V Kanjogera, 1916–31

Political System	Sovereigns and Regents*
Saint Christopher	Queen Elizabeth II, 1983–
Saint Lucia	Queen Elizabeth II, 1979–
Saint Vincent	Queen Elizabeth II, 1979
Senegal	Queen Aline Sitoe Diatta of the Diola Tribe in Casamance, 1936–43
Sierra Leone	Queen Elizabeth II, 1961–71
	Paramount Chiefess Madam Yoko of Kpaa Mende and Seneghum, 1878–1908
	Paramount Chiefess Madam Matolo of Nongowa and Panguma, 1898–1908
	Paramount Chiefess Madam Hamonya of Nongowa and Pangum, 1908–18
	Paramount Chiefess Madam Ella Koblo Bulama of Kaiyamba, 1953–
	Madame Gulama, Mende Chieftain, 1960s–86
	Paramount Chief Honoria Bailor-Caulker of Shenge, 1961–99
	Paramount Chiefess Madam Boi Sei Kenja III of Imperri, 1963
	Paramount Chiefess Madam Kadiyatta Gata of Jong, 1963
	Paramount Chiefess Madam Tity Messi of Kwameba Krim, 1963
	Paramount Chiefess Madam Tiange Gbatekaka of Gaura, 1963
	Paramount Chiefess Madam Benya of Small Bo, 1963
	Paramount Chiefess Madam Mammawa Sama of Tunika, 1963
	Paramount Chief Madam Theresa Vibbi of Koya, 2001
	Paramount Chief Madam Margaret Thompson Seibureh of Bum, 1998
	Paramount Chief Madam Hawa Yakubu Ngokowa II of Selenga, 2001
	Paramount Chief Veronica B. Gbani III of Valunia, 2001
	Paramount Chief Madam Hawa Kpanabon Sokan IV of Imperri, 2001

Political System	Sovereigns and Regents*
Sierra Leone, cont.'d	Paramount Chief Madam Mattu Kaikai Yimbo of Timbale, 2001
	Paramount Chief Madam Edna Gamanga Fawundu of Mano Sakrim, 2001
	Paramount Chief Madam Mamie G. Gamanga of Simbaru, 2001
	Paramount Chief Madam Sall S. Lamin Gendemeh of Malegohun, 2001
	Paramount Chief Madam Mathilda Lansana Minnah of Yekomo Kpukumu Krim, 2001
	Paramount Chief Madam Baindu Sowa of Sowa, 2001
	Paramount Chief Madam Thompson-Seibureh, 2000
	Paramount Chief Madam Susan Caulker, 2000
South Africa	Queen Elizabeth II, 1952–61
	Chief Mali II of Khaha, 1928–43
	Rain Queen Khetoane Modjadji III, 1896–1959
	Rain Queen Makoma Mujaji IV, 1959–80
	Rain Queen Mokope Modjadji V, 1981–2001
	Acting Paramount Chief Elizabeth Tshatshu of the imiNtinde-line, 1941–46
	Acting Paramount Chief Nofikile a Ngongo of the imiDushane ka Ndlambe line of the Xhosas, 1943–57
	Acting Paramount Chief Nonayithi Jalia a Mthathi of the imiQhayi line, 1953–?
	Chief Sibongile Zungu, Madlebe Tribe in KwaZulu Natal, 1991–
	Acting Paramount Chieftainess Mathokoana Mopeli of the Bakwena Clan in the Qua Qua Homeland, 1993–
	Acting Chieftainess Fikele Lydia Nkosi, 1997–?
	Acting Paramount Chief Bhongolethu a Makhungu Dlamini of West amaPondo, 1997–2001
	Chieftainess Nolitha Matiwana of Emboland, 1997–2001
	Chieftainess Noiseko Gayilla of the Amanbombo Tribe at Keiskammahoek, ca. 2000–

Political System	Sovereigns and Regents*
South Africa (cont.)	Acting Chieftainess Noluntu of aba Thembu, 2000–
	Senior Chieftainess Nopharkamisa Mditshwa of the pondomise Tribe, ?–2000
	Chiefess N. Mopeli of Thababosiu, 2000
	Chiefess M.H. Mota of Phomolong, 2000
	Chiefess Mpungose Lilly Busiswe (Ibamba) of Mpungose, 2000
	Chiefess Nancy Tseane Mamaila of Mamaila, 2000
	Chiefess Anna Mpitso Shongoane of Shongoane, 2000
	Chiefess Angelina Ramadimetja Chaune of Ditlou Machidi, 2000
	Chiefess Dina ngwanamohule Seloane of Batau-Ba-Seloane, 2000
	Chiefess Eugine Bhekintina Zulu of Mandhlakazi, 2000
	Chief (Hosi) Philla Shilubana of the Valoyi, 2002–
	Rain Queen Makobo Modjadji VI, 2003–5
Spain	Maria Christina of Austria, Queen, Regent of Spain, 1885–1902
Swaziland	Joint Head of State The Ndlovukati Nukwase Nxumalo Ndwandwe, 1938–57
	Joint Head of State The Ndlovukati Lomawa Nxumalo Ndwandwe, 1925–38
	Reigning Queen Mother Latotsibeni Gwamile Mduli/ laMvelase, 1899–1921, Joint Head of State, 1921–25
	Joint Head of State, The Queen Mother, Zihlathi Ndwandwe, 1957–75
	Joint Head of State, The Queen Mother, Seneleleni Ndwandwe, 1975–
	Reigning Queen Mother, Dezliwe Shongwe, 1982–83
	Queen Regent and Head of State Ntombi Latfwala, 1983–86, Reigning Queen Mother, 1985–86, Joint Head of State and Queen Mother, 1986–
Tahiti	High Chiefess Te-ha'apapa III of Huahine French Polynesia, around 1909

Political System	Sovereigns and Regents*
Tanzania	Queen Elizabeth II, 1961–62
	Chief Sala of Nkokolo, 1934–62
	Chief Ng'endo of Ipito, 1934–62
	Chief Musonga II of Ipito, until 1934
	Chief Mugalula II of Kiwele, 1929–62
	Chief Ng'endo of Nkokolo, around 1926
	Chiefess Mukunde of Wikangulu, until 1922
	Chief Msavila I of Kiwele, 1893–1924
	Chief Muyelaansime of Nkokolo, 1903
Thailand	Regent Queen H.M. Somdetch Pra Nang Chao Sirikit Phra Baromma Rajini Nath, 1956
	Temporary Royal Regent HRH The Princess Mother Somdet Phra Srinagarindra Boromarajajonani, 1950–95
	Regent, Royal Princess, Maha Chakri Sirindhorm, 1977
	Queen Regent Sri Bajarindra, 1897–1916
Timor Leste	Liurai Clara Assi of Fatu Mean, ca. 1952 (substate)
	Liurai Bai Buti of Irelelo, ca. 1952 (substate)
	Princess Regnant Raja Liurai Rapubut of Atabai of Paselera, 20th c. (substate)
Tonga	Kuini/queen and President of the Privy Council, Queen Salote Mafile'o Piloevu Veiongo Tupou III, 1918–65
	Queen Regnant Halaevalu Mata'aho, 1998–99
	Princess Regent Salote Mafile'o Pilolevu Tuku'aho Tuita, 1998–99
Uganda	Queen Elizabeth II, 1962–63
	Joint Regent Queen Mother of Buganda, 1897–1914
United Kingdom	Queen Victoria, 1837–1901; Empress of India
	Queen Elizabeth II, 1952–
Viet Nam	Princess Daiana Cong Huyen Ton Nu Dai Trang, Member of The Imperial Grand Council, 2004–
Zambia	Senior Chieftainess Nkomeshya of the Soni People of Lusaka Province, 1979–
	Chieftainess Kabulwebulwe of the Nkoya People in the Mumbwa District, ?–2000

Political System	Sovereigns and Regents*
Zambia, cont'd	Senior Chieftainess Waotiwikas in the Nakonde Area, ?–2000
	Senior Chieftainess Waitwikas of Nakonde, 2000
	Chieftainess Kabulwebulwe of the Nkoya People in the Mumbwa District, 2000
	Chieftainess Nio Sikori of the AmaRharbe Kingdom, 2000
	Chief Elizabeth Mulenje, Senior chieftainess of the Soli People, ca. 1979–?
	Chieftainess Mphamba Esther Nyirenda of the Tumbuka People of the Lundazi District, 1997–2000
	Chieftainess Waitwikas of the Namwanga Tribe of the Nakonde District, before 2000–
	Chieftainess Kabulwebulwe of the Nkoya People in the Mumbwa District, before 2000–
	Chieftainess Nio Sikori of the AmaRharbe Kingdom, 2000–
	Chieftainess Nawaitwika of the Namwanga Tribe in the Nakonde, 2002–
	Chieftainess Chiawa of the Goba in the Kafue District, ca. 2005–
	Chieftainess Mboanjikana of the Lozi Tribe in the Kalabo District, ca. 2005–

*Does not include Governor Generals, titular rulers, exiled rulers, or rulers of unrecognized nations as of 2006.

NOTES

Chapter 1

1. For a valuable, pathbreaking explication of the role of immigration in the context of American political development, see Daniel J. Tichenor, *Dividing Lines: The Politics of Immigration Control in America* (Princeton, NJ: Princeton University Press, 2002).

2. Political scientist Nancy Burns points out that one of the crucial differences between race and sex discrimination is the invisibility of the latter at the aggregate level. While "race has been a key feature, a key driving force, of the American political tradition . . . [gender] has . . . been off-stage, in action in everyday life—in the understanding of women's fitness for political roles, in the ways institutions outside of politics allocate advantages to men." Nancy Burns, "Gender in the Aggregate, Gender in the Individual, Gender and Political Action," *Politics and Gender* 3, no. 1 (2007): 104–24, citing Karen Stenner (2001) at 106–7.

Constitutional law scholar Reva Siegel concurs, arguing that a distinction between race and sex discrimination in American political development is the existence of a clearly understood narrative of harm in the case of African Americans and their association with the legacy of slavery in contrast with a comparatively absent narrative of harm in the case of women. Discrimination against women, she argues, is too often seen as consensual, if not beneficially protective of women, and, hence considered to be no harm at all. This, despite the obvious lack of equity between men and women in virtually all sectors of American society, yesterday and today. Reva B. Siegel, "Collective Memory and the Nineteenth Amendment: Reasoning about the 'Woman Question' in the Discourse of Sex Discrimination," in *History, Memory, and the Law*, ed. Austin Sarat and Thomas Kearns (Ann Arbor: University of Michigan Press, 1999).

3. Available at http://www.nationmaster.com/index.php.

4. Nancy Burns, Kay Lehman Schlozman, and Sidney Verba, *The Private Roots of Public Action: Gender, Equality, and Political Participation* (Cambridge, MA: Harvard University Press, 2001), 340. However, women compared to men are not yet represented

equally at the top ranks of business and the professions, a problem that deserves continuing attention. Virginia Valian, *Why So Slow? The Advancement of Women* (Cambridge, MA: MIT Press, 1999).

5. This ranking takes into account nations that are tied with one another. That is, there are seventy-two nations that have a higher percentage of women in their national legislatures than does the United States.

6. See chapter four for a discussion of women's executive political leadership.

7. The term *liberal* has many meanings. As Julia O'Connor and others note, in the United States, "liberalism" connotes what might be termed "social liberalism," referring to a commitment to use the resources of the state to reduce economic inequalities in distinction to "conservatism," or what is sometimes referred to as "neo-liberalism," which refers to a minimalist conception of the state when it comes to social provision for those in need and a reliance upon private institutions. Julia S. O'Connor, Ann Shola Orloff, and Shelia Shaver, *States, Markets, and Families: Gender, Liberalism, and Social Policy in Australia, Canada, Great Britain, and the United States* (New York: Cambridge University Press, 1999), 3. In this project, I refer to the American state as *liberal* in the neoliberal sense of the word, given that "social liberalism" has not prevailed as evidenced by a relative lack of social provision in the United States compared to most other comparable democracies.

8. Descriptive political representation, on the one hand, refers to the idea that a democratic representative legislature is "a microcosm of the entire population and can readily be substituted for a democratic convocation of the whole people." Janet Clark, "Getting There: Women in Political Office," in *Different Roles, Different Voices*, ed. Marianne Githens, Pippa Norris, and Joni Lovenduski (New York: HarperCollins, 1994), 99. Substantive representation, on the other hand, refers to whether officeholders represent the interests and goals of their constituencies, regardless of whether the officeholders are descriptively similar to the people who elect them. For some, therefore, the key issue is not what sex a person is (a socially constructed biological classification), but rather what gender a person is (a socially constructed behavioral role classification). Female gender roles are associated with issues such as support for welfare provision and the promotion of world peace, while male gender roles are associated with issues such as fiscal conservatism and military security. However, some male officeholders are substantively more supportive of welfare and world peace than some women. Hence, substantive representation of female gender role issues can sometimes be best accomplished by electing a man, rather than a woman, to public office. Generally, however, researchers find that there is a positive correlation between descriptive and substantive representation. For a convincing treatment of the way women's descriptive representation fosters their substantive representative, see Michele L. Swers, *The Difference Women Make* (Chicago: University of Chicago Press, 2002).

9. Pippa Norris, ed. *Passages to Power: Legislative Recruitment in Advanced Democracies* (Cambridge: Cambridge University Press, 1997); Richard E. Matland and Michelle M. Taylor, "Electoral System Effects on Women's Representation: Theoretical Arguments and Evidence from Costa Rica," *Comparative Political Studies*, 30, no. 2 (1997): 186–210; Ian McAllister, "Australia," in *Passages to Power: Legislative Recruitment in Advanced Democracies*, ed. Pippa Norris (Cambridge: Cambridge University Press, 1997); Susan Welch and Donley T. Studlar, "Multi-Member Districts and the Representation of Women: Evidence from Britain and the United States," *Journal of Politics*, 52, no. 2 (1990): 391–412.

10. Frances Rosenbluth, Rob Salmond, and Michael F. Thies, "Welfare Works: Explaining Female Legislative Representation," *Politics and Gender* 2 (2006): 167.

11. Ibid., 166.

12. The basis for women's domain in the home, as Janet Clark notes, gives women family responsibilities that are often believed to be irrelevant to participation in public office. In addition, because of women's family roles, they may not be as likely to have occupations that are viewed as suited for running for public office, such as being lawyers, being in the military, or being in business. Clark, "Getting There: Women in Political Office," in *Different Roles, Different Voices,* ed. Githens, Norris, and Lovenduski. Others point to the sexual division of labor in production and reproduction, arguing that the problems of women's underrepresentation in government will only be resolved "when men and women shared equally in the full range of paid and unpaid work." Anne Phillips, *Democracy and Difference* (University Park: Pennsylvania State University Press, 1993).

13. Jennifer L. Lawless and Richard L. Fox, eds. *It Takes a Candidate: Why Women Don't Run for Office* (New York: Cambridge University Press, 2005).

14. Max Weber is noted for defining the state as the entity having a monopoly on the legitimate use of coercive force, including violence, to be exercised for maintaining law and order domestically and internationally. Max Weber, "The Profession and Vocation of Politics," in *Weber: Political Writings*, ed. Peter Lassman and Ronald Speirs (Cambridge: Cambridge University Press, 1994), 310–11.

15. Characteristics acquired at birth, such as one's class and sex, can sometimes be modified and altered, but generally are not and/or only with great difficulty. Hence, for example, most people retain the social class background that marks their birth. Also, while it is possible to transform to some degree the sex classification that one acquires at birth by means of sex change surgery and/or hormonal regimens, this is difficult for most people to do. For this reason, race, class, and sex are considered static, ascriptive characteristics determined arbitrarily as a consequence of the economic, social, religious, political, and genetic context of a person's birth.

16. For an excellent analysis of Ferraro's campaign and for the obstacles faced in general by women running for public office, see Linda Witt, Karen M. Paget, and Glenna Matthews, eds., *Running as a Woman: Gender and Power in American Politics* (New York: Free Press, 1995); Barbara Palmer and Dennis Simon, *Breaking the Glass Ceiling: Women and Congressional Elections* (New York: Routledge, 2006).

17. The Bush-Ferraro Vice-Presidential Debate, October 11, 1984, Commissioner on Presidential Debates, available at http://www.debates.org/pages/trans94.html, emphasis added.

18. Ibid.

19. Ibid.

20. Panel presentation at the Aspen Institute Workshop on Women and Political Leadership, organized by Laura Liswood, Secretary General, The Council of Women World Leaders, Washington, DC, July 20, 2005.

21. Geraldine Ferraro with Linda Bird Francke, *Ferraro: My Story* (New York: Bantam Books, 1985), 201, 147.

22. Marian Burros, "Now Is the Time to Come to the Aid of Your Favorite Cookies," *New York Times*, July 15, 1992.

23. Nadine Brozan, "Chronicle," *New York Times*, August 8, 1992.

24. Mark Leibovich, "Rights vs. Rights: An Improbable Collision Course," *New York Times*, January 13, 2008, accessed at www.nytimes.com/2008/01/13/weekinreview/13leibovich.html?_r=1&sq=hillaryclinton.

25. I am indebted to Mary Katzenstein and Stephen Skowronek for bringing to my attention the relevance of the language of representation when referring to maternal public policies (private correspondence and discussion). In the "varieties of capitalism" literature, most argue that what works best from economic perspectives is a country that is characterized *either* by a "liberal market economy," such as the United States, in which the market is relatively free of government stipulation in the organization of business and in the control of financial institutions, *or* one in which the state coordinates markets and corporate hierarchies, as in Sweden or Germany—but, not both. That is, hybrid capitalism is not predicted to work well. See Peter A. Hall and David Soskice, eds., *Varieties of Capitalism: The Institutional Foundations of Comparative Advantage* (New York: Oxford University Press, 2001); Bob Hancke and Martin Rhodes, eds., *Beyond Varieties of Capitalism: Conflict, Contradictions, and Complementarities in the European Economy* (New York: Oxford University Press, 2007); Peter A. Hall and David Soskice, "An Introduction to Varieties of Capitalism," in their *Varieties of Capitalism*. However, others find that hybrid capitalism can perform well, as is exemplified by the Danish case. John L. Campbell and Ove K. Pedersen, "The Varieties of Capitalism and Hybrid Success," *Comparative Political Studies* 40, no. 3 (2007): 307–32.

26. Karen Orren and Stephen Skowronek, *The Search for American Political Development* (Cambridge: Cambridge University Press, 2004), 113.

27. For an analysis of how voting choices result from both personal attitudes and social, contextual attributes, see Paul Allen Beck, Russell J. Dalton, Steven Greene, and Robert Huckfeldt, "The Social Calculus of Voting: Interpersonal, Media, and Organizational Influences on Presidential Choices," *American Political Science Review* 96, no. 1 (2002): 57–73.

28. Melissa S. Williams, *Voice, Trust, Memory: Marginalized Groups and the Failings of Liberal Representation* (Princeton, NJ: Princeton University Press, 1998); Anne Phillips, *The Politics of Presence* (Oxford: Clarendon Press, 1995).

29. Arend Lijphart, *Electoral Systems and Party Systems: A Study of Twenty-Seven Democracies* (Oxford: Oxford University Press, 1994). Lijphart has developed complex ways to test the operation of different types of democracy, using typologies categorizing them as consociational, federal, and majority-versus-non-majority rule. For example, see Arend Lijphart, "Non-Majoritarian Democracy: A Comparison of Federal and Consociational Theories," *Publius* 15, no. 2 (1985): 3–15; Lijphart, *Patterns of Democracy: Government Forms and Performance in Thirty-Six Countries* (New Haven, CT: Yale University Press, 1999).

30. Virginia Sapiro, "Democracy Minus Women Is Not Democracy: Gender and World Changes in Citizenship," in *Citizenship and Citizenship Education in a Changing World*, ed. Orit Ichilov (London: Woburn Press, 1998), 174–90; Clark, "Getting There: Women in Political Office," in *Different Roles, Different Voices*, ed. Githens, Norris, and Lovenduski.

31. Clark, "Getting There: Women in Political Office," in *Different Roles, Different Voices*, ed. Githens, Norris, and Lovenduski, 99.

32. Susan J. Carroll, *The Impact of Women in Public Office* (Bloomington: Indiana University Press, 2001); Swers, *The Difference Women Make*.

33. Clark, "Getting There: Women in Political Office," in *Different Roles, Different Voices*, ed. Githens, Norris, and Lovenduski, 100.

34. Alana Jeydel and Andrew J. Taylor, "Are Women Legislators Less Effective? Evidence from the U.S. House in the 103rd–105th Congress," *Political Research Quarterly*, 56, no. 1 (2003): 19–27.

35. Valerie R. O'Regan, *Gender Matters: Female Policymakers' Influence in Industrialized Nations* (Westport, CT: Praeger, 2000). John D. Griffin and Michael Keane find that descriptive representation promotes the voting participation of African Americans when the candidate running corresponds with constituents' liberal issue position. "Descriptive Representation and the Composition of African American Turnout," *American Journal of Political Science*, 50, no. 4 (2006): 998–1012. Similarly, Susan Banducci et al. find that descriptive representation has a number of positive impacts on minority political participation, including an increase in political knowledge, an increase in constituent contact with representatives, an increase in voting, and a more positive view of the responsiveness of government. Susan A. Banducci, Todd Donovan, and Jeffrey A. Karp, "Minority Representation, Empowerment, and Participation," *Journal of Politics*, 66, no. 2 (2004): 534–56.

36. Kira Sanbonmatsu, *Where Women Run: Gender and Party in the American States* (Ann Arbor: University of Michigan Press, 2006), 182.

37. Catharine A. MacKinnon, *Toward a Feminist Theory of the State* (Cambridge, MA: Harvard University Press, 1989); Georgina Waylen, "Women and Democratization: Conceptualizing Gender Relations in Transition Politics," *World Politics* 46, no. 3 (1994): 327–54; Richard Ogmundson, "Does It Matter if Women, Minorities, and Gays Govern? New Data concerning an Old Question," *Canadian Journal of Sociology* 30, no. 3 (2005): 315–24; Manon Tremblay and Réjean Pelletier, "More Feminists or More Women? Descriptive and Substantive Representations of Women in the 1997 Canadian Federal Elections," *International Political Science Review* 21, no. 4 (2000): 381–405.

38. Carroll, *The Impact of Women in Public Office*, xiii.

39. Lise Togeby, "The Gender Gap in Foreign Policy Attitudes," *Journal of Peace Research* 31, no. 4 (1994): 375.

40. After controlling for income and skills, gender accounts for 8% to 17% of the variance in support for social spending policies. Torben Iversen, *Capitalism, Democracy, and Welfare* (New York: Cambridge University Press, 2005), 104–5.

41. Political theorist Jane Mansbridge extends the analysis of the principle of representation in the context of democratic theory and practice to include this four-fold typology: (1) *promissory representation*, which refers to whether elected officials implement their campaign promises once in office; (2) *anticipatory representation*, in which elected officeholders focus on what they think their constituents will care about in forthcoming elections; (3) *gyroscopic representation*, in which those elected to political office look within themselves for decision-making principles as based on their own backgrounds, experiences, and what they perceive to be "common sense"; and (4) *surrogate representation*, which occurs when officeholders represent voters outside their own districts. Jane Mansbridge, "Rethinking Representation," *American Political Science Review*, 97, no. 4 (2003): 515.

42. Political scientist Birte Siim focuses on how particular social discourses about citizenship and gender set a context influencing women's political representation. Birte Siim, *Gender and Citizenship: Politics and Agency in France, Britain, and Denmark* (New York: Cambridge University Press, 2000). This book extends that idea by focusing on how specific public policies set a political context influencing women's political representation.

43. Feminist research is fraught with disagreement over the meaning of gender and sex as well as the instrumental and normative consequences entailed in their use. For an unusually insightful discussion, see Mary Hawkesworth, "Confounding Gender," *Signs* 22, no. 3 (1997): 649–85. Also see Toril Moi, *What Is a Woman? And Other Essays* (New York: Oxford University Press, 1999). In this research, I use the term *gender* to refer

to both sex and gender differences unless it is specifically the physical sex differences between women and men that require analytical attention.

44. Political scientist Sue Tolleson-Rinehart, for example, found that, "gendered expectations of women in politics . . . [were] centered on motherhood." Sue Tolleson-Rinehart, "Do Women Leaders Make a Difference?" in *The Impact of Women in Public Office*, ed. Carroll, 163. So, too, does Jeffrey Koch note that voters are more likely to believe that female candidates are better able to deal with "compassion issues," such as health care, education, welfare, and the environment, than are men running for political office, assumptions that result from the "assignment of character traits to candidates on the basis of gender." Jeffrey W. Koch, "Gender Stereotypes and Citizens' Impressions of House Candidates' Ideological Orientations," *American Journal of Political Science* 46, no. 2 (2002): 453–62. As Leone Huddy and Nayda Terkildsen observe, at higher levels of political office, the gender stereotypes applied to women become negative because voters believe that the characteristics required to be a leader are masculine ones, such as being "tough, aggressive, and assertive," rather than the characteristics typically associated with women, such as being "warm, gentle, kind, and passive." Leonie Huddy and Nayda Terkildsen, "The Consequences of Gender Stereotypes for Women Candidates at Different Levels and Types of Office," *Political Research Quarterly*, 46, no. 3 (1993): 503–4. For a discussion about how gender beliefs constitute a set of cultural rules and a social system defining relationships between people, see Cecilia L. Ridgeway and Shelley J. Correll, "Unpacking the Gender System: A Theoretical Perspective on Gender Beliefs and Social Relations," *Gender and Society*, 18, no. 4 (2004): 510–31.

45. Ann Shola Orloff, "Gender and the Social Rights of Citizenship: The Comparative Analysis of Gender Relations and Welfare States," *American Sociological Review*, 58, no. 3 (1993): 303–28.

46. Paul S. Herrnson, J. Celeste Lay, and Atiya Kai Stokes, "Women Running 'as Women': Candidate Gender, Campaign Issues, and Voter-Targeting Strategies," *Journal of Politics* 65, no. 1. (2003): 245.

47. Virginia Sapiro, "If U.S. Senator Baker Were a Woman: An Experimental Study of Candidate Images," *Political Psychology* 3, nos. 1/2 (1981–82): 62.

48. Herrnson, Lay, and Stokes, "Women Running 'as Women,'" 245. As Danny Hayes terms it, candidates "own traits," and it is this "trait ownership" that "provides a baseline" for voters' expectations. Since most people are only minimally attentive to politics, they use presumptions about trait ownership as a shortcut when making assessments of candidates. Danny Hayes, "Candidate Qualities through a Partisan Lens: A Theory of Trait Ownership," *American Journal of Political Science* 49, no. 4 (2005): 908–10. Deborah Alexander and Kristi Andersen found that the attribution of gendered stereotypes to candidates running for political office increases when voters have little information. Deborah Alexander and Kristi Andersen, "Gender as a Factor in the Attribution of Leadership Traits," *Political Research Quarterly* 46, no. 3 (1993): 527–45. Research by Fred Cutler also confirms that voters employ heuristic shortcuts to determine the policy positions of candidates as inferred from socioeconomic characteristics, particularly in situations where there is low information about the issue orientations of those running for office. Fred Cutler, "The Simplest Shortcut of All: Sociodemographic Characteristics and Electoral Choice," *Journal of Politics* 64, no. 2 (2002): 466–90. In addition, research shows that people process information about political candidates based on preconceptions. Specifically, voters use their cognitive expectations about candidates as a filter for analyzing—or not analyzing—actual information about candidates. The result is that voters ignore information about candidates that conflicts with preconceived expectations and are

overly attentive to information that conforms to what they expected in the first place. See David Moskowitz and Patrick Stroh, "Expectation-Driven Assessments of Political Candidates," *Political Psychology* 17, no. 4 (1996): 695–712. In the case of women running for political office, this would mean that voters filter out information that is contrary to prior expectations that women are more caring and maternal than men, thereby reinforcing gender stereotypes in the electoral process.

49. Joan C. Tronto, *Moral Boundaries: A Political Argument for an Ethic of Care* (London: Routledge, 1993), 134, 127, 105, 161–62.

50. "American Time Uses Survey," Bureau of Labor Statistics; the complete 2005 study can be found at http://www.bls.gov/tus/home.htm.

51. "A Woman's Work Is Never Done," *Atlantic Monthly*, December 2004, available at http://www.theatlantic.com/doc/200412/primarysources.

52. Alison Morehead, "Governments, Workplaces, and Households," *Family Matters*, 70 (Autumn 2005): 4.

53. Monika L. McDermott, "Voting Cues in Low-Information Elections: Candidate Gender as a Social Information Variable in Contemporary United States Elections," *American Journal of Political Science* 41, no. 1 (1997): 271. When assessing the way voters attribute to women empathetic and compassionate issue stances, some refer to those traits as "feminine" rather than as "maternal." However, "maternal" is a more appropriate word for child care and education, and any other care-work issue is "feminine" because caring for people is *work*, social reproductive labor, in the terminology of sociologists. A feminine person, however culturally determined, need not be an empathic, compassionate, much less a social reproductive worker. Care-work as "work," takes energy, time, and skill, including such skills as empathy and compassion. That the public perceives this type of work as being done by women more than by men is why social reproductive labor can be defined as social maternalism. Many maternal women—and maternal men—are anything but feminine, and any glance at today's glossy magazines and commercial advertisements for feminine products will find little reference to how these products are related to the care-work of those in need. Hence, instead of "feminine," let's start using "social maternalism" as a more accurate term for how the public perceives women's sex group difference from men.

54. Kim Fridkin Kahn and Ann Gordon, "How Women Campaign for the U.S. Senate," in *Women, Media, and Politics*, ed. Pippa Norris (New York: Oxford University Press, 1997).

55. Carey Goldberg, "A Pregnant Candidate Discovers She's an Issue," *New York Times*, Monday, April 21, 2008, available at http://query.nytimes.com/gst/fullpage .html?res=9806E2D81330F936A25756C0A96E958260&sec=&spon=&pagewanted=all.

56. Ibid. The association of women with biological maternalism also is evident by the extraordinary time and effort it has taken to establish employment policies that exclude questions about women's pregnancy intentions when interviewing for jobs. As was reported in the American Political Science Association, *PS: Political Science and Politics*, by a faculty member in the political science department at the University of Michigan, who chose to remain anonymous, the idea that a woman should not be hired because she "might get pregnant in a year or two"—and asking her about this in an interview—is not only an offensive form of sex discrimination, it is illegal. Title VII of the Civil Rights Act of 1964 prohibits employers from asking about family attributes, which includes questions about dating, marriage, or family planning, precisely because such questions could translate easily into discrimination on the basis of one's sex (Anonymous 2002).

57. Available at http://www.guide2womenleaders.com/womeninpower/womeninpower01.htm.

58. As political scientist S. Laurel Weldon notes, public agencies and policies are crucial mechanisms for the representation of minorities or other marginalized groups. Women's policy agencies, for example, are institutions that, at least in part, "reflect women's perspective." Given adequate political authority, economic resources, and a mobilized women's movement, such institutions "can improve substantive representation for women by providing a mechanism by which women's distinctive perspective can be articulated," S. Laurel Weldon, "Beyond Bodies: Institutional Sources of Representation for Women in Democratic Policymaking," *Journal of Politics* (2002): 1153, 1154, 1158, 1160. So, too, can the state represent traits associated with women when it adopts public policies that do so.

59. Vernon Bagdanor *The Monarchy and the Constitution* (New York: Oxford University Press, 1995).

60. Because of this fusion of maternal duties with state office, monarchies, however merely symbolic or ceremonial they may be, *visibly include women* in the state's performance of political governance. It has not escaped scholars that a woman who serves as regent in hereditary monarchies can generate more favorable public attitudes toward women's political inclusion. Although it is common to associate the Victorian period with the repression of women and of sexuality, Helen Irving notes that there was another dimension to the queen's persona that served as an "important female symbol" and a catalyst for Australian women's greater involvement in politics. The Australian states were federated around the time of the queen's death, and her reign, Irving observes, "was immensely useful to Australian women . . . [because] she symbolized the ability of women to occupy a position of power, and to exercise political judgement." Helen Irving, ed., *A Woman's Constitution: Gender and History in the Australian Commonwealth* (Sydney: Hale and Iremonger, 1996), 34.

61. John Stuart Mill, *The Subjection of Women* (1869), available at http://melbecon.unimelb.edu.au/het/mill/women.htm, last accessed April 20, 2008, 1.

62. Ibid., 28.

63. Ibid.

64. Burns, Schlozman, and Verba, eds., *The Private Roots of Public Action*. It is also the case that when women run for political office, they garner more support from women voters. Eric Plutzer and John F. Zipp, "Identity Politics, Partisanship, and Voting for Women Candidates," *Public Opinion Quarterly* 60, no. 1 (1996): 30–57.

65. She used the "U.S. News" section of LexisNexis, with the search phrases "women candidates" and "election." The year 1998 was omitted from her analysis. Dolan, *Voting for Women*, 135.

66. This probability of 0.19 is the impact coefficient of a logit analysis for 1990–2000, controlling for woman incumbency, party identification, party correspondence between the woman candidate and the voter, political ideology, and the year 1994 for the time period 1990–2000. See table 6.1, in ibid., 141. She found that the impact of a gendered political context was most pronounced for respondents who had a "low awareness" of politics.

67. Ibid., 134–35.

68. Ibid.

69. Kim Fridkin Kahn, *The Political Consequences of Being a Woman: How Stereotypes Influence the Conduct and Consequences of Political Campaigns* (New York: Columbia University Press, 1996), 1.

70. Ibid., 119–23.

71. Ibid., 125. Susan Banducci and Jeffrey Karp find that there is an impact on voting behavior when women are leaders of political parties. Susan A. Banducci and Jeffrey A. Karp, "Gender, Leadership, and Choice in Multiparty Systems," *Political Research Quarterly* 53, no. 4 (2000): 815–48.

72. Public attitudes influence the adoption of public policies through the mediation of interest groups, social movements, political parties, and candidates running for political office.

73. Sometimes policies can generate a backlash effect that weakens rather than strengthens their initial acceptance. Generally, though, once policies are in place, their very existence reinforces their bases of support.

74. Women can do much in the way of voluntary activities and social movement advocacy from informal positions outside the state, as the work of Theda Skocpol and others established. See Theda Skocpol, *Protecting Soldiers and Mothers: The Political Origins of Social Policy in the United States* (Cambridge, MA: Harvard University Press, 1992). However, women's power from these informal positions necessarily stops short of their electoral representation as officeholders.

75. Linda Kerber, "The Republican Mother: Women and the Enlightenment—An American Perspective," *American Quarterly*, 28, no. 2 (1976): 187–205.

76. Joanna L. Grossman, "Women's Jury Service: Right of Citizenship or Privilege of Difference?" *Stanford Law Review* 46, no. 5 (1994): 1118. The Sixth Amendment states that "[i]n all criminal prosecutions, the accused shall enjoy the right to a speedy and public trial, by an impartial jury . . ."

77. Quoted in ibid.

78. Grossman, "Women's Jury Service," 1117.

79. Ibid., 1121.

80. Quoted in Grossman, "Women's Jury Service," 1121.

81. *Powers v. Ohio*, 499 U.S. 400 (1991).

82. Quoted in Grossman, "Women's Jury Service," 1122.

83. The case involved an African American man who had been convicted of murder by a jury from which all African Americans had been barred by a West Virginia law that specified that only "white male persons who are twenty-one years of age and who are citizens of this State were eligible to serve as jurors." Laurence H. Tribe, *American Constitutional Law* (Mineola, NY: The Foundation Press, 1988), 1466. The Court viewed such state-level legislation as a clear violation of the Equal Protection Clause, which specifically guaranteed that "all persons, whether colored or white, shall stand equal before the laws of the States, and, in regard to the colored race, for whose protection the amendment was primarily designed, that no discrimination shall be made against them by law because of their color . . ." Quoted in Tribe, *American Constitutional Law*, 1466. The same principle, of course, would apply to the subordinate racial group. What is unconstitutional, therefore, is to use race as a criterion for eligibility to be in a jury pool.

84. For an excellent analysis of jury duty in relation to women's equality in the United States, see Gretchen Ritter, *The Constitution as Social Design: Gender and Civic Membership in the American Constitutional Order* (Stanford, CA: Stanford University Press, 2006), chap. 4.

85. Leslie Freidman Goldstein, *The Constitutional Rights of Women: Cases in Law and Social Change* (Madison: University of Wisconsin Press, 1989), 105.

86. Hoyt, quoted in Goldstein, *The Constitutional Rights of Women*, 108.

87. Ibid., 107–8.

88. Ibid., 108.

89. *Brown v. Board of Education*, 347 U.S. 483 (1954).

90. *Taylor v. Louisiana*, 419 U.S. 522 (1975).

Chapter 2

1. Gwendolyn Mink, "From Welfare to Wedlock: Marriage Promotion and Poor Mothers' Inequality," *The Good Society* 11, no. 3 (2002): 69. As Mink notes, the right to marry and to choose one's intimate, sexual relationships is at the core of the privacy rights protected by the Due Process Clause of the Constitution. Yet welfare policies regulate marriage as if it were "a necessary condition of worthy adult citizenship." Ibid., 68. The impact of welfare regulation, as Mink argues, is to treat "poor single mothers as a separate caste, subject to a separate system of law. Poor single mothers are the only people in America whose decisions to bear children are punished by government. They are the only people in America of whom government may demand the details of intimate relationships. And they are the only mothers in America compelled by law to make room for biological fathers in their families," Mink, "The Lady and the Tramp (II): Feminist Welfare Politics; Poor Single Mothers, and the Challenge of Welfare Justice," *Feminist Studies* 24, no. 1 (1998): 58. Also see Cathy Marie Johnson, Georgia Duerst-Lahti, and Noelle H. Norton, *Creating Gender: The Sexual Politics of Welfare Policy* (Boulder, CO: Lynne Rienner, 2007).

2. For example, see Karen Seccombe, *"So You Think I Drive a Cadillac?" Welfare Recipients' Perspectives on the System and Its Reform* (Boston: Allyn and Bacon, 1998); Dorothy Roberts, "Irrationality and Sacrifice in the Welfare Reform Consensus," *Virginia Law Review* 81, no. 8 (1995): 2607–24; Roberts, *Killing the Black Body: Race, Reproduction, and the Meaning of Liberty* (New York: Pantheon, 1998); Roberts, *Shattered Bonds: The Color of Child Welfare* (New York: Basic Civitas Books, 2002); Ange-Marie Hancock, *The Politics of Disgust: The Public Identity of the Welfare Queen* (New York: New York University Press, 2004); Mink, "From Welfare to Wedlock," 68–73.; Randy Albelda, "Fallacies of Welfare-to-Work Policies," *Annals of the American Academy of Political and Social Science* 577 (September 2001): 66–78; Mink, "Violating Women: Rights Abuses in the Welfare Police State," *Annals of the American Academy of Political and Social Science* 577 (September 2001): 79–93; Jyl J. Josephson, *Gender, Families, and the State: Child Support Policy in the United States* (Lanham, MD: Rowman and Littlefield, 1997); Margrit Eichler, *Family Shifts: Families, Policies, and Gender Equality* (Toronto: Oxford University Press, 1997); Mink, *Welfare's End* (Ithaca, NY: Cornell University Press, 1998); Mink, ed., *Whose Welfare?* (Ithaca, NY: Cornell University Press, 1999).

In addition, scholars point out from cross-national perspectives how welfare provision can reinforce women's traditional, domestic roles and identities rather than facilitating the extension of women's identities to include nontraditional roles in the market, if not in politics. As Mary Daly notes, for example, Germany's welfare provision is geared toward encouraging women to remain in the home as wives and mothers rather than to take on competitive roles in the market. Mary Daly, *The Gender Division of Welfare* (Cambridge: Cambridge University Press, 2000).

3. Lee Ann Banaszak, "The Gendering State and Citizens' Attitudes toward Women's Roles: State Policy, Employment, and Religion in Germany," *Politics and Gender* 2 (2006): 32.

4. Ibid., 33.

5. Ibid., 49–52.

6. Jason Wittenberg, *Crucibles of Political Loyalty: Church Institutions and Electoral Continuity in Hungary* (New York: Cambridge University Press, 2006), 237.

7. "Freedom House: About Us," available at www.freedomhouse.org/template .cfm?page=2, accessed November 5, 2006.

8. Freedom House, *Freedom in the World 2005* (Lanham, MD: Rowman and Littlefield, 2005), 775 (emphasis added).

9. Ibid.

10. As political scientists Ronald Englehart and Pippa Norris note, the key dividing difference between Western-oriented countries and Muslim ones is not support for democratic institutions or procedures, but rather the application of individual equality to women in particular and to sexual orientations in general. People living in the West have become more liberal in their views about women's equality with men and more supportive of "sexual liberalization" in contrast to "Muslim nations [that] have remained the most traditional societies in the world," when it comes to gender equality and sexual mores. Ronald Ingelhart and Pippa Norris, "The True Clash of Civilizations," *Foreign Policy* 135 (March/April 2003): 54–65.

11. Some comparativists, such as Diane Sainsbury, examine welfare policies in a broader frame of reference than I do in this project. She is interested, for example, in the variety of regimes that fall under the rubric "welfare state" and includes in her definition of this type of state formation a regime that is a national-level institution that redistributes benefits to those in need by means of social insurance programs, tax policies, pensions, and family-work related policies, such as publicly funded child-care policies. Her main concern is redistributed outcomes, not the way public policies constitute symbols that convey to the public the political meaning of the maternal traits voters associate with women. Hence, her examination of welfare policies includes more than care-work per se, but less than my definition of state maternalism, which also includes gender quotas and hereditary monarchies. See Diane Sainsbury, *Gender, Equality, and Welfare States* (Cambridge: Cambridge University Press, 1996).

12. *Oxford English Dictionary, 2002, CD*, "mother, v.," Definition 2.b., 1901, *Blackw. Mag.* October, 449.

13. Ann Shola Orloff, "Gender and the Social Rights of Citizenship: The Comparative Analysis of Gender Relations and Welfare States," *American Sociological Review* 58, no. 3 (1993): 303–28.

14. For an interesting discussion of care-work as labor, see Eileen Boris and S. J. Kleinberg, "Mothers and Other Workers: (Re)Conceiving Labor, Maternalism, and the State," *Journal of Women's History* 15, no. 3 (2003): 104.

15. Scholars identify three major delivery systems: the family, the market, and the state. Margarita Leon Borja, "Reconciling Work and Family: Impact on Gender and Family," European University Institute, 2002. As Jenson notes, it is important not to equate unpaid work with care-work, since care-work also can be paid for as a market commodity. In her framework, she suggests a typology that would distinguish between where care is provided (the family, charities, the market, the state), who cares (women or men), and who pays (women, men, charities, or the state). Jane Jenson et al., *Who Cares? Women's Work, Childcare, and Welfare State Redesign* (Toronto: University of Toronto Press, 2001).

16. Lise Vogel, *Woman Questions: Essays for a Materialist Feminism* (London: Routledge, 1995).

17. The family in general and women in particular are not the only resources for care-work. We can also say that the *market*, or, commercial resources of a country and financial resources of people, also is a resource for care-work. People who are employed and who receive sufficient financial remuneration from the market or have other financial resources can purchase the materials and services necessary to satisfy their dependency needs. Thus, a person who earns sufficient funds can purchase food, shelter, clothing, health care, and education. For people without access to family resources or market resources, that is, for the poor, traditionally, when the poor lack both family and market resources to satisfy their dependency needs, those needs are met by charitable institutions, such as churches and nonprofit assistance organizations. Charitable institutions provide food, clothing, shelter, health care, and education to those who lack family or market resources. However, charities generally are not analyzed as a major delivery system for a society's welfare needs.

18. Alva Myrdal, *Nation and Family: The Swedish Experiment in Democratic Family and Population Policy* (Cambridge, MA: MIT Press, 1941), 340.

19. Orloff, "Gender and the Social Rights of Citizenship," 303–28.

20. Myrdal, *Nation and Family*, 340.

21. For the power of language in the context of law, see Stephen M. Feldman, *American Legal Thought from Premodernism to Postmodernism: An Intellectual Void* (New York: Oxford University Press, 2000); for the importance of constitutional text, see Laurence H. Tribe and Michael C. Dorf, *On Reading the Constitution* (Cambridge, MA: Harvard University Press, 1991).

22. Jenson et al., *Who Cares? Women's Work, Childcare, and Welfare State Redesign.*

23. Gosta Esping-Andersen, *The Three Worlds of Welfare Capitalism* (Princeton, NJ: Princeton University Press, 1990), 18. Social citizenship is a component of the social democratic approach to welfare rights as promulgated by William Beveridge and Richard Titmuss as well as Marshall. See Martin Hewitt, *Welfare, Ideology, and Need: Developing Perspectives on the Welfare State* (Savage, MD: Barnes and Noble Books, 1992).

24. T. H. Marshall and Tom Bottomore, *Citizenship and Social Class* (1950; London: Pluto Press, 1992).

25. Madonna Harrington Meyer, *Care Work: Gender, Labor, and the Welfare State* (New York: Routledge, 2000).

26. Wendy Sarvasy "Social Citizenship from a Feminist Perspective," *Hypatia* 12, no. 4 (1997): 55.

27. Esping-Andersen *The Three Worlds of Welfare Capitalism*, 20.

28. Esping-Andersen employs the idea of a residual welfare state from the work of Titmuss.

29. Esping-Andersen, *The Three Worlds of Welfare Capitalism*, 19.

30. Ibid.

31. Ibid., 27+.

32. Ibid., 27.

33. Ibid.

34. Ibid.

35. Julia S. O'Connor, Ann Shola Orloff, and Sheila Shaver, eds., *States, Markets, Families: Gender, Liberalism, and Social Policy in Australia, Canada, Great Britain, and the United States* (New York: Cambridge University Press, 1999), 23; Helga Maria Herne, *Welfare State and Woman Power* (Stockholm: Scandinavian University Press, 1988).

36. Ibid.

37. Eileen Boris and Peter Bardaglio, "The Transformation of Patriarchy: The Historic Role of the State," in *Families, Politics, and Public Policy*, ed. Irene Diamond (New York: Longman, 1983), 70–72.

38. Ibid., 78–88.

39. Diane Sainsbury, *Gender, Equality, and Welfare States* (Cambridge: Cambridge University Press, 1996).

40. Gwendolyn Mink, *The Wages of Motherhood: Inequality in the Welfare State, 1917–1942* (Ithaca, NY: Cornell University Press, 1995); Elinor Ann Accampo, Rachel G. Fuchs, and Mary Lynn Stewart, *Gender and the Politics of Social Reform in France, 1870–1914* (Baltimore: Johns Hopkins University Press, 1995); Linda Gordon, *Pitied But Not Entitled: Single Mothers and the History of Welfare* (Cambridge, MA: Harvard University Press, 1994); John Myles and Jill Quadagno, "Envisioning a Third Way: The Welfare State in the Twenty-First Century," *Contemporary Sociology* 29, no. 1, Utopian Visions: Engaged Sociologies for the 21st Century (2000): 156–67; Sylvia Bashevkin, "From Tough Times to Better Times: Feminism, Public Policy, and New Labour Politics in Britain," *International Political Science Review* 21, no. 4, Women, Citizenship, and Representation (2000): 407–24; Robert A. Moffitt, Robert Reville, and Anne E. Winkler, "Beyond Single Mothers: Cohabitation and Marriage in the AFDC Program," *Demography* 35, no. 3 (1998): 259–78; Diane Sainsbury, *Gender and Welfare State Regimes* (New York: Oxford University Press, 2000).

41. Sainsbury, *Gender and Welfare State Regimes*; Bashevkin, "From Tough Times to Better Times."

42. Jill Quadagno, "Race, Class, and Gender in the U.S. Welfare State: Nixon's Failed Family Assistance Plan," *American Sociological Review* 55, no. 1 (1990): 11–28; Bashevkin, "From Tough Times to Better Times."

43. Seth Koven and Sonya Michel, eds., *Mothers of a New World: Maternalist Politics and the Origins of Welfare States* (New York: Routledge, 1993).

44. Patrick Wilkinson, "Review: The Selfless and the Helpless: Maternalist Origins of the U.S. Welfare State," *Feminist Studies* 25, no. 3 (1999): 571–97.

45. Myles and Quadagno, "Envisioning a Third Way," 156–67; Paul Pierson, ed., *The New Politics of the Welfare State* (Oxford: Oxford University Press, 2001).

46. For a succinct discussion of a democratic state in relation to a principle of economic justice, see Stephen Nathanson, *Economic Justice* (Upper Saddle River, NJ: Prentice-Hall, 1998).

47. Rogers Smith seems to believe one can deduce ideology from the content and format of written constitutions: "The liberal strains in American thought were similarly visible in the states' fondness for written constitutions with bills of rights that summarized Lockean principles of individual rights, social compacts, and separated powers. They, too, blended such general principles with procedural rights drawn from English legal traditions and saw all these measures as simultaneously expressive of Enlightenment doctrines of the rights of man and the libertarian heritage specific to Anglo-Saxon peoples." Rogers M. Smith, *Civic Ideals: Conflicting Visions of Citizenship in U.S. History* (New Haven, CT: Yale University Press, 1997).

48. Vivien Hart, *Bound by Our Constitution: Women, Workers, and the Minimum Wage* (Princeton, NJ: Princeton University Press, 1994), 5.

49. Daniel P. Franklin and Michael J. Baun, eds., *Political Culture and Constitutionalism: A Comparative Approach* (Armonk, NY: M. E. Sharpe, 1995), 2.

50. Axel Hadenius, *Democracy and Development* (Cambridge: Cambridge University Press, 1992), 175. Even when states do not have written constitutions—such as New Zealand, Great Britain, and Israel—nevertheless, there is agreement about "constitutional rules . . . [and] constitutional conventions," which some "define as 'non-legal rules regulating the way in which legal rules shall be applied.'" William B. Gwyn, "Political Culture and Constitutionalism in Britain," in *Political Culture and Constitutionalism*, ed. Franklin and Baun, 21.

51. I include the constitutionalization of care-work as a definition of the welfare state for two reasons. First, as I have discussed, constitutions signify the most fundamental conception of the state in its most permanent form. For this reason, I interpret constitutional affirmation of the state's provision of welfare benefits to denote a public vision of the state as an entity whose proper role is to be a caregiver, that is, to protect positive rights that guarantee what the state will do to help people as well as negative rights that guarantee what the state will not do to hurt people. Second, the constitutions of the world's countries predate the arrival of women in any large percentages to their national legislatures. Thus, including the constitutionalized provision of welfare to the needy can be viewed as a cause of women's access to political office, not merely an effect of women's political representation in leadership positions, despite the assumed reinforcement of welfare policies we should expect, once women are in office.

52. Candace Johnson Redden, "Health as Citizenship Narrative," *Polity* 34, no. 3 (2002): 355–70; Candace Johnson Redden, "Health Care as Citizenship Development: Examining Social Rights and Entitlement," *Canadian Journal of Political Science* 35 (March 2002): 103–25.

53. Many other indications of welfare provision could have been gathered for the 190 countries in this study such as more detailed types of legislative policies for child care and family leave, but health-care funding by the government in conjunction with constitutionalization is a more viable measure of welfare provision might be suitable is no doubt true. However, what I was looking for was a measure of welfare provision, because it is comparable across all 190 countries studied and gets at a basic need that all people share, namely support for health care problems.

54. These democracies have a per capita income of $11,000 or more (in the year 2000), and are at least 50% urban.

55. France and Japan, though they are two countries that contribute at a high level on the funding domain, are not included in the final tally as a welfare state because of their failure to constitutionalize the state's duty to provide for the welfare needs of people.

56. Christopher Howard, *The Hidden Welfare State: Tax Expenditures and Social Policy in the United States* (Princeton, NJ: Princeton University Press, 1997).

57. Christopher Howard, *The Welfare State Nobody Knows: Debunking Myths about U.S. Social Policy* (Princeton, NJ: Princeton University Press, 2006); Howard, *The Hidden Welfare State*.

58. Howard, *The Hidden Welfare State*.

59. What is more, when the issue is taken to court, the Supreme Court has ruled that there is no affirmative right to economic assistance as citizens, much less as residents, in the United States, even for such a basic need as education.

60. Susan Pedersen, *Family, Dependence, and the Origins of the Welfare State in Britain and France, 1914–1945* (New York: Cambridge University Press, 1993). Women obtained the right to vote in the United Kingdom in 1918 compared to 1944 in France. For a discussion of the weakness of women's rights compared to Great Britain, see Noëlle

Renoir, "The Representation of Women in Politics: From Quotas to Parity in Elections," *International and Comparative Law Quarterly* 50 (2001): 217–47.

61. Of course, the United Kingdom does not have a formal constitution. However, the International Constitutional Law Project, organized and directed by A. Tschentscher, provides a "compilation of information material originally provided by the British Embassy for purposes of publication," which stands in lieu of a written constitution. Available at www.servat.unibe/ch/law/icl/info/html.

62. As political scientist Birte Siim notes, the explanation for why women lag behind men in terms of their political representation in France despite generously funded social policies is due to the French republican heritage that stresses universalism and individualism, thereby undermining political claims based on particularized group identities. Birte Siim, *Gender and Citizenship: Politics and Agency in France, Britain, and Denmark* (New York: Cambridge University Press, 2000). The French republican heritage is evident in its constitution, in contrast to Britain's constitution that incorporates a monarchy as a component of the state along with recognition of positive group needs as a responsibility of the state.

63. The *OED*, for example, defines female as "belonging to the sex which bears offspring." *Oxford English Dictionary*, 2002, CD, "female, *a.* and *n.*," definition A. *adj*. I. As biologist Ann Fausto-Sterling argues, there are a multitude of sexual identities and, therefore, it is incorrect to view sex classification in terms of bipolar categories of "male and female." Anne Fausto-Sterling, *Sexing the Body: Gender Politics and the Construction of Sexuality* (New York: Basic Books, 2000).

However, Fausto-Sterling does not address fertility issues in relation to expanding sex classifications. Despite the fluidity of the social construction of sex categories, given the current state of reproductive technology, the bearing of offspring still requires a bipolar combination of a male and female human being to contribute sperm and ova, respectively, to the conception of a fertilized ovum. After conception, the bearing of an offspring requires a parent who is female with the requisite chromosomes, organs, and hormones to be pregnant and to give birth. Thus, this book adopts sex classification as female as one definition of maternalism.

Deirdre Condit argues that rather than focus on what women can do as female, namely, bear offspring, a more appropriate focus is on what men cannot do. She argues that reproductive technology may make it possible in the not too distant future for men to bear children. And, were this to come to pass—and men exercised that new option—the extension of childbearing as a capacity to men would be the best way to deconstruct "identity, biology, and even materiality" as derived from bodily differences. Deirdre M. Condit, "Androgenesis and Mothering Human Identity," in *21st Century Mothering*, ed. Andrea O'Reilly (Cambridge: Cambridge University Press, 2009, forthcoming).

64. Joan Wallach Scott, *Parité! Equality and the Crisis of French Universalism* (Chicago: University of Chicago Press, 2005). Anna van der Vleuten also sees the French case as one defined by a norm of "equality," which is the idea that every citizen has the right to be "treated equally." In her view, in France, this norm is combined with a national identity fixated on the French Revolution, yielding the view that France has a "duty to serve as a role model for all civilized nations." Anna van der Vleuten, *The Price of Gender Equality: Member States and Governance in the European Union* (Hampshire, England: Ashgate, 2007), 12–13. For a fascinating analysis of how gender difference figured into the French social model of solidarity and citizenship after World War I, see Laura Frader, *Breadwinners and Citizens: Gender in the Making of the French Social Model* (Durham, NC: Duke University Press, 2008).

65. Wilma Rule, "Electoral Systems, Contextual Factors, and Women's Opportunity for Election to Parliament in Twenty-Three Democracies," *Western Political Quarterly* 40 (1987): 477–98; Richard E. Matland, "Women's Representation in National Legislatures: Developed and Developing Countries," *Legislative Studies Quarterly* 23, no. 1 (1998): 109–25; Pippa Norris, "Women's Legislative Participation in Western Europe," *Western European Politics* 8, no. 4 (1985): 90–101; Lane Kenworthy and Melissa Malami, "Gender Inequality in Political Representation: A Worldwide Comparative Analysis," *Social Forces* 78, no. 1 (1999): 235–68; Aili Mari Tripp and Alice Kang, "The Global Impact of Quotas: On the Fast Track to Increased Female Representation," *Comparative Political Studies* 41, no. 3 (2008): 338–61; Miki Caul, "Political Parties and the Adoption of Candidate Gender Quotas: A Cross-National Analysis," *Journal of Politics* 63, no. 4 (2001): 1214–29.

66. Available at www.quotaproject.org/displayCountry.cfm?CountryCode=FR; South Africa is included in this measure.

67. The *OED* defines "family" as "the group of persons consisting of the parents and their children, whether actually living together or not; in a wider sense, the unity formed by those who are nearly connected by blood or affinity" . . . "those descended or claiming descent from a common ancestor: a house, kindred lineage. *Oxford English Dictionary*, 2002, CD, "family, n.," Definition I. 3a, 4a. Similarly, the primary definition of "kinship" is the "quality of state of being kin" as established by "relationship by descent; consanguinity." *Oxford English Dictionary*, 2002, CD, "kinship, n.," Definition 1.a. When women give birth, therefore, they generate families and kinship groups. The association of "family" and women's capacity to be pregnant and give birth is obvious. As the *OED* notes, to be "in the family way" means "to be pregnant" and "to put in the family way" means "to make pregnant." *Oxford English Dictionary*, 2002, CD, "family, n.," Definition II. 10 b.

68. A notable exception is the work of Jeremy D. Mayer and Lee Sigelman, "Zog for Albania, Edward for Estonia, and Monarchs for All the Rest? The Royal Road to Prosperity, Democracy, and World Peace," *PS* (September 1999): 771–74, their tongue-in-cheek tone notwithstanding.

69. Vernon Bagdanor, *The Monarchy and the Constitution* (New York: Oxford University Press, 1995).

70. Historian Sarah Hanley attributes the success of monarchical state-building, that is, political centralization, in France in the sixteenth and early seventeenth centuries as founded upon a "family-state compact," which she defines as a "conflation of private and public power, or family-state governance" that resulted from the sale by the royal government of judicial and other political offices to family networks. This type of fusion of the family with the state in a monarchical system extends that fusion from how the pool of eligible rulers is defined to how the bureaucratic apparatus of the state is determined. Sarah Hanley, "Engendering the State: Family Formation and State Building in Early Modern France," *French Historical Studies* 16, no. 1 (1989): 4–7.

71. These percentages are based on democratic monarchies open to women. Excluded are Japan and Liechtenstein.

72. André Poulet notes that a queen was far from exempt from ideology of the times that defined women to be subordinate to men. André Poulet, "Capetian Women and the Regency: The Genesis of a Vocation," in *Medieval Queenship*, ed. John Carmi Parsons (New York: St. Martin's Press, 1993), 93.

73. Barbara J. Harris, "Women and Politics in Early Tudor England," *Historical Journal* 33, no. 2 (1990): 274.

74. Antonia Fraser, *The Warrior Queens* (New York: Alfred A. Knopf, 1989).

75. Janet Nelson, "Women at the Court of Charlemagne: A Case of Monstrous Regiment?" in *Medieval Queenship*, ed. Parsons, 59.

76. Parsons, ed., *Medieval Queenship*; Fraser, *The Warrior Queens*.

77. Ibid.

78. Allison Heisch, "Queen Elizabeth I and the Persistence of Patriarchy," *Feminist Review* (1981): 50.

79. Quoted in Heisch, "Queen Elizabeth I and the Persistence of Patriarchy," 50.

80. Lisa Anderson, "Absolutism and the Resilience of Monarchy in the Middle East," *Political Science Quarterly* 106, no. 1 (1991): 1–15.

81. Monarchies that bar women from accession and regency, however, destroy the very principle that symbolizes the fusion of women's maternal identities with the state in the first place. Thus in this study, only countries with monarchies that allow women to ascend to the throne as sovereigns or permit women to serve in other sovereign roles, such as regents, are credited as monarchies as a type of state maternalism.

82. Helen Fisher, *The First Sex: The Natural Talents of Women and How They Are Changing the World* (New York: Ballantine Books, 2000), 155.

83. Susan J. Carroll, *Women as Candidates in American Politics* (Bloomington: Indiana University Press, 1985); Michele L. Swers, *The Difference Women Make* (Chicago: University of Chicago Press, 2002); Susan J. Carroll, ed., *The Impact of Women in Public Office* (Bloomington: Indiana University Press, 2001).

84. Chou Bih-er, Cal Clark, and Janet Clark, *Women in Taiwan Politics: Overcoming Barriers to Women's Participation in a Modernizing Society* (Boulder, CO: Lynne Rienner, 1990), 151, 157.

85. Mohamad Tavakoli-Targhi, "Women of the West Imagined: The Farangi Other and the Emergence of the Woman Question in Iran," in *Identity Politics and Women*, ed. Valentine M. Moghadam (Boulder, CO: Westview Press, 1994), 98.

86. Khawar Mumtaz, "Identity Politics and Women: 'Fundamentalism' and Women in Pakistan," in *Identity Politics and Women*, ed. Valentine M. Moghadam (Boulder, CO: Westview Press, 1994), 235–36.

87. Hanna Papanek, "The Ideal Woman and the Ideal Society: Control and Autonomy in the Construction of Identity," in *Identity Politics and Women*, ed. Moghadam, 43; Tavakoli-Targhi continues, stating that "woman's veil was constituted as a marker of identity [in Iran] and that it was a product of cultural and political encounters among the Iranian traditionalists, reformists, and revolutionaries. These contestations led to the Constitutional Revolution of 1905–1909 and the emergence of Islamist (Mashru'ahkhvah) and Secular-nationalist (Mashrutahkhvah) camps. These antagonistic camps had as their sub-test two conflicting images of the West. One viewed the West as Farang-I ba Farhang (the cultured Farang) and the other as Kufristani (the land of the infidels). One was grounded in a positive notion of freedom (azadi) anchored to the memories of the French Revolution and called for the educating and unveiling of Iranian women constructed on the indecency and corruption of European women and sought to protect Iranian women and the nation of Islam from the malady of the deviant gaze (mafasid-I harzah chashmi) which would result in fornication (zina), sedition (fitnah), bloodshed (khunrizi), syphilis, and the discontinuation of the human race. These antagonistic articulations of European women have remained the organizing elements of twentieth-century Iranian modernist and Islamicist political discourses. The Islamization of Iran since 1979 was grounded in the rejection and condemnation of unveiled women as European dolls ('Arusak-I Faragni)." Tavakoli-Targhi, "Women of the West Imagined," in *Identity Politics and Women*, ed. Moghadam. Binnaz Toprak argues that "Islamic fundamentalism in Turkey is primarily

concerned with the status of women and defines the parameters of Islamic community in terms of a sexual differentiation of social and familial roles. The movement sees the defining characteristic of a Muslim society in its conception of women that in turn shapes the social organization without which Islam would have become a purely individualistic faith since it does not recognize priesthood. Fundamentalist politics reflect a struggle to redefine women's status in Turkish society." Binnaz Toprak, "Women and Fundamentalism: The Case of Turkey," in *Identity Politics and Women*, ed. Moghadam, 293. Also, as Papanek notes, national control over women's body can be a way to project "feelings of lost identity." Papanek "The Ideal Woman and the Ideal Society," in *Identity Politics and Women*, ed. Moghadam. As Papanek notes, "Much has also been written about "westitis" or "westoxication" through which some Iranian writers have used the allegory of disease to express their feelings of lost identity. Not only are these notions useful for projecting responsibility on others—in this case "the West"—but, as Afsaneh Najmabadi notes, "the allegories used by Al-e Ahmad to diagnose a general social illness found their most resonant reading onto the body of woman, on her public physical appearance. In its extreme expression, un-Islamicly dressed woman became the sickness itself. [ft 55] In other words, continuing a pattern of attributing blame to women (for instance, as temptresses of men) as justification for male control of female behavior (to protect men against their own impulses), here the attribution of blame to external forces is continued by further projections onto women. This, in turn, justifies the expansion of men's control over women." Papanek "The Ideal Woman and the Ideal Society," in *Identity Politics and Women*, ed. Moghadam, 63–64. [ft 55: Afsaneh Najmbadi, "Hazards of Modernity and Morality," p. 15, emphasis added (74).]

Some equate the need to control women in postcolonial states as stemming from the need to find some area in which control is possible. As Khawar Mumtaz notes, "In Pakistan, as in most other post-colonial states, the rapid transformation of the economic and social structures has resulted in a state of confusion and lack of control by men. In this shifting and bewildering reality the only area where control is possible is the domestic space, hence the compelling need to exercise it over women." Mumtaz, "Identity Politics and Women," in *Identity Politics and Women*, ed. Moghadam, 235–36. That is, the state uses the "ideal of womanhood" to symbolize the "ideal state" and "as a *tool* to control and manipulate individual conformity to state policy." Papanek "The Ideal Woman and the Ideal Society," in *Identity Politics and Women*, ed. Moghadam, 43.

88. Nancy E. Cott, *Public Vows: A History of Marriage and the Nation* (Cambridge, MA: Harvard University Press, 2000), 5.

89. Ibid., 156.

90. Louise Chappell, *Gendering Government: Feminist Engagement with the State in Australia and Canada*. (Vancouver: University of British Columbia Press: 2002), 4.

91. Ibid., 4–5.

92. Mala Htun, *Sex and the State: Abortion, Divorce, and the Family under Latin American Dictatorships and Democracies* (New York: Cambridge University Press, 2003).

93. Joni Lovenduski, "Introduction," in *Feminizing Politics*, ed. Joni Lovenduski (Cambridge: Polity Press. 2005), 4.

94. Amy G. Mazur, *Theorizing Feminist Policy* (Oxford: Oxford University Press, 2002), 1.

95. John Brueggemann "The Power and Collapse of Paternalism: The Ford Motor Company and Black Workers, 1937–1941" *Social Problems* 47, no. 2 (2000): 222.

96. Ibid., 223.

97. Deborah M. Weiss "Paternalistic Pension Policy: Psychological Evidence and Economic Theory," *University of Chicago Law Review* 58, no. 4 (1991): 1276.

98. Quoted in Christopher Wolfe, "Liberalism and Paternalism: A Critique of Ronald Dworkin," *Review of Politics* 56, no. 4 (1994): 616.

99. Paul Burrows, "Patronising Paternalism," *Oxford Economic Papers* (n.s.) 45, no. 4 (1993): 542.

100. Meera Kosambi, "Gender Issues and State Intervention in India," *Feminist Review* 63, Negotiations and Resistances (Autumn 1999): 98–100.

101. Nira Yuval-Davis, *Gender and Nation* (London: Sage Publications, 1997).

102. Eileen L. McDonagh, "Race, Class, and Gender in the Progressive Era: Restructuring State and Society," in *Progressivism and the New Democracy*, ed. Sidney Milkis and Jerome M. Mileur (Amherst: University of Massachusetts Press, 1999), 160.

103. Ibid.

104. Ibid.

105. Papanek, "The Ideal Woman and the Ideal Society," in *Identity Politics and Women*, ed. Moghadam, 47–48.

106. Robin West, *Caring for Justice* (New York: New York University Press, 1997), 23.

107. Larry Jay Diamond, "Thinking about Hybrid Regimes," *Journal of Democracy* 13, no. 2 (2002): 23.

108. Ibid., referencing Thomas Carothers, "The End of the Transition Paradigm," *Journal of Democracy* 13 (January 2002): 9, 18.

109. Curtis R. Ryan and Jillian Schwedler, "Return to Democratization or New Hybrid Regime? The 2003 Elections in Jordan," *Middle East Policy* 11, no. 2 (2004): 148.

Chapter 3

1. Paul Pierson, "When Effect Becomes Cause: Policy Feedback and Political Change," *World Politics* 45, no. 4 (1993): 595.

2. Suzanne Mettler and Joe Soss, "The Consequences of Public Policy for Democratic Citizenship: Bridging Policy Studies and Mass Politics," *Perspectives on Politics* 2, no. 1 (2004): 55–73.

3. Ibid., 57.

4. Ibid.

5. Ibid.

6. Torben Iversen, "Political leadership and Representation in West European Democracies: A Test of Three Models of Voting," *American Journal of Political Science* 38, no. 1 (1994): 47.

7. Mettler and Soss, "The Consequences of Public Policy for Democratic Citizenship," 57.

8. Ibid., 57n26.

9. Ibid., 57nn27, 28, 29.

10. Ibid., 57.

11. Ibid.

12. Ibid., 55.

13. Ibid., 56.

14. Ibid.

15. Ibid.

16. Ibid., 58.

17. Quoted in Pierson, "When Effect Becomes Cause," 595; and quoted in Mettler and Soss, "The Consequences of Public Policy for Democratic Citizenship," 58, respectively.

18. Anne Schneider and Helen Ingram, "Social Construction of Target Populations: Implications for Politics and Policy" *American Political Science Review* 87, no. 2 (1993): 344.

19. In ibid., 345.

20. Mettler and Soss, "The Consequences of Public Policy for Democratic Citizenship," 58.

21. Schneider and Ingram, "Social Construction of Target Populations," 340.

22. Joe Soss, "Lessons of Welfare: Policy Design, Political Learning, and Political Action," *American Political Science Review* 93, no. 2 (1999): 376.

23. The state is a central concept in political science, a virtual synonym for what is meant by "political." For an interesting discussion that would do well to expand our view to recognize the way "politics occurs universally in human relations," see Ruth Lane, "Pitkin's Dilemma: The Wider Shores of Political Theory and Political Science," *Perspectives on Politics* 2, no. 3 (2004): 460.

24. Andrea Louise Campbell, *How Policies Make Citizens: Senior Political Activism and the American Welfare State* (Princeton, NJ: Princeton University Press, 2005), 2, 1–7.

25. As Suzanne Mettler argues, the inclusion of mass publics, such as African American men, in social programs, such as the GI Bill, had an impact on their subsequent civic engagement. By extension, exclusion from social programs had the reverse impact, that is, exclusion reduces subsequent civic engagement. Suzanne Mettler and Ira Katznelson disagree as to how inclusive the GI Bill was for African American men, and, thus, it is little surprise that they also disagree as to whether content and/or administration of the GI Bill impacted positively or negatively upon the subsequent incorporation of African Americans into American society. See Ira Katznelson, *When Affirmative Action Was White: An Untold History of Racial Inequality in Twentieth-Century America* (New York: W. W. Norton, 2005).

26. Campbell, *How Policies Make Citizens*, 5.

27. Ibid., 1, emphasis added.

28. Suzanne Mettler, *Soldiers to Citizens: The G.I. Bill and the Making of the Greatest Generation* (Cambridge: Oxford University Press, 2005); Katznelson, *When Affirmative Action Was White*; Pierson, "When Effect Becomes Cause," 595–628.

29. Jacob S. Hacker, *The Divided Welfare State: The Battle over Public and Private Social Benefits in the United States* (New York: Cambridge University Press, 2002); Sven Steinmo, Kathleen Thelen, and Frank Longstreth, eds., *Structuring Politics: Historical Institutionalism in Comparative Analysis* (New York: Cambridge University Press, 1992); Theda Skocpol, *Protecting Soldiers and Mothers: The Political Origins of Social Policy in the United States* (Cambridge, MA: Harvard University Press, 1992); Daniel P. Carpenter, *The Forging of Bureaucratic Autonomy: Reputations, Networks, and Policy Innovation in Executive Agencies, 1862–1928* (Princeton, NJ: Princeton University Press, 2001).

30. Campbell, *How Policies Make Citizens*, 5; Mettler, *Soldiers to Citizens*. Campbell observes that public policies such as Social Security and Medicare foster a political "group identity" among recipients that enhances their propensity to engage in politics. Public policies also have interpretative influences that create feelings of inclusion—that is, citizenship—by signifying to the recipients how the government and others regard their value to society. For instance, political scientist Suzanne Mettler has demonstrated that

public policies such as the GI Bill that reward those who have served in the military convey the message that the government (and the society the government represents) values those who have engaged in such service for their country. Andrea Louise Campbell, "Policy Feedbacks and the Political Mobilization of Mass Publics" (2008), Department of Political Science, MIT, unpublished paper.

31. Pippa Norris and Ronald Inglehart, "Cultural Barriers to Equal Representation," *Journal of Democracy* 12 (July 2001): 126–40.

32. Pamela Paxton and Sheri Kunovich, "Women's Political Representation: The Importance of Ideology," *Social Forces* 82, no. 1 (2003): 87–114.

33. Quoted in ibid., 91.

34. The term used in Campbell, citing Pierson, is *resource* rather than *instrumental*. Campbell, *How Policies Make Citizens,* 1, citing Pierson, "When Effect Becomes Cause."

35. Campbell, *How Policies Make Citizens,* 2, citing Pierson "When Effect Becomes Cause"; Schneider and Ingram, "Social Construction of Target Populations," 334–47.

36. Ann Shola Orloff, "Gender and the Social Rights of Citizenship: The Comparative Analysis of Gender Relations and Welfare States," *American Sociological Review* 58, no. 3 (1993).

37. Miki Caul Kittilson, "In Support of Gender Quotas: Setting New Standards, Bringing Visible Gains," *Politics and Gender* (2005): 638.

38. Ibid., 643–44.

39. Helen Irving, *A Woman's Constitution: Gender and History in the Australian Commonwealth* (Sydney: Hale and Iremonger, 1996), 34.

40. Ibid.

41. Ibid., 35.

42. Ibid., 37. Similarly, consider the contemporary case of Japan, one of the world's leading economic powers, but also a country that has an extraordinarily low percentage of women elected to its national legislature, only 4.6%, despite having high scores affirming individual equality, a competitive electoral system, and a ceremonial monarchy open only to women. The public in Japan expresses the view that opening the ceremonial Japanese monarchy up so that women could inherit the right to rule would dispose voters to be more favorable toward the election of women political leaders. This view surfaced, for example, when the current Princess of Japan gave birth to a baby girl, after considerable difficulties in producing an offspring. However, although eight women ruled as empresses in Japan in centuries past, since 1889, Japan's monarchy has been open only to men.

After Crown Princess Masako gave birth to a baby girl, Prime Minister Koizumi and 83% of the Japanese people supported amending the Japanese Constitution to allow a woman to succeed to the imperial throne, a policy this study found to enhance women's access to electoral office. In the words of Junko Kamikita, a homemaker, "It would be good to have a woman as the symbol of our state, just like Queen Elizabeth or Prime Minister Thatcher. If we have a female symbol of state, the Japanese people's notions [about women in politics] would change." Peggy Hernandez, "Japan fetes birth of a princess who may yet rule," *Boston Globe,* Sunday, December 2, 2001, A3; Howard W. French, "Japan Royal Birth Stirs Talk of Return to Empress," *New York Times,* Sunday, December 2, 2001, A3. The *New York Times* editorial page concurs, declaring that a Japanese empress "would send a positive message to all Japanese women," Editorial, *New York Times,* December 2, 2001, A22.

Similarly, political scientist and Japanese expert, Sherry Martin, when asked if she thought opening the Japanese monarchy up to women would have a positive impact on the public's acceptance of women in position of elected political leadership, answered "yes." Personal conversation with author, spring 2005.

43. As political scientists Pamela Paxton and Sheri Kunovich note, the two basic ways to explain women's election to political office is in terms of the "supply" of female candidates and the "demand" for female candidates. Paxton and Kunovich, "Women's Political Representation," 87–114; Susan Welch and Dudley, "The Opportunity Structure for Women's Candidacies and Electability in Britain and the United States," *Political Research Quarterly* 49, no. 4 (1996): 861–74.

In this book, I test the policy feedback impact of public policies as it affects the "demand" for female candidates as measured by public attitudes about the suitability of women as political leaders. The feedback effect should also increase the "supply" of female candidates. This is because research shows that women are more interested than are men in policy issues that are directly feminist (such as abortion rights) or generally oriented toward the well-being of people (such as peace, education, and health policies). When the government adopts public policies that correspond more to women's policy orientations, the feedback effect should be to increase women's identification with the government and to bolster women's views that they themselves are suitable for officeholding positions in the government. Thus, though it is outside the scope of this book to test, the increase in public attitudes about the suitability of women as political leaders resulting from the government's adoption of public policies representing maternal traits should translate into a greater "supply" of women candidates running for political office.

44. Social democracy as it derives from socialist political perspectives also often includes prescriptions for government ownership of basic utilities in society, such as railroads, electrical facilities, etc., as well as a government commitment to reduce class inequalities, which go beyond my focus on welfare provision.

45. Robert J. Hill, "Turning a Gay Gaze on Citizenship, Sexual Orientation, and Gender Identity: Contesting/ed Terrain," in *Citizenship, Democracy, and Lifelong Learning,* ed. Carolyn Medel-Añonuevo and Gordon Mitchell (Hamburg, Germany: UNESCO Institute for Education, 2003), 99–139.

46. David T. Evans, *Sexual Citizenship: The Material Construction of Sexualities* (London: Routledge, 1993), 63.

47. Brenda Cossman, *Sexual Citizens: The Legal and Cultural Regulation of Sex and Belonging* (Stanford, CA: Stanford University Press, 2007), 2, 6.

48. Ibid., 7; Shane Phelan, *Sexual Strangers: Gays, Lesbians, and the Dilemmas of Citizenship* (Philadelphia: Temple University Press, 2001), cited in Cossman, *Sexual Citizens,* 7.

49. David Bell and Jon Binnie, *The Sexual Citizen: Queer Politics and Beyond* (Cambridge: Polity Press, 2000), 10.

50. Ruth O'Brien, *Bodies in Revolt: Gender, Disability, and a Workplace Ethic of Care* (London: Routledge, 2005).

51. Ibid., 3.

52. Ibid., 55, citing Sacks.

53. Pensions to government employees or public officials are not counted as an affirmation of welfare provision to people in general.

54. Mona Lena Krook and Diana O'Brien, "The Politics of Group Representation: Quotas for Women and Minorities Worldwide," paper presented at the Midwest Political Science Association meeting, 2007.

55. "Introduction," *World Value Survey,* available at http://wvs.isr.umich.edu.

56. Variable D059.

57. There are several reasons why I evaluate the meaning of this attitudinal survey data by determining the ratio of those who "strongly agree" (that is, strong opponents of women's ability to lead) to those who "strongly disagree" (that is, those who strongly support women's political leadership). The people who express the strongest attitudes are the ones who are more likely to act on those attitudes. I calculate the ratio of these two groups rather than just compare the raw numbers because a ratio quantifies the dynamic social relationship between the two factions, which can reveal important information about a society. A ratio close to one can indicate a highly polarized population, where strong supporters and strong opponents of women's political leadership are present in roughly equal numbers. A ratio closer to zero than to one indicates a society where those who strongly believe in women's leadership capabilities are outnumbered by strong opponents of women's ability to lead. Finally, a ratio much larger than one can suggest that the society in question is one where women's capabilities as political leaders are strongly recognized by a majority of the populace.

58. Susan B. Hansen, "Talking about Politics: Gender and Contextual Effects on Political Proselytizing," *Journal of Politics* 59, no. 1 (1997): 73, 89.

59. Available at www.iup.org/wmn-e/world.htm.

60. In the WVS, 2000, these two variables are A029 and A034, respectively.

61. In the WVS, 2000, these two variables are D077 and D073, respectively.

62. In a 1998 cross-national analysis of the impact of proportional representation, economic development, women's participation in the labor force, and women's cultural standing on women's political representation, Richard Matland found that these factors had little impact on less-developed nations, but that once nation-states passed a certain "threshold" of development, these factors exerted a much more significant positive impact on women's representation in legislatures. Richard E. Matland, "Women's Representation in National Legislatures: Developed and Developing Countries," *Legislative Studies Quarterly* 23, no. 1 (1998): 109–25.

63. Helen Fisher, *The First Sex: The Natural Talents of Women and How They Are Changing the World* (New York: Ballantine Books, 2000), 152, and Anne Phillips, *Democracy and Difference* (University Park: Pennsylvania State University Press, 1993), 106.

64. Type of job, education, and income are recoded from variables (X036), (X025R), (X047R), respectively, WVS, 2000.

65. Pippa Norris found that in 2000, women were elected to national legislatures in a slightly higher percentage in Catholic countries than in Protestant ones (14.3% to 13.6%), despite the fact that many researchers use "Catholicism" as a proxy for a "traditional society" that is presumed to be less supportive of women as political leaders than a nontraditional one. Pippa Norris, *Electoral Engineering: Voting Rules and Political Behavior* (Cambridge: Cambridge University Press, 2004), 205–6. Valerie O'Regan found that Catholic influences were positive sources of support for public policies benefiting women in her study of twenty-two industrial nations. Valerie R. O'Regan, *Gender Matters: Female Policymakers' Influence in Industrialized Nations* (Westport, CT: Praeger, 2000).

Chapter 4

1. I am indebted to Robert Price for first drawing my attention to the presidential campaign of Gracie Allen in 1940.

2. William Carroll, *Gracie Allen for President 1940* (San Marcos, CA: Coda Publications, 2000), 7.

3. Ibid., 11.

4. Ibid., 95.

5. Ibid., 14.

6. Ibid., 76.

7. Aristotle defined a citizen of a state as "He who has the power to take part in the deliberative or judicial administration of any state." *Politics, Book III,* available at http://www.fordham.edu/halsall/ancient/aristotle-politics1.html.

8. Janet Clark, "Getting There: Women in Political Office," in *Different Roles, Different Voices,* ed. Marianne Githens, Pippa Norris, and Joni Lovenduski (New York: HarperCollins, 1994), 99.

9. Ibid.

10. Jane Mansbridge, "Quota Problems: Combating the Dangers of Essentialism," *Politics and Gender* 1, no. 4 (2005).

11. Virginia Sapiro, *The Political Integration of Women: Roles, Socialization, and Politics* (Urbana: University of Illinois Press, 1983).

12. It is usual at this point in the discussion of the distinction between descriptive and substantive representation to invoke the example of Margaret Thatcher, a woman, who as prime minister is noted for her opposition to welfare provision spending and her support of military endeavors, such as the invasion of the Falkland Islands.

13. Kira Sanbonmatsu, *Where Women Run: Gender and Party in the American State* (Ann Arbor: University of Michigan Press, 2006), 182.

14. David Canon, *Redistricting and Representation: The Unintended Consequences of Black Majority Districts* (Chicago: University of Chicago Press, 1999).

15. See Anne Phillips, *The Politics of Presence* (Oxford: Clarendon Press, 1995); Jane Mansbridge, "Rethinking Representation," *American Political Science Review* (2003), and "Should Blacks Represent Blacks and Women Represent Women? A Contingent 'Yes,'" *Journal of Politics* (1999); Iris Marion Young, *Inclusion and Democracy* (New York: Oxford University Press, 2000); Manon Tremblay and Jackie F. Steele, "Paradise Lost? Gender Parity and the Nunavut Experience," in *Representing Women in Parliament: A Comparative Study,* ed. Marian Sawer, Manon Tremblay, and Linda Trimble (New York: Routledge, 2006), 223; Marian Sawer, Manon Tremblay, and Linda Trimble, "Introduction: Patterns and Practice in the Parliamentary Representation of Women," in *Representing Women in Parliament,* ed. Sawer, Tremblay, and Trimble, 16.

16. Mansbridge, "Quota Problems," 627.

17. Susan J. Carroll, ed. *The Impact of Women in Public Office* (Bloomington: Indiana University Press, 2001), xiii.

18. Michele L. Swers, *The Difference Women Make* (Chicago: University of Chicago Press, 2002).

19. Ibid., 126–27.

20. Debra L. Dodson, "Acting for Women," in *The Impact of Women in Public Office,* ed. Carroll, 226.

21. Carroll, ed., *The Impact of Women in Public Office,* 3.

22. Quoted in Eliza Newlin Carney, "Weighing In," in *Different Roles, Different Voices,* ed. Githens, Norris, and Lovenduski, 93.

23. FWCW Platform for Action, "Women in Power and Decision-Making," G.181, available at www.un.org/womenwatch/daw/beijing/platform/decision.htm.

24. R. Darcy, Susan Welch, and Janet Clark, *Women, Elections, and Representation,* 2nd ed. (Lincoln: University of Nebraska Press, 1994), 169.

25. Nurith Aizenman, "Where Do Women Have Power?" *Marie Claire* (Spring 2000): 199.

26. Ibid. There is some disagreement about how strong a relationship exists between descriptive and substantive representation. Political scientist Weldon questions the effectiveness of descriptive representation for ensuring the policy-outcomes preferences of marginalized groups. S. Laurel Weldon, "Beyond Bodies: Institutional Sources of Representation for Women in Democratic Policymaking," *Journal of Politics* 64, no. 4 (2002): 1162. Similarly, political scientist Beth Reingold's study of state legislatures found that descriptive representation does not garner much for women in the way of advancing their substantive interests. Beth Reingold, *Sex, Gender, and Legislative Behavior in Arizona and California* (Chapel Hill: University of North Carolina Press, 2000). However, even though she disputes the value of descriptive representation in general, she does find that it has powerful substantive impacts on the policy priorities of men and women in legislative office, and that women legislators do view themselves in particular as representing women and women's interests. In Arizona, for example, there was a marked difference between the issues focused on by women and men legislators, with the women oriented toward what are usually considered to be "women's issues," such as health care and educational programs, while the men focused more on "men's issues," such as tax reform, budgeting, and agricultural policies, Ibid., 130–33.

27. Nancy Burns, Kay Lehman Schlozman, and Sidney Verba, *The Private Roots of Public Action: Gender, Equality, and Political Participation* (Cambridge, MA: Harvard University Press, 2001), 351–52. In addition to getting into office women who endorse a feminist agenda and increasing women's political participation, others argue that women's descriptive representation is associated with different leadership styles. As Helen Fisher notes, in a 1996 Gallup poll, respondents in twenty-one out of twenty-two countries believed that electing women to office not only would improve policies and improve society because women were more interested in "community health, public education, children, day care, families, and the elderly," a policy focus that would improve the way government works, but also that women had a unique leadership style. Helen Fisher, *The First Sex: The Natural Talents of Women and How They Are Changing the World* (New York: Ballantine Books, 2000), 155.

28. Burns, Lehman Schlozman, and Verba suggest that this is because the visibility of women's political campaigns provides American women with a model of politics as a woman's game, not just a man's game. Burns, Schlozman, and Verba, *The Private Roots of Public Action*, 10.

29. Christina Wolbrecht and David E. Campbell, "Leading by Example: Female Members of Parliament as Political Role Models," *American Journal of Political Science* 51 (2007): 921–39; David E. Campbell and Christina Wolbrecht, "See Jane Run: Women Politicians as Role Models for Adolescents," *Journal of Politics* 68 (2006): 233–47.

30. "leadership," n. Oxford Reference Online, www.oxfordreference.com.ezp1.harvard.edu.

31. Scholars who study women's political leadership as action typically focus on the biographies of particular women leaders, or on types of women leaders, or on the leadership styles of women compared to men, or the policy consequences of women's political leadership.

32. The literature is vast, but see Richard A. Seltzer, Jody Newman, and Melissa Voorhees Leighton, *Sex as a Political Variable* (Boulder, CO: Lynne Rienner, 1997); Susan J. Carroll, *Women as Candidates in American Politics* (Bloomington: Indiana University Press, 1995); Kay Lehman Schlozman, Nancy Burns, and Sidney Verba, "Gender and the

Pathways to Participation: The Role of Resources," *Journal of Politics* 56 (1994): 963–90; Kay Lehman Schlozman, Nancy Burns, Sidney Verba, and Jesse Donahue, "Gender and Citizen Participation: Is There a Different Voice?" *American Journal of Political Science* 39, no. 2 (1995): 267–93.

33. Bystydzienski, *Women Transforming Politics*, 1.

34. Tamir, *Liberal Nationalism*, xiii.

35. Pamela Radcliff, "Citizens and Housewives: The Problem of Female Citizenship in Spain's Transition to Democracy," *Journal of Social History* 36, no. 1 (2002): 80.

36. Theda Skocpol, *Protecting Soldiers and Mothers: The Political Origins of Social Policy in the United States* (Cambridge, MA: Harvard University Press, 1992).

37. Mary Fainsod Katzenstein, *Faithful and Fearless: Moving Feminist Protest inside the Church and Military* (Princeton, NJ: Princeton University Press, 1998).

38. Georgina Waylen, "Women and Democratization: Conceptualizing Gender Relations in Transition Politics," *World Politics* 46, no. 3 (1994): 327–54; Maxine Molyneux, "The 'Woman Question' in the Age of Perestroika," *Agenda* 10 (1991): 89–108.

39. Virginia Sapiro, "Democracy Minus Women Is Not Democracy," in *Citizenship and Citizenship Education in a Changing World*, ed. Orit Ichilov (London: Woburn Press, 1998).

40. See Jane Mansbridge, "Feminism and Democracy," *American Prospect* 1 (1990).

41. Barbara C. Burrell, *A Woman's Place Is in the House* (Ann Arbor: University of Michigan Press, 1994), 151–52.

42. For example, see Brenda Cossman, *Sexual Citizens: The Legal and Cultural Regulation of Sex and Belonging* (Stanford, CA: Stanford University Press, 2007); David T. Evans, *Sexual Citizenship: The Material Construction of Sexualities* (London: Routledge, 1993).

43. Ruth O'Brien, *Bodies in Revolt: Gender, Disability, and a Workplace Ethic of Care* (London: Routledge, 2005).

44. Andrea Louise Campbell, *How Policies Make Citizens: Senior Political Activism and the American Welfare State* (Princeton, NJ: Princeton University Press, 2005), 3. Other economic resources, such as education, confer political skills upon recipients, provide more information about politics, and tend to generate greater interest in politics among recipients, all of which enhances their inclusion in the political system, which is to say, their "citizenship." Campbell, *How Policies Make Citizens*, 4.

45. I am indebted to Mary Katzenstein and Stephen Skowronek for pointing me in the direction of thinking about political institutions in term of the representative performance of gender. Private correspondence, November 2005.

46. Frances Rosenbluth, Rob Salmond, and Michael F. Thies, "Welfare Works: Explaining Female Legislative Representation," *Politics and Gender* 2 (2006): 165.

47. Ibid.

48. Scholars have assessed the connection between gender quotas and principles of representation in a democratic political system using at least three major rationales for gender quotas: (1) to promote *democratic political systems*, (2) to promote a well-functioning *market system* within nation-states, and (3) to promote *isomorphic nation-states* as a foundation of international relations. To this list, this book adds a fourth: (4) gender quotas as the *institutionalization of reproductive labor* as a constitutive component of a nation's legislative political institutions.

49. Ann Towns, "Understanding the Effects of Larger Ratios of Women in National Legislatures: Proportions and Gender Differentiation in Sweden and Norway," *Women and Politics* 25, nos. 1 and 2 (2003): 10.

50. Quoted in ibid., 11. Yet another way scholars evaluate the meaning of gender quotas is the way gender quotas increase the *isomorphism* of political systems internationally by making men and women more similar to each other within each political system and by producing more similarity between political systems. As Ann Towns argues, it is not just any similarity that seeks to be advanced by the adoption of gender quotas. Rather, it is a specific similarity, namely, characteristics used to define a nation-state as "modern, capitalist democracy" in contrast to an "unprofitable," "traditional" state. According to this democratization view, gender quotas are seen as a modernizing mechanism affecting both the economic, political, and cultural norms of a political system. Consequently, some scholars interpret gender quotas to be about "'modern' statehood."

The chief characteristic of a nation-state that makes it "traditional," according to the international isomorphic view, that must be overcome if the nation-state is to join an international community of "modern" political systems, is the cultural value attributed by national cultures to the separation of women into the private sphere of the family and men into the public sphere of the state. As the UNDP notes, "traditional understandings of space as private and public, women generally being relegated to the former . . . lie at the very heart of most of the difficulties women face entering politics." Similarly, the Inter-American Commission on Women also targets the "'socio-cultural patterns' that inhibit women from taking part in 'modern society.'" The most serious sociocultural principle that obstructs women's participation in politics, according to SADC, is "age old attitudes and stereotypes that assign women to the private, and men to the public domain." A solution, therefore, to this problem, is to mandate the inclusion of women in the public sphere of the state, if only as "transitory electoral reforms" that are best viewed as affirmative action initiatives. Towns, "Understanding the Effects of Larger Ratios of Women in National Legislatures," 2–4, 7.

51. Lisa Baldez, "Critical Perspectives on Gender and Politics," *Politics and Gender* 2 (2006): 104.

52. Ibid., 105.

53. Ibid.

54. These patterns hold even when controlling for the Nordic countries.

55. Proportional representation is an electoral system where election results seek to achieve a close correspondence between the percentage of votes that a group of candidates (for instance, candidates belonging to the same party) receives and the number of seats that are allocated to that group in a national legislature. Variations of proportional representation are used in many political systems, including Israel, the Netherlands, Finland, the European Parliament for EU countries, Australia, Germany, Mexico, and Brazil. Proportional representation systems are in contrast to plurality voting systems, such as is used in the United States, where the "winner takes all," despite the slenderness of the electoral margin. Thus, in the 109th Congress that recently concluded, the Republican Party led the Senate despite having the direct support of only 17% of eligible voters. See http://en.wikipedia.org/wiki/Proportional_representation. Darcy, Welch, and Clark, *Women, Elections, and Representation*, 92–93; Linda K. Richter, "Exploring Theories of Female Leadership in South and Southeast Asia," *Pacific Affairs* (1990): 532–33; Pippa Norris, "Political Recruitment," in *Different Roles, Different Voices*, ed. Githens, Norris, and Lovenduski, 114; Pippa Norris, "Conclusions: Comparing Passages to Powers," in *Passages to Power: Legislative Recruitment in Advanced Democracies*, ed. Pippa Norris (Cambridge: Cambridge University Press, 1997); Wilma Rule, "Electoral Systems, Contextual Factors, and Women's Opportunity for Election to Parliament in Twenty-Three Democracies," *Western Political Quarterly* 40 (1987): 477–98, 444; Pippa

Norris, "Women's Legislative Participation in Western Europe," *Western European Politics* 8 (1985): 90–101; Pamela Paxton, "Women in National Legislatures: A Cross-National Analysis," *Social Science Research* 26 (1997): 442–64; Lane Kenworthy and Melissa Malami, "Gender Inequality in Political Representation: A Worldwide Comparative Analysis," *Social Forces* 78, no. 1 (1999): 235–68; Andrew Reynolds, "Women in the Legislatures and Executives of the World Knocking at the Highest Glass Ceiling," *World Politics* 51 (July 1999): 547–72; Ian McAllister and Donley T. Studlar, "Electoral Systems and Women's Representation: A Long-Term Perspective," *Representation* 39, no. 1 (2002): 3–14; Pamela Paxton, Melanie Hughes, and Jennifer Green, "The International Women's Movement and Women's Political Representation, 1893–2003," *American Sociological Review* 71 (2006): 898–920. Also, for excellent overviews of quotas and their impact, see Drude Dahlerup, ed., *Women, Quotas, and Politics* (London: Routledge: 2006), and Drude Dahlerup and Lenita Freidenvall, "Quotas as a 'Fast Track' to Equal Representation for Women: Why Scandinavia Is No Longer the Model," *International Feminist Journal of Politics* 7, no. 1 (2005): 26–48. Research points to the way political structures also influence women's acquisition of the right to vote, see Holly J. McCammon, Karen E. Campbell, Ellen M. Granberg, and Christine Mowery, "How Movements Win: Gendered Opportunity Structures and U.S. Women's Suffrage Movements, 1866 to 1919," *American Sociological Review* 66, no. 1 (2001): 49–70.

56. Chou Bih-er, Cal Clark, and Janet Clark, *Women in Taiwan Politics: Overcoming Barriers to Women's Participation in a Modernizing Society* (Boulder, CO: Lynne Rienner, 1990), 96,153.

57. Other structural factors found to be important include incumbency, which is one of the major boosts to getting elected; if one is already in office, one has more of a chance to be reelected. This is a Catch 22 for women, however. Since they are not in office already, they cannot be incumbents to the same degree as men. Thus, women candidates tend to lack the incumbency boost. Clark, "Getting There," 107. As R. Darcy and colleagues point out, voters and party leaders do not discriminate against women, and, also, women can raise as much money as men. The real problem, therefore, it's that women are not incumbents. Clark, "Getting There," 89–92; and Darcy, Welch, and Clark, *Women, Elections, and Representation*, 89–92.

58. Fisher, *The First Sex*, 152; Anne Phillips, *Democracy and Difference* (University Park: Pennsylvania State University Press, 1993), 106.

59. Percentages are rounded off from unstandardized regression coefficients.

60. In proportional representation electoral systems, each political party determines its priorities and then lists its candidates according to that predetermined ranking. In a closed list, instead of voting for candidates, voters vote for an entire list. Based on election results, each party receives a proportion of seats in the legislature corresponding to the proportion of votes that party received. Each party uses the rank order on its list to determine who the representatives will be. When voters are allowed to vote for candidates directly, as when open lists are in effect, voters often have the choice to vote for one candidate or to vote for a number of candidates, indicating their rank preference for each.

61. These patterns hold even when controlling for the Nordic countries.

62. These patterns hold even when controlling for the Nordic countries.

63. The statistical significance slightly exceeds 0.10. (These patterns hold even when controlling for the Nordic countries.)

64. The unit of analysis for public attitudes is at the respondent level, and the unit of analysis for women's election to national legislatures is at the country level, making it difficult to analyze both data sets in the form of a structural equation assessing both

the direct and indirect effects of public attitudes on women's election to political office. Hence, to simulate a structural equation model, the measure of public attitudes used in this equation is the estimated ratio for each country of those who strongly agree that women are suitable as political leaders to those who strongly disagree as predicated by the data analysis of public attitudes reported in chapter 3. The estimated ratio is used as a proxy for a structural equation model that would use a somewhat comparable measure.

65. These patterns hold even when controlling for the Nordic countries.

66. Numbers rounded off to the nearest whole number.

67. Even today, women do not have full access to all types of military action. For instance, women are not permitted to serve on submarines, or to participate in special forces such as Navy Seals. And although women can serve as commanding officers, they are barred from infantry assignments, as well as Special Operations, Artillery, Armour, and Forward Air Defense. Women can fly military aircraft, but make up 2% of all pilots in the U.S. military.

68. Quoted in www.dukenews.duke.edu/dialogue/liswood426.html.

69. Quoted in ibid.

70. Worldwide Guide to Women in Leadership, available at www.guide2womenleaders.com/Presidents-Chronological.htm.

71. Table 4.4 includes contemporary nation-states, but does not include territories and political systems no longer in existence, with the exception of East Germany.

72. This percentage includes only contemporary political systems; it does not include East Germany.

73. This book claims that it is the failure of the United States—as a liberal democracy in which the state performs, at least to some degree, public policies representing a principle of individualism that the government should treat all people the same "in spite of" their ascriptive group differences—to maternalize its state by performing public policies representing a principle of maternal group difference in which the government treats people differently "because of" ascriptive group difference derivative of a definition of maternalism. That is, the failure of the United States to adopt gender quotas, welfare provision, or to have retained its hereditary monarchy at its founding.

The question I now raise is whether we can ascertain if democratic maternal state action also promotes women's election to executive leadership positions? This is a more difficult question than that of legislative leadership because of data difficulties. Women, as noted, have been elected to positions of executive political leadership, defined as either the chief executive leader (prime minister or president) and/or second in command (defined as either deputy prime minister or vice president). However, the time range involved in this collection of women who have been elected to executive political leadership positions is a long one, indeed. Years. If we were to try to test statistically the relationship between state style—whether the state is intergendered or not—and women's election to executive leadership positions, we run into several problems. First, we do not have attitudinal measures of the public's view of women's suitability as political leaders before the year 2000. Thus, we cannot measure how state style—the intergendered state—indirectly affects women's election to executive political office over the range of years for which we have such data.

Second, even if we were to skip the public attitudes component of our model that is diagrammed in figure 3.1, we are still left with another data problem, namely, the small variation on the dependent variable, percent of nations that elect a woman as an executive leader per year. That is to say, the percentage of political systems on a yearly basis that elect women to positions of executive political leadership varies from no nations to one nation to a maximum of several nations. This is a very small amount of variation on the "dependent variable," percent women elected to executive political leadership positions, and the small size of this variation makes it difficult from a statistical point of view to verify the impact of maternal state action as an explanation of that small amount of variation in the dependent variable, especially when we are missing a measurement of the intervening variable, public attitudes, for virtually the entire range of years in which we are interested.

Thus, what follows, admittedly, is not a systematic statistical analysis of the relationship between maternal state action and women's election to positions of executive political leadership, but rather a set of observations to be added to the way others have observed patterns cross-nationally in the election of women to executive positions of political leadership.

74. Hendrik Hertzberg, "Dynastic Voyage," *New Yorker*, October 29, 2007.

75. Ibid.

76. Ibid.

77. Lisa Solowiej and Thomas L. Brunell, "The Entrance of Women to the U.S. Congress: The Widow Effect," *Political Research Quarterly* 56, no. 3 (2003): 283.

78. Ibid.

79. Ibid.

80. Irwin N. Gertzog, "The Matrimonial Connection: The Nomination of Congressmen's Widows for the House of Representatives," *Journal of Politics* 42, no. 3 (1980): 820–33; Solowiej and Brunell, "The Entrance of Women to the U.S. Congress: The Widow Effect," 284.

81. Quoted in Solowiej and Brunell, "The Entrance of Women to the U.S. Congress: The Widow Effect," 283.

82. Michelle Goldberg "A Tainted Milestone," *Guardian* online, December 3, 2007, available at http://commentisfree.guardian.co.uk/michelle_goldberg/2007/12/tainted_milestone.html.

83. Ibid.

84. Terry Golway, "Dynasties," *America* 198, no. 2 (2008): 9.

85. Ibid.

Chapter 5

1. Nicholas Kristof, "When Women Rule," *New York Times*, February 10, 2008.

2. Quoted in Kristof, "When Women Rule."

3. Given the American liberal democratic and republican heritage, it is usual to view monarchies and systems of inherited status inequalities as tyrannous and absolutely injurious to the well-being of the disadvantaged. As some suggest, however, it is a mistake to assume that relationships of inequality are necessarily characterized solely by adversarial and conflictual norms. Rather, historical research reveals that those in dominant and subordinate positions are often extremely reluctant to engage in antagonistic behavior toward one another, preferring to develop relationships based on cooperation and trust. This holds, researchers find, even when the degree of inequality is dramatic, as in slavery.

4. Frank Prochaska, *Royal Bounty: The Making of a Welfare Monarchy* (New Haven, CT: Yale University Press, 1995).

5. Available at www.woodlands-junion.kent.sch.uk/customs/easter/maundythrusday.htm, last accessed April 16, 2008.

6. Available at www.nio.gov.uk/the-queen-attends-royal-maundy-service-in-historic-visit-to-armagy/media-detail.htm?newsID=1501, last accessed April 16, 2008; see www.woodlands-junion.kent.sch.uk/customs/easter/maundythrusday.htm, last accessed April 16, 2008.

7. Available at www.royal.gov.uk/output/page4947.asp, last accessed April 17, 2008.

8. Prochaska, *Royal Bounty*.

9. George Boyer, "English Poor Laws," available at http://eh.net/encyclopedia/article/boyer.poor.laws.england, last accessed April 18, 2008.

10. E. P. Thompson, *Customs in Common: Studies in Traditional Popular Culture* (New York: The New Press, 1993), 21.

11. Ibid., 47.

12. Joan R. Gundersen, "Independence, Citizenship, and the American Revolution," *Signs* 13, no. 1 (1987): 60.

13. Ibid.

14. Nancy Fraser and Linda Gordon, "A Genealogy of Dependency: Tracing a Keyword of the U.S. Welfare State," *Signs* 19, no. 2 (1994): 309, 311, 324–25.

15. Gundersen, "Independence, Citizenship, and the American Revolution," 65.

16. The view that "anyone" who works hard enough can "do anything" is encapsulated in the American Horatio Alger myth. For an analysis of the relationship of this myth to American political development, see Carol Nackenoff, *The Fictional Republic: Horatio Alger and American Political Discourse* (New York: Oxford University Press, 1994).

17. Gosta Esping-Andersen, *Why We Need a New Welfare State* (Oxford: Oxford University Press, 2002), 3.

18. Ibid.

19. John Gerring, Philip Bond, William T. Barndt, and Carola Moreno, "Democracy and Economic Growth: A Historical Perpsective," *World Politics* 57 (April 2005): 324.

20. Georgina Waylen, "Gender and Democratic Politics: A Comparative Analysis of Consolidation in Argentina and Chile," *Journal of Latin American Studies* 32, no. 3 (2000): 765–66; Georgina Waylen, "Women and Democratization: Conceptualizing Gender Relations in Transition Politics," *World Politics* 46, no. 3 (1994): 327–54.

21. As political scientist Jacob Hacker notes, we might expect an "antistatist political culture" to retard the subsequent development of a welfare state based on government spending. Jacob S. Hacker, *The Divided Welfare State: The Battle over Public and Private Social Benefits in the United States* (New York: Cambridge University Press, 2002), 279. The American Revolutionary heritage has long been associated with an antistatist, anticentral, government, antifederal government at least in part as a legacy of rejecting a monarchical form of government that epitomizes a strong, if not absolute, executive branch, and centralization of executive authority. Although Hacker does not discuss the relevance of a monarchical heritage—or its destruction—in his analysis of historical legacies, we can add that to the list of what counts for subsequent development of state welfare provision. Hacker seeks to address the lack of publicly funded health care in the United States by arguing that we need to reformulate how we study welfare policies to include privately funded ones, such as Social Security. Hacker, *The Divided Welfare State*, 23. While this is an important perspective, from the vantage point of studying women's political inclusion, it makes a difference whether welfare is privately or publicly provided because it is the latter, not the former, that teaches the public that maternal traits associated with women denote a location in the public sphere of political governance, not merely the home or the market.

22. Robert D. Putnam, *Making Democracy Work: Civic Traditions in Modern Italy* (Princeton, NJ: Princeton University Press, 1993).

23. Steven D. Roper and Florin Fesnic, "Historical Legacies and Their Impact on Post-Communist Voting Behavior," *Europe-Asia Studies* 55, no. 1 (2003): 119–31.

24. The United States does have one absolute ascriptive qualification for the presidency, namely, birth in the United States, and also requires that a person be at least thirty-five years old. However, in general, the American political system eschews a reliance on ascriptive status as a qualification for political office. Notably, when considering our sister in revolutionary crime, France, it is significant that the acceptance of gender quotas in that country required a "universal" framing rather than a sex-specific definition. To gain acceptance of gender quotas, proponents argued that a universal feature of human beings is their male- or femaleness, and, thus, to represent human beings as a universal category requires representing both their male- and femaleness. See Joan Wallach Scott, *Parité! Equality and the Crisis of French Universalism* (Chicago: University of Chicago Press, 2005).

25. Out of thirty countries that endorsed and then abolished slavery during their history, the United States was the twentieth country to abolish slavery, which it did in 1865. Sweden was the first country to do so in 1335 and Mauritania was the last country to do so in 1980. The countries that abolished slavery and the date (in parentheses), that they did so, in chronological order, are: Sweden (1335, including Finland); Portugal (1761); England and Wales (1772); Scotland (1776); Haiti (1791); Upper Canada (1793); France (1794–1802); Chile (1811); Argentina (1813); Ecuador, Colombia, Panama, Venezuela (Fran Colombia, 1821–54); Mexico (1829); British Empire (1833); Mauritius (1835, under British rule); Denmark (1848); France (including all colonies, 1848); Peru (1851); Romania (1855); the Netherlands (1863); United States (1865); Cuba (with Puerto Rico, 1873–80); Brazil (1888); Korea (1894; hereditary slavery ended in 1886); China (1910); Burma (1929); Ethiopia (1936); Tibet (1959); Saudi Arabia (1962); and Mauritania (1980).

26. Ratified February 3, 1870.

27. Judith Apter Klinghoffer and Lois Elkis, "'The Petticoat Electors': Women's Suffrage in New Jersey, 1776–1807," *Journal of the Early Republic* 12, no. 2 (1992): 159.

28. William Blackstone, "Of the Right of Persons," *Commentaries on the Laws of England*, 4 vols. (Philadelphia: Young Biran and Abraham Small, 1803).

29. Mary Beth Norton, *Liberty's Daughters: The Revolutionary Experience of American Women, 1750–1800* (Toronto: Little, Brown, 1980), 45–46.

30. Klinghoffer and Elkis, "'The Petticoat Electors,'" 172.

31. Ibid., 160, 188.

32. The four new states were Wyoming, Utah, Idaho, and Nevada.

33. Of course, formal political rights can be undermined, as they were in the case of African American men who gained a constitutional right to vote by means of the Fifteenth Amendment, only to have Southern states negate that gain by passing non-race-specific legislation, such as poll taxes, literacy, and other such requirements that disproportionately disenfranchised African Americans. See Richard M. Valelly, *The Two Reconstructions: The Struggle for Black Enfranchisement* (Chicago: University of Chicago Press, 2004).

34. These countries are: Australia, Austria, The Bahamas, Belgium, Canada, Denmark, Finland, France, Germany, Greece, Iceland, Ireland, Israel, Italy, Japan, Luxembourg, the Netherlands, New Zealand, Norway, Portugal, Spain, Sweden, Switzerland, United States, and the United Kingdom.

35. The policy feedback model introduced at the outset of this chapter does not attribute instrumental impacts upon women's election to national public office to the presence in a political system of a hereditary monarchy. Rather, that form of state maternalism is hypothesized as having only interpretative impacts on public attitudes about the suitability of women as political leaders, which then indirectly affects the election of women to national political office.

However, in the absence of attitudinal data for the late nineteenth and early twentieth centuries, I will use the presence of hereditary monarchies as a surrogate for attitudes about the suitability of women as political leaders on the grounds that the presence of a monarchy in the democracies included in this discussion were all open to women; thereby, all of the monarchies represent the principle that women are suitable as political leaders, since women could, and did, assume political positions as sovereigns.

36. In the case of Spain, in 1936 a Personal Rule System was established after the military uprising by General Franco. However, in 1947, the Law of Succession defined Spain to be a monarchy, though without a monarchy, though with a designated heir to the throne. In 1975, with Franco no longer on the scene, the monarchy was reestablished as provided for by law that Franco himself had acknowledged. In 1978, a parliamentary monarchy was confirmed by constitutional provision. Hence, Spain never revolted against a monarchy by demolishing it in principle as a legitimate form of government. Rather, the royal succession, while remaining in place, simply did not assume monarchical political office. For this reason, I classify Spain as a political system that retained its monarchy. Arthur S. Banks, *Political Handbook of the World, 1991* (Binghamton, NY: CSA Publications, 1975–91), 623–24.

37. By 1871, Germany was formulated into an Empire by Wilhelm I, and on June 15, 1888, twenty-nine-year-old William II took over as German Emperor and King of Prussia. This rule lasted into the twentieth century with the conclusion of World War I in 1918. When Germany was defeated by the Allied powers at that time, William II bore the brunt of the ensuing ill will and near anarchy fell across the country. The association of William II with Germany's involvement in World War I, along with its defeat, inspired the German military forces to mutiny against the monarchy. William II conceded that he needed to abdicate his political power, if governmental order was to be reinstated. Thus, on November 9, 1918, he abdicated his position as Emperor of the German Empire and as King of Prussia and went into exile in Holland, a country that had been neutral in World War I. Queen Wilhelmina protected him, refusing to extradite him despite constant demands on the part of the Allied forces to do so. Even the Treaty of Versailles, Article 227, called for his return to Germany so that he could be prosecuted for "a supreme offence against international morality and the sanctity of treaties." The United States had launched propaganda that was responsible, at least in part, for the perception by the victorious countries that the responsibility for World War I lay at the feet of William II.

William II was never executed as a particular monarch, however, nor was the monarchy as an institution demolished ideologically in Germany. Rather, Germany transitioned from a monarchical state to a liberal democratic one on the basis of what I can term a principle that was ideologically *neutral* from the perspective of the people of Germany. Thus, even with the abdication and exile of William II, Germany did not ideologically demolish or distance itself from its monarchical heritage. To the contrary, when William II died on June 5, 1941 of a pulmonary embolism, the German government sent an honor guard of German soldiers to stand at the gates to his estate in Doorn, Holland. What is more, when the German Constitution of 1871 was amended on October 28, 1918, the original goal had been to create a constitutional monarchy in Germany similar to the one in Great Britain. The plan was to have a parliamentary democracy in which the Chancellor would be responsible to the German Parliament, the Reichstag, rather than to the Kaiser. From 1919 to 1933, the government of Germany was known as the Weimar Republic (due to the fact that it was in the city of Weimar where the national assembly had convened to draft the country's new constitution after World War I), but in fact the formal term by which is was constituted was the Deutsches Reich (German Empire). The term Weimar Republic is that used by historians, but the German government at this point was not a republic, but rather a constitutional monarchy. Until his death, William II retained his monarchical titles, and it was his fervent hope that he would be able to return someday to Germany as its monarch. "Germany," Encyclopædia Britannica, 2008. Encyclopædia Britannica Online, accessed April 25, 2008, available at http://www.britannica.com/eb/article-58194; "History of Weimar Republic—Germany 1919–1933—and the Rising of Hitler. The Roaring Twenties in Germany and World Economic Crisis," GermanNotes Online, available at http://www.germannotes.com/hist_weimar_republic.shtml, accessed April 4, 2008; "Background Note: Germany," U.S. Department of State online, accessed April 24, 2008, available at http://www.state.gov/r/pa/ei/bgn/3997.htm.

The story of Austria's Empire is similar to that Germany's. Greece had a monarchy as late as 1972, which in 1974, people *voted* against restoring, a far cry from an ideological revolution that involves executing the sovereigns and killing their families. Italy had a monarchy until 1946, at which time, after an *election*, the people of Italy established a Republic to replace their monarchy. Again, it was a far cry from a bloody revolution to demolish one's monarchy. And Portugal had a monarchy until 1910, when a Republic was declared.

38. Finland, for example, was ruled by Sweden's monarchy and by Russia's monarchy, but never claimed an indigenous monarchical family-kinship group of its own. Finland achieved political independence in 1917 by breaking away from the Russian Empire without ever acquiring its own monarchical heritage and established its own, modern parliamentary systems of political governance on the basis of a constitution in 1919. Never having its own monarchy, Finland did not have monarchs to exile, much less to execute. Nor did Finland, therefore, have to face the ideological problem of what to do with an indigenous monarchy. Thus, the major goal for Finland was simply the political one of gaining independence from occupying powers, such as Sweden and Russia.

Ditto for Iceland. It was settled in the late ninth and early tenth centuries by peoples from Nordic regions, and in 930 CE, the ruling chiefs in Iceland established the first parliament in the world and a republican constitution. Although Iceland remained independent until 1262, it established a union with the Norwegian monarchy on the basis of a treaty. In the late fourteenth century, when Norway and Denmark were united under the Danish crown, Iceland was passed over to Denmark. Iceland formally became a sovereign, independent republic after World War II, on June 17, 1944. In so doing, Iceland simply bypassed having a monarchy of its own with its own Icelandic ruling family-kinship group, and consequently also bypassed the need to exile its own monarchy, much less demolish its own monarchy by means of executions and/or ideological fervor.

Ditto for Ireland. Ireland's history begins as early as 8000 BCE with hunter-gatherers whom archaeologists believe arrived via a land bridge from Britain and continental Europe. By 600 CE, the indigenous pagan religion that had developed over the centuries was subsumed by Christian missionaries, such as St. Patrick. Although some regional dynasties developed, by 800 CE, Viking invaders were wreaking havoc upon them. However, it was with the invasion of Richard de Clare, 2nd Earl of Pembroke in the mid-thirteenth century that Ireland was to mark the initiation of 800 years of English political involvement in Ireland. By the sixteenth and seventeenth centuries, the Protestant British monarchy had gained full control of Ireland, whose people had remained for the most part Catholics. Sectarian and political conflict became the norm henceforth. By 1801, all pretense that Ireland had any political autonomy was destroyed as it became an integral unit of a new United Kingdom of Great Britain and Ireland, as specified by the Act of Union.

Ireland, therefore, never developed a monarchical heritage of its own, where its own ruling family-kinship group could claim to represent the Irish people. To the contrary, it was the foreign monarchy of the United Kingdom that ruled Ireland, as had the foreign monarchies of Sweden and Russia ruled Finland. Eventually, in 1922, after the Irish War of Independence, twenty-six counties of western and southern Ireland seceded from the United Kingdom to establish the independent Irish Free State, now recognized legally as the Republic of Ireland. As is well known, the remainder of the island, that is, Northern Ireland, remains a political unit of the United Kingdom, though a substantial percentage of its population is Catholic and identifies with the Irish Republic, leading to continuing conflict to this very day. However, from our point of view, what is significant about Ireland is that it never overthrew an indigenous monarchy of its own because it never had one.

Ditto for Switzerland. And modern Israel was founded in 1948 without the political incorporation of the monarchies of ancient, biblical Israel. See www.mongabay.com/reference/country_studies/finland/HISTORY.html.

By contrast, although the United States did not have a territorial monarchy operating within its own boundaries, it *did have* a national and ethnic monarchy. I say this because the people who colonized the American territories were ethnically and nationally English, and, hence, were under the political authority of their own ethnic and national group, England. Louis Hartz, of course, is notable for asserting that the United States did have an indigenous monarchy because its monarchy was territorially located across the Atlantic Ocean from the American colonists. Louis Hartz, *The Liberal Tradition in America: An Interpretation of American Political Thought since the Revolution* (New York: Harcourt, Brace, 1955). I disagree, however, because in terms of their country of origin, language, and religious heritage, the American colonists did have an indigenous monarchy despite the fact that the location of the monarchs was outside their colonial territory.

39. This omits Israel, which was not a state until 1948, and, hence, had no opportunity to enfranchise women prior to 1920.

40. Paul Pierson, *Dismantling the Welfare State? Reagan, Thatcher, and the Politics of Retrenchment* (Cambridge: Cambridge University Press, 1994), 1.

41. Paul Pierson, "Increasing Returns, Path Dependence, and the Study of Politics," *American Political Science Review* 94, no. 2 (2000): 263.

42. Ibid., 265.

43. James Mahoney, "Path Dependence in Historical Sociology," *Theory and Society* 29, no. 4 (2000): 513.

44. Guide to women world leaders, Web site. I am indebted to Deanne Kallgren for her assistance in developing this database of 4,180 women executive leaders.

45. William L. Langer, Peter N. Stearns, general editors, *The Encyclopedia of World History: Ancient, Medieval, and Modern, Chronologically Arranged* (Cambridge: James Clarke, 2001). Langer dates Ancient Period as commencing with 3500 BCE and periods prior to that as Prehistoric.

46. Katherine Crawford, "Catherine de Médicis and the Performance of Political Motherhood," *Sixteenth Century Journal* 31, no. 3 (2000): 645–46.

47. Ibid., 651–53, 662–63.

48. Inge Skovgaard-Petersen in collaboration with Nanna Dansbolt, "Queenship in Medieval Denmark," in *Medieval Queenship*, ed. John Carmi Parsons (New York: St. Martin's Press, 1993), 35.

49. Ibid., 36.

50. Lois L. Huneycutt, "Female Succession and the Language of Power in the Writings of Twelfth-Century Churchmen," in *Medieval Queenship*, ed. Parsons, 190.

51. János M. Bak, "Roles and Functions of Queens in Arpádian and Angevin Hungary (1000–1386 A.D.)," in *Medieval Queenship*, ed. Parsons, 19.

52. Huneycutt, "Female Succession and the Language of Power in the Writings of Twelfth-Century Churchmen," in *Medieval Queenship*, ed. Parsons, 199–200.

53. Available at www.guide2womenleaders.com/womeninpower/Womeninpower0000.htm.

54. Available at www.guide2womenleaders.com/womeninpower/Womeninpower1200.htm.

55. Available at www.guide2womenleaders.com/womeninpower/Womeninpower00000.htm.

56. Langer and Stearns, *The Encyclopedia of World History: Ancient, Medieval, and Modern Chronologically Arranged*.

57. Available at www.guide2womenleaders.com/womeninpower/Womeninpower00000.htm.

58. Available at www.guide2womenleaders.com/womeninpower/Womeninpower000.htm.

59. Available at www.guide2womenleaders.com/womeninpower/Womeninpower1150.htm.

60. Available at www.guide2womenleaders.com/womeninpower/Womeinpower01.htm.

61. Kathleen A. Dolan, *Voting for Women: How the Public Evaluates Women Candidates* (Boulder, CO: Westview Press, 2004), 134.

62. Ibid., 134–35.

Chapter 6

1. Quoted in Diane Carman, "Women Hope to Say Hail to the 'Chief,'" *Denver Post*, available at www.thewhitehouseproject.org/v2/press/20050918-denverpost.html, September 18, 2005.

2. Quoted in ibid.

3. Carman, "Women Hope to Say Hail to the 'Chief.'"

4. Quoted in John H. Fund, "A TV Show and Its Political Party," *Wall Street Journal Online*, September 30, 2005, available at http://opinionjournal.com/taste/?id=110007338.

5. The "could" and "should" duo haunts all aspects of women's aspirations for a more equal participation in American society. For a discussion of how both interfere with women's athletic achievements historically and still today, see Eileen McDonagh and Laura Pappano, *Playing with the Boys: Why Separate Is Not Equal in Sports* (New York: Oxford University Press, 2007).

6. Orestes Brownson, quoted in Paula S. Rothenberg, *Racism and Sexism: An Integrated Study* (New York: St. Martin's Press, 1988), 199.

7. Ibid., 198.

8. With regard to "just doing it" when it comes to voting, see, for instance, *Minor v. Happersett* (1874). In 1872, Virginia Minor—president of the Missouri branch of the National Women's Suffrage Association (NWSA)—attempted to register to vote in St. Louis. State registrar Reese Happersett denied her the ability to register. With her husband Francis, who had laid out a legal rationale for woman suffrage based on the Fourteenth Amendment's equal protection clause at the 1869 NWSA convention, Virginia Minor challenged her inability to register to vote in court, arguing that "there can be no half-way citizenship." In a 9-0 decision, the Supreme Court denied her claim on the grounds that there is no constitutionally guaranteed right to vote, and arguing that if the privileges and immunities clause of the Fourteenth Amendment indeed gave all citizens the right to vote, there would not have been a need for the Fifteenth Amendment, which explicitly gave blacks the vote.

9. According to the Center for American Women in Politics at Rutgers, forty-seven women have been elected or appointed to fill congressional seats vacant after the death of their husbands—eight in the Senate and thirty-nine in the House. Among governors, Nellie Taylor Ross (1925–27) won a special election in Wyoming after the death of her husband, "Ma" Ferguson (1925–27, 1933–35) was elected governor of Texas as a surrogate for her husband who could not succeed himself, as was Lurleen Wallace (1967–69) in Alabama. It was not until 1975 that the first woman was elected governor in her own right—Ella Grasso in Connecticut. Thus, the opening gambit of "Commander-in-Chief" is all too true to life, namely, that before women are allowed to officially take on new roles as leaders, they must somehow get themselves into positions of political leadership—not necessarily by the same means as men. This can be seen by the fact that many of the first women to serve as governor, senator, and congressional representative in this country were appointed to those positions, or were filling in after the death of a husband who had been formally elected.

10. Four western states—Idaho, Colorado, Utah, and Wyoming—entered the Union in the late nineteenth century without voting qualifications that excluded women, but all other states did exclude women from their electorates and none of these states in the course of the nineteenth century dropped being male as a qualification for voting rights.

11. Eileen L. McDonagh, "Race, Class, and Gender in the Progressive Era: Restructuring State and Society," in *Progressivism and the New Democracy*, ed. Sidney Milkis and Jerome M. Mileur (Amherst: University of Massachusetts Press, 1999), 157; Eileen L. McDonagh, "The 'Welfare Rights State' and the 'Civil Rights State': Policy Paradox and State Building in the Progressive Era," *Studies in American Political Development* 7, no. 2 (1993).

12. McDonagh, "Race, Class, and Gender in the Progressive Era," in *Progressivism and the New Democracy*, ed. Milkis and Mileur, 159–60.

13. *Lochner v. New York*, 198 U.S. 45 (1905).

14. A public policy that provides care to people is called "maternal" not because its beneficiaries are women but because it represents an activity that the public associates with women's identities as social maternalists who typically provide more care to others than do men.

15. Theda Skocpol, *Protecting Soldiers and Mothers: The Political Origins of Social Policy in the United States* (Cambridge, MA: Harvard University Press, 1992).

16. Joanne L. Goodwin, *Gender and the Politics of Welfare Reform: Mothers' Pensions in Chicago, 1911–1929* (Chicago: University of Chicago Press, 1997); Dorothy Roberts, "Irrationality and Sacrifice in the Welfare Reform Consensus," *Virginia Law Review* 81,

no. 8 (1995), 2620. Also see Lisa Dodson, *Don't Call Us Out of Name: The Untold Lives of Women and Girls in Poor America* (Boston: Beacon Press, 1998).

17. Gwendolyn Mink, *The Wages of Motherhood: Inequality in the Welfare State, 1917–1942* (Ithaca, NY: Cornell University Press, 1995), 26. Robert Lieberman analyzes how racial biases also undermined New Deal efforts to provide for the dependency needs of people. Robert C. Lieberman, *Shifting the Color Line: Race and the American Welfare State* (Cambridge, MA: Harvard University Press, 1998).

18. Kurt Schock, "People Power and Political Opportunities: Social Movement Mobilization and Outcomes in the Philippines and Burma," *Social Problems* 46, no. 3 (1999): 355–75.

19. Johanna Brenner and Barbara Laslett, "Gender, Social Reproduction, and Women's Political Self-Organization," *Gender and Society* 5, no. 3 (1991): 312.

20. Philip J. Ethington, "Recasting Urban Political History: Gender, the Public, the Household, and Political Participation in Boston and San Francisco during the Progressive Era," *Social Science History* 16, no. 2 (1992): 303.

21. Elisabeth S. Clemens, *The People's Lobby: Organizational Innovation and the Rise of Interest Group Politics in the United States, 1890–1925* (Chicago: University of Chicago Press, 1997).

22. Michael Katz, *In the Shadow of the Poorhouse: A Social History of Welfare in America* (New York: Basic Books, 1986), 194.

23. Thomas K. McCraw, *Regulation in Perspective: Historical Essays* (Cambridge, MA: Harvard University Press, 1981); Thomas K. McCraw, *Prophets of Regulation: Charles Francis Adams, Louis D. Brandeis, James M. Landis, and Alfred E. Kahn* (Cambridge, MA: Belknap Press of Harvard University Press, 1984).

24. William Dean Howells, quoted in Robert H. Bremner, *From the Depths: The Discovery of Poverty in the United States* (New York: New York University Press, 1956), 104.

25. Ibid., 124–25; Katz, *In the Shadow of the Poorhouse*.

26. Samuel Mencher, *Poor Law to Poverty Program: Economic Security Policy in Britain and the United States* (Pittsburgh: University of Pittsburgh Press, 1974), 275, 299; see also Katz, *In the Shadow of the Poorhouse*.

27. Robert Fogel, "Panel: Culture, History, and Social Theory," discussion comments, annual meeting of the Social Science History Association, 1992.

28. The exaggeration of laissez-faire principles of individualism as a cause of social distress is more coterminous with late-nineteenth-century Spencerian notions linking Adam Smith with Darwin than it is with initial principles of liberalism per se. Andrew Ross, "Is Global Culture Warming Up?" *Social Text* 28 (1991): 15, 18.

29. John D. Buenker, *Urban Liberalism and Progressive Reform* (New York: W. W. Norton, 1978), chap. 2.

30. Debates continue to rage, of course, about whether enough welfare legislation passed in the Progressive Era and whether it was passed as an attempt to assist, co-opt, or socially control the disadvantaged. Gabriel Kolko, *The Triumph of Conservatism: A Reinterpretation of American History, 1900–1916* (New York: The Free Press, 1963). Yet, given the tenacity of the American laissez-faire context, there is reason to credit Progressive Era welfare achievements as those marking a major departure from previous norms restricting the use of government as an instrument for advancing welfare policies. Richard L. McCormick, *The Party Period and Public Policy: American Politics from the Age of Jackson to the Progressive Era* (New York: Oxford University Press, 1986), 269.

31. James Weinstein, *The Corporate Ideal in the Liberal State, 1900–1918* (Boston: Beacon Press, 1968), x.

32. Richard Hofstadter, *The Age of Reform* (New York: Vintage Books, 1955).

33. McCormick, *The Party Period and Public Policy*; McCraw, *Regulation in Perspective*; McCraw, *Prophets of Regulation*; Morton Keller, *Regulating a New Economy: Public Policy and Economic Change in America, 1900–1933* (Cambridge, MA: Harvard University Press, 1990); Robert H. Wiebe, *The Search for Order, 1877–1920* (New York: Hill and Wang, 1967).

34. State-level mothers' pensions and passage by Congress of the Sheppard-Towner Act are exceptions. Skocpol, *Protecting Soldiers and Mothers*, 10.

35. Samuel P. Huntington, *American Politics: The Promise of Disharmony* (Cambridge, MA: Harvard University Press, 1981); Wiebe, *The Search for Order*.

36. Ann Vanderpol, "Dependent Children, Child Custody, and the Mothers' Pensions: The Transformation of State-Family Relations in the Early 20th Century," *Social Problems* 29, no. 3 (1982): 229–30.

37. Eugene Tobin, *Organize or Perish: America's Independent Progressives, 1913–1933* (New York: Greenwood Press, 1986), 8.

38. The scope and coverage of this federal legislation virtually halted further state level action, as did the Supreme Court, ruling in *Erie R. Co. v. N.Y.*, 233 U.S. 671 (1914), that congressional action in this field precluded additional state laws, even where state legislation attempted to set higher standards. Elizabeth Brandeis, *History of Labor in the United States, 1896–1932* (New York: Macmillan, 1935), 549.

39. Roy Lubove, *The Struggle for Social Security, 1900–1935* (Pittsburgh: University of Pittsburgh Press, 1986), 54.

40. U.S. Department of Labor, 1914, 123; James Weinstein notes that labor unionists often opposed workmen's compensation legislation, believing that it would only "pension off the worker during his period of disablement at something less than his regular wages," in contrast to what might be won by employees in court. Weinstein, *The Corporate Ideal in the Liberal State*, 43.

41. Arthur S. Link, *Wilson: The New Freedom* (Princeton, NJ: Princeton University Press, 1956), 256.

42. The Supreme Court first ruled congressional child labor legislation unconstitutional in *Hammer v. Dagenhart* (1917) and again in *Bailey v. Drexel* (1922). Many state statutes remained on the books, however, throughout the Progressive Era. Alan Dawley, *Struggles for Justice: Social Responsibility and the Liberal State* (Cambridge, MA: Belknap Press of Harvard University Press, 1991), 282–83.

43. Scholars note that we must temper evaluation of the "success" of mothers' pensions with recognition of their complexity, if not limitations. Linda Gordon, ed., *Women, the State, and Welfare* (Madison: University of Wisconsin Press, 1990); Linda Gordon, *Woman's Body, Woman's Right: Birth Control in America*, rev. ed. (New York: Penguin Books, 1990). Barbara Nelson and Gwendolyn Mink, for example, illuminate how policies within the welfare domain contained anti-civil-rights principles adversarial to the interests of the very groups meant to benefit from them. Barbara Nelson, "The Gender, Race, and Class Origins of Early Welfare Policy and the U.S. Welfare State: A Comparison of Workmen's Compensation and Mothers' Aid," in *Women, Change and Politics*, ed. Louise Tilly and Patricia Gurin (New York: Russell Sage Foundation, 1990), 413–35; Gwendolyn Mink, *The Wages of Motherhood: Inequality in the Welfare State, 1917–1942* (Ithaca, NY: Cornell University Press, 1995).

The association of mothers' pensions with pauperism in many states at the turn of the century, for example, meant that women receiving these benefits also were susceptible to civil restrictions on paupers operating in many states at the turn of the century, which included limitations on where they could live, their right to marry, and their right to vote, as Nelson points out (Nelson, "The Gender, Race, and Class Origins of Early Welfare Policy and the U.S. Welfare State"). While Mothers' Aid was the first public assistance program to challenge the premise of pauperism attributing economic distress to an individual's own weak character, nonetheless, if a "state classified Mothers' Aid within its Poor Laws, and if pauperism disenfranchised one, then Mothers' Aid could disenfranchise its recipients." Ibid.

The anti-civil-rights elements embedded in welfare policies are a preview of the defining feature of Progressive Era reform discussed above: institutionalization of an anti-civil-rights state in conjunction with a pro-welfare state.

44. Skocpol, *Protecting Soldiers and Mothers*.

45. Linda K. Kerber, *Women of the Republic: Intellect and Ideology in Revolutionary America* (Chapel Hill: University of North Carolina Press, 1997).

46. Orestes A. Brownson, *The Works of Orestes A. Brownson*, vol. 18, *Politics*, ed. Henry F. Brownson (Detroit: Thorndike Nourse Publishing, 1885), 388.

47. Aileen S. Kraditor, *The Ideas of the Woman Suffrage Movement, 1890-1920* (New York: Columbia University Press, 1967).

48. Alexander Keyssar, *The Right to Vote: The Contested History of Democracy in the United States* (New York: Basic Books, 2000).

49. Ibid., 188.

50. Ellen Carol DuBois, *Harriot Stanton Blatch and the Winning of Woman Suffrage* (New Haven, CT: Yale University Press, 1997).

51. Anna Howard Shaw, "Re: Suffrage," speech, Cornell University, Ithaca, NY (1912 or 1913), Anna Howard Shaw Papers, Schlesinger Library, Harvard University, p. 24.

52. Anna Howard Shaw, "Is Democracy a Failure," speech delivered at the New York State woman suffrage convention, March 3, 1911, Anna Howard Shaw Papers, Schlesinger Library, Harvard University.

53. Shaw, "Re: Suffrage."

54. Ibid.

55. Carrie Chapman Catt, "The Most Interesting Person I Ever Met" (1917), Carrie Chapman Catt Papers, Schlesinger Library, Harvard University.

56. Carrie Chapman Catt, "An Appeal for Liberty" (1915), Carrie Chapman Catt Papers, Schlesinger Library, Harvard University.

57. Carrie Chapman Catt, "The Widow's Mite" (1919), Carrie Chapman Catt Papers, Schlesinger Library, Harvard University.

58. Carrie Chapman Catt, "Women and the Presidency" (1916), Carrie Chapman Catt Papers, Schlesinger Library, Harvard University.

59. Carrie Chapman Catt, untitled speech (1917), Carrie Chapman Catt Papers, Schlesinger Library, Harvard University.

60. Carrie Chapman Catt, "The Nation Calls" (1919), Carrie Chapman Catt Papers, Schlesinger Library, Harvard University.

61. Carrie Chapman Catt, remarks to "Chairman and gentlemen of the Committee on Woman Suffrage" (1917), Carrie Chapman Catt Papers, Schlesinger Library, Harvard University.

62. Carrie Chapman Catt, "Suffrage" (probably 1903), Carrie Chapman Catt Papers, Schlesinger Library, Harvard University.

63. *Congressional Record*, House of Representatives, 63rd Congress, 3rd Session (January 12, 1915), 1409.

64. Ibid., 1410.

65. Ibid., 1415.

66. Ibid., 1409.

67. Ibid., 1415.

68. J. Stanley Lemons, "The Sheppard-Towner Act: Progressivism in the 1920s," *Journal of American History* 55, no. 4 (1969): 776.

69. Ibid.

70. Ibid.

71. Ibid., 777–78.

72. Ibid., 778.

73. Ibid.

74. Ibid., 779.

75. As Lemons notes, it is ironic that the only woman in the House at this time, Alice Robertson, was an antisuffragist and, consequently, opposed the Sheppard-Towner Act. Ibid., 778.

76. Ibid., 782.

77. Ibid.

78. Ibid., 779.

79. Quoted in ibid., 784.

80. Ibid., 779.

81. Quoted in ibid., 781.

82. Quoted in ibid., 780.

83. Harold Maslow, "The Background of the Wagner National Health Bill," *Law and Contemporary Problems* 6, no. 4 (1939): 611.

84. The amount was $2,158,000. Ibid.

85. Lemons, "The Sheppard-Towner Act: Progressivism in the 1920s," 784.

86. *Adkins v. Children's Hospital*, 261 U.S. 525 (1923).

87. Quoted in Joan G. Zimmerman, "The Jurisprudence of Equality: The Women's Minimum Wage, the First Equal Rights Amendment, and *Adkins v. Children's Hospital, 1905–1923*," *Journal of American History* 78, no. 1 (1991): 221.

88. Kelley was admitted to the Illinois bar in 1894. Zimmerman, "The Jurisprudence of Equality," 191n2.

89. Ibid., 193.

90. Ibid., 195.

91. Ibid., 196.

92. Ibid., 217.

93. Ibid., 224.

94. Suzanne Mettler, *Dividing Citizens: Gender and Federalism in New Deal Public Policy* (Ithaca, NY: Cornell University Press, 1998), 22.

95. Quoted in Mettler, *Dividing Citizens*, 231.

96. Mettler, *Dividing Citizens*, 213.

97. Ibid., 213–14.

98. Ibid., 82–83. Restricting benefits to full-time workers in the paid labor force also discriminated against a disproportionate percentage of African Americans. For an insightful analysis of the racial bias built into the construction and administration of New Deal policies, see Robert C. Lieberman, *Shifting the Color Line: Race and the American Welfare State* (Cambridge, MA: Harvard University Press, 2001).

99. Mettler, *Dividing Citizens*, 153–54.

100. Ibid., 25.

101. Ibid.

102. Ibid., 119.

103. Ibid., 139.

104. Ibid., 164.

105. Ibid., 230.

106. Robert C. Post and Reva B. Siegel, "Legislative Constitutionalism and Section Five Power: Policentric Interpretation of the Family and Medical Leave Act," *Yale Law Journal* 112, no. 8 (2003): 5.

107. Ibid., 24.

108. Quoted in Post and Siegel, "Legislative Constitutionalism and Section Five Power," 3.

109. According to the U.S. Department of Labor Web site, available at http://www.dol.gov/esa/whd/fmla, covered employers (employing more than fifty employees, or a public agency) must grant an eligible employee (has been employed for at least 1,250 hours of service during the twelve-month period immediately preceding the commencement of the leave) up to a total of twelve work weeks of unpaid leave during any twelve-month period for one or more of the following reasons: for the birth and care of the newborn child of the employee; for placement with the employee of a son or daughter for adoption or foster care; to care for an immediate family member (spouse, child, or parent) with a serious health condition; or to take medical leave when the employee is unable to work because of a serious health condition.

Chapter 7

1. David Cohen, "Much Apu about Nothing," *The Simpsons*, FOX, May 5, 1996.

2. Senator Barack Obama, "A More Perfect Union" (speech, Constitution Center, Philadelphia, PA, March 18, 2008).

3. The idea of a hybrid state that represents both individualism and maternalism in its public policies is similar to legal scholar Judith Baer's argument about a feminist postliberalism that includes a concept of needs along with rights when identifying a just political system. Judith Baer, *Our Lives before the Law: Constructing a Feminist Jurisprudence* (Princeton, NJ: Princeton University Press, 1999). Also see Linda C. McCain, *The Place of Families: Fostering Capacity, Equality, and Responsibility* (Cambridge, MA: Harvard University Press, 2006). For a discussion of how the constitutional basis of individual rights could be altered to include a group-based, instrumental dimension, see Vikram David Amar and Alan Brownstein, "The Hybrid Nature of Political Rights," *Stanford Law Review* 50, no. 3 (1998): 915–1014.

4. The literature is vast, but for classic, pioneering statements, see Susan Muller Okin, *Justice, Gender, and the Family* (New York: Basic Books, 1989), and Carole Pateman, *The Sexual Contract* (Stanford, CA: Stanford University Press, 1988).

5. For an interesting discussion of exceptions, see Gerda Lerner, *The Creation of Patriarchy* (New York: Oxford University Press, 1986).

6. Joan Kelly, "Did Women Have a Renaissance?" in *Women, History, and Theory: The Essays of Joan Kelly* (Chicago: University of Chicago Press, 1984). The material that follows appeared in "Modernization and Political Inclusion: The Case of Women Leaders," *Harvard International Review* (Fall 1999). In terms of contemporary political processes of change, the analogous question is whether "democratization is progress for women?" Some leading scholars say, "no." See Georgina Waylen, "Women and Democratization: Conceptualizing Gender Relations in Transition Politics," *World Politics* 46, no. 3 (1994): 327–54; Mala Htun, *Sex and the State: Abortion, Divorce, and the Family under Latin American Dictatorships and Democracies* (Cambridge: Cambridge University Press, 2003).

7. Kelly, "Did Women Have a Renaissance?" ix–xiv, 20. Historian Joan Wallach Scott views basic reinterpretations of the impact of historical periodization on women, such as Kelly's, to be in the same intellectual camp as those who argue that women's political participation was dampened as a result of the "Age of Democratic Revolutions," that the development of the nuclear family constituted constraints on women's ability to develop their emotional and intellectual selves, and that the ascendancy of medicine brought with it the destruction of women's sense of autonomy and community in areas of reproductive and family experiences. Joan Wallach Scott, "Women in History: The Modern Period," *Past and Present* 101 (November 1983): 145–46.

8. Kelly, "Did Women Have a Renaissance?" 22.

9. Ibid., 23.

10. In the medieval period the Christian Church had reserved love as the idealization of that which was beautiful and had defined the proper object of love as being none other than Christ himself. Sexuality, or the reproduction of the species, was, in fact, considered important and necessary, but was a more utilitarian and secular kind of activity and was, presumably, reserved for marriage and the family. The separation of marriage and reproductive sexuality from the idealization of beauty and the feeling of love that would accompany such idealization was the official position of the Church. The fact that courtly love came into being in this medieval context meant that there was a defiance of Church authority in this respect. Courtesans and the knight and the lady represent a defiance of the separation of sexuality from the feeling and spirit of love.

11. The lack of consent characterizing the relationship between men and women of different classes simply highlights the principle of consent operating between members of the same class. Thus, though men of the nobility were viewed as having absolute sexual rights of access to lower-class women, the prevalence of this class distinction is one of the reasons it was so important to distinguish horizontal relationships within the nobility on the basis of consent. Otherwise, the class distinctions would fade—an impossible thought in feudal times. Thus, the posture of the knight bending and kneeling before his lady was to emphasize the consensual nature of the relationship between this man and woman, in particular that the woman's involvement was not on the basis of sexual force, but consensual, willful agreement.

12. Kelly, "Did Women Have a Renaissance?" 27.

13. Ibid.

14. Ibid., 28.

15. It is for this reason that women's chastity became a condition of their presence in the private sphere of the home in marked contrast to the invitation for sexual cooperation and complementarity and equality that existed in feudal times.

16. Joan B. Landes, *Women and the Public Sphere: In the Age of the French Revolution* (Ithaca, NY: Cornell University Press, 1988), 2, 17.

17. Steven C. Hause with Anne R. Kenney, *Women's Suffrage and Social Politics in the French Third Republic* (Princeton, NJ: Princeton University Press, 1984), 22, 170–71.

18. Ibid., 1.

19. Ibid.

20. Landes, *Women and the Public Sphere*, 93.

21. Ibid., 204. Others extend the concern that liberal principles can retard rather than advance women's rights to more current democratization processes. Political scientist Elizabeth Dore, for example, considers the institutionalization of liberal values in Latin America in the nineteenth century to be a step backward for women as new, privatized property laws resulted in the loss of access to communal lands by indigenous women, and a secularized court system reinforced the patriarchal family. Elizabeth Dore, "One Step Forward, Two Steps Back: Gender and the State in the Long Nineteenth Century," in *Hidden Histories of Gender and the State in Latin America,* ed. Elizabeth Dore and Maxine Molyneux (Durham, NC: Duke University Press, 2000).

22. Jean Bethke Elshtain, *Public Man, Private Woman* (Princeton, NJ: Princeton University Press, 1981), 318–37.

23. Anne Phillips, *Democracy and Difference* (University Park: Pennsylvania State University Press, 1993), 105, 11. Other theorists point to the way liberalism's focus on the individual as the basic unit of society disadvantages women because the abstract, universal individual almost inevitably is, by default, defined in terms of norms that apply more to men than to women. As the late Susan Okin argued, a consequence of the feminist challenge to orthodox political theory has been "an extraordinary denial of women's unique relationship to pregnancy that turns arguments over abortion into a discussion of the relationship between parents and foetuses, and hardly seems to register that women have a different relationship to the foetus than men." Susan Moller Okin, *Justice, Gender, and the Family* (New York: Basic Books, 1989). Anne Phillips concurs, arguing that the "individuals of liberal theory are presented as if they refer indiscriminately to women or men, but have written into them a masculine experience and a masculine norm. Their abstraction cloaks a masculine body." Phillips, *Democracy and Difference*, 46.

24. They note that "liberalism, free speech, free markets, citizenship, family and gender relations, popular sovereignty, representative government, federalism, the separation of powers, checks and balances, globalization—all build and turn on the distribution of authority." Karen Orren and Stephen Skowronek, *The Search for American Political Development* (Cambridge: Cambridge University Press, 2004), 123.

25. Ibid., 127, 131.

26. As Louis Hartz asserts, for Americans, the reality of atomistic social freedom, what we would term the principle that the government should treat all individuals equally "in spite of" their ascriptive group differences, "is instinctive to the American mind, as in a sense the concept of the polis was instinctive to Platonic Athens." Louis Hartz, *The Liberal Tradition in America: An Interpretation of American Political Thought since the Revolution* (New York: Harcourt, Brace, 1955), 62.

27. As Hartz notes, it was impossible even for Southern defenders of slavery to claim that slaves had no human attributes. Even Greek political philosophers, such as Aristotle, had never made such a claim. Hartz, *The Liberal Tradition in America*, 15.

28. Ibid., 169.

29. Ibid.

30. Ibid., 156, 173.

31. Alexis de Tocqueville, *Democracy in America*, ed. Isaac Krammick, trans. Gerald Bevan (New York: Penguin Classics, 2003); Gunnar Myrdal, *An American Dilemma: The Negro Problem and Modern Democracy*, 2 vols. (New Brunswick, NJ: Transaction Publishers, 1996); Samuel P. Huntington, *American Politics: The Promise of Disharmony* (Cambridge, MA: Harvard University Press, 1981).

32. Huntington, *American Politics*.

33. Orren's basic argument is the following:

> At the time the United States entered upon full-scale industrialization after the Civil War, its politics contained, at the core, a belated [residual] feudalism, a remnant of the medieval hierarchy of personal relations, a particularized network of law and morality—a system of governance—that the word "feudalism" conveys. It had been dislodged neither by the American Revolution nor by the advent of the U.S. Constitution, but remained embedded within American government—a state within a state—dividing power, limiting the reach of legislation, setting the bounds of collective action, well into the current [twentieth] century. This belated feudalism is the missing historical link between nineteenth-century liberal ideology and twentieth-century liberal politics.

Karen Orren, *Belated Feudalism: Labor, the Law, and Liberal Development in the United States* (Cambridge: Cambridge University Press, 1991), 3–4.

34. Ibid., 25.

35. Ibid., 69.

36. Ibid., 74.

37. Ibid.

38. Orren's thorough analysis of how common-law-based judicial decision-making favored the employer over the employee leaves little doubt that feudal remnants of master-servant norms prevailed in American labor law until well into the twentieth century. She notes, for example, that the ancient feudal premise that workers were hired for an "entire" period of labor was applied to American workers. According to this principle, workers were not entitled to receive wages until the entire period for which they were to labor had been fulfilled. This provision made it possible for employers "to goad employees into quitting near the end of a term or pay period, and thereby benefit from their earlier labor without having to pay." Orren, *Belated Feudalism*, 74, 85.

39. Ibid., 107.

40. Ibid., 123–24.

41. 301 U.S. 1 (1937)

42. Orren, *Belated Feudalism*, 29, 209.

43. Ibid., 209.

44. Ibid., 215.

45. Smith's "multiple traditions" thesis is that there are three basic sets of principles that American political actors have drawn upon since the very founding of the American state, namely, liberal principles stressing the inherent equality of rights-bearing individuals; democratic republican principles stressing the value of common civic institutions; and ascriptivist American principles that use such characteristics as people's race, sex, and religion to create inegalitarian hierarchical social orders based on heredity. Rogers M. Smith, *Civic Ideals: Conflicting Views of Citizenship in U.S. History* (New Haven, CT: Yale University Press, 1997), 2–6.

46. Ibid., 36–37.

47. Gretchen Ritter, *The Constitution as Social Design: Gender and Civic Membership in the American Constitutional Order* (Stanford, CA: Stanford University Press, 2006), 3, 21.

48. Ibid., 259, 295.

49. Philosopher Martha Nussbaum concurs that liberal theory, while valuable, has "not yet given satisfactory answers to deep problems exposed by feminist thinkers . . . [namely] the need for care in times of extreme dependency; and the political role of the family." Martha Nussbaum, "The Future of Feminist Liberalism," *Proceedings and Addresses of the American Philosophical Association* 74, no. 2 (2000): 48.

50. "The Monarchist Mission and Credo," The Monarchist Society of America, available at home1.gte.net/eskandar/monarchistsociety.html#mission.

51. Ibid.

52. Available at www.worldfreeinternet.net/monarchy, accessed December 7, 2007.

53. Ibid.

54. Ibid., italics in text.

55. Accessed at www.freepages.genealogy.rootsweb.ancestry.com/~apassageintime/uel.html; www.mysteriesofcanada.com/Canada/united_empire_loyalists.htm.

56. BBC Monitoring/BBC, June 1, 2004.

57. Ibid.

58. In Iran, thousands of monarchist demonstrators clashed with police in February 2001, the first demonstration on such a grand scale since the 1979 Islamic revolution. The monarchists, in opposition to the radical Islamists who are currently in power, are pro-American and support the Reza Pahlavi, who lives in exile in the United States and who is the son of the late Shah. Monarchists claim that a constitutional monarchy "has historical roots in our country," and that there is nothing "wrong with being pro-American"(Deutsche Presse-Agentur, February 9, 2001). More recently, a group of nearly sixty Iranian monarchists encamped on a Lufthansa jet in a Belgian airport and went on a hunger strike, refusing to leave until the United States and other nations sign a pledge promising that they will stop cooperating with the current Islamic government in Iran, which they claim is a terrorist regime. These protestors engaged in this action to "highlight their support for the late Shah of Iran" and to draw attention to the serious political problems currently plaguing Iran (Associated Press, March 10, 2005, BC cycle).

In Russia, on the eighty-fifth anniversary of the execution of the Russian royal family, a rally of about six hundred people gathered in Moscow to urge the revival of the monarchy. A poll indicated that 32% of the people in Russia favor reinstating a monarchy (BBC Monitoring International Reports, July 17, 2003). In Italy, several monarchist groups are actively promoting a return to a monarchy, despite the fact that the heir apparent has sworn his allegiance to the republic. Nevertheless, there is a monarchist party in Italy, Unione Monarchica Italiana (UMI) that currently represents seventy thousand Italians (ANSA English Media Service, December 16, 2003).

In the Czech Republic there is also an effort to restore the monarchy. As Peter Placak, founder of the most famous Czech monarchist association, the Czech Crown, stated, "A ruler who does not interfere in everyday politics is protected from scandalisation, can stand above parties. He can best represent society both outside and inside the country" (quoted in Czech News Agency, January 7, 2004). Similar efforts to restore a monarchy are underway in Uganda, where a constitutional amendment has been proposed that would establish a coexistence between republicans and monarchists who represent regions within Uganda (AllAfrica, Inc., Africa News, February 3, 2003; February 15, 2005).

In Israel, there is also discussion about the creation of a Jewish monarchy. A group called the Monarchists has been conducting extensive research for the past several years about the lineage of several families in order to determine who has the closest bloodline to the biblical King David, which would be a requirement for any future Jewish king. All agree that the best candidate to be "king of Israel" is Rabbi Yosef Dayan from Psagot. This is because it is assumed that one must trace one's lineage not only back to David, but also only through a male line to David. Dayan is the best candidate because "he has two documented ancient sources which draw a direct line between him and the males in his family to King David some 3,000 years ago" (*Jerusalem Post*, January 12, 2005). Although many people can show that they are descendants of David, they cannot show that they are descendants through the male line. It appears that the monarchists in Israel envision overthrowing the presiding democratic government and replacing it with a monarchy. Dayan, in particular, has been a vehement opponent of Israeli prime ministers, such as Ariel Sharon, even to the extent of placing a death curse on Sharon while he was prime minister. Nevertheless, this modern-day Sanhedrin, composed primarily of Kahane sympathizers, remains actively engaged in assessing the prospects for establishing anew a Jewish kingdom (*Jerusalem Post*, January 12, 2005).

59. Quoted in Neil Conan, "Monarchy," *Talk of the Nation,* Public Broadcasting Radio, December 12, 1998, transcript of radio program.

60. Ibid.

61. Jeremy D. Mayer and Lee Sigelman, "Zog for Albania, Edward for Estonia, and Monarchs for All the Rest? The Royal Road to Prosperity, Democracy, and World Peace," *PS* (September 1999): 771.

62. Quoted in Mayer and Sigelman, "Zog for Albania, Edward for Estonia, and Monarchs for All the Rest? 771.

63. Cited in ibid.

64. Mayer and Sigelman, "Zog for Albania, Edward for Estonia, and Monarchs for All the Rest? 771, citing Barry Came, "Downsizing Royalty," *Maclean's* (March 23, 1998): 32–34 and Thomas Nairm, *The Enchanted Glass: Britain and Its Monarchy* (London: Vintage Press, 1994).

65. Mayer and Sigelman, "Zog for Albania, Edward for Estonia, and Monarchs for All the Rest? 772.

66. Ibid., 773. Others seriously advance the virtues of monarchy as a politically stabilizing influence. In political contexts where there is polarized ethnic and religious diversity, for example, some believe that attachment to a constitutional monarchy can stand for a symbol of national unity and contribute to national stability. Those analyzing contemporary politics, for example, also note the stabilizing effects of monarchical systems, even when those systems are patriarchal in their construction. In the Middle East, for example, political analysts view a new network of young, male monarchs as holding the promise for providing constructive leadership and smooth transitions to new rulers. King Hassan II, who had ruled Morocco for thirty-eight years prior to his death in July 1999, was peacefully succeeded by his thirty-six-year-old son, King Mohammed VI. Similarly, King Abdullah at the age of thirty-seven assumed the rulership of Jordan upon the death of his father, King Hussein, in February of 1999 with the enthusiastic support of the people of Jordan.

Other Middle East monarchs who exemplify the way inherited rule can present an option for stable political transition and rulership are Sheik Hamad bin Issa, forty-nine,

who in March of 1999 succeeded his father as the Emir of Bahrain and Sheik Hamad
bin Khalifa, who at the age of forty-nine successfully staged a bloodless coup in 1995
to depose his father as Emir of Qatar. Such peaceful monarchical succession stands in
dramatic contrast to the 1969 and 1970 violent coups that marked the accession to political rule of Muammar al-Qaddafi in Libya, Mr. Assad in Syria, and Saddam Hussein in
Iraq. In addition, the 1975 assassination of King Faisal of Saudi Arabia and the assassination of President Anwar el-Sadat of Egypt in 1981 as bases for political turnovers also
stand in contrast to the way Middle East monarchies have by-passed such events. Some
nonmonarchical Arab rulers have even begun to suggest that when they die, their sons
should take over as ruler, apparently believing that whatever opposition there might be
to such a plan, that opposition nevertheless is preferable to the power struggles that have
characteristically marked nonmonarchical shifts in rulers (Douglas Jehl, "In Morocco,
Too, a Young King for a New Generation," *New York Times*, Tuesday, July 27, 1999, A3).

Political scientist Jeffrey Marshall concurs, adding that monarchies also can symbolize political legitimacy. He believes that people who claim constitutional monarchies are
undemocratic do so on the basis of a very "narrow view of democracy" (quoted in Neil
Conan, "Monarchy," *Talk of the Nation*, Public Broadcasting Radio, December 12, 1998,
transcript of the radio program). In his opinion, a key element of democracy is "about
governing in accordance with the wishes of the majority of the people." He observes that
in Japan and in quite a large number of countries in Europe and Africa people appear to
think that monarchy is a good system. As he notes, "Queen Elizabeth II is head of a
Commonwealth composed of fifty-four nations, which want the Queen to continue as
their head" (quoted in ibid.). The referendum recently held in Australia confirms that
assessment, given that a measure to detach Australia from the monarchy of Great Britain
failed to pass.

67. Lisa Baldez, "The Pros and Cons of Gender Quota Laws: What Happens When
You Kick Men Out and Let Women In?" *Politics and Gender* 2, no. 1 (2006): 103, emphasis in text.

68. Ibid.

69. As Bernard Bailyn notes, in colonial times, prior to the founding of the American
state, people were familiar with Locke and Montesquieu. Bernard Bailyn, *Faces of Revolution: Personalities and Themes in the Struggle for American Independence* (New York:
Alfred A. Knopf, 1990), 190. As Andrew Rehfeld observes, at the very least, Locke had an
indirect influence on the charters for both North and South Carolina, as Locke was the
recording secretary for the very commission that wrote the Carolinas' charter. Andrew
Rehfeld, "Silence of the Land: On the Historical Irrelevance of Territory to Congressional
Districting and Political Representation in the United States," *Studies in American Political Development* 15 (Spring 2001): 62n37, 62.

70. Some believe that James Madison patterned the Tenth Federalist with David
Hume's *Essays* in mind. Stanley Elkins and Eric McKitrick, *The Age of Federalism: The
Early American Republic, 1788–1800* (New York: Oxford University Press, 1993), 86.
Others believe that although Enlightenment ideas contributed an important liberal context to the thinking of the Founders, "they were not the immediate sources of the ideas,
fears, and beliefs that directly shaped Americans' responses to particular events or guided
the specific reforms they undertook." Bernard Bailyn, *Faces of Revolution: Personalities
and Themes in the Struggle for American Independence* (New York: Alfred A. Knopf,
1990), 202.

71. Elkins and McKitrick, *The Age of Federalism*, 86.

72. Bailyn, *Faces of Revolution*, 221.

73. Ibid., 196.

74. Elkins and McKitrick, *The Age of Federalism*, 11.

75. Ibid., 12.

76. Ibid.

77. Bailyn, *Faces of Revolution*, 217.

78. Donald S. Lutz, "The Theory of Consent in the Early State," in *Republicanism, Representation, and Consent: Views of the Founding Era*, ed. Daniel J. Elazar (New Brunswick, NJ: Transaction Books, 1979), 19.

79. Jean Yarbrough, "Representation and Republicanism," in *Republicanism, Representation, and Consent*, ed. Elazar, 79–80.

80. Ibid., 80.

81. Ibid., 79.

82. Bailyn, *Faces of Revolution*, 194.

83. Quoted in Lutz, "The Theory of Consent in the Early State," in *Republicanism, Representation, and Consent*, ed. Elazar, 18.

84. Quoted in Rehfeld, "Silence of the Land," 69.

85. Rehfeld "Silence of the Land," 54.

86. Ibid., 56.

87. Ibid., 59.

88. Ibid., 69.

89. Ibid., 79.

90. Ibid.

91. Ibid., 55.

92. Ibid.

93. Each state may determine how to choose its Electors. Originally, state legislatures chose the state's Electors, but, now, the people of the state make that choice in the general election.

94. Jytte Klausen and Charles S. Maier, eds., *Has Liberalism Failed Women? Assuring Equal Representation in Europe and the United States* (New York: Palgrave Press, 2001).

95. Alan Wolfe and Jytte Klausen, "Identity Politics and Contemporary Liberalism," in *Festschrift für Claus Offe* (Cambridge, MA: Center for European Studies, Harvard University, 2000), 17.

96. Nira Yuval-Davis, *Gender and Nation* (London: Sage, 1997), 58.

97. Yael Tamir, *Liberal Nationalism* (Princeton, NJ: Princeton University Press, 1995); John Rawls, *A Theory of Justice* (Cambridge: Belknap Press of Harvard University Press, 2005), *Political Liberalism* (New York: Columbia University Press, 1995); Ronald Dworkin, *Taking Rights Seriously* (Cambridge, MA: Harvard University Press, 2007).

98. Young cited in Tamir, *Liberal Nationalism*, xxvii–xxviii. Legal scholar Lucinda Finley makes a similar claim when she advocates "enlarging the meanings of words and the conceptions of human nature underlying existing theories of equality and rights," cited in Adelaide H. Villmoare, "Review: Feminist Jurisprudence and Political Vision," *Law and Social Inquiry* 24, no. 2 (1999): 443–76.

99. See Ruth O'Brien, *Bodies in Revolt: Gender, Disability, and a Workplace Ethic of Care* (London: Routledge, 2005).

100. Martha Minow, *Making All the Difference: Inclusion, Exclusion, and the American Law* (Ithaca, NY: Cornell University Press, 1991), 111.

101. Jennifer Nedelsky, "Law, Boundaries, and the Bounded Self," *Representations* 30 (Spring 1990): 167.

102. Ibid., 169.

103. When it comes to women, the goal is not to draw boundaries around them to protect them from men, and certainly not to bind them within the separate sphere of the home. Boundaries and separatism more often than not go hand in hand with sexism. Keller quoted in Nedelsky, "Law, Boundaries, and the Bounded Self," 178. As Keller notes, "Fear of merger and self-dispersion motivates all insistence on separate selfhood . . . in such fear of self-loss lurks a profound fear of women. . . . In the hive and the anthill we see fully realized the two things that . . . most [people] dread for our own species—the dominance of the female and the dominance of the collective." Keller quoted in Nedelsky, "Law, Boundaries, and the Bounded Self," 178.

104. Rick Santorum, *It Takes a Family: Conservatism and the Common Good* (Wilmington, DE: ISI Books, 2005); Hillary Rodham Clinton, *It Takes a Village*, 10th anniversary ed. (New York: Simon and Schuster, 2006); Rebbeca M. Blank, *It Takes a Nation: A New Agenda for Fighting Poverty* (Princeton, NJ: Princeton University Press, 1998).

Appendix 1

1. Joyce Carol Oates, "Out of the Machine," originally published as the second part of "With Norman Mailer at the Sex Circus," *Atlantic Monthly*, July 1971.

2. Ibid.

3. Ibid.

4. For an insightful analysis of essentialism, including the differences within essentialism, see Diana Fuss, *Essentially Speaking: Feminism, Nature, and Difference* (New York: Routledge, 1989).

5. Quoted in Deirdre M. Condit, "Anrogenesis and Mothering Human Identity," in *21st Century Mothering*, ed. Andrea O'Reilly (Cambridge: Cambridge University Press, 2009, forthcoming).

6. Quoted in ibid.

7. Quoted in Ayako Doi, "Japan's Hybrid Women," *Foreign Policy* 139 (November/December 2003): 78.

8. Sherilyn MacGregor, "From Care to Citizenship: Calling for Ecofeminism Back to Politics," *Ethics and the Environment* 9, no. 1 (2004): 56.

9. Martha Nussbaum, "The Future of Feminist Liberalism," *Proceedings and Addresses of the American Philosophical Association* 74, no. 2 (2000): 50.

10. Jane Mansbridge, "Quota Problems: Combating the Dangers of Essentialism," *Politics and Gender* 1, no. 4 (2005): 630.

11. Ibid.

12. Ibid.

13. Personal correspondence, November 2007.

14. Ibid.

15. Anonymous reviewer of book manuscript, November 2007.

16. The idea of modal behaviors rather than essentialist identities maps onto what political scientist Karen Beckwith refers to as the concept of gender as a category and as a process. As a process, gender refers to the "behaviors, conventions, practices, and dynamics engaged in by individuals, organizations, movements, institutions, and nations." Karen Beckwith, "A Common Language of Gender?" *Politics and Gender* (2005): 630.

As an analytical category, it is appropriate to focus on gender specifically in "situations where all the actors are male (e.g., the military) or where the primary actors are female (e.g., care-work)," ibid. The point of this book is that maternalism, both biological and social, at this point in time—and for the foreseeable future—is an area of human activity where the primary actors are female. In this sense, therefore, it is permissible to focus on women's association with maternalism without running the risk of essentializing them.

17. Yet because there are also group tendencies, including biological, if not social, maternalism, until the deconstruction of the public's association of women with maternalism is achieved, the public will continue to associate women with biological and social maternalism, whether or not women candidates—much less women in general—want those identities in the first place. For an example of the need to challenge public perceptions about gender characteristics in the context of sports policies in order to ensure that women and men will not be victims of stereotyping, see Eileen McDonagh and Laura Pappano, *Playing with the Boys: Why Separate Is Not Equal in Sports* (New York: Oxford University Press, 2008).

18. Ange-Marie Hancock, "When Multiplication Doesn't Equal Quick Addition: Examining Intersectionality as a Research Paradigm," *Perspectives on Politics* 5, no. 1 (2007): 67.

19. Ibid., 66, italics added.

20. Kimberlé Crenshaw, "Mapping the Margins: Intersectionality, Identity Politics, and Violence against Women of Color," *Stanford Law Review* 43, no. 6 (1991): 1244–45.

21. Ibid.

22. Ange-Marie Hancock, *The Politics of Disgust: The Public Identity of the Welfare Queen* (New York: New York University Press, 2004), 20.

23. Kimberlé Crenshaw, "Demarginalizing the Intersection of Race and Sex: A Black Feminist Critique of Antidiscrimination Doctrine, Feminist Theory, and Antiracist Politics," *University of Chicago Legal Forum* (1989): 139+.

24. Jane Junn, "Square Pegs and Round Holes: Challenges of Fitting Individual-Level Analysis to a Theory of Politicized Context of Gender," *Politics and Gender* 3 (2007): 127.

25. Ibid. For an excellent analysis of the intersection of race, class, gender, and nation in the context of welfare provision policies, see O'Connor, Orloff, and Shaver, *States, Markets, and Families*.

26. Dorothy E. Roberts, "Punishing Drug Addicts Who Have Babies: Women of Color, Equality, and the Right of Privacy," *Harvard Law Review* 104, no. 7 (1991): 1419–82. Also see Laura Gomez, *Misconceiving Mothers: Legislators, Prosecutors, and the Politics of Prenatal Drug Exposure* (Philadelphia: Temple University Press, 1997) and Marie Ashe, "The 'Bad Mother' in Law and Literature: A Problem of Representation," *Hastings Law Journal* 43 (1992): 1017–37.

27. Dorothy Roberts, *Killing the Black Body: Race, Reproduction, and the Meaning of Liberty* (New York: Pantheon, 1998), 138.

28. Ibid.; Dorothy Roberts, "Black Women and the Pill," *Family Planning Perspectives* 32, no. 2 (2000): 92–93.

29. Dorothy Roberts, *Shattered Bonds: The Color of Child Welfare* (New York: Basic Civitas Books, 2002).

30. The limits of intersectional perspectives for examining the possible existence of common denominators that cut across groups of women differentiated by their class, race, or other ascriptive identities is a theme of many critiques of multiculturalism. As political theorist Sarah Song notes, efforts to accommodate "sexist practices within minority

cultures . . . [can] boomerang back to threaten struggles toward gender equality within the wider society." Sarah Song, "Majority Norms, Multiculturalism, and Gender Equality," *American Political Science Review* 99, no. 4 (2005): 478. Also see Susan Moller Okin, *Is Multiculturalism Bad for Women?* (Princeton, NJ: Princeton University Press, 1999). In addition, as Mala Htun establishes, the differing ways race and gender are represented in groups necessitates a different analysis for each. Gender is a crosscutting identity that is present in all groups, while ethnicity and race are concentrated in distinct groups. For this reason, she finds different types of quotas work, specifically gender quotas for women and legislative reserve seats for ethnic minorities. Mala Htun, "Is Gender like Ethnicity? The Political Representation of Identity Groups," *Perspectives on Politics* 2, no. 3 (2004): 439–58. For an insightful analysis of how race and gender intersect as a process of marginalization in the U.S. Congress, see Mary Hawkesworth, "Congressional Enactments of Race-Gender: Toward a Theory of Raced-Gendered Institutions," *American Political Science Review* 97, no. 4 (2003): 529–50. From the perspective of this project, it is noteworthy that Hawkesworth focuses on "gendering" as a process, not "sexing," where the latter specifically refers to physical, biological definitions of sex difference, as analyzed by Anne Fausto-Sterling, *Sexing the Body: Gender Politics and the Construction of Sexuality* (New York: Basic Books, 2000). This project includes a focus on sex defined as the biological difference between men and women required for biological reproduction. In this respect, we can agree with Hawkesworth that "racing" and "gendering" can be viewed as the result of the "actions of individuals" supplemented by "laws, policies, and organizational norms." Hawkesworth, "Congressional Enactments of Race-Gender," 531. However, gendering does not exhaust the ways the public views women, whatever their race, because the public also sexes individuals by reference to the biological differences between men and women required for biological reproduction. When examining public attitudes about gender, therefore, it behooves us to include attention to sex difference as a biological difference.

31. Max Weber, *Politics as a Vocation* (Philadelphia: Fortress Press, 1965).

32. Jennifer Lawless, "Women, War, and Winning Elections: Gender Stereotyping in the Post–September 11th Era," *Political Research Quarterly* 57, no. 3 (2004): 479–90.

33. T. H. Marshall and Tom Bottomore, eds., *Citizenship and Social Class* (Sterling, VA: Pluto Press, 1992).

34. Catharine A. MacKinnon, *Are Women Human? And Other International Dialogues* (Cambridge, MA: Harvard University Press, 2006), 4.

35. Ibid., 122–23.

36. Uday Singh Mehta, *Liberalism and Empire: A Study in Nineteenth-Century British Liberal Thought* (Chicago: University of Chicago Press, 1999).

37. Kymlicka quoted in Melissa S. Williams, *Voice, Trust, Memory: Marginalized Groups and the Failings of Liberal Representation* (Princeton, NJ: Princeton University Press, 1998), 185.

38. Catharine A. MacKinnon *Sexual Harassment of Working Women* (New Haven, CT: Yale University Press, 1979).

39. James Conniff, "Burke, Bristol, and the Concept of Representation," *Western Political Quarterly* 30, no. 3 (1977): 329.

40. Ibid., 338.

41. Ibid., 330. Burke did recognize limits to virtual representation. First, there must be some connection between virtual representation and what would be direct representation by the people, otherwise the incongruence between who are represented and who are the representatives will be too great. Thus, Burke believed, for example, that the Irish

Catholics were so different from the Protestant British as to make virtual representation of the Irish Catholics by the British impossible. Second, Burke believed that even if there were a familiar connection between the people and their representatives, that connection would have to have some substantial interaction to be feasible. Thus, Burke, for example, believed that although the American colonists and the British shared a familiarity with each other, the geographic distance separating them was so great as to make virtual representation impossible. Thus, he thought the Americans should be left alone by the British to be largely self-governing. Ibid., 338.

42. Anne Phillips, "Must Feminists Give Up on Liberal Democracy?" *Political Studies* 40, Special Issue (1992): 68–82.

INDEX

Page references followed by t, i, *or* g *refer to tables, illustrations, and graphs, respectively.*

Franco, Francisco, 285n36
Franklin, Daniel P., 265n49
Fraser, Antonia, 46, 268n74
Fraser, Nancy, 141, 283n14
Freedom House, 31, 71, 97, 263nn8–9
"Freedom House: About Us," 263n7
free rider problems, 60
Freidenvall, Lenita, 280n55
Frelinghuysens, Frederick, 126
Frelinghuysens, Rodney, 126
Frelinghuysens family, 126
French, Howard W., 273n42
French Revolution, 205–6
Fuchs, Rachel G., 265n40
Fund, John H., 288n4
Fuss, Diana, 302n4
FWCW Platform for Action, 276n23

Gabon, 120*t*
Gambia, The, 3*t*, 120*t*, 241*t*
Gandhi, Indira, 123, 128
Gandhi, Rajiv, 123
Gandhi, Sonia, 123
GDP, 104, 105, 106–8*t*
gender: as category, 302–3n16; as component of American political development, 210–11; as crosscutting identity, 304n30; difference in interest in issues by, 12–13; as process, 302n16, 304n30; as salient to identity of women running for executive office, 168; sex vs., 13–14, 257n43, 304n30; spending policies and, 13, 257n40; as static, ascriptive characteristic, 255n15
gendered electoral environment, 20–21, 171, 260n66
gendered information, 20
gender ideology, 63–64
gendering the government, 51
gendering the nation, 49–50, 270n87
gender quotas: adoption of in democratized monarchies, 102, 138–39, 158*t*; as affirmative action policy, 68, 304n30; as biological maternalism, 17–18, 31, 38–39*t*, 42–45, 71, 97, 101, 102–3; in Canada, 119; citizen-centered atmosphere promoting, 62; in democracies comparable to United States, 132*t*, 133; effect of hereditary monarchies on adoption of, 138–39, 157, 158*t*, 159–60;

effect on civic capacities, 100–101; effect on number of women elected to legislatures, 102, 103*t*, 104–5, 106–8*t*, 109, 134–35*t*; effect on public attitudes toward women as leaders, 74, 75, 76*t*, 77*g*, 81, 82*t*, 172; effect on women's political prospects, 6, 43–45, 65–66, 137; enforcement of, 44; as form of biological citizenship, 69; in France, 123, 284n24; governments incorporating, 38–39*t*; in hybrid states, 55, 56–57*t*; increase in isomorphism of political systems by, 279n50; in India, 123; influence of historical legacies on adoption of, 142–43; as maternal public policy, 17–18, 71, 102–3, 157; in Nordic nations, 126; public attitudes concerning, 21, 214–15; rationales for, 278n48; as social maternalism, 17–18, 101; as solution for motherless state, 211, 214–19; United States lacking policies of, 22; in Western democracies, 124–25*t*; women in legislature and, 48–49; women's election to political office and, 43–45
gender roles, 30, 262n2
gender stereotypes, 14–15, 20, 202, 226, 230, 258n44, 258n48
genuine welfare states, 34
Georgia (nation-state): institution of neither maternal nor democratic policies, 120*t*; monarchist movement in, 213; view of women as political leaders in, 73*t*; women elected to executive positions in, 113*t*; woman suffrage in, 151*t*
Georgia (US state), 146, 148*t*, 178, 179
German Democratic Republic (GDP), 30, 113*t*
Germany: constitutionally guaranteed equality in, 130*t*; constitutional provision for and funding of health care, 38*t*, 124*t*; as corporatist welfare regime, 34; ERA for sex equality in, 132*t*, 135*t*; eugenic policies in, 54; fade away monarchy of, 152, 153*t*, 155*t*, 156*t*, 158*t*, 285n37; gender quotas in, 102, 124*t*; institution of democratic and maternal policies, 121*t*; maternal public policies of, 56*t*, 124*t*, 132*t*, 135*t*, 158*t*; proportional representation in, 279n55;

political candidates: campaign focuses,
    15; gendered political context and,
    20–21; maternalism and, 13–16; voter
    assumptions based on trait ownership,
    258n48; women as hybrid candidates,
    7–10
political citizenship, 68, 96, 97, 186–88
political context: effect of women in po-
    litical office, 20–21; effect on women
    elected as executive leaders, 123; of he-
    reditary monarchies, 19–20; masculine
    state, 6, 231; maternal political envi-
    ronments, 171–73; patterns character-
    izing women's election, 10–11, 20–21,
    128, 202, 220–21, 233–34; of United
    States in Progressive Era, 178; war
    atmosphere, 231. See also hybrid state;
    specific nation
political democracies, 102, 103t
political development in America, 206–11,
    297n33
political leadership, 94–96, 175–78. See
    also deputy prime minister (women);
    monarchs; president; prime minister
    (women); regents (women); religious
    sovereigns (women); sovereigns
    (women); vice president (women)
political learning model of policy analysis,
    62, 63–64, 272–73n30
political offices, 2, 254n5. See also specific
    office such as president
political participation, 63–67
political parties, 6
political recruitment, 94–95
political representation of women, 90–94
political rights: Freedom House's
    evaluation of, 31, 71, 97; guaranteed
    by democracies, 75, 230; as measure of
    liberal democracy, 97
political structures: effect on number of
    women elected to legislatures, 6, 102,
    104, 105, 106–8t; gender quotas as,
    17–18; types of, 103
politics, as woman's game, 20–21
poll taxes, 180, 284n33
Poor Laws, 140
popular sovereignty, 215–16
Portugal: abolition of slavery, 284n25;
    constitutionally guaranteed equal-
    ity in, 131t; constitutional provision

for and funding of health care, 38t,
    48, 124t; destruction of hereditary
    monarchy in, 153, 153t, 155t, 156t,
    158t, 286n37; ERA for sex equality in,
    132t, 135t; gender quotas in, 38t, 102,
    124t; institution of democratic and
    maternal policies, 121t; maternal public
    policies of, 56t, 124t, 132t, 135t, 158t,
    159–60; same-sex marriage rights in,
    237t; woman suffrage in, 151–52, 155t,
    284n34; women elected to executive
    positions in, 116t, 124t; women in
    legislature of, 3t, 48, 124t, 156t
positive group rights: definition of, 28,
    68–69; in democracies comparable to
    United States, 133; effect on number
    of women elected to legislatures, 102,
    103t; effect on public attitudes toward
    women as leaders, 86; effect on wom-
    en's political prospects, 74; Freedom
    House's evaluation of, 31, 71, 97; in
    hereditary monarchies, 139–41; influ-
    ence of historical legacies on adoption
    of, 142; institution of in Progressive
    Era, 182–86; not represented in United
    States, 129. See also gender quotas;
    maternal public policies; welfare
    provision
positive group rights principle, 139–41
Post, Robert C., 294nn106–8
Post-Classical Period, 163, 164g
postmaterialist values, 6
Poulet, André, 268n72
poverty, 182, 183–84, 192–93
Powers v. Ohio, 24, 261n81
pregnancy: association with women,
    15–16; family-kinship networks gener-
    ated by, 18–19, 45–46; as female role,
    13, 46; female sex classification and, 42,
    267n63; New Deal and, 198; as role of
    women in dynasties, 16–17, 45, 169; of
    teenagers, 15; view of in feudal socie-
    ties, 204; view of in Renaissance, 205;
    welfare policies and, 262n1; women
    candidates and, 16; women's need for
    leave for, 232. See also biological ma-
    ternalism; biological reproductive labor;
    childbearing
president: ascriptive qualifications in
    United States, 284n24; as commander-

Selassie, Ermias Sahle (prince of Ethiopia),
213
Seltzer, Richard A., 277n32
Seneca Falls conference, 179, 190
Senegal, 4t, 117t, 121t, 248t
separatism, 302n103
September 11, 2001, terrorist attacks, 230
Serbia & Montenegro: institution of
democratic and maternal policies, 121t,
122t; monarchist movement in, 213;
women elected to executive positions
in, 117t; women in legislature of, 4t
sex: class as overriding characteristic in
monarchies, 168, 171; constitutionally
guaranteed equality in contemporary
democracies, 130–31t, 132t; effect on
attitudes toward women as leaders, 78,
80, 82t, 86; gender vs., 13–14, 257n43,
304n30; limitation of voting rights by,
146–47, 148–49t, 150g
sexism, 27–29, 302n103
sexual citizenship, 69–70, 96
sexual division of labor, 255n12
sexual harassment, 232
sexuality, 203–4
Seychelles, 4t, 120t
Shagshag (queen of Mesopotamia), 163
Sharon, Ariel, 299n58
Shaver, Sheila, 35, 254n7, 264–65nn35–36,
303n25
Shaw, Anna Howard, 188, 189, 190,
292nn51–54
Sheppard, Morris, 193
Sheppard-Towner Act, 192–96, 291n34,
293n75
Siegel, Reva, 253n2, 294nn106–8
Sierra Leone, 3t, 120t, 248–49t
Sigelman, Lee, 214, 268n68, 299nn61–66
Siim, Birte, 257n42, 267n62
Simon, Dennis, 255n16
Simpsons, The (TV show), 201–2
Singapore, 4t, 120t
single cause fallacy, 201–2
Sixth Amendment to U.S. Constitution,
23–24, 261n76
Skocpol, Theda, 95, 181, 261n74, 272n29,
278n36, 289n14, 291n34, 292n44
Skovgaad-Petersen, Inge, 288nn48–49
Skowronek, Stephen, 10–11, 206, 256n26,
296nn24–25

slavery, 1, 145, 207, 284n25, 296n27
Slovakia, 5t, 121t
Slovenia, 4t, 237t
Smith, Adam, 290n28
Smith, Rogers M., 297–98nn45–46
social citizenship: definition of, 33–34; Kelley's work for, 196–97; measurement of, 97; mothers' pension legislation as, 181–82; positive group rights and, 70; in Progressive Era, 182–86; rights of, 33–34, 96; Sheppard-Towner Act as, 192–96; social maternalism as form of, 69, 226; welfare provision as measure of, 36, 68–69, 214
social conventions, 226
social democracy, 69, 274n44
social democratic policies, 96–97
social democratic welfare regime, 34–35
social feminists, 188–89
social justice measures, 185
social liberalism, 254n7
social maternalism: as avenue to New Deal benefits, 198; care-work as, 14, 32, 69; definition of, 14; delivery systems of, 32, 263n15; effect of policy representing on attitudes toward women as leaders, 75, 76t, 77, 80–81, 82–83t, 84–86; effect on female candidates, 14–15; as female activity, 302–3n16, 303n17; femininity vs., 259n53; as form of social citizenship, 69; needs of women as, 27–28; New Deal and, 197–98; public policies associated with, 31; reductionism and, 225; as a requirement for female candidates, 9–10; Sheppard-Towner Act and, 192–96, 291n34, 293n75; social democracy incorporating policies representative of, 69; of state, 17, 22, 32–34, 65; United States lacking policies representing, 22, 23; welfare policies representing, 17, 32–37, 38–39t, 40–42, 97; as women's domain, 186. See also hereditary monarchies; welfare provision
social movements, 99, 182
social reproductive labor: ADC provisions and, 198; association with women, 13–15; definition of, 13–14; Family Medical and Leave Act and, 199–200; mothers' pension legislation and, 181–82, 183, 185, 198, 291–92n43,

in, 73*t*; women elected to executive positions in, 117*t*; women in legislature of, 3*t*

Tajikistan, 5*t*, 117*t*, 120*t*

Tamir, Yael, 95, 220, 278n33, 301nn97–98

Tanzania, 3*t*, 73*t*, 120*t*, 251*t*

Tavakoli-Targhi, Mohamad, 49–50, 269n85, 269n87

tax policies, 30, 40, 277n26

Taylor, Andrew J., 12, 256nn34

Taylor, Michelle M., 254n9

Taylor v. Louisiana, 26, 262n90

television, 66, 175–76, 177, 201–2

Temporary Assistance to Needy Families (TANF), 29, 199

Tenth Federalist, 300n70

Terkildsen, Nayda, 258n44

Texas, 289n9

Thailand, 120*t*, 251*t*

Thatcher, Margaret, 110, 169, 276n12

Thatcher factor, 169

Thelen, Kathleen, 272n29

theory of actual representation, 217

Thies, Michael F., 99, 254n10, 278nn46–47

Thirteenth Amendment to U.S. Constitution, 145

Thompson, E. P., 140, 283nn10–11

Tiaa (queen of Egypt), 167

Tibet, 284n25

Tichenor, Daniel J., 253n1

Timor Leste, 3*t*, 120*t*, 251*t*

Title VII of Civil Rights Act, 6–7, 231, 232, 233, 259n56

Tobin, Eugene, 185, 291n37

Tocqueville, Alexis de, 207, 297n31

Togeby, Lise, 12–13, 257n39

Togo, 120*t*

Tokkrson-Rinehart, Sue, 258n44

Tonga, 120*t*, 251*t*

Toprak, Binnaz, 269–70n87

Towner, Horace, 193

Towns, Ann, 278–79n49–50, 279n50

transgender surgery, 13, 69

Tremblay, Manon, 257n37, 276n15

Tribe, Laurence H., 261n83, 264n21

Trimble, Linda, 276n15

Trinidad & Tobago, 4*t*, 117*t*, 121*t*

Tripp, Aili Mari, 268n65

Tronto, Joan C., 14, 259n49

Tschentscher, A., 267n61

Tunisia, 3*t*, 120*t*

Turkey, 73*t*, 120*t*, 269n87

Turkmenistan, 5*t*, 117*t*, 120*t*

Tuvalu, 121*t*

Uganda: constitutional amendment to restore monarch of, 298n58; institution of maternal but not democratic policies, 120*t*; monarchist movement in, 213; view of women as political leaders in, 73*t*; women elected to executive positions in, 117*t*, 251*t*; women in legislature of, 2, 4*t*

Ukraine, 117*t*, 122*t*, 151*t*

Ulipia Serverina (regent of Roman Empire), 166

UNDP, 279n50

Unione Monarchica Italiana, 298n58

unions, 99, 291n40

United Arab Emirates, 120*t*

United Empire Loyalists, 212

United Kingdom: constitutionally guaranteed equality in, 131*t*; constitutional provision for and funding of health care, 37, 38*t*, 41; ERA for sex equality in, 132*t*, 135*t*; gender quotas in, 38*t*, 124*t*; as hereditary monarchy, 38*t*, 124*t*; institution of democratic and maternal policies, 122*t*; International Constitutional Law Project of, 267n61; maternal public policies of, 56*t*, 124*t*, 132*t*, 135*t*, 158*t*; retention of monarchy of, 66, 152, 153*t*, 155*t*, 156*t*, 158*t*; same-sex marriage rights in, 129, 131*t*, 132*t*, 135*t*; voting rights of women in, 41, 266n60; woman suffrage in, 151*t*, 155*t*; women elected to executive positions in, 118*t*, 124*t*; women in hereditary executive positions in, 251*t*; women in legislature of, 4*t*, 124*t*, 156*t*

United Nations Fourth World Conference on Women (FWCW), 93–94

United Nations Universal Declaration of Human Rights, 31

United States: abolition of slavery, 284n25; adoption of English common law, 146–47; adoption of gender quotas and women's election to legislature of, 105; adoption of welfare provisions and women's election to legislature of, 105;